# VMware®
# Private Cloud
# Computing
# with vCloud
# Director®

# VMware®
# Private Cloud
# Computing
# with vCloud
# Director®

**Simon Gallagher**

**with Aidan Dalgleish**

SYBEX®

A Wiley Brand

Acquisitions Editor: Mariann Barsolo

Development Editor: Tom Cirtin

Technical Editor: Aidan Dalgleish

Production Editor: Dassi Zeidel

Copy Editor: Liz Welch

Editorial Manager: Pete Gaughan

Production Manager: Tim Tate

Vice President and Executive Group Publisher: Richard Swadley

Vice President and Publisher: Neil Edde

Book Designer: Maureen Forys, Happenstance Type-O-Rama

Proofreader: Rebecca Rider

Indexer: Jack Lewis

Project Coordinator, Cover: Katherine Crocker

Cover Designer: Ryan Sneed

Cover Image: © istockphoto.com/loops7

Dear Reader,

Thank you for choosing *VMware Private Cloud Computing with vCloud Director*. This book is part of a family of premium-quality Sybex books, all of which are written by outstanding authors who combine practical experience with a gift for teaching.

Sybex was founded in 1976. More than 30 years later, we're still committed to producing consistently exceptional books. With each of our titles, we're working hard to set a new standard for the industry. From the paper we print on, to the authors we work with, our goal is to bring you the best books available.

I hope you see all that reflected in these pages. I'd be very interested to hear your comments and get your feedback on how we're doing. Feel free to let me know what you think about this or any other Sybex book by sending me an email at nedde@wiley.com. If you think you've found a technical error in this book, please visit http://sybex.custhelp.com. Customer feedback is critical to our efforts at Sybex.

Best regards,

Neil Edde
Vice President and Publisher
Sybex, an Imprint of Wiley

Best regards,

This book is dedicated to my wonderful wife Carol; without her continual and selfless support this book would not have been possible. Also to our amazing children, Abigail and Rowan, for not asking too many times why Daddy spends all day and night in his office with all those computers.
—Simon

I'd like to thank my VMware colleagues, Alan Renouf, Christope Decanini, Gary Blake, Timo Sugliani, Adrian Roberts, Duncan Epping, and Kamau Wanguhu, for their editorial contributions to some of the chapters in this book. John McGinn, Stephen Beck, and Matt Stepanski from my management team for being supportive of me taking part in this project. And last but not least, my partner, Jane Seabridge, for putting up with me working late evenings and weekends.
—Aidan

# Acknowledgments

I'd like to thank Aidan Dalgleish of VMware for his technical editing and for writing two chapters of this book. Thanks also go to Dan Senior, Brian Keats, and Michael Smith of Colt Technology Services for the involvement in real-world vCloud projects; Stuart Thompson, Martyn Storey, Peter Holditch, and David Hill. And a special thanks to  Servers Plus, for excellent service in my hour of hardware need; and the entire London VMware User Group for their continued encouragement in the production of this book.

I'd also like to thank the Sybex & Wiley book teams for their patience and diligent efforts in producing this book.

*—Simon Gallagher*

# About the Authors

**Simon Gallagher** first read about VMware Workstation in a magazine article in 2000. He was instantly hooked and used it to build various complex network and server labs for his studies. Simon built his first ESX server at version 2.5 and, in his work for a managed services provider, built complex test and development environments for customers. Simon saw an opportunity to create a multitenant environment using ESX 3 to deliver customer solutions faster, cheaper, and more flexibly, so he ended up building a very early implementation of a cloud.

Simon has since gone on to work for some of the largest technology & service providers in the world (including VMware), designing and delivering cloud solutions for customers using VMware technology.

Since his university days, Simon has maintained a large and ever-evolving home lab environment. When he found you could virtualize ESX itself, he spent a lot of his own time and money on the various incarnations of his vTARDIS project (`http://vinf.net/vTARDIS`).

In late 2007 Simon began attending the London VMware User Group (VMUG) on the advice of a colleague and was impressed at the technical content and approachability of all the attendees. In 2011 he joined the steering committee for the London VMUG to assist with finding content and helped organize (and presented at) their first ever national UK event, which attracted over 300 attendees. He has been awarded the vExpert title annually by VMware since 2009 and continues to blog and contribute to the London VMUG and the wider community. You can follow Simon Gallagher's blog at `http://vinf.net` and follow him on Twitter: `@vinf_net`.

**Aidan Dalgleish** is a consulting architect with the VMware Global Center of Excellence. He has more than 12 years of experience working with IT hardware and software solutions. Before joining VMware, he served a financial services company as an infrastructure design consultant. There he architected solutions to support business needs, including a bespoke browser–based virtual desktop infrastructure (VDI) broker solution—prior to the release of VMware View®—to support satellite and offshore office locations. At VMware, he has guided partners and customers in deploying VMware solutions ranging from datacenter migrations and VMware View deployments to bespoke multisite disaster recovery solutions with vSphere PowerCLI automation. Aidan is also among the first VMware Certified Design Experts (VCDX 010). You can follow Aidan Dalgleish's blog at `http://www.vcloudscape.com` and follow him on Twitter: `@AidersD`.

# Contents at a Glance

# Contents

# Foreword

Cloud computing is possibly the most incendiary term of recent years, if not all time, in our industry. Many people have spent a lot of time trying to formulate concrete definitions of the aspects as they see them. Others have argued long and hard both publicly and privately about the same and continue to do so.

Cloud computing is the combined result of technical advances in computing, network, storage, management, security, application development, and many more areas, which means a lot of people can lay claim to invention and involvement. One thing we know for certain is that change in our industry is continual and accelerating. This certainty of change is a source of challenge for all, and for many it has culminated into the question of "How do I do *cloud*?"

One thing you can be certain of is that many of the workloads you have today will not be going anywhere, whereas new ones will arrive with "cloudy" characteristics and requirements. Your challenge will be to build a platform that can handle both.

Virtualization is only the first step to the road of abstraction, pooling, and automation that leads you to the agility promised by cloud computing. We have been abstracting, pooling, and automating in computing since we started, whether it was abstracting and pooling disks into arrays or abstracting and pooling computing resources into clusters.

The key difference between a collection of virtualized servers and a private cloud lies in automation and management. This is a step-change involving both technology and process changes. This book will help you take that step.

—*Joe Baguley*
*Chief Technologist, EMEA*
*VMware*

# Introduction

There is a significant shift in the industry: IT, which once served as a one-use tool to help get a specific job, is becoming a wide-ranging competitive advantage that enables your business to do things that weren't possible before and to reach new markets directly.

Delivery of IT within businesses has become a formalized service, and cloud computing is about making that service easier to consume by the business. Modularity and reuse of standard components has been commonplace in software development for years, allowing subsequent generations of developers to build on the work of their predecessors through the use of abstraction. Cloud computing, and specifically the implementation of a private cloud, seeks to extend this concept of reusable and easy-to-consume elements to infrastructure that can be delivered and consumed across multiple computers, datacenters, and even continents without the consumer having to understand every nuance of its implementation.

VMware is the established market leader in virtualization, a technology borne of the need to do more with less and drive efficiency through the sharing of physical resources. VMware technology is a core tool in delivering cloud computing and is being extended and expanded to build a layered stack of services and standard interfaces.

In this book we'll take a look at the end-to-end implementation of a private cloud using VMware vCloud Director. vCloud Director is VMware's strategic tool in the cloud computing space. It is able to take the well-established enterprise footprint of VMware vSphere and provide a simple roadmap to cloud computing in both the private and public cloud space.

## Who Should Read This Book

As the title implies, this book is intended for people who are trying to learn the why, what, and how of building a private cloud on VMware technologies. A good example is an infrastructure architect or systems administrator tasked by the CIO with implementing "cloud" in their organization—yesterday.

The typical reader has spent a number of years administering VMware and Windows/Linux systems (2–5yrs), and they understand the principles of virtualization and know where to look for deep-dive VMware, Microsoft, and Linux materials.

This is an end-to-end guide to implementing private clouds in an enterprise. Smaller organizations may need to deliver a more agile platform to support rapidly changing business requirements and to deliver lower cost of operations through simplified deployment and resource sharing. Larger enterprises will likely be trying to satisfy diverse business-led IT teams with on-demand provisioning but keep everything under cost and management control.

People who are unfamiliar with vCloud Director will have a lot of new concepts to learn, and although the learning curve is steep, we introduce concepts (the what and why) before diving into the implementation details (the how).

## What You Will Learn

In this book you'll explore the core concepts of cloud computing and how they apply to a private, public, and hybrid implementation.

You'll learn about the functionality that vCloud Director delivers and how to design and implement it. You'll also learn about the services you can deliver to your consumers through real-world examples and how they integrate into your enterprise landscape and can be automated. You'll explore the challenges that new products like vCloud Director can bring in terms of business continuity.

## Additional Resources

At present there are few published materials on vCloud Director outside of official VMware documentation, but the virtualization community has a long tradition of dedicated and passionate bloggers, speakers, and contributors producing timely content in easily digestible chunks. Writing a book on a new product like vCloud Director has been something of a moving target, seeking to capitalize on the emerging cloud computing market. VMware has maintained an aggressive release cadence for the vCloud Director product, which is now in its second major release in three years, and we encourage the reader to use this book in conjunction with these online materials to dive deep where required. Although the core concepts and architecture will remain broadly consistent across future releases, these online resources will prove invaluable in keeping abreast of new functionality, issues, and features. This book points you to the best of them, but the best way to stay informed of breaking news in the virtualization world is to follow the VMware Planet v12n RSS feed (`www.vmware.com/vmtn/planet/v12n/`). For those of you familiar with social media tools like Twitter, the virtualization community is also active there on a daily basis.

Eric Siebert also maintains a painstakingly categorized online directory of links to online blog content called the vLaunchPad at `http://vlp.vsphere-land.com/`.

In terms of the wider community and outside of official conferences like VMworld, there are a lot of free user groups. User groups are where like-minded professionals meet face to face to discuss the issues of the day, developments in the industry, and real-world experiences.

CloudCamp (`www.cloudcamp.com`) touts itself as an "unconference" held all around the world several times a year. People share their experiences in an independent manner through five-minute presentations known as lightning talks. CloudCamp is fiercely vendor-neutral in terms of content and operates a lighthearted red-card process to flag participants that get overly "pitchy" in their presentations.

The VMware User Group (VMUG) is an independent organization created to assist with managing, developing, and staging local VMUG meetings. VMUG provides a mix of sponsored and community content and opportunities for face-to-face networking with your peers, ranging from a handful to over a thousand attendees. You can check the VMUG website (`http://vmug.com`) to locate your local chapter.

The VMware Community platform, including VMware Technology Network (VMTN), is a wealth of peer-to-peer online assistance. It is an excellent forum in which to ask a question or debate an issue.

## What You Need

To get the most from this book, you'll need to have a reasonable understanding of VMware vSphere and your server platform of choice, be it Windows and/or Linux, and general networking and storage concepts like VLANs and storage area networks, ideally gained in a hands-on manner.

In order to actually implement vCloud Director in your organization, you'll need a number of vSphere environments and shared storage and networking hardware; as you'll see in Chapter 5, the specific hardware choices will depend on your design requirements and criteria.

# What Is Covered in This Book

*VMware Private Cloud Computing with vCloud Director* is organized to provide you with a solid grounding in the concepts of cloud computing, and it explores how and where you can apply those concepts to your organization. The book focuses on well-understood technologies such as VMware virtualization and the vCloud Director suite to build a private cloud.

◆ **Part I: Private Cloud Foundations**

   ◆ **Chapter 1: What Makes a Private Cloud?**  This chapter explains what a cloud is (and what it isn't), and explores many of the services and delivery models of cloud computing. You'll learn the key concepts of the platform: abstraction, virtualization, and cloud computing, and the NIST definition of cloud computing.

   ◆ **Chapter 2: Developing Your Strategy**  You'll need commitment and buy-in to embark on a successful private cloud project. Chapter 2 helps you understand what you need in terms of organization and strategy.

   ◆ **Chapter 3: Introducing VMware vCloud Director**  The technical requirements for vCloud Director are covered in Chapter 3. vCloud Director is a suite of products made up of many moving parts; as such, you'll need to have a well-planned infrastructure to be successful.

◆ **Part II: Designing Your Cloud Service**

   ◆ **Chapter 4: Defining the Service Catalog**  A service catalog is a place to store and share the components for building cloud services. It's the vehicle to deliver application and operating system instances so that your consumers can deploy, customize, and use them. Chapter 4 explains the elements of the service catalog and key concepts, such as the vApp, OS templates, the role of media files, and end-to-end automation.

   ◆ **Chapter 5: Platform Design for vCloud Director**  You'll learn how to develop design goals for providers and consumers and how to build a list of requirements on which to base your design. Other topics include design constraints, common architecture decisions, availability and performance, management pod design, and resource pod design.

◆ **Chapter 6: Building a Cost Model**  You'll learn about the economics of cloud computing, including how to build a cost matrix, the difference between cost and price, how to standardize units of consumption, and the ins and outs of software and service-providing licensing, including Microsoft's Service Provider Licensing Agreement and the VMware Service Provider Program.

◆ **Part III: Building the Cloud**

◆ **Chapter 7: Installing VMware vCloud Director**  This chapter begins by showing you how to obtain the necessary binary files—vCloud Director, vShield Manager, and Adobe Flash—and the license key you'll eventually need. Among the many other topics addressed are DNS configuration, the dedicated vCenter Server installation, vShield Manager, the vCloud Director database, vCloud Director installation, SSL certificates, and additional cell server installation.

◆ **Chapter 8: Delivering Services**  Delivering services is the *raison d'être* of a private cloud. You'll learn to build the resource pod; associate vShield Manager with your resource pod; create an organization to map to a business unit, department, or division; create a service catalog to afford self-service among your consumers; and deliver your private cloud to your consumers.

◆ **Chapter 9: Consuming Services**  This chapter describes the various means by which consumers will build, customize, and deploy vApps. Topics include creating and customizing a vApp, uploading a vApp to the catalog, deploying a vApp on a vApp network, and deploying a vApp with an IP load balancer.

◆ **Chapter 10: Integrating Automation**  Automation is the key to successfully performing the day-to-day tasks of maintaining your vCloud. This involves leveraging the vCloud APIs, learning to use the powerful VMware vSphere PowerCLI command-line tool, configuring VMware vCenter Orchestrator for automating workflows, and configuring a RabbitMQ message broker.

◆ **Part IV: Operating the Cloud**

◆ **Chapter 11: Managing Your Cloud**  This chapter explores the differences between managing vSphere and vCloud and how enterprise operational frameworks fit with vCloud. Other topics include managing change; putting together your operations team to serve users; monitoring performance; ensuring that your system is fulfilling your SLA; protecting the platform from malware; and troubleshooting vCloud Director.

◆ **Chapter 12: Business Continuity**  What could be more important than the continuation of your enterprise? You'll explore the tasks that are crucial to ensuring business continuity, including backing up consumer workloads and understanding the special challenges of vCloud Director when recovering from a disaster.

## How to Contact the Authors

We encourage feedback from you about this book, and we're genuinely interested in how people adopt private cloud principles in their organizations. We welcome your ideas, experiences, and war stories.

Simon maintains a blog on virtualization and cloud technologies at `http://vinf.net` where he posts as regularly as possible on topics that interest him. His email address is `simon@vinf.net`. He is also a semi-regular on Twitter and can be reached as `@vinf_net` if you can squeeze your message into 140 characters!

Aidan works for VMware and can be contacted on twitter as `@aidersD`.

Sybex strives to keep you supplied with the latest tools and information you need for your work. Please check their website at `www.sybex.com`, where we'll post additional content and updates that supplement this book if the need arises. Enter **vCloud Director** in the Search box (or type the book's ISBN—**9781118180587**), and click Go to get to the book's update page: `www.sybex.com/go/vmwareprivatecloud`.

# VMware® Private Cloud Computing with vCloud Director®

# Part I

# Private Cloud Foundations

# Chapter 1

# What Makes a Private Cloud?

Over the last few years, many people have struggled to understand what cloud computing is. Most folks have their own ideas about what it means, and various organizations have tried to formulate official definitions. Many niche and mainstream vendors have ridden the cloud computing wave, often contributing little more than confusion and marketing hype. "Cloud washing" is a term frequently used to describe vendors sexing up and repackaging existing solutions as "clouds"—often with only the most tenuous links to the concepts of cloud computing. Today, however, the most widely accepted definition is that of the National Institute of Standards and Technologies (NIST), which is a federal technology agency that works with industry to develop and apply technology, measurements, and standards.

In this chapter, you will learn to:

- ♦ Understand the great abstraction layer
- ♦ Define cloud computing
- ♦ Understand services and delivery models

## Understanding the Great Abstraction Layer

In the early days of the computer, having once assembled systems by hand, people spent endless days debugging problems and trying to reproduce intermittent errors to produce a stable environment to work with.

Fast-forward 30 years. People still assemble systems by hand, and they still spend endless hours debugging complex problems.

So, does that mean that nothing has changed? No, the fundamental drive of human endeavor to do more still persists, but look what you can do with even the most basic computer in 2013 compared to the 1980s.

In the '80s, your sole interface to the computing power of your system was a keyboard and an arcane command line. The only way you could exchange information with your peers was by manually copying files to a large-format floppy disk and physically exchanging that media.

Thirty years later, our general usage patterns of computers haven't changed that significantly: We use them to input, store, and process information. What *have* changed significantly are the massive number of sources and formats of input and output methods—the USB flash drive, portable hard disks, the Internet, email, FTP, and BitTorrent, among others. As a result, there is a massive increase in the expectations of users about what they will be able to do with a computer system.

This increase in expectation has only been possible because each innovation in computing has leap-frogged from the previous one, often driven by pioneering vendors (or left-field inventors) rather than by agreed standards. However, as those pioneering technologies established a market share, their innovations became standards (officially or not) and were iterated by future innovators adding functionality and further compatibility. In essence, abstraction is making it easier for the next innovator to get further, faster, and cheaper.

The history of computing (and indeed human development) has been possible because each new generation of technology has stood on the shoulders of its predecessors. In practical terms, this has been possible because of an ongoing *abstraction of complexity*. This abstraction has also made it feasible to replace or change the underlying processes, configurations, or even hardware without significantly impacting applications that rely on it. This abstraction eventually became known as an application programming interface (API)—an agreed demarcation point between various components of a system.

Here's an example. Ask the typical 2013 graduate Java developer how a hard disk determines which files, sectors, and tracks to read a file from over a small computer system interface (SCSI) interface. You'll probably get a shrug and "I just call `java.io.FileReader` and it does its thing." That's because frankly, they don't care. And they don't care because they don't need to. A diligent design and engineering team has provided them with an API call that masks the underlying complexities of talking to a physical disk—reading 1s and 0s from a magnetic track, decoding them and turning them into usable data, correcting any random errors, and ensuring that any errors are handled gracefully (most of the time). That same application is ignorant of whether the file is stored on a SCSI or a SATA (Serial Advanced Technology Attachment) disk, or even over a network connection, because it is abstracted.

If you map this out, your Java application follows steps similar to these through the stack:

1. The Java developer creates the user code.
2. The developer runs the Java function `java.io.FileReader`.
3. The framework converts the Java function into the appropriate operating system (OS) API call for the OS the code is running on.
4. The operating system receives the API call.
5. The operating system job scheduler creates a job to accomplish the request.
6. The kernel dispatches the job to the filesystem driver.
7. The filesystem driver creates pointers, determines metadata, and builds a stream of file content data.
8. The disk subsystem driver packages file data into a sequence of SCSI bus commands and makes the hardware register manipulations and CPU interrupts.
9. The disk firmware responds to commands and receives data issued over a bus.
10. The disk firmware calculates the appropriate physical disk platter location.
11. The disk firmware manipulates the voltage to microprocessors, motors, and sensors over command wires to move physical disk heads into a predetermined position.
12. The disk microprocessor executes a predetermined pattern to manipulate an electrical pulse on the disk head, and then reads back the resulting magnetic pattern.

**13.** The disk microprocessor compares the predetermined pattern against what has been read back from the disk platter.

**14.** Assuming all that is okay, a Successful command is sent back up the stack.

Phew! Most techies or people who have done some low-level coding can probably follow most of the steps down to the microcontroller level before it turns into pure electrical engineering. But most techies can't master all of this stack, and if they try, they'll spend so long mastering it that they won't get any further than some incomplete Java code that can only read a single file but is implemented as an instance of code that doesn't exist outside of a single machine—let alone become the next social networking sensation or solve the meaning of life.

Abstraction allows people to focus less on the nuts and bolts of building absolutely everything from raw materials and get on with doing useful "stuff" using basic building blocks.

Imagine you are building an application that will run across more than one server. You must deal with the complexities of maintaining state of user sessions between multiple servers and applications. If you want to scale this application across multiple datacenters and even continents, doing so adds another layer of complexity related to concurrency, load, latency, and other factors.

So if you have to build and intimately understand the processing from your users' browser down to the microcontroller on an individual disk, or the conversion of optical or voltage pulses to data flows down cables and telecommunications carrier equipment across the world to move data between your servers, you have a lot of work cut out for you.

## Abstraction and Cloud Computing

Abstraction is a key feature of cloud computing, and cloud computing is an evolution of computer science to date, allowing people to build applications that transcend the traditional disciplines and complexities of computer science and engineering by turning them into abstract constructs that can be manipulated from code by a developer, a user, or even more code. That's a bold statement, but cloud computing is allowing people with little knowledge (or interest) in how the latest x86 CPU architecture executes UNPCKHPS instructions, or even how operating systems access files, to build solutions and services that span the globe overnight because they don't have to understand all the plumbing.

In technical terms, this is known as "moving up the stack," and it's going to be a running theme of this book. We're not saying that people focusing on low-level engineering and complex microtechnology problems aren't valuable; indeed, without their diligent efforts things wouldn't be getting cheaper, faster, or better. And in the real-world trenches of the corporate datacenter, the middle tier still needs people to manage and maintain infrastructure, servers, switches, power, cooling, backup, and so forth. However, this abstraction and continual improvement is commoditizing these elements, as technologies become more mature and start to manage much of this day-to-day maintenance and provisioning themselves "by design." The typical system administrator will be required to understand the application stack and the business, and focus on delivering a service and innovation.

In the early days of computing, people were dedicated to managing the physical placement and retrieval of data on storage devices. But today modern disk arrays deal with this placement (and even automatic policy-based tiers) transparently to the user. When was the last time you wondered which disk platter your file ended up on within a SCSI disk? Or even within an entire disk array? Abstract this into the cloud computing model where your storage is just a web service call that distributes the data you pass as an HTML payload across several geographically diverse datacenters, across many different disk arrays, and across many different physical disks. Technology has evolved to the stage where we trust it to be largely self-managing.

## Virtualization and Cloud Computing

In the computer world, the concept of self-management has been brought to the traditional server estate through virtualization. Autonomously-managed virtual servers can move around a physical datacenter and distribute workload automatically across the physical infrastructure.

As Figure 1.1 shows, application frameworks like the open source Spring Framework and Microsoft's .NET Framework have been introduced to abstract the growing complexity of the operating system and provide database and web services that developers can work with directly. Expand this concept to cover database and application workloads being moved around geographically diverse datacenters, automatically ensuring resilience by spawning redundant copies, or automatically restarting failed processes, operating systems, and even servers.

**FIGURE 1.1**
The functionality of the software "stack," from low-level server components to the cloud, grows by increasing abstraction of functionality.

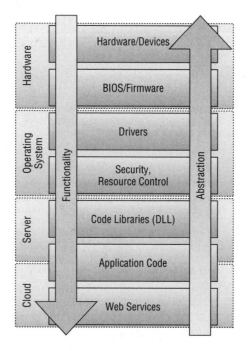

We have the foundation of most of this abstraction today in the shape of VMware vSphere and its complementary technologies, but applications have been bound by their tight dependencies to a physical server operating system, framework, and services. Tweaking typical applications to run seamlessly on multiple server instances and scale up and down based on demand is a complicated piece of engineering and development work in itself. Cloud computing, and particularly VMware vCloud Director and vFabric, provides a services layer above the infrastructure engineering to enable you to build and maintain cloud solutions.

Like many technological developments, cloud computing isn't an overnight solution to this problem; it's an evolution of tools and frameworks to support the next generation of applications that are capable of leveraging these frameworks. That said, cloud isn't just for the Web 2.0/3.0

world; there are a number of things that cloud computing can offer to the traditional enterprise to build on the foundations of virtualization to improve business agility and streamline operations. This is what *private cloud* is about. To understand what a cloud is, you need to look at the key attributes.

# Defining Cloud Computing

The National Institute of Standards and Technology (NIST) has a well-accepted definition of cloud computing that we will use in this book. NIST has defined a list of the key attributes that define cloud computing; they also have a number of working groups and special publications at their website:

    http://csrc.nist.gov/publications/PubsSPs.html#800-145

The NIST definition of cloud computing is based on the following attributes:

◆ On-demand self-service

◆ Broad network access

◆ Resource pooling

◆ Rapid elasticity

◆ Measured service

In this section, we will discuss each of these attributes and see how they map to the practical tools and processes we have available today.

## On-Demand Self-Service

> *A consumer can unilaterally provision computing capabilities, such as server time and network storage, as needed automatically without requiring human interaction with each service's provider.*
>
> —From the NIST definition of cloud computing

On-demand self-service is an abstract concept. It relates to provisioning processing time, such as submitting a batch job, requesting an email account, or requesting an entire server operating system instance from a shared platform. The "without requiring human interaction" phrase relates to the provision of APIs and integrations to allow program code to interact with the platform.

As you know, operating system APIs allow end-user applications to request memory allocations or open files within the scope of a single server. In a similar way, cloud services provide a higher-level abstraction that allows an end-user application running in a cloud to programmatically request more resources, more infrastructure like networks or storage, or even more instances of itself to facilitate horizontal scaling, and potentially makes it possible for those additional resources to be brought online anywhere in the world, rather than just inside a single physical server.

**NOTE**  On-demand self-service is provided by VMware vCloud Director, backed by custom orchestrations for end-to-end functionality and automation that we will discuss in later chapters.

## Broad Network Access

*Capabilities are available over the network and accessed through standard mechanisms that promote use by heterogeneous thin or thick client platforms (e.g., mobile phones, laptops, and PDAs).*

—From the NIST definition of cloud computing

Broad network access is arguably of less relevance to the private cloud, since it is geared more toward platform as a service/software as a service (PaaS/SaaS) solutions rather than infrastructure and services. However, by definition it means that services in cloud computing are more centralized to datacenters and service centers—which has been a key trend in IT for years. A number of the other attributes—particularly resource pooling, discussed next—are not broadly feasible without resources being physically in the same location.

## Resource Pooling

*The provider's computing resources are pooled to serve multiple consumers using a multi-tenant model, with different physical and virtual resources dynamically assigned and reassigned according to consumer demand. There is a sense of location independence in that the customer generally has no control or knowledge over the exact location of the provided resources but may be able to specify location at a higher level of abstraction (e.g., country, state, or datacenter). Examples of resources include storage, processing, memory, network bandwidth, and virtual machines.*

—From the NIST definition of cloud computing

Resource pooling is the gathering of traditionally discrete physical resources like CPU, memory, and disk storage into a singly managed entity. This entity is then shared by a number of consumers. Controls can be placed to grant and limit access by a single consumer so as not to be detrimental to the experience of other consumers.

If a provider chooses to do so, resources can be overcommitted, whereby consumers are allocated more virtual resources than physically exist in the underlying infrastructure. This approach works on the general principle that not all consumers need all of the resources they request all of the time. This model needs to be carefully managed and balanced to ensure that sufficient resources exist to provide an agreed level of service while maintaining practical headroom for day-to-day operations.

The resource pooling concept is key to the economics of cloud computing, a topic we will cover in detail later in this book. Virtualization is a major technology in delivering this capability in a cost-effective and flexible manner.

Within the scope of this book, resource pooling is delivered mainly by vSphere and specific functionality of the underlying ESX hypervisor. vCloud Director provides a number of resource and security abstractions to the user to make this concept easy to understand without them having to grasp the underlying physical resources in a multitenant environment.

## Rapid Elasticity

*Capabilities can be rapidly and elastically provisioned, in some cases automatically, to quickly scale-out, and rapidly released to quickly scale in. To the consumer, the capabilities available for provisioning often appear to be unlimited and can be purchased in any quantity at any time.*

—From the NIST definition of cloud computing

Elasticity describes the ability to add and remove allocated resources to a discrete unit of consumption. In practical terms, this involves adding CPU, memory, and storage resources—either by adding or removing physical resources within a single discrete server (known as vertical scaling) or by adding further discrete virtual server instances (known as horizontal scaling).

Virtualization plays a key role in delivering rapid elasticity, particularly within the scope of a discrete server. This type of elasticity is hard in the physical world as it typically requires high-end "hot-add" hardware and a human engineer to add/remove physical hardware to a single server, a process that is neither rapid nor cheap.

Rapid elasticity in the purely physical world can be achieved in a limited sense if you can deal with adding and removing physical servers for a consumer (horizontal scalability) and you have applications that can support this. This model requires excellent technical orchestration and creative commercial models to be cost-effective and is usually found in the hosting/service-provider space where they have a scale of operation that makes this feasible. Virtualization is rapidly replacing the need for such providers to carry this sort of "ready-to-go" hardware inventory.

Within the scope of this book, rapid elasticity is delivered by vSphere and the underlying ESX hypervisor as well as a layer of orchestration for physical and in-guest provisioning.

### Measured Service

*Cloud systems automatically control and optimize resource use by leveraging a metering capability at some level of abstraction appropriate to the type of service (e.g., storage, processing, bandwidth, and active user accounts). Resource usage can be monitored, controlled, and reported, providing transparency for both the provider and consumer of the utilized service.*

—From the NIST definition of cloud computing

Measured service is key to some of the economic and financial aspirations for cloud computing. Enabling a pay-as-you-go model for consumption of resources ensures that a number of new commercial models are opened up for consumption by organizations. This is often more about the ability to do charge-back or show-back—where you can bill (or report on) the actual or potential cost to provide a set of services to a business unit either to recover cost or to demonstrate usage.

Within the scope of this book, the attribute of measured service is provided by vCenter Chargeback (which is part of VMware vCloud).

## Is Virtualization Cloud Computing?

*Virtualization is a tool, cloud computing is a business model.*

—Joe Baguley, Chief Cloud Technologist, VMware

Virtualization is an enabling technology for cloud computing, but many of the attributes of cloud computing contained in the NIST definition can be delivered on entirely physical platforms through high levels of orchestration—and ironically, it is just this model that Google is rumored to use: thousands upon thousands of physical servers commanded by a tightly controlled orchestration engine to move, provision, and de-provision workloads around the globe.

Similarly high-end computer systems like IBM mainframes and the HP Superdome have hardware-level partitioning that can dedicate physical computing resources at a hardware level to individual processes or services. However, such systems come at a significant up-front cost to the would-be cloud service provider or enterprise.

Where virtualization has become critical to cloud computing is in the economic realm: Virtualization makes x86 hardware significantly more flexible and transparently scalable way beyond its original single-user personal computer design goals.

Innovation in the virtualization space, such as with the VMware Distributed Resource Scheduler, vMotion, and hot-add virtual hardware, has allowed traditional 1:1 workloads to move vertically and horizontally within the boundaries of a single x86 server. This innovation has meant that levels of functionality previously only offered on high-end supercomputers have become available at a lower price point and in a manner that means systems can be built incrementally through horizontal scaling.

This horizontal scaling can often be directly tied to a revenue stream within a business model, which reduces start-up risk and makes it easier to demonstrate return on investment (ROI).

## Are Traditional Services Cloud Computing?

There is much discussion (usually from vendors of such services) over whether or not traditional services like co-location, managed, or hosted services are cloud computing; they are defined and compared with cloud computing as follows:

*Co-location*, where an organization houses its own servers in a datacenter operated by a service provider, is technically the furthest from the NIST cloud definition. Provisioning of services is manual, and the compute infrastructure (consisting of the servers, network, storage, etc.) is either purchased or paid for up-front. As a result, infrastructure typically exhibits little elasticity from a commercial point of view to the provider and consumer.

Power, cooling, and physical space are pooled resources with the co-location facility, shared by many tenant organizations. They aren't directly related to providing computer services (although without them, there would be little ability to provide a service!).

*Managed services*, where a service provider runs a service like email or an application suite on the behalf of an organization, are akin to traditional outsourcing. The provider brings their domain experience in hosting this type of application, and the organization benefits from contractual service-level agreements and a scale of economies. Rather than providing entirely dedicated support resources, the service provider often pools the human technical support resources responsible for running the service among multiple customers, thus reducing the cost to individual consumers.

Most managed services are run on infrastructure dedicated to a customer. The customer may not own the underlying physical infrastructure, instead choosing to lease or rent it from the service provider. But they have full control of it and can implement a truly custom implementation. This is usually done in order to maintain an agreed contractual service level agreement or security boundary and so is less elastic than most cloud definitions would allow for.

This isn't to say you can't run managed services *on* a cloud provider. In this instance, the managed service provider is a further human service layer between the end-user organization and the cloud provider's facilities (in some cases, they may even be the cloud provider, muddying the waters further). The managed service provider adds experience and can provide a custom end-to-end service with the advantages of cloud infrastructure (such as on-demand self-service, elasticity, and pay-as-you-go flexibility).

Managed services provided on a cloud platform is a common model. A managed service provider building and managing a solution for an organization on a public cloud is a good halfway point for getting a custom service in an off-the-shelf/do-it-yourself cloud world. As increasing numbers of service providers adopt this approach, the cost of computing resources will become the commodity, whereas the managed services will become the value-added that service providers use to attract customers.

*Hosting* is most often seen in the world of websites and web services. A service provider typically has an infrastructure that they provide to a broad range of customers, making available a limited set of off-the-shelf features such as standard scripts and applications that customers can utilize. There is little flexibility in traditional hosting. You choose the type of application you want and it is provided in a fixed configuration. You are given limited access to the system and typically afforded user rather than root privileges. This arrangement resembles the SaaS model, which we will discuss later in the "Understanding Services and Delivery Models" section of this chapter.

A number of variants exist such as virtual private hosting, where you are given a virtual machine for which you have full control—this is getting into cloud territory. Such services are usually charged on a fixed rental basis with a minimum contractual term, rather than the measured usage, no-commitment approach you get with most cloud providers—for example, $99 a month for a Windows instance with 4 GB of RAM, a 1 GHz CPU, and 20 GB hard disk from a hosting provider versus $0.40 per hour for individual SQL transactions with a cloud provider.

## Understanding Services and Delivery Models

There are a number of ways in which cloud services can be delivered. In this section we review the commonly accepted definitions of the various services and their delivery models.

The *X as a Service* (XaaS) models are important concepts to understand and predate the definition of cloud services. XaaS defines the *type* of service being delivered; delivery models describe *how* those services are delivered and to whom (see Figure 1.2).

To understand delivery models, you must grasp the concepts of consumer and provider:

**Consumer**   A consumer is the user—the person or organization that requests, uses, and releases resources and services. This involves the processing of data using the services provided. In some instances, the consumer may be another application or software process rather than a human consumer.

**Provider**   A provider is the person or organization that deals with delivering and provisioning the resources and services to the consumer. This involves installing hardware and software and typically using automation and workflows to simplify the process for the consumer while delivering a low operational cost to the provider.

**FIGURE 1.2**
The relationship
between services
and delivery models

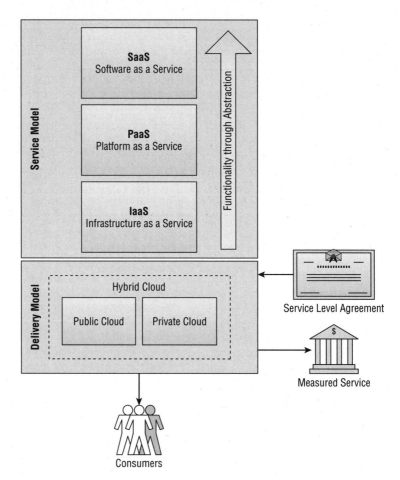

## Infrastructure as a Service (IaaS)

*The capability provided to the consumer is to provision processing, storage, networks, and other fundamental computing resources where the consumer is able to deploy and run arbitrary software, which can include operating systems and applications. The consumer does not manage or control the underlying cloud infrastructure but has control over operating systems, storage, and deployed applications; and possibly limited control of select networking components (e.g., host firewalls).*

—From the NIST definition of cloud computing

This definition describes a model for a service providing infrastructure—typically consisting of computing, network, and storage resources—to a user in a transparent manner. This model allows the consumer to request resources in units of CPU hours, network subnets, or giga-bytes of storage allocated in disk volumes to a specific server instance running the requested operating system. Many outsourcing, hosting, and managed service providers have run this type of model for years, whereby a consumer can request a server of a particular specification and configuration and the provider deals with the complexities of ordering, taking delivery, racking, installing the operating system, and updating inventory and management tools before handing over control to the consumer—as well as managing its overall life cycle of updates, upgrades, and refreshes.

The consumer has a fixed unit of capacity because it is bounded by a single server (or a resource allocation in the instance of a virtual server) that the consumer owns outright or rents over a fixed period—typically measured in months or years. However, they pay a fixed amount regardless of how much of the allocated resource they consume.

When delivering Infrastructure as a Service (IaaS) on a cloud (be it public, private, or hybrid), this resource allocation is provided on a self-service basis. Self-service, speed of delivery, and measured service attributes dictate that infrastructure be delivered in an entirely automated fashion from a shared pool of computing, storage, and network capacity. The consumer only pays for what they consume, rather than a fixed, contracted allocation over an agreed term.

The provider abstracts the complexity in providing this underlying infrastructure. Examples include the creation of a virtual local area network (VLAN), firewalls, storage allocation, server instances, installation of the operating system, applications, management tools, and integration with a billing system or configuration management tool. To achieve economies of scale in cloud platforms, this is accomplished by calling on a pool of virtualized, multitenant physical resources driven by an automation tool.

IaaS is a foundational layer for other higher-level services like PaaS and SaaS. In basic terms, nothing can be delivered without infrastructure to run it, but the infrastructure is abstracted to allow higher-level services to build on it without having to invest significant time in the complexities of building and managing servers, networks, and storage for each tenant service.

## Platform as a Service (PaaS)

*The capability provided to the consumer is to deploy onto the cloud infrastructure consumer-created or acquired applications created using programming languages, libraries, services, and tools supported by the provider.*

*The consumer does not manage or control the underlying cloud infrastructure including network, servers, operating systems, or storage, but has control over the deployed applications and possibly configuration settings for the application-hosting environment.*

—From the NIST definition of cloud computing

Developers have spent a lot of time in traditional infrastructure liaising with infrastructure people trying to build applications that can scale and that are highly available in the event of infrastructure problems. In reality, delivering such solutions has proven to be a difficult path—both infrastructure and development teams strive to engineer in redundancy and availability features. Sometimes these efforts result in overengineering of solutions with little material benefit—which drives up total cost of ownership. Also, because of the tight dependencies between applications and the underlying servers, storage, and networks required to deliver reliable high availability and scalability, someone has to intimately understand how the code works, as well as how the lower-level services are configured—and the limitations of both.

Platform as a service (PaaS) seeks to build on the IaaS foundation and abstract discrete blocks of infrastructure into platform services, such as database, message queueing, and caching that can be consumed by application code to deliver services to consumers.

In the traditional model, developers work with infrastructure people to design, deliver, and test various third-party applications like Oracle databases, IBM's MQSeries, BizTalk, and SQL Server on discrete infrastructure to build services dedicated to the service being delivered. The delivery of more and more services leads to discrete silos of infrastructure and platforms being implemented for each service, which drives up the overall total cost of ownership for the provider and in turn for the consumer as the provider seeks to recoup the cost, or the consumer funds the end-to-end process.

PaaS seeks to simplify this process and deliver services that provide an agreed level of availability and performance that is usually defined by a service level agreement (SLA). This goal is often accomplished through multitenancy of software solutions built on an IaaS foundation, whereby the PaaS layer is able to request and adjust resources from the IaaS layer through self-service (typically accomplished programmatically using an API).

PaaS is the first layer where services in the cloud world become self-aware. The PaaS layer is engineered to understand its load and availability requirements (defined by the SLA) and has built-in logic to know when it needs more (or fewer) resources. It handles such requests to the IaaS layer and distributes jobs accordingly.

PaaS is characterized by providing a scalable abstraction of application services that developers can consume. Developers and their creations are the primary consumers of PaaS and not users (although users indirectly benefit from PaaS through the services they consume).

---

### PaaS and the Private Cloud

Today, PaaS is just emerging in the private cloud space whereas a plethora of PaaS services are available in the public cloud space—thanks to Amazon and its Amazon Web Services (AWS), Google and its Google App Engine, and Microsoft and its Azure platforms. These platforms provide a growing stack of PaaS services for databases, message queuing, and caching. But they are all currently limited to public cloud implementations, hosted on Amazon-, Google-, or Microsoft-provided infrastructure that is available to anyone with a credit card and a user account.

There is currently no way to take a solution that you have built on AWS, App Engine, or Azure and run it internally in your enterprise without having to build and maintain an API-compatible clone of the PaaS services that AWS, App Engine, or Azure provide—an expensive and nontrivial task.

PaaS solutions are for *green-field applications*—they provide the underlying plumbing for Web 2.0/cloud-generation applications and require developers to learn a new programming method and framework to deliver a solution (although not necessarily a different programming language as they all support most modern languages or their variants).

VMware has made a number of strategic acquisitions in the PaaS space in the past few years, and the vFabric and Cloud Foundry product lines promise to deliver the ability to seamlessly move an application-level workload between public and private cloud platforms. In part this is accomplished by having a common VMware IaaS layer (vCloud Director and vSphere) that is present and available to both public and private cloud implementations.

With those acquisitions the stage is set for a battle between the VMware/Spring (vCloud/vFabric) world and the Microsoft (.NET/Azure) world over the coming few years. This book focuses on the VMware cloud stack.

## Software as a Service (SaaS)

*The capability provided to the consumer is to use the provider's applications running on a cloud infrastructure.*

*The applications are accessible from various client devices through either a thin client interface, such as a web browser (e.g., web-based email), or a program interface. The consumer does not manage or control the underlying cloud infrastructure including network, servers, operating systems, storage, or even individual application capabilities, with the possible exception of limited user specific application configuration settings.*

—From the NIST definition of cloud computing

Services provided on a software as a service (SaaS) basis are often multitenant and leverage lower-level services like IaaS and PaaS to deliver services that are directly used by consumers.

Email and collaboration solutions are the most commonly encountered examples of SaaS. Consumers interact directly with services and are typically measured (and charged) on a per-user or per-minute/per-gigabyte basis.

SaaS solutions typically present the least flexible but ready-to-use solutions for consumers, who use the functionality provided as instructed. Consumers cannot typically modify and extend these services—for example, to integrate with an in-house legacy application.

SaaS is closest to off-the-shelf commercial software but is provided online on an ongoing measured basis rather than a one-off purchase model. That isn't to say that providers can't build custom solutions that leverage IaaS and PaaS building blocks to provide a solution on a SaaS basis to consumers; in fact, that is essentially what SaaS vendors like SalesForce.com, Gmail, and Microsoft Business Productivity Online Standard Suite do.

Now that you have a good understanding of the various service models, we'll look at the various delivery models for those services. Each cloud service can be delivered in a different way depending on where the service is physically housed and to whom it is provided.

## Public Cloud

*The cloud infrastructure is provisioned for open use by the general public. It may be owned, managed, and operated by a business, academic, or government organization, or some combination of them. It exists on the premises of the cloud provider.*

—From the NIST definition of cloud computing

Amazon Elastic Compute Cloud (EC2) is the most widely used public cloud service. Both EC2 and AWS provide a set of IaaS and PaaS services for developers to build cloud applications on.

EC2 is open to the public over the Internet, and developers can start using the service with little more than an Amazon account and a credit card. EC2 has a diverse customer base and is deployed in several global locations. EC2 maintains a library of standard operating systems—mainly Linux- and open source–based, although Windows is also available.

Users pay for EC2 on a per-CPU hour basis or per-gigabyte of data stored or transferred in/out of the cloud. EC2 supports an extensive API to allow users or even applications to provision and adjust computing, network, or storage resources.

This IaaS offering is complemented by AWS. AWS is a PaaS layer that includes database, content delivery, file storage, and message queuing services, among other innovations.

Many providers offer public cloud services that are open to tenants from any business type. Their core business model may be built on a theory similar to investment banking: Having a wide spread of industries and customer types means there is less chance of them all requiring high levels of resources at the same time. These providers are essentially betting that while there are peaks and troughs in demand, the overall spread of load is averaged out. This spread helps providers keep operating costs low. This model has been a common one in the networking and telecommunications world for a long time.

## Private Cloud

*The cloud infrastructure is provisioned for exclusive use by a single organization comprising multiple consumers (e.g., business units).*

*It may be owned, managed, and operated by the organization, a third party, or some combination of them, and it may exist on or off premises.*

—From the NIST definition of cloud computing

The private cloud is our main focus in this book. The concept of the private cloud takes much of the bleeding-edge innovation going on within the public cloud space and applies it to technologies and ideas used by the typical enterprise in a measured and controlled manner. In the private cloud model, tenants of the system are typically business units or departments rather than separate businesses. All tenants gain self-service provisioning, and by consuming pooled and elastic resources, the overall business can realize savings in infrastructure costs.

Most public cloud solutions are green-field builds, where there are no real legacy systems and infrastructure to consider. They can be also designed from the ground up with scalability and elasticity in mind. The private cloud delivers an underlying infrastructure that can support this model but also allows legacy and current application implementations to benefit from cloud attributes while their services evolve into true cloud applications.

vCloud Director builds on the existing vSphere suite of products to make it possible to build cloud services with a familiar base. vCloud Director gives IT departments the ability to leverage existing investment in infrastructure, operations, and virtualization to build a private cloud.

**WARNING**    Keep in mind that vCloud Director isn't just a vSphere component you can install into an existing vSphere environment to make a private cloud. To be successful in building a private cloud, you must take into account many more technical and operational factors and plan for them in your design. We will tackle these factors in later chapters.

## Hybrid Cloud

*The cloud infrastructure is a composition of two or more distinct cloud infrastructures (private, community, or public) that remain unique entities, but are bound together by standardized or proprietary technology that enables data and application portability (e.g., cloud bursting for load balancing between clouds).*

—From the NIST definition of cloud computing

The hybrid cloud is, as you would imagine, a cross between a public and a private cloud. It describes an implementation where an organization selectively chooses to deploy services hosted with a public cloud provider like Amazon or one of the VMware vCloud partners as well as running services on a private cloud in-house.

Ideally there should be a single interface between the public and private services, as well as an API for automation and integrations between the two to facilitate moving workloads as seamlessly as possible between public and private infrastructures. As of this writing, VMware leads this space with the vCloud product and service provider program. Because the core vCloud Director product is common across service providers and end-user organizations, the consumer is able to leverage a high-level of integration and common components to make solutions portable and interoperable between private and public clouds. You'll learn more about this topic later in the book.

The hybrid cloud is likely to be the most common deployment model for enterprises in the coming years. As organizations dip their toes into the cloud world, the hybrid cloud allows them the flexibility to selectively deploy solutions that benefit from public cloud capabilities with a public provider. Where they feel they have security or compliance or legacy architecture constraints that prevent such solutions from being hosted in a public, multitenant platform, the same vSphere technologies can be used to operate a more controlled private cloud.

As the application portfolios of organizations evolve to take advantage of cloud service attributes like PaaS and SaaS, applications may become natural candidates to be implemented in the public cloud to achieve a lower cost of running or to meet vastly varying load.

### Community Cloud

*The cloud infrastructure is provisioned for exclusive use by a specific community of consumers from organizations that have shared concerns (e.g., mission, security requirements, policy, and compliance considerations).*

*It may be owned, managed, and operated by one or more of the organizations in the community, a third party, or some combination of them, and it may exist on or off premises.*

—From the NIST definition of cloud computing

The community cloud is less a focus in this book. You can view it as a variant of the private cloud—as a private cloud that is shared among a number of enterprises. An example is the infrastructure shared among a group of banks that are working collaboratively and that share a common set of security compliance requirements.

## Summary

Abstraction is a way of allowing you to build on the work of others without having to understand the entire end-to-end stack of technologies. Developers provide demarcation points such as APIs to allow the fine details of underlying technologies to change and shift as they evolve without impacting solutions that are built on them.

The NIST definition of cloud computing provides clear guidance on the various attributes that define cloud computing. It serves to ground any discussion of technologies and solutions through a common definition and allows you to compare traditional delivery methods for IT services such as managed services and hosting.

A number of services and delivery models appear within the definition of cloud computing. While we have spent some time defining what a cloud is, avoid getting too hung up on the definition—instead, think about what it is that you want to do with your service, what you want out of it, and how you can achieve it.

A key takeaway from this chapter is that cloud computing is much more than just technology; it is a business model. Cloud computing is a way of providing services (internally or externally) that allows more creative commercial and operational models to be used that enable creative and innovative solutions.

Agility, or the ability to react quickly to changing requirements, is also a key driver for the adoption of cloud computing. By enabling self-service through automation, providers can empower consumers to provision, manage, and deploy their own solutions without administrative intervention on a day-to-day basis.

To put things into perspective, a December 2011 Gartner survey on the single biggest driver for implementing a private cloud revealed that 59 percent of respondents said their main driver was speed and agility, whereas 21 percent indicated cost:

    http://blogs.gartner.com/thomas_bittman/2012/02/28/private-cloud-and-hot-tubs/

# Chapter 2

# Developing Your Strategy

As we touched on in the previous chapter, cloud computing is really all about applications and data. This is a pretty big shift from the pure infrastructure/development split that has dominated most IT departments in the last 20 years. The cloud enables consumers to manage infrastructure through abstractions. This fact may seem like a scary prospect, but it's important to appreciate that infrastructure isn't going away with cloud computing. It's becoming simpler than ever before for your users to consume services, which in turn frees you from a lot of repetitive tasks like provisioning and changing machines for consumers.

Careful design, planning, management, and operations are still necessary, but in many ways you are free from the day-to-day activities of "keeping the lights on" and can focus on finding effective and innovative ways of doing business. This is the "moving up the stack" concept we touched on in Chapter 1, "What Makes a Private Cloud?" To get the most out of cloud computing, you'll need to understand more about your applications and their life cycles than you've ever considered relevant before.

Once you've decided to embark on the journey to the cloud, you need to ask yourself a few questions: What are the business drivers behind this move? Is the purpose commercial, technical, or operational, or is it something else entirely?

In this chapter, you will learn to:

- ◆ Work out your overall strategy

- ◆ Build detailed requirements

- ◆ Manage the life cycle of your cloud and its services

- ◆ Understand how your users will want to use your cloud platform through the development of use cases

- ◆ Develop a team

## Developing Your Strategy

You'll need to develop a good strategy for your organization's adoption of cloud computing. Understand what your endgame is and what the business drivers are for getting there.

We have seen several common business drivers across all industry sectors considering cloud computing. These are best summarized as follows:

**Business Focus**   This driver allows the business to concentrate less on funding, managing, and building infrastructure and IT services and instead choose to maintain in-house expertise of industry-specific services and solutions that are built on commodity/standard infrastructure building blocks. This driver is often paired with an outsourcing arrangement and combined with one or more of the other common drivers that follow.

**Commercial**   This driver is the ability to do more with less—to spend less on operations with efficient sharing, automation, and allocation of an elastic pool of resources.

**Agility**   Agility is the ability to react quickly to changes in requirements, enabling consumers to provision their own services rather than rely on a dedicated and manual process.

**Portability**   Portability allows you to move services from one IT service provider to another through the adoption of a standardized set of interfaces for application and infrastructure provision.

**Cutting Edge**   The wish to demonstrate to competitors and prospective customers that you have a competitive edge over the rest of the industry by adopting cutting-edge technology solutions, even if it isn't strictly delivering direct business benefit.

Another key decision point in setting your strategy is the delivery model you'll use. The scope of this book is the private cloud. But when you consider your overall strategy, you might need to take a hybrid approach (see Figure 2.1). Many organizations, for example, operate in regulated industries, like finance and healthcare, where there are regulatory and legal constraints that define where data can be stored and how it is accessed. Is the private cloud an interim solution until you can move applications to the true public cloud? Or do you have technical, legal, and business constraints that will prevent this?

**FIGURE 2.1**
Common cloud use cases and deployment models

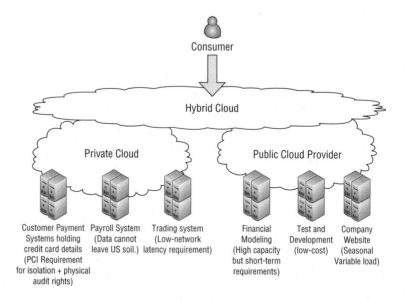

If the latter, is it more likely that you'll operate in a hybrid model with core services hosted on your private cloud while spin-off operations and noncore services are hosted on a public cloud but with a single point of administration?

The end state might be a public cloud, with applications that develop over their life cycle into true cloud-enabled applications. Or perhaps the private cloud model may unlock enough commercial and business agility that it meets all of your requirements for the foreseeable future so there is little motivation to move to a fully public model.

It's worth setting out a 3–5-year plan with regular review checkpoints. You can plan for at least the next 3 years of the life cycle now, and take comfort in the fact that the technologies underpinning the private cloud present a flexible and modular architecture that you can rework to accommodate a future change in direction if required without massive reengineering.

Committing to a multiyear strategy is risky in the IT industry because things change so quickly. Keep in mind that, as we discussed earlier in this book, cloud computing is an evolution of what has gone before. It is an iteration of previous delivery and consumption models rather than a radical change to the capabilities of technology itself.

# Buy or Build?

A key decision in deciding your private cloud strategy is how you will implement it. Will you build it from the components and manage it in-house, or will you buy a service from a provider (hosted either on-premise or with a service provider's datacenter)? Both are valid models for the private cloud. A service provider's datacenter is a logical but dedicated extension of your own. You might decide to buy the platform as a managed service; in this instance, the provider builds a dedicated discrete infrastructure and management (so it is a private cloud) for your requirements but commercially or operationally provides it on an IaaS basis. This section explores a number of factors you should consider early in your strategy process.

## Deciding to Buy

If you are evaluating options to buy your private cloud as a service from a provider, there are a number of areas where you should focus your due-diligence efforts to ensure you understand the service's costs and limitations.

This approach is different from buying a public cloud service; you should see it more as building a dedicated platform from common infrastructure building blocks from your chosen service provider and consuming it as a managed service. View this process as a partnership with the service provider, and depending on your requirements, it may be an entirely custom design or it may leverage a number of standard infrastructure components that the provider supplies in a fixed configuration.

### SERVICE LEVEL AGREEMENT

Service providers typically express the availability levels on offer in terms of an availability percentage. Table 2.1 shows how those percentage figures break down into periods of unplanned downtime during a month and a year.

**TABLE 2.1:** Availability, expressed as "nines" and allowable downtime

| AVAILABILITY % | DOWNTIME PER YEAR | DOWNTIME PER MONTH* | DOWNTIME PER WEEK |
|---|---|---|---|
| 90% ("one nine") | 36.5 days | 72 hours | 16.8 hours |
| 95% | 18.25 days | 36 hours | 8.4 hours |
| 97% | 10.96 days | 21.6 hours | 5.04 hours |
| 98% | 7.30 days | 14.4 hours | 3.36 hours |
| 99% ("two nines") | 3.65 days | 7.20 hours | 1.68 hours |
| 99.5% | 1.83 days | 3.60 hours | 50.4 minutes |
| 99.8% | 17.52 hours | 86.23 minutes | 20.16 minutes |
| 99.9% ("three nines") | 8.76 hours | 43.8 minutes | 10.1 minutes |
| 99.95% | 4.38 hours | 21.56 minutes | 5.04 minutes |
| 99.99% ("four nines") | 52.56 minutes | 4.32 minutes | 1.01 minutes |
| 99.999% ("five nines") | 5.26 minutes | 25.9 seconds | 6.05 seconds |
| 99.9999% ("six nines") | 31.5 seconds | 2.59 seconds | 0.605 seconds |
| 99.99999% ("seven nines") | 3.15 seconds | 0.259 seconds | 0.0605 seconds |

Source: http://en.wikipedia.org/wiki/High_availability

Most service providers will only offer a service level agreement (SLA) that excludes scheduled downtime—that is, your 99.95 percent metric applies only to unplanned downtime outside of scheduled maintenance windows. So it is important to understand what the maintenance windows entail and the periods they cover.

It's useful to ask what commitments the service provider is able to make during that maintenance window. For example, the provider may commit to providing reduced resilience during that window, rather than a total outage, by removing one of two power feeds. Assuming your equipment is dual-connected to the power feeds, you lose the resilience during the scheduled maintenance but not the overall service.

Some providers may be willing to offer a different service-credit condition during maintenance windows. Although resiliency is reduced, the service-credit condition may still be in force if the main power feed fails while the backup feed is offline for maintenance.

Some SLAs may also define normal business hours for support requests. Doing so is especially important if your organization spans several time zones.

You should understand what performance guarantees (if any) are being offered by the provider and how compliance is measured and reported. Your provider will likely have various tiers of SLAs.

It may be possible to mix and match discrete parts of your infrastructure to an appropriate SLA tier. But consider that your overall service is only as good as the weakest link in the chain. If your virtual computing infrastructure can provide a 99.99 percent SLA but the storage or networking services can only deliver 99.9 percent, then the best you can offer for your overall service is 99.9 percent and you may be wasting any extra money spent on providing the computing capability at a higher SLA.

Also pay attention to provisioning and request timescales and the headroom built into whatever capacity you have contracted for. Determine how far the provider will let you scale before there is a change in cost or further commercial commitment required.

## Service Credits

What are your chances of getting some compensation if the provider is unable to deliver the SLA you have signed up for? How will terms of performance or availability commitments be monitored and reported? Are they expecting you to do this or will they provide this reporting to you?

You should also exercise caution wherever you see very high percentage SLAs (like 99.999 percent or even 100 percent in some cases). This level of service is hard to achieve even with the best engineered technologies and skilled staff on standby. Often those higher-level SLAs are giving you access to a service credit condition if they fail to deliver that availability metric rather than a real guarantee that your service will be available to those levels.

The overhead risk cost of providing those service credits will be factored into the price you pay the provider. Take into account that most service-credit conditions with cloud providers typically cover only what you are paying the provider for the service during the downtime incurred, rather than the actual financial loss you incur through the loss of business.

## Disaster Recovery

Be sure that you understand the scope of the disaster recovery services being offered (or not) by your chosen provider. Business continuity and disaster recovery (BC/DR) is a complicated subject and can be specific to your business and IT systems. Know the boundaries of your service.

For example, many providers do not provide a commitment to house or rebuild and restore your systems if they have a catastrophic failure at a datacenter site. Instead, they will rely on your solution and business to plan, budget, and provide resources accordingly.

Many providers will be glad to work with you to define and manage a full BC/DR solution and plan, but be aware it's generally not part of the basic service they offer.

## Cost Structure

Understand how and when you are being monitored for usage. Is the service provider measuring peak, average, or a fixed allocation of resources over a fixed period?

When you are looking to buy a cloud service from a provider, don't expect to be allowed to see the details of how costs are constructed. This is essentially the provider's "special sauce" and they may not be willing to share the commercial secrets (or infrastructure skeletons!) that allow them to deliver service at a particular cost.

## Deciding to Build

If you are evaluating building your private cloud in-house from the ground up, you need to consider a number of factors before you arrive at the most appropriate solution.

### GREENFIELD OR REENGINEER?

Your organization is likely to have a large existing datacenter footprint—a mix of network, storage, and computing infrastructure that you have acquired over a period of time. Various elements of that existing infrastructure will be at various stages of their life cycle, making management as a single unit difficult.

vCloud Director has a number of design considerations, and we don't recommend that you layer it over an existing vSphere installation. The networking features make it important to design the network appropriately to ensure you can scale the platform without significant reengineering of the platform to accommodate future expansion.

### HARDWARE PLATFORM

IT departments typically buy servers on a per-project basis. The private cloud is geared toward a shared pool of resources. Many organizations don't have this model in place and aren't able to use this model because specific infrastructure is owned by business units or groups.

You'll need to choose a hardware platform for each of the stacks within your solution. Unless you plan on buying massive amounts of infrastructure up front, it makes sense to purchase infrastructure that can be scaled in a modular fashion.

We'll cover the vCloud Director design criteria and decisions in Chapter 5, "Platform Design for vCloud Director."

### DATACENTER FACILITIES

Because you're likely to be deploying your cloud platform on new infrastructure, ensure you have the physical space and power/cooling capacity to host it. It's likely you'll need to run it alongside your current-state infrastructure for some time (that is, until you can migrate everything into your private cloud).

As part of your design to provide agility and elasticity, you may be considering consolidated technologies like blade servers and converged input/output (I/O) for your networking and storage traffic. This strategy can pose challenges within your datacenter, especially where your current design places constraints over power density and you have a significant investment in existing structured cabling that may not meet the requirements of modern 10GbE converged I/O technologies.

### VIRTUAL OR PHYSICAL SERVERS

As we discussed in the previous chapter, a number of delivery and service models are available for cloud computing. We discussed how virtualization has been a useful tool in enabling more flexible infrastructure, which has facilitated a more commodity-based approach to providing infrastructure. Although virtualization is almost a given for most cloud computing solutions, it's important to realize that the two are not mutually exclusive—there are ways of maintaining a hybrid physical/virtual solution within a cloud computing solution.

Leveraging physical infrastructure requires a much more holistic view to automation since you must deal with technical and human systems, purchase order systems, datacenter facilities teams, firmware, and OS and application build processes, among other factors.

Elements of cloud computing using physical infrastructure work on very different time-scales compared to virtual infrastructure unless you can maintain a healthy pool of hardware ready for use. If you have to physically order equipment and wait for it to be delivered and commissioned, then that isn't necessarily the rapid elasticity attribute we discussed in Chapter 1. However, modern blade and server hardware is making it easier than ever to carry out complex hardware-level provisioning tasks through converged I/O technologies and centralized management toolsets in ways that were impossible with older technologies.

This sort of model is usually best left to a service provider who can leverage a pool of physical hardware on a rental basis for a diverse range of customers. It's much harder to justify this sort of solution within an enterprise due to the costs involved and the quantity of idle hardware unless there are sound business reasons. It's more than likely you'll need to adopt a high level of virtualization, although you may want to supplement it with services provided on physical hardware that are tied to automated provisioning processes.

The native vCloud Director product is only capable of managing virtual resources, such as virtual machines and vShield firewalls. A number of plug-ins are available that work with external automation engines to manipulate non-VMware infrastructure. In Chapter 10, "Integrating Automation," we'll show how you can use vCenter Orchestrator to deal with these sorts of end-to-end automations and interfaces.

## Application Stack Considerations

It's critical that you consider the application stacks you'll be deploying into your cloud solution. You must grasp the distinction between current-state and cloud-generation applications.

Some vendors are adopting the term *legacy* for your current-state applications. You may think that looking at your current-state applications, using the term legacy is unfair. After all, many systems have only recently migrated from the big-iron midrange and mainframe platforms that were previously known as legacy to commodity x86 infrastructure. This may seem to be a cynical marketing ploy by vendors; however, there is a valid, if commercially focused sentiment, that nothing ever stands still. As you'll see later in this chapter, planning for the next cycle is important.

Current-state applications are your line-of-business applications, your client-server applications, and to some extent the n-tier web services that you have implemented. These applications are typically deployed in vertically scaled silos of discrete computing capacity; they generally rely on the infrastructure and operating system layer to deal with availability, disaster recovery, and performance management.

Such availability and performance management is provided through clustering, load balancing, and disk-level redundant array of independent disks (RAID). Few facilities exist within the application code itself to deal with failure of a discrete server component or service other than maybe an internal error handling and retry protocol. Figure 2.2 shows the traditional enterprise model for application deployment.

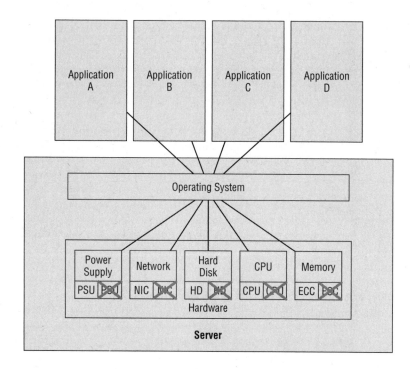

These applications typically exist in a single datacenter location and are unaware of where they are executing and how they should resume services from an alternative location in the event of a datacenter-level failure. This job is left to the infrastructure and operational functions of an organization.

Sometimes underlying infrastructure like a spanned layer 2 network and replicating storage is used to present a logical infrastructure across more than one physical location (see Figure 2.3). But the key point remains: The application itself is unaware of the underlying locations of infrastructure for providing service.

Likewise, performance is managed in a vertical sense within the scope of a discrete server. Most modern applications can request extra capacity (processes, threads, memory, CPU cycles, etc.) from an operating system, but this is always within the scope of a discrete server. If the maximum capacity of that discrete server is reached, it cannot be increased without a manual upgrade performed by an operations team manually adding faster CPUs, more RAM, disks, and so forth. If one discrete server is running at full capacity and other servers are lightly utilized, most current-state applications cannot automatically redistribute the processing load to other servers because they all maintain separate binaries and configurations.

Virtualization, particularly vSphere, has alleviated some of these issues of scalability and availability and provided an easy-to-implement solution to the elasticity dictated by cloud computing by consolidating multiple discrete silos of x86 capacity into a single overall capacity. When discrete servers are implemented as virtual machines on a vSphere cluster, they consume resources (CPU cycles, memory) from a shared pool managed by the Distributed Resource Scheduling (DRS) feature. DRS takes this concept a step further by allowing individual virtual machine workloads to be balanced and migrated between physical compute resources without downtime to offer the best possible performance of individual servers within the constraints of physically available resources.

**FIGURE 2.3**
An example of using low-level infrastructure technologies to transparently present a single logical datacenter that spans multiple physical locations to applications

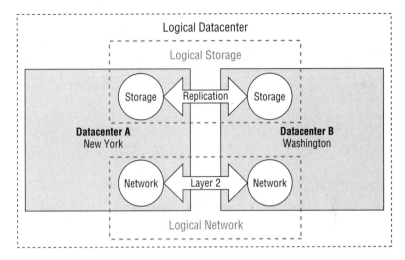

But all of these approaches are still bound by the maximum capacity of a single host. With current technologies, virtual machines (and by implication the applications they contain) can only scale vertically within the capacity of a single host. As such, individual hosts have to be sized to support the largest possible workload. If a high degree of vertical computing elasticity is required, doing so can be costly, or even physically impossible, with current hardware, especially when you factor in extra hosts for redundancy and failover.

Virtualization has extended the life cycle of a number of legacy applications by providing a more flexible virtual infrastructure platform and breaking the tight coupling between hardware, operating system, and application. However, the way these applications are architected has not fundamentally changed—just the delivery model.

Next-generation cloud applications are defined by several key attributes that allow them to rise above the limitations of the current approaches described here. This section explores those attributes.

## Design for Failure

Design for failure blurs the line of abstraction that current-state applications leverage to deliver availability and performance. Cloud application developers take more ownership of the way the applications are implemented and deployed: across multiple datacenters or discrete hosts. The applications are engineered to be tolerant of a loss of connection to service components like databases. Message queuing and buffering are common approaches, where an n-tier application is capable of rerouting requests to other subsystems when it determines that one subsystem has become unavailable.

In current-state applications, design for failure is either handled at the infrastructure level through IP/application traffic manipulation or via operating system–level features like clustering—tools typically deployed in an enterprise to provide transparent application availability in the event of an individual host failure (see Figure 2.4).

**FIGURE 2.4**
Various infrastructure-
level tools like IP load
balancing and clustering

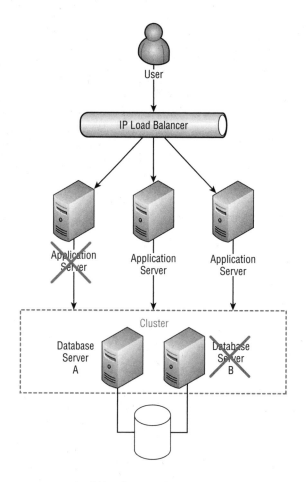

Cloud applications are state-aware and self-healing in this sense. They can request new application instances to work around a detected failure. Building this self-awareness into the application allows developers to make decisions inside code to intelligently work around failures and changes in load and performance characteristics. In Figure 2.5, note how the job dispatchers work around a failed instance by spawning a new instance of the application. The code deals with an increase in database load by spawning a new instance of a database server and loading it with data.

This design makes much more sense: In the traditional approach to infrastructure, people had to make assumptions about what was required for an application, usually based on observed behaviors and criteria.

## Scale-Out Elasticity

Where applications are built to handle large workloads, a degree of parallelism is factored into their architecture, distributing jobs or processes across a number of worker processes and essentially managing a job dispatch and distributed execution function. If a job fails or does not complete in a timely fashion, it may be re-sent to an alternative worker or retried.

**FIGURE 2.5**
A next-generation
cloud application

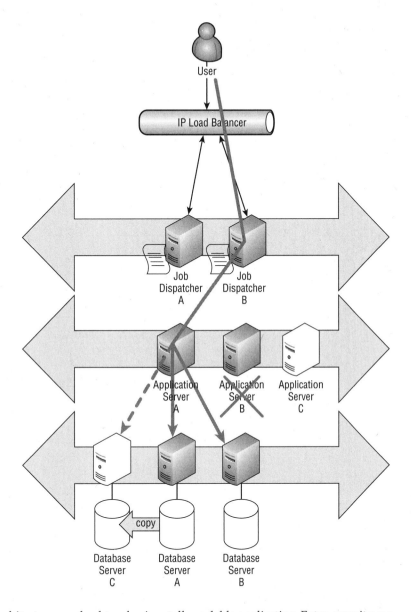

This type of architecture can lead to a horizontally scalable application. Extra capacity can be brought on stream and released in units of discrete virtual servers and processes. Using this method avoids the up-front hardware cost or a developer having to understand the low-level symmetric multiprocessing (SMP) approaches to accomplishing this sort of scalability on a vertically scaled system.

The application simply requests new server/application instances from the cloud infrastructure via the automation interfaces. It de-provisions those instances when they are no longer required to service a higher-than-usual load level. As shown in Figure 2.6, the application achieves elasticity by scaling application servers horizontally under load and scaling back the number of database server instances when load decreases.

**FIGURE 2.6**
A next-generation cloud application

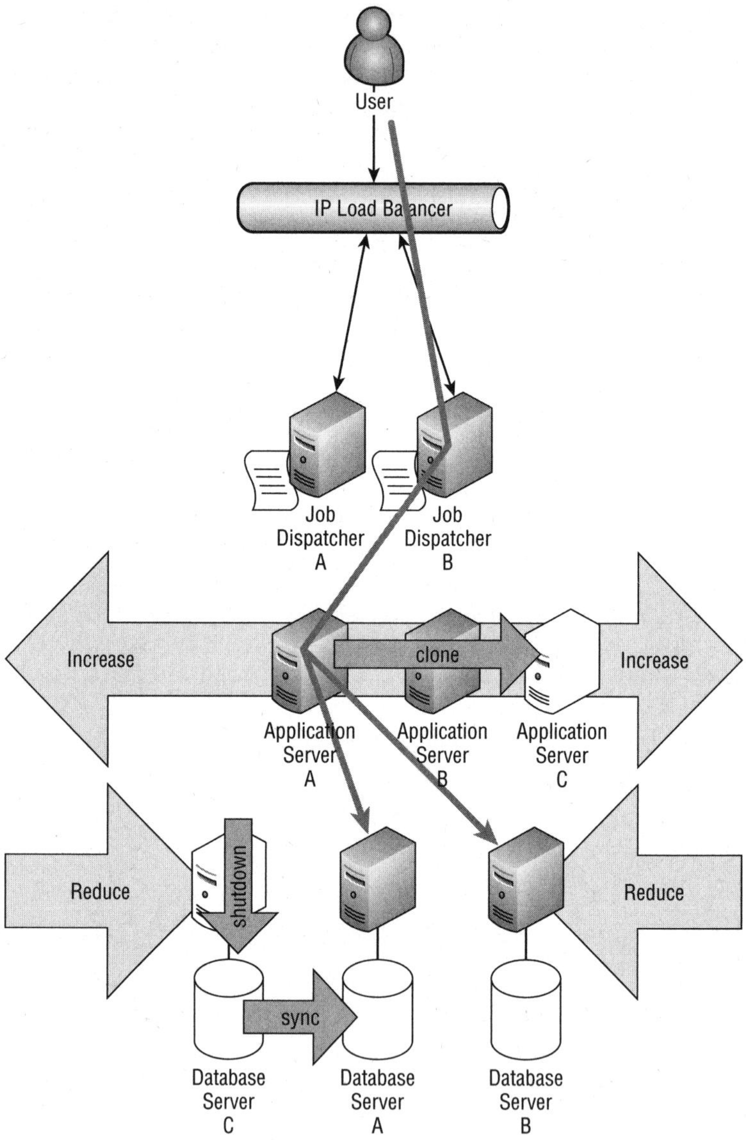

## Framework (PaaS)

Cloud applications heavily rely on frameworks to accomplish their goals. As discussed in Chapter 1, frameworks abstract lower-level hardware and operating system facilities into high-level constructs that can be manipulated by code and that are easy to consume for your users.

Platform as a service (PaaS) provides many opportunities for delivering next-generation cloud applications for your private cloud. PaaS allows you to build high-level abstractions for common building blocks like message queuing. The use of databases allows developers to focus less on managing individual server instances and more on interfacing with a service broker or API to carry out their requests.

# Gathering Requirements

Before you embark on building anything, you'll need to gather some requirements to inform your design process. It is important to learn what your consumers need and how they intend to use the platform. In this section, we'll look at some useful methods for doing so.

## Documenting Requirements

You should aim to break down your requirements into two categories:

**Nonfunctional Requirements**   Mainly geared toward desired levels of service (SLAs) expressed in terms of performance, availability, response time, and similar factors.

**Functional Requirements**   Describe what the solution should be capable of doing; for example, the system should be capable of supporting Windows 2008 R2 x64 virtual machines.

It's useful to categorize your requirements using MoSCoW (Must, Should, Could, Won't) notation, which helps make your requirements specific. MoSCoW notation is also useful for tracking by whom and when each requirement was registered.

An example of each type of MoSCoW classification is shown here; you should aim to make the statements as specific as possible:

**Must**   The infrastructure (blade, SAN, core network switch) solution must meet a 99.99 percent availability metric for unplanned downtime.

**Should**   The solution should support the same set of operating systems that are currently supported by the operations team.

**Could**   The solution could support Windows 8.

**Won't**   The solution won't support non-x86 machine architectures.

## Define Use Cases

Use cases are helpful ways to define in a detailed way what your consumers will want to do and how they will want to do it.

### WHO ARE YOUR USERS?

It's important to identify who your users are. You need to understand their roles in the business. Are you catering to a community of developers who want to focus on flexibility for test and development scenarios? Or do you need to provide services to lines of business or operating units, who will be deploying applications and solutions?

## WHAT DO THEY DO?

Equally important is understanding what your users do today. Are you proposing a replacement for some legacy system (manual or technological), or are you proposing something entirely new?

Developers like to deploy and tweak code, whereas business users like to consume services that are simple and cost-efficient to use. Identifying this type of information is crucial to determining how your solution will be used.

## WHAT WOULD THEY LIKE TO DO?

What users would like to do is the most fundamental question that you must ask yourself before you go anywhere near Visio or the whiteboard; otherwise, your project is doomed to fail. You may already know the answer—they may be sponsoring your project. However, even in that case you should still talk to them to gain a better and more specific understanding of what they want to do. A lot of misconceptions exist over what the "cloud" is and what it can and can't do.

In our experience, there is no substitute for face-to-face interaction at this phase of the project. Not only does it build trust and understanding, but it's much more efficient to express abstract concepts and dive in and out of detail in a highly interactive setting at such a key stage of your project.

You have to talk to them—but not in the usual way we infrastructure people approach developers: "I'm the infrastructure guy; you developer types tell me how many CPUs, IOPS, and servers you want so I can build something you can't complain about."

Or, if your user is from a business-focused unit, not in the typical way we infrastructure people approach them: "You want it to print invoices, provide bulletproof secure web access, and make toast, coffee, and croissants—and you want it to cost $5, and you want it tomorrow?"

You need to understand how they use things, what things they use, where they want them, and ultimately how much they have to spend.

Use cases are all about understanding this. A mockup tool (or just a plain old whiteboard) can be used to draw some diagrams or a flowchart of the types of activities users would like to perform.

# Executive Sponsorship

From the outset you'll need to have secured executive sponsorship for your project. Your executive sponsor may be the chief information officer (CIO) or chief technology officer (CTO), but could be a line-of-business head, someone who wants to take services from the IT team rather than buy servers. If you're struggling to get traction within the IT team, then there is nothing more compelling than the business itself asking for this sort of solution, rather than "another" IT-driven initiative (or science project, as I've heard them referred to by "the business," which hopefully doesn't reflect your organization's appreciation of the IT department!).

## Dealing with "the Directive"

You may already have your sponsor in the shape of your CIO or business unit head who has read much of the trade press and "wants the cloud, yesterday." If this is the case, you seemingly already have your sponsor—although we urge caution; try to understand your sponsor's expectations for what cloud computing is going to deliver in your organization. Many vendors are pushing cloud computing as a way to do everything cheaper and faster—words that appeal to any executive. But it's not all about technology; people and process are far more important success factors in your project, and you'll need to determine whether cloud computing is the magic bullet that will deliver what they want in a cost-effective manner.

You may even be skeptical of the technological or operational benefits yourself. We encourage you to keep an open mind in trying to understand their vision. Be constructive in suggesting where you think challenges may exist, or where you think politics or technology could impact the feasibility of the project.

In our experience, a key delineator between a successful professional and someone who is seen by upper management as an eternal pessimist or luddite is the ability to raise concerns with a proposed approach but at the same time clearly articulate a realistic alternative. It's easy to complain and object; it's a lot harder (but ultimately much more constructive) to object in a positive way that suggests a realistic alternative solution. Change is inevitable in business—and in IT the cycles of change are much shorter than in other professions.

It's also critical to avoid thinking of cloud computing as a drive to reduce your operational headcount or costs. Although lowering costs is a valid business goal, it's also a way of taking a lot of the day-to-day repetitive work out of your operations through automation. Automation enables IT staff to do something that adds benefit to the business, allowing them more time to focus on projects rather than business as usual. This may sound like a well-used truism that is trotted out by management, and it is often overused to justify technology spending. However, if you think about the way the IT industry is moving—increasingly making use of lower-cost headcount to perform operational tasks, often through offshoring or outsourcing—you should see an opportunity to implement cloud computing as a way of developing your career and moving up the stack to stay relevant in a changing world rather than being left to compete with a cheaper workforce.

It often takes an outside view to spur fresh thinking. If everything in your "as is" platform is delivering maximum business benefit, would people be asking for something different or challenging the way you operate? You should view such challenges as constructive and an opportunity for your own professional development if nothing else.

## "The Pitch": Into the Dragon's Den

If you are without an existing executive sponsor and are looking to drive interest in a project to implement a private cloud as an infrastructure or operations person, then you need to go to them equipped with some clear thinking. To your executive audience, such clear thinking is generally about advantages, numbers, and timescales.

There are a number of ways to approach this challenge, and it depends on your organization:

**Socializing**  If you work in a relatively informal organization and have direct access to the potential sponsors, a great way to plant the seed of your idea is by "socializing" it—mentioning your idea in a casual setting, maybe the watercooler, that period before or after a regular meeting, or maybe even the bar after work. These conversations typically start with "Have you ever thought about…" or "I was talking to X about…." From there you have to rely on your interpersonal skills to maintain interest and sell your idea. But avoid bringing technology into it; mention firmware or vSphere and you're likely to be labeled as a nerd. Instead, keep the conversation brief, open, and most importantly, two-way.

**Working the Chain of Command**   If you don't have direct access to your potential sponsors, work your way up the management chain with the same approach. Doing so can be time-consuming and you risk your idea spawning off as someone else's great idea. Losing credit is a risk, but try not to let your ego take control. Sometimes it's a necessary evil, and after all, you're the one with the real facts who people will lean on when it comes to making it happen. And that will be recognized by the people who matter, right?

**WARNING**   Try to avoid email, IM, and other electronic means to pitch these ideas. You do need to see the whites of their eyes for this sort of conversation.

Assuming your socialization or other efforts have been successful enough to gain access to your potential sponsors, schedule a brief meeting to deliver your initial pitch. If you can position the goal of this meeting as trying to gain their feedback on a concept, it will help your sponsor feel brought into your idea (even if it subsequently becomes their idea) and will remove some of the initial barriers of just straight-out presenting a "take it or leave it" position.

You should aim to get your pitch scheduled with your executive well in advance. Avoid known busy periods like quarter-end where possible, and make sure you distribute an agenda as part of the scheduling process. This agenda should be a one-page overview of what you are proposing; condense the facts, keep it brief, and keep it simple and free of product. Adhere to the following formula:

**Current State**   1–2 paragraphs outlining how services are currently provisioned and managed with average timescales and/or costs.

**Proposed Solution**   1–3 paragraphs outlining in broad terms what you can do with a private cloud, focusing on the deliverable benefits. If it helps, refer to the key attributes of cloud computing discussed in Chapter 1 and relate them to pain points or inefficiencies in your current operation.

**Capital Cost**   Capital cost (CAPEX) rounded up to the nearest $1,000; indicate the likely life cycle of the platform (such as 3–4 years).

**Operational Cost**   Operational cost (OPEX) rounded up to the nearest $1,000 (or whatever is appropriate to the scale of your business); compare to what the current spend is.

**Schedules**   Round up timescales to the nearest whole month (or week, or whatever makes sense for your business). Wherever possible, avoid making statements like "implemented by Q3, 2014" because that immediately sets an expectation of a hard deadline. If your project takes 6–12 months to gain budgetary/purchase approval, you're off on the wrong foot from the start. Keep it to realistic implementation timescales.

**WARNING**   For some organizations, it may make more sense to express the timescale as a number of man-days of effort. But we advise against doing this at the opening stage; there is far more work to do to get to this level of detail yet.

Aim to deliver your "pitch" in under 10 minutes, with a further 15 minutes allowed for Q&A. Your intended audience consists of busy people and you'll need to be able to summarize the proposition as much as possible to gain and hold their interest. As long as you know the detail behind the summary, it's a good sign if they question you deeper; it means they're not dismissing your proposal out of hand and you may have piqued their interest.

Structure your pitch along similar lines to the one-pager that you provided as an agenda for the meeting but layer in more detail and evidence. In the vein of keeping it an open two-way discussion, seek your executive's feedback. Time management will be key here, and make sure you get through your material in case there is heavy Q&A. There is nothing more likely to kill your proposal than getting mired in the "why and why not" and not making it to the "how much and how long" because you've run out of time.

Where there are synergies with existing initiatives or scope to integrate with other projects, specifically mention these; all too often IT organizations are seen as going off and doing things in isolation from the rest of the business. But be careful; such integrations could derail your own timescales if there is a high dependency. Maybe a better way to position your proposal is that the private cloud you are suggesting implements services that can be consumed by project X if they were to develop suitable interfaces to provide elasticity and/or cost savings through pooled resources.

Also, don't forget to briefly introduce yourself if you are outside your normal direct management chain and throw in that you were involved in project X (you know, the successful one that saved the company so much money). Doing so helps build credibility, but don't get too carried away and never exaggerate.

It's a well-used phrase, but *death by PowerPoint* is a serious disease! You'll need to produce some slides, if only to give the executive something to take away. You should aim for no more than five slides with succinct and accurate bullet points, as well as a few "backup" slides to support your arguments and provide more detail. The following sections provide suggestions for the presentation.

**TIP**   In our experience, executives love printed-out PowerPoint slides much more than printed Word documents, maybe because people can be less verbose in PowerPoint.

## Explaining the Current State of Your Organization

Use a single slide to answer the question "How do you do things now?" Don't focus on why the current state of your organization is bad, expensive, or wasteful; simply focus on the facts in a nonpolitical manner. Try to take a broad view of the organization rather than blaming department X for the delays in Y. Where you can quantify timescales, costs, and so forth, do so—for example: "Today our silos of infrastructure are only 30 percent utilized, whereas some business units peak over 130 percent."

## Proposing Your Solution

Create two slides to explain what your ideas, if implemented, will do for your business. Keep it simple, keep it concise—a set of well-written bullet points is all that's required. This is essentially your sales pitch for your executive sponsor: The private cloud will allow greater sharing of resources and speed up provisioning times for services by X%/hours/days/years. It can deliver self-service.

Initial work you have done in identifying use cases and requirements here is critical. If you can present specific examples of what people would like to do, or need to do, it helps relate your proposal to your business and avoids giving the impression that you are just a techie wanting funding for one of your expensive science projects.

Diagrams are great visual tools, but this is not the audience for Layer 3 network or rack diagrams. If it's relevant, show a services stack like that shown in Figure 2.7, which illustrates how you can leverage functionality to deliver building blocks.

**FIGURE 2.7**
The various layers that comprise a cloud service

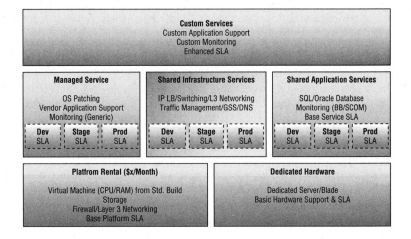

## PRESENTING THE NUMBERS

Use this slide to show the cost and savings of your proposed private cloud. Understand what your current baseline provisioning and operating cost is for services, and explain what you're proposing to change and why. Have an outline of what it's going to cost to build your private cloud, what the benefits will be, and how you can make it pay for itself, or at least cover its cost.

At this stage you're in the early days, so you'll have to use ball-park estimates. Don't flash up a bill of materials part-code breakdown; keep it neat and concise. We suggest the high-line items shown in Table 2.2, but be prepared to break them out, depending on your audience (see our discussion on backup slides in a moment). If you have been to a supplier and got ball-park pricing, great; otherwise, use your judgment. But be careful—there is massive scope for discounting on infrastructure purchases from suppliers. At this stage you should keep it to list pricing but clearly state that and mention in the delivery that you expect discounts of X% (based on your typical purchases). Don't be tempted to low-ball the pricing at this stage. If your commercial business case is marginal, a slight fluctuation in pricing could cause the whole project to fail. There is always a deal to be done with a supplier when you get to a final level of detail and specification if you have a commercial constraint that makes or breaks a project—although, of course, be realistic in your expectations.

**TIP**    If your project is going to save money over a period of time, then it's definitely worth calling this out; if it's not straight operational savings, you need to think in business terms what impact being more agile could have to your business. Can you deliver X% more sales if you can provision things in one hour? If you are going to take this approach, it's worth getting some feedback from your business to learn what they see as realistic.

**TABLE 2.2:**    Cost estimates

| As is | As is | To be |
|-------|-------|-------|
| Compute | N/A Existing | CAPEX $ |
| Storage | N/A Existing | CAPEX $ |
| Network | N/A Existing | CAPEX $ |
| Build | N/A Existing | CAPEX $ |
| Operate | OPEX/Month $ | OPEX/Month $ |

## How Long, Who, and When?

Make one slide that shows who you need to deliver this project, not necessarily specific named headcount, but certainly a list of the teams and roles you need to be involved. In larger projects, an organizational chart of the project team would help explain your positioning.

As mentioned earlier, avoid statements like "by Q3, 2014" but present a timeline with realistic estimates of budgetary/design and build cycles. We like to work on the basis of this meeting as the start of the project, with suitable periods for more detailed development of plans. Your mileage may vary and you'll need to adjust the presentation for your own organization. For example, some organizations work to fixed budgetary/project start dates within the financial year; if you have those constraints, make sure you show them on the timeline.

Although we suggested keeping your pitch to five slides at most, we strongly recommend that you have a set of backup slides with further detail. You can use these slides as a way to back up statements you've made if you're called out on them, or to provide further technical detail to validate your thinking if you're presenting to a technically savvy/interested executive.

The key slides we like to keep in our back pocket are explained in the following sections.

## Case Study

If you can find a case study of a similar organization (and, ideally a competitor) implementing a private cloud, then that's golden material. Some organizations like to lead, and some like to follow (allowing those that went before to make the mistakes they can learn from). Having this in your slide deck can be a useful way of dealing with the "So, who else is doing this?" question.

## Cost Breakdown

Include some slides with a detailed cost breakdown, such as the number of man-days in the build, broken out by role (not named individual) with a nominal day-rate against them. A good way of obtaining this day-rate is to look at the commercial rates being offered for similar roles on job websites that offer contract roles and add 10–20 percent (that 10–20 percent is a typical agency markup). Either way, the resource for your project will need to come from somewhere. Even if you free up dedicated internal resources for the project, their roles will need to be backfilled (either by a contractor or other flexible resource, which will have an associated cost as well).

### LOGICAL DIAGRAMS

While we've said you should avoid products and technical content in the main deck, the backup slides are an ideal location. In some organizations, the CIO/CTO has a good appreciation of technology and will want to look in more detail at what you are proposing because they are interested or want to see how it aligns with another strategy they have in their mind. Sometimes they just ask the questions to see if you are bluffing, so it doesn't hurt to have the material ready to go.

Have a diagram showing key facts like the number of servers, switches, and storage arrays; what sort of bandwidths are proposed between them; and callout notes showing what each major component can scale to if required (for example, core switch uplinks 2 ×10GbE initially with the capability to increase to 8 × 10GbE or SAN, populated with 24 × 144 GB SAS disks, with the capability to host up to 192 SAS disks).

**NOTE**    If you're successful in your initial pitch, you'll need to move into the next phase: a detailed planning exercise that we will discuss elsewhere within this book.

## Overcoming Hurdles

Come prepared with real-world examples of your competitors or similar organizations adopting cloud computing. Such examples will be helpful in positioning your proposal against what your competitors are doing.

Also point out that it's just an iteration of how you currently do things, a strategic step toward the next generation of applications. You currently do virtualization—this is just a management/abstraction layer to make it easier to consume. Implementing a private cloud now will position you for the long-term future and deliver some benefits in the short term. The toolsets you propose also allow hybrid operation.

There is also the argument that if you don't do it, your users will go and do it anyway, working around existing IT procurement/provisioning processes by going direct to Amazon Elastic Compute Cloud (EC2) with a credit card, often referred to as "shadow IT." By being proactive in this space, you'll get a head start on giving your users options to manage these platforms within your own boundaries, rather than having them pick them up from Amazon at some point in the future.

When you are presenting the numbers for your proposal, it's worth tying the technical and commercial benefits of building a private cloud against the longer-term commercial impact of shadow IT. For example, implementing a private cloud will improve provisioning times 600 percent (half a day), satisfying developers and removing their need to use Amazon EC2. Furthermore, you potentially leverage existing internal infrastructure, making it more cost effective, or offer additional infrastructure to be leveraged elsewhere.

### CLOUD? OUR AUDITORS WILL GO NUTS!

You need to describe the concepts of the private cloud. Explain how it's taking a lot of the commercial and business agility features of the public cloud and applying them to a private setting that is much better controlled and auditable.

With a private cloud, you are essentially getting a productized version of the technology concepts and knowledge that trailblazers like Amazon and Google have built without having to take a significant financial and technical risk.

Because your private cloud is under your control, you can design it to meet the requirements of your own auditors. In a public cloud setting, getting access from a provider for your auditor is often impossible. A public cloud provider typically delivers a black box from a service and infrastructure point of view, and very rarely will you be able to physically inspect their facilities and internal processes for compliance with your requirements.

You can realize levels of business agility in a private cloud setting similar to those found in the public cloud because a lot of the concepts, such as elasticity and self-service, have been productized into standard interfaces that your consumers and applications can leverage without requiring human intervention. Technology supporting the private cloud is refined to enable infrastructure to be self-managing within definable constraints and controls.

In a private cloud setting, you own the underlying control of the provisioning and oversubscription elements. You can control at a granular level which services can run uncontended and those for which it is feasible to run in contention with each other while still delivering an appropriate level of service.

Because you own and control the cost/performance ratio of your private cloud, you can also demonstrate that control in an open-book fashion to internal or external customers to document how you guarantee service availability and performance. Doing so is less possible in the black box and commercially sensitive public cloud.

### But Amazon Will Sell Me This for Like $1 a Day

It's true that public cloud services are becoming very common, and they have compelling price points. But it's important to consider how they get to these price points, and while in the short term those low costs seem tempting, charges can ramp up when you operate at a scale over an extended period of time compared to the cost to acquire and operate your own private cloud.

They are typically selling a commodity service with a fixed specification. The process is akin to procuring an off-the-shelf product with fixed functionality and limited scope for customization.

If you can accept all their standard terms and conditions, functionality, and standard SLA, then that's going to work well for you. However, most businesses looking at private cloud solutions are doing so because they have more specific or special requirements, particularly when they look at public cloud providers' contractual positions on liability and damages. You get what you pay for, and it doesn't necessarily match your business's requirements once you look into the details.

# Life Cycle

A key part of planning any new IT system is to understand its life cycle. It's generally considered unrealistic to expect an IT system to last forever. As such, you need to define its useful lifetime. Often this is driven by the support life cycle of products used to build the system, but in-service upgrades are not impractical ways to extend life cycles and move on to currently supported products.

It is important to set out a roadmap for your cloud platform. Treating discrete IT systems as a product is not a new concept; service providers have done this for decades. They do this for a reason: to ensure that they are managed entities and that the provider has control of the return on investment (ROI) of the system. They understand the point at which something becomes an established product and has recouped its development costs. But it also allows service providers to clearly communicate to consumers that the system will evolve over time and may be replaced with something else. In turn, your tenant consumers will need to factor this into their own planning.

Considering that a common driver for implementing a private cloud is to realize some of the commercial advantages of the public cloud in a private setting, you'll need to learn this approach to product management and apply it to services within your own borders.

In terms of your cloud, you have two types of products for which you'll need to carefully plan and manage their life cycle:

**The Platform**   The infrastructure providing the computing, storage, and network capabilities and the management, APIs, and automation that surround it

**The Service Catalog**   The various service elements you'll be making available to your consumers (virtual machine builds, database services, web services, etc.)

The life cycle of the platform itself is closely tied to the vendors and products you use to build it. The service catalog is tied to what you are planning to offer your internal users. Both can have their life cycles managed independently, as long as you provide some capability for backward compatibility/interoperability.

Product management (and thus life cycle) has some key stages, which are illustrated in Figure 2.8.

**FIGURE 2.8**
Product life cycle

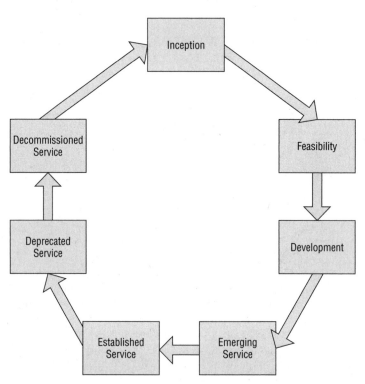

## Inception

Inception is the stage where you think up the idea for a product, be it a storage-on-demand solution, a website provisioning tool, or a virtual machine build. This stage typically involves producing estimates for resources and materials required to develop the product along the lines of "the pitch" that we discussed earlier in the section "'The Pitch': Into the Dragon's Den" It also produces a high-level product specification, sometimes expressed in MoSCoW notation, and provides expected use cases.

## Feasibility

The feasibility stage essentially evaluates what is proposed. The proposed benefits (be they commercial or strategic) are weighed against the cost of developing and producing it.

The main output of this stage is a developed business case that the product team can use to obtain support from stakeholders and essentially the people who will sign the check. If the business case is not clear in terms of its strategic or commercial benefit or carries a large risk (operational, legal, or strategic), then the idea may be discontinued. The feasibility stage is essential to avoid burning resources on ideas that are unlikely to realize reasonable commercial or strategic benefit; in essence the idea fails early at a minimal cost, rather than midstream at a significant cost.

## Development

With clear buy-in from the business stakeholders, you can develop the idea into a practical solution. There are a number of approaches to this type of project—agile and waterfall, among others—and your choice of methodology may come down to internal standards or technical or commercial constraints. For example, you may not be able to take an agile iterative approach with a large user community if competitive constraints exist dictating that you need to keep the solution "secret" until it is ready to launch.

When you are dealing with the platform elements of your service, it is less common to apply an agile approach than when you are developing service catalog entries, but doing so is possible. You need to treat your individual sprints (or iterative units of work) as delivering discrete components of the infrastructure—for example, making the platform available for use by consumers but with limited capacity and no high-availability functionality.

Those layers of infrastructure are built upon in an iterative manner as sprints deliver further elements, such as high availability, further capacity, and integration with external management or monitoring solutions.

## Emerging Service

The emerging service phase is when you launch your service incrementally to the users. Google is an adopter of this model, applying the "beta" tag to most services. This is a way of setting expectations with users for availability or reliability, while encouraging a community of technically savvy users to try your service.

If you are delivering an infrastructure as a service (IaaS) solution, for example, by this stage you could be offering your consumers access to the provisioning portal, allowing them to deploy virtual machines, adjust configurations, and develop their own tools and interfaces.

However, this is done with the expectation that this is a "beta" service—availability and stability are not guaranteed.

If your consumers are developing toolsets and interfaces, you should have the interfaces and APIs developed to an agreed level. Both parties should bear in mind that there might be changes to the way these APIs work in the established service.

In this phase, you should aim to deliver as good an experience as possible to the user and deliver functionality incrementally where possible based on feedback from your consumers' actual use of the service.

## Established Service

Once you're confident your service is ready for "prime-time" or it has achieved a critical mass of users with a low (enough) occurrence of problems, it has achieved established status.

By this stage, you should have a good idea of what works and what doesn't work with your user community. It's important that you apply that experience in a forward-thinking model to the next major iteration of your service. In essence you'll be going back to the inception stage of the life cycle but for the next major revision of your service.

This doesn't have to be a total write-off and replacement of your service. But it's useful to start from a clean slate, asking yourself what you would have done better, what other capabilities your consumers are requesting, and how you would implement them.

**WARNING** You should carefully evaluate requests for functionality for cost and benefit. This is an important part of ongoing management of this service as a product: identifying what delivers the best value and enhances the experience for those using the platform. You must be able to spot those that are pure "science project" requests—features and functionality that would be cool, but of little use to most people.

As you go through the feasibility stage, you may have to revise and iterate the proposal, reducing the scope and factoring in upgrades to existing systems rather than a total replacement.

It's also critical to consider backward compatibility for both your platform and service catalog entities. This is a significant part of communicating the life cycle of your solution from the outset; as you move to become a more formal service provider/consumer model of service consumption, such "contracts" (formal or otherwise) are important for both sides to understand.

Because the cloud is heavily focused on self-service, the provider doesn't necessarily have much involvement with the solution built by the consumer. So both parties must have a clear understanding of what will be supported and for how long. Sharing the roadmap is important to providers as they gain feedback, validation, and direction from the user and to consumers as they can build their own individual service and commercial plans around it.

## Deprecated Service

This is the stage where the provider is still offering a service but places it into a deprecated state with a clear end-of-life date, indicating that it is still fully supported but is actively being replaced. New solutions should not be deployed on deprecated services unless absolutely necessary (and with agreement from the provider). However, you should not place services into a deprecated state unless there is an alternative service for the consumer; otherwise you risk increasing the amount of painful future transition for both parties.

### Decommissioned Service

The decommissioned service phase is the point where you make your product/service unavailable for new installations and remove any instances from production. By this point, your users should have migrated to your replacement products (by the date that you clearly communicated to them).

This can be a significant effort, but it's an important consideration when you look at the team you'll need to manage your cloud.

## Building the Right Team

Deploying a private cloud is different in many ways from building and maintaining traditional infrastructure. There is a much tighter focus on automation and self-service.

It's well recognized in the industry that a high level of virtualization and automation typically blurs the traditional line between storage, network, computing, and application silos. Being successful in implementing and managing these sort of solutions requires a much broader skillset to avoid paralysis through finger pointing and a better appreciation and understanding of the entire stack operating as a single entity.

Add to the mix the fact that your consumers are not only users but also applications that are empowered by an API to manipulate, request, and release capacity from the infrastructure

We've already discussed the requirement for a product/portfolio management function of a cloud solution. There are a number of important roles in the management and operation of a private cloud; here we'll discuss those individual roles.

The roles are split into two tiers of management and operations (see Figure 2.9), along traditional lines. Depending on the scale of your organization, these individual roles could be held as additional responsibilities by people across the business, or a dedicated resource could provide this function. It is important to clearly define and communicate who owns which role.

**NOTE**   We'll discuss the management tier roles here, and in later chapters we'll tackle the operational aspects as you look to operationalize your cloud platform.

### Product/Portfolio Manager

The Product/Portfolio Manager role looks after the definition and life cycle of cloud products. As we discussed earlier, products are implementations of solutions within the setting of your private cloud, and they are instrumental in defining and managing the commercial, service, and contractual (SLA) aspects of those products.

### Change Manager

The change manager is also an important part of the team. Although this may not be change management in the traditional process-heavy Information Technology Infrastructure Library (ITIL) sense, these concepts are still critical. The high levels of automation dictated by cloud computing mean that decisions and changes are generally made automatically by autonomous systems. Those changes are made within an agreed framework of allowed capacity and capability. Nevertheless, change control in cloud computing is important to manage changes to those automation systems and underlying infrastructure. Adjustments to capacities are seen as business-as-usual change if they are within the agreed headroom capacity.

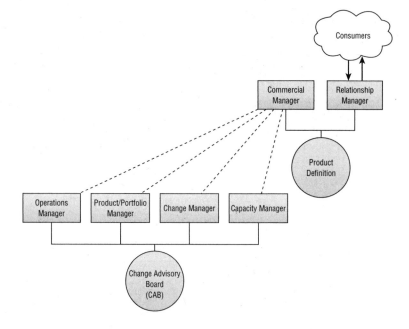

## Capacity Manager

Capacity planning is front and center in cloud computing as it is essentially what makes the economics work for the platform and its tenants. Capacity managers need to maintain forward forecasts of capacity and ensure capacity is ahead of growth while ensuring that pragmatic capacity headroom is maintained across the platform. As such, they need a close working relationship with the business interfaces to be familiar with upcoming projects and initiatives and the impact they will have on capacity plans.

Capacity planning is more important than it has been in the past due to the multitenant nature of the platform. Everybody is sharing the same underlying infrastructure, so you need to make sure you are ahead of the curve of demand and usage.

Conversely, it's also important to ensure that idle capacity is well utilized but that you are not massively overprovisioning for short-term large demand.

For example, if you have a marketing project that is going to need a 40 percent uplift in capacity but for a relatively short period of time (like one month), then it's generally going to be uneconomic to procure and manage that equipment for your private cloud and expect the capacity to be taken up by a business-as-usual increase once the project has finished unless that project covers the entire cost of the uplift (which breaks a lot of the principles and economic advantages of cloud computing).

In these sorts of scenario, a hybrid cloud model may be more appropriate because it leverages public cloud providers to handle this burst/peak capacity. vCloud Director is uniquely positioned to make this feasible through the vCloud partner ecosystem of service providers and the vCloud Connector tool.

## Commercial Manager

There is a Commercial Manager role, which is responsible for ensuring the profitability and/or return on investment of the platform. Depending on the scale of the implementation, this role could be held by a dedicated resource (it is typically the model in a service provider) or as part of the duties of the CIO and finance teams to monitor, project, and manage the commercial aspects of operating the platform. They have an awareness of all the constituent elements of the total cost of ownership, for example:

◆ Power/cooling

◆ Hardware (computer, storage, networking, etc.)

◆ Cabling, racks, datacenter facilities

◆ Operations costs (business as usual [BAU] support), such as how much it costs to run the platform on a daily basis, factoring in staff overheads, cover for holidays, service desk, on-call or 24/7 support costs, developer support, and on-call application support resources

## Operations Manager

There is an Operations Manager role, looking after the day-to-day technical and service operations of the platform, managing technical staff, and dealing with problems, incidents, and escalations. The ITIL model for operations is certainly still applicable here and provides an excellent framework for dealing with incidents and problems in a controller manner.

## Relationship Manager

Depending on the scale of your organization, the Relationship Manager role may be held by a CIO or there may be a dedicated relationship manager in large organizations. A key part of this role is getting close to "the business" to better understand requirements and plans; it is almost an internal consultant/advisor position and is the go-to person for the business to assist in the early stages of planning and proposing the services they want to offer and translating them into technical requirements, costs, and plans.

# Summary

It's crucial to define your strategy for implementing a private cloud and understand common business drivers to allow you to match them to your own organization. You also must consider some of the implications, options, and constraints of building your own platform or contracting with a service provider, particularly in relation to the commercial and service-level commitments being offered.

Gaining executive sponsorship for your project is obviously important to its success and hopefully you take away some methods for presenting your plans with an open mind, understanding their needs and balancing them with the advantages they offer your organization, as well as your own opportunities for professional development.

Creating a structure for managing the life cycle of the cloud platform itself and its tenant services is essential, as is understanding its importance as you move to a more formalized provider/consumer relationship with your end-users.

The importance of managing your services as discrete products can't be overemphasized. Services will grow, shrink, and change across their life cycle. The way cloud computing formalizes a provider/consumer relationship means that more care needs to be taken to communicate and manage life cycles of the platform and the service catalog, as IT staff are less in control of the solutions being built by consumers; they are merely enabling the layer for innovation. But your consumers are highly dependent on the various technical interfaces they utilize.

A number of roles are involved in managing a private cloud effectively. These roles act more like a service provider in paying closer attention to the commercial and product/service attributes of the platform than traditionally happens in IT.

These roles don't have to be dedicated people, depending on the scale of your organization. These roles could be seen as responsibilities in addition to a normal role, and some people may hold more than one of these roles at the same time.

There is no one-size-fits-all approach to building a private cloud, but you should feel suitably equipped with the various options and considerations to enable you to make informed decisions and begin to embark on designing your private cloud.

# Chapter 3

# Introducing VMware vCloud Director

VMware vSphere has become the de facto hypervisor for virtualizing production servers in the last 10 years. As organizations realize the underutilization of most x86 workloads, they look to run those workloads with less hardware and consolidate to increase efficiency and reduce cost. The increased agility that virtualization delivers was initially perceived as a side effect, but with the growth in virtualization, this agility is moving center stage and becoming a critical reason to virtualize.

Seeking to further enhance their hypervisor offering and secure its place among open source competitors (who were making significant progress in the emerging public cloud space), VMware started working on what was initially known as project Redwood. VMware's goal was to deliver a product that provided the technical underpinnings of the flexible infrastructure that enabled cloud computing.

VMware introduced the concept of the virtual datacenter at VMworld in 2009. The company subsequently released vCloud Director 1.0 in August 2010, and a further release titled 1.5 launched in August 2011.

The most current release is vCloud Director 5.1. The skip in version numbering brings the vCloud product in line with vSphere 5.1, which was released at the same time, and reflects VMware's ongoing effort to unify various components into product suites. vCloud 5.1 is essentially the second major release of the vCloud Director product.

Part of the key value proposition of vCloud is that it takes a suite approach to building a cloud, building on the established vSphere line of products, integrating them to drive savings in operational efficiency, agility, support, training, and deployment time while using common tools.

In this chapter, you will learn to:

◆ Use the various components of the vCloud suite

◆ Understand how the components interact

◆ Use vCloud Director networking concepts

## Heriarchical Management

vCloud Director is a management and abstraction layer that sits above vSphere (see Figure 3.1). vSphere provides the low-level resource virtualization, high availability, and networking functionality.

**FIGURE 3.1**

The vCloud family

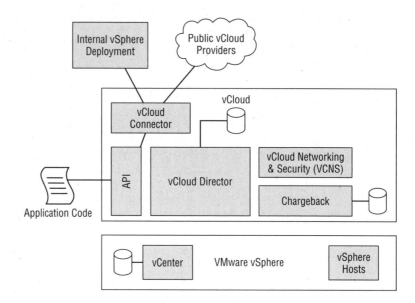

vCloud Director adds a REST-based API and browser-based management and provisioning portal that provides flexible self-service access to consumers, and also allows for end-to-end integration between vCloud and external components to be built programmatically.

With the 5.1 release, the vShield product line has been rebranded as VMware vCloud Networking and Security (vCNS). (This rebranding isn't entirely consistent across the product suite, and you will often find references to vShield Edge rather than vCNS Edge; treat those terms as interchangeable.) vCNS is fundamental to the networking functionality available within vCloud and is one of the core technologies that provides multitenant capabilities by allowing for segregated networks between virtual machines (VMs) on common hosts.

vCloud Director also supports optional components like vCenter Chargeback, which provides a billing engine and usage metering functionality, and vCloud Connector, which allows you to extend your vCloud infrastructure by integrating it with public vCloud providers or other private vSphere and vCloud implementations.

You'll notice that the products are mostly interdependent in the delivery of the service. If you remove one element, your tenant VMs continue to run but your consumers lose the ability to isolate, administer, and reconfigure via the vCloud Director interfaces.

**NOTE** The only exceptions to this are vCenter Chargeback and vCloud Connector, which are not technically required components of your private cloud. However, if you want to be able to provide usage-based billing or resource utilization reports to your consumers or extend your infrastructure with external VMware-based deployments, you will need them.

vCloud Director leverages supported builds of the vCNS virtual firewall product to provide a higher level of network virtualization and abstraction. This allows isolated and multitenant networks to be implemented between virtual networks by controlling the traffic between port groups through application of firewall rules. It also provides DHCP, VPN, and NAT functionality if required.

Using the vCNS Edge vCNS Edge Gateway virtual firewall and router appliances with the underpinning network encapsulation and automation technologies allows vCloud Director to provide multitenancy by providing isolated layer 2 networks in software. If required these isolated networks can be inter-connected using virtual layer 3 firewalls to control traffic flow and enforce security policies. Because the logical network and firewalls are under the control of vCloud Director this can be configured automatically from the interface without any manual configuration at the network layer.

Isolated or shared networks known as vApp and organization networks can be configured and provisioned by the consumer without requiring an administrator to set up specific VLANs and port groups per tenant. Such resources are requested from a pre-provisioned pool and the relevant configurations enacted in vCenter by vCloud Director. Although there is a high-level of self-service for the consumer system, administrators have a higher level of control and are tasked with configuring the more complex network setups and integration with external networks.

Creation and allocation of external physical networks is a system administrator task, usually carried out when an organization is created. The system administrator can create one or more Edge Gateway(s), which then allows an organization administrator to create routed organization networks to external networks.

## Understanding How vCloud Director Works

vCloud Director manages one or more vCenter instances for your private cloud. It maintains its own database of metadata about the objects it manages. As such, you should exercise caution when manipulating resources directly in vCenter. vCloud Director–created objects have a Globally Unique Identifier (GUID) appended to their display name, thus making them easy to spot. But if you edit such an object in vCenter, you may experience issues when trying to administer it from vCloud Director.

vSphere 5.0 and later will warn users when they attempt to modify an object that is managed by vCloud Director from the vSphere Client. The split of administration between vCenter and vCloud Director is illustrated in Figure 3.2.

Note how the lower-level tasks, such as creating VMFS volumes, adding hosts, and configuring the cluster, are handled in the normal way by the vCenter administrator. Higher-level tasks, related to VMs, virtual networks, and so forth, are handled by vCloud Director.

Likewise, vCloud Director acts as an orchestration layer managing other parts of the vSphere ecosystem—for example, to provision virtual firewall instances, vCloud Director communicates with the vCNS Manager.

## Exploring the Interfaces

vCloud Director presents three types of interfaces, each targeted at different types of consumers:

**Consumer Portal**   The consumer portal is targeted at consumers wishing to deploy and use VMs or create entries in the service catalog. It presents a view of the objects to which the consumer has access.

As you would expect in a multitenant environment, the consumer is able to see only the objects that are part of their organization. For example, an organization administrator can see everything within the organization (including vApps they didn't create or don't own), but a vApp author or user can see only their own vApps or vApps shared with them by other users. They would not be able to see other objects within the organization.

Consumers typically administer their organization via an organization's specific subsite under the /cloud/org/ URL—for example, https://vcloud.vinf.corp/cloud/org/ *myOrganization*.

**FIGURE 3.2**
vCenter- and
vCloud Director–
administered
objects

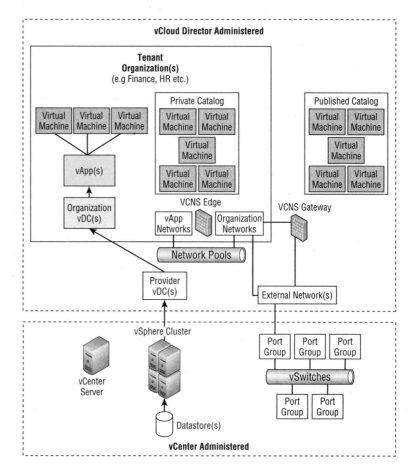

**Administrator Portal**    The administrator portal lets the system administrator adjust and configure vCloud Director properties, such as network pools and physical computing resources. It also allows the administrator to create and configure tenant organizations and their resource allocations. Administrators at this level are able to open and modify consumer organizations if required.

Administrators access the vCloud administrative portal by accessing the root site at https://vcloud.vinf.corp/cloud/.

**Application Program Interface (API)**    This is an API for developers to interface their code with. It also provides access to all the functionality available via the UI and exposes advanced functionality, such as extending VM disks. This enables consumers to initiate complex provisioning tasks from the cloud directly within their own applications, thus allowing them to deploy or remove further application instances from the catalog.

This API is a very powerful interface but one that is based around an industry standard REST request/response model for web services. vCloud Director handles the lower-level integrations with vSphere through abstractions of their own particular APIs. For example, vCloud deals with vSphere's SOAP-based API and vCNS Manager's REST API while presenting a single REST API to vCloud consumers. This makes it easier for developers to work with logical objects, rather than dealing with low-level infrastructure concepts and configurations.

Each of these interfaces can be tied to a different type of authentication method, including a local username/password, or federated to a consumer's own Active Directory or Lightweight Directory Access Protocol (LDAP) directory system. Integration with the consumer's own directory assumes an appropriate level of network access between management elements of vCloud and the consumer's infrastructure. In provider-hosted or complex network environments, this access is typically achieved over a virtual private network (VPN) connection from provider to consumer.

**NOTE**    This level of integration requires LDAP access to the corporate directory from the vCloud Director cell servers that carry out the request on the consumer's behalf.

# Exploring vCloud Director's Core Components

As you've seen, vCloud Director is composed of various elements of the VMware product portfolio. The vCloud Director product acts as an orchestration engine, dealing with the backend integrations and presenting abstracted objects to consumers via its own set of interfaces.

Let's take a look at the various components of vCloud Director and the roles they perform.

## Cell Servers

The cell server(s) are where the core of vCloud Director functionality exists. Cell servers provide the orchestration and consumer interfaces.

You can have one or more cell servers within your vCloud Director service. They are implemented as stateless web applications, so you can scale out to meet increasing demand. Keep in mind, though, that cell servers handle only lightweight tasks, such as controlling provisioning and providing a consumer user interface. Although cell servers deal with uploading and downloading OVF and ISO files from consumers, most of the heavy-lifting of provisioning is offloaded to the underlying vSphere components. Cell servers are really managers, requesting tasks from other components and monitoring and reporting progress.

Multiple cell servers are typically deployed for high-availability reasons, rather than load. As a result, unless you are supporting many, many thousands of concurrent consumers administering their vCloud services, you're unlikely to need more than two or three cell servers.

Cell servers are typically implemented as VMs. It is technically possible to install a cell server on a physical host, but there is no real reason to do so, especially if you have adopted the management cluster approach that we discussed in Chapter 5, "Platform Design for vCloud Director."

A cell server is a 64-bit Red Hat Enterprise Linux (RHEL) VM with the vCloud Director software installed. The vCloud Director software is officially supported on the following OS platforms:

◆ RHEL 5 Update 4 (64-bit)

◆ RHEL 5 Update 5 (64-bit)

- RHEL 5 Update 6 (64-bit)

- RHEL 5 Update 8 (64-bit)

- RHEL 6 Update 1(64-bit)

- RHEL 6 Update 2 (64-bit)

The vCloud Director software will run on other distributions like CentOS for testing purposes only and you don't require production support.

A vCloud Director installation is a security and management boundary for vCloud, and it has a unique identifier number associated with it. If you implement or work with multiple vCloud Director instances (for example, using vCloud Connector), we recommend that you change the unique identifier from the default to avoid conflicts.

It is useful to note, however, that if the vCloud Director cell server were to fail, the underlying VMs and tenants would continue to function but you would lose the ability to administer the vCloud service or connect to the console via the vCloud portal. If you have a small number of consumers, this may not be too much of an issue, but given that cloud computing is designed to handle scale, this level of availability is an important consideration for your design.

**WARNING** Shortly after the release of vCloud Director 1.5 and with version 5.1, VMware provides a vCloud Director appliance. The appliance has a built-in database or the ability to connect to an external database server. It comes as a preconfigured operating system with the vCloud Director binaries ready to run. Although this is a useful evaluation tool, you should exercise caution as it is not supported for production use.

## Database

vCloud Director, like many applications, needs its own database to store its metadata and configuration settings. Version 1.0 of vCloud Director supported only an Oracle database, but version 1.5 added support for Microsoft SQL Server.

Given that the database is critical to the function of vCloud Director, this database should be provided by a database server that can guarantee a degree of high availability. Database clustering technologies like Oracle RAC and SQL Clustering were not officially supported until version 5.1, but these options are now available.

## vCenter

vCloud Director leverages the functionality delivered in vSphere and, as such, uses vCenter to manage and request virtual resources. vCenter in turn controls and requests these resources from the ESX hosts and clusters it manages.

vCloud Director v5.1 can manage up to 25 vCenter installations from a single vCloud Director instance. This is how vCloud Director can manage up to 30,000 VMs from a single installation. It essentially manages, consolidates, and abstracts resources managed by vCenter.

**NOTE** Although a single vCloud installation can manage 25 vCenter Server instances, it can't achieve the same total scale as 25 x vCenter Server installations because vCloud Director has its own limits that in some cases are reached before those of vSphere and vCenter. These are documented in the vSphere 5 Configuration Maximums document available here:

https://www.vmware.com/pdf/vsphere5/r51/vsphere-51-configuration-maximums.pdf

## vCloud Networking and Security Services

vCNS is a separate suite of network and security products. The Edge appliance and manager is bundled with vCloud Director. It is split into two editions: Standard and Advanced. The Advanced edition adds support for high availability, load balancing, and data encryption.

vCNS Edge is part of the vCNS suite of products which includes Edge, App, and Endpoint. Only Edge is directly used and compatible with vCloud Director 5.1. vCNS Edge is implemented as a virtual appliance and comes in two variants:

◆ vCNS Edge

◆ vCNS Edge Gateway

vCNS Edge supports a maximum of two network segments and is typically used to connect vApp networks to organization networks. It supports basic NAT functionality. vCNS Edge appliances are deployed by consumers automatically as part of the networking configuration for vApps.

vCNS Gateway is more aligned to a traditional firewall appliance like a basic Cisco ASA. It supports VPN termination, high availability, and IP load balancing, as well as firewall and NAT functionality. vCNS Edge Gateway appliances are deployed by the system administrator and configured for organizations and Organization (Org) vDCs. The gateways can support a number of virtual NICs to allow a multitier organization network configuration and integration with up to 10 external networks.

vCNS Edge appliances are self-contained, secure virtual appliances. However, like most of the vCloud Director components, the intention is that the vCNS appliances not be administered directly via their own command-line interface but be controlled centrally from the vCNS Manager, which is controlled by vCloud Director.

vCNS Manager is another appliance that exists as part of the vCloud Director control pane. vCloud Director communicates with vCNS Manager via an API, which deals with deploying or destroying vCNS Edge appliances on your clusters. Each appliance then downloads and applies its specifically determined configuration from the vCNS Manager appliance.

vCNS Edge is bundled as part of vCloud Director in its standard form and is able to perform the basic firewall functionality. You need an advanced license if you want to do IP-based load balancing and terminating of IPSEC VPNs. The latter capability opens up some interesting use cases for hybrid cloud models.

### vCNS Manager

vCloud relies heavily on vCNS Edge and Gateway appliances to support complex network configurations and multitenancy. Each vCloud installation needs to be associated with one or more vCNS Manager appliances. There is a 1:1 relationship between the vCNS Manager and a vCenter Server. The vCNS Manager appliance is typically deployed in a management pod, and vCloud Director communicates with it via a REST API. The vCNS Manager then deploys and configures vCNS Edge and Gateway appliances into tenant organizations.

There is no built-in high availability for vCNS Manager, but it can be protected by VMware High Availability (HA) if it is deployed on a suitably equipped vSphere cluster.

Because the vCNS Manager maintains its own configuration database, it is important to back up its contents. You can configure the backup from the vCNS Manager's browser-based management UI using FTP.

## Chargeback Manager

To deliver the metered usage attribute of cloud computing, you need a way to measure usage. vCenter Chargeback Manager works on the principle of *collectors*. Each collector gathers details of resource allocations from various points within the vCloud product suite, such as vCenter, vCNS Manager, and vCloud Director. The collector then attributes resource allocation to individual organizations defined within vCloud Director.

Chargeback Manager records resource allocation rather than actual usage statistics. Even in the pay-as-you-go allocation model, it records resource allocation when vApps are powered on, rather than CPU resource consumed.

Unlike most current products focused on resource monitoring and reporting, Chargeback Manager understands the organization structure within vCloud Director and is thus able to attribute resource allocations recorded in its database against organizations defined within vCloud Director. This data mapping is used to generate billing reports.

Chargeback Manager is implemented as a software package that installs on a supported Windows platform. No appliance-based implementation is currently available. We recommend that Chargeback Manager not be co-located with other vSphere services like vCenter and that you install it on a dedicated OS instance, typically within a management pod. You can install Chargeback Manager on a physical machine, but this isn't a common approach.

Chargeback Manager contains a number of flexible definitions of cost models and charging plans. Administrators can choose which out-of-the-box cost models and plans to apply to their organization, or they can create their own. This capability allows for a flexible set of billing policies.

Configurations and utilization data are held in a database, which can be hosted on an Oracle or a Microsoft SQL Server.

Chargeback Manager needs a number of different credentials to access the various subcomponents of vCloud such as databases and vCenter. These credentials are statically set within the Chargeback Manager UI.

## Application Programming Interface

As we've discussed in earlier chapters, one of the distinguishing features of cloud computing is the opening of the infrastructure to manipulation by applications themselves. The cell servers provide a REST-based API for your applications and tools to interact with via the external interface.

## Virtual Datacenter Objects

One of the main advantages of vCloud Director is that it abstracts the underlying infrastructure technologies provided by the hardware and vSphere and turns them into easy-to-consume objects, each with a standard set of attributes and methods to interact with.

**WARNING** These objects are created and managed from vCloud Director; you should not attempt to modify their properties directly from the vCenter interface.

The following are the most important objects to understand at this stage of your vCloud Director project.

### ORGANIZATION

The organization object represents a security and administrative boundary, as shown in Figure 3.3. It defines its own list of users or an external authentication source and optionally contains an allocation of resources known as an organization vDC into which vApps can be created.

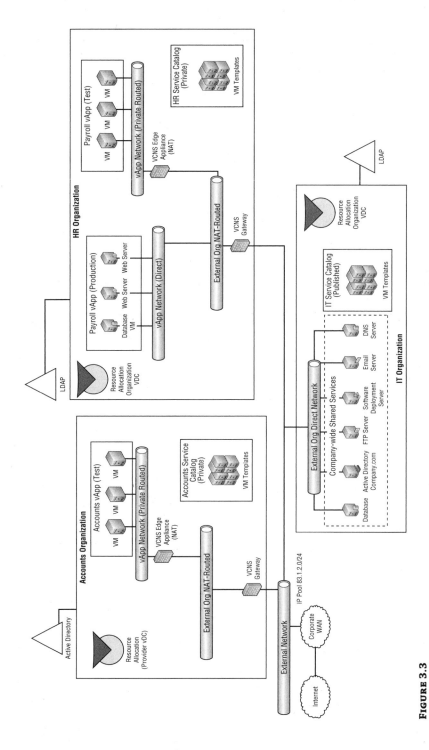

**FIGURE 3.3**

An example of organizations within vCloud Director

Figure 3.3 shows a highly simplified implementation of organizations within a private cloud. Individual departments are represented as organizations with private resources, and shared services are provided by an overall IT organization.

The remaining virtual datacenter objects are concerned with allocating physical resources to organizations.

### PROVIDER VIRTUAL DATA CENTER

The provider virtual datacenter (PvDC) represents your raw computing capacity. It is typically a dedicated vSphere cluster that is made available to vCloud Director to manage.

Each vSphere host in the cluster automatically has an agent deployed to it when it is prepared for use by vCloud Director. The agent facilitates the extra functionality required by vCloud Director such as network isolation.

Mapping a PvDC to a vCenter resource pool is also a supported model, but doing so is not recommended unless you have a specific reason.

A more typical model is to represent various clusters with different availability characteristics (and hence service level agreement [SLA] capabilities) as different PvDCs, as shown in Figure 3.4.

**FIGURE 3.4**

The PvDC model

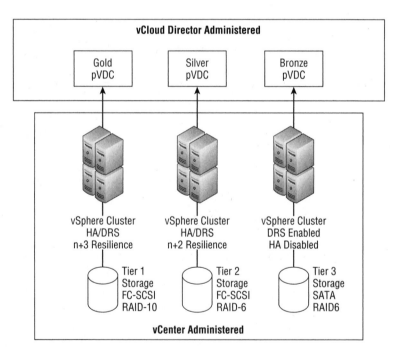

### ORGANIZATION VIRTUAL DATA CENTER

Each organization can be allocated one or more Org vDCs into which they can instantiate instances of vApps from the catalog. You would do this to determine the amount and performance/availability characteristics of resources available to your organization by mapping to a share of a PvDC.

An organization can have multiple Org vDCs, which is a mapping between an Org vDC and one or more provider vDCs. You may choose to provide a Gold, Silver, and Bronze vDC offering with the availability and performance characteristics shown in Figure 3.5.

**FIGURE 3.5**
Placement of vApps and relationship to Org vDC and PvDC objects

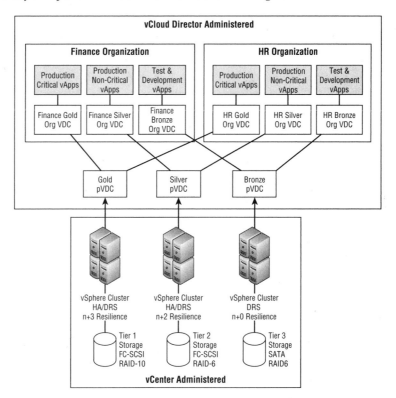

In vSphere terms, the Org vDC maps to a resource pool within an individual vSphere cluster that is automatically created by vCenter based on a request from vCloud Director. The Org vDC defines how many resources are available to the organization and what caps and limits are applied.

An Org vDC supports one of three different resource allocation models. These models govern how and if computing resources are allocated to tenant organizations.

**Pay As You Go (PAYG)**  Under the PAYG resource model, there is effectively an unlimited set of resources available to consumers. Resources are not allocated for a vApp until it is powered on. The resources are limited to the underlying PvDC, but this limit can be expanded by the provider by adding further vSphere hosts.

PAYG is a first-come, first-served type model that allows the provider to control the level of overcommitment by adjusting the percentage of requested resources guaranteed to the virtual machines.

**Allocation Pool**  The allocation pool resource model works by allocating a defined quantity of CPU and memory resource and then defining how much of that is guaranteed.

This model configures an amount of burst or peak CPU and RAM capacity. If capacity (up to the allocation) is available in the PvDC, it is available for use within the Org vDC but the reservation is always guaranteed.

For example, you may allocate 10 GHz of CPU capacity but choose to guarantee 50 percent of it. This approach ensures that you will always have at least 5 GHz available as well as the ability to "burst" up to 10 GHz if it is available in the PvDC.

**Reservation Pool**   The reservation pool model is similar to traditional hosting or co-location models. The consumer requests and pays for a fixed allocation of resources, regardless of how much of those physical resources they consume. The reservation pool is a fixed specification and cost container.

In vSphere terms, this equates to a fixed 100 percent reservation of resources for the vApp.

**WARNING**   You cannot change the allocation model of an Org vDC without destroying it and re-creating it. To do so, you would need to move all tenant VMs to an alternative Org vDC first. In the current release, you cannot do this with the machines online and you must shut them down first.

These models implement native vSphere features for resource allocation and control. However, they place a higher-level abstraction over the vSphere resource settings to make them simpler to consume and administer than accomplishing the same thing directly by configuring resource pools and individual VMs in vCenter.

You can map these allocation models by vCenter Chargeback Manager to track usage and generate appropriate costs based on resource allocation.

## Catalog

The catalog is a logical construct representing collections of VMs available to be deployed by consumers. If consumers are given appropriate permissions, they are able to upload and share their own VMs. Catalogs contain collections of media files, VMs, and vApps that your consumers can choose to copy into their own organization catalog or deploy directly.

Catalogs can be configured within vCloud Director by an administrator so that they can be shared just within an organization or published so they can be shared with other organizations.

## vApp

A vApp is a unit of deployment within vCloud Director. A vApp contains one or more VMs and details of their associated networking configuration.

vCloud Director vApps differ from traditional vSphere VM templates in that they contain preconfigured firewall virtual appliances and details of a number of internal and external networks that they connect to.

vApps are deployed and uploaded to the catalog via the API or vCloud interface, which implements a web browser–based Java upload/download applet.

You should not confuse vSphere 4.0 and later vApps that you can define in vCenter with vCloud Director vApps. They are different implementations of a similar idea and are not compatible. We will take a deeper look at these differences in Chapter 10, "Integrating Automation."

## vCloud Networking

Networking is one of the most complex topics in vCloud Director. But if you understand the principles of port groups and VLAN tagging from vSphere, you shouldn't find it too hard to understand the extra features and automations vCloud Director provides.

vCloud Director includes functionality to configure guest VM IP addresses and network properties like DNS servers and gateways via the guest customization process. In order for networking to function correctly, you should avoid setting or changing the IP address directly within the guest.

A number of network types are defined as objects within vCloud Director. Each has a number of properties associated with it, such as the IP address range, subnet mask, default gateway, and DNS servers.

In addition to the traditional vSphere type port group VLAN-based networking, vCloud Director offers a couple of proprietary extensions designed to provide cloud-scale networking for organizations. Let's take a closer look.

### vCloud Network Isolation (VCNI)

vCloud Director 1.0 shipped with vCloud Director Network Isolation (VCNI; sometimes referred to as VCDNI or VCD-NI in older documents). This is proprietary MAC-in-MAC encapsulation, as shown in Figure 3.6. This technology is designed to dynamically create and pass traffic within a vSphere cluster (PvDC) across one or more physical transport VLANs using an agent installed on the ESX host.

**FIGURE 3.6**
VCNI MAC-in-MAC encapsulation over transit VLAN between two ESX hosts

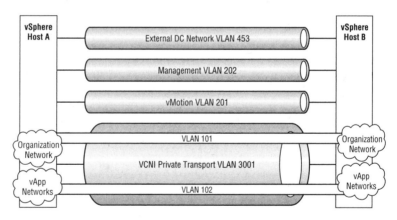

### Virtual Extensible Local Area Network (VXLAN)

vCloud Director 5.1 introduced an additional type of overlay network called Virtual Extensible Local Area Network (VXLAN). VXLAN is a collaboratively developed standard between Cisco and VMware and published by the Internet Engineering Task Force (IETF) standards body. It is designed to offer scalability benefits by not consuming significant numbers of physical network VLANs and provides a network overlay functionality on top of a traditional Layer 3 network. It provides a way of encapsulating, virtualizing, and extending Layer 2 networks across multiple physical datacenters using traditional Layer 3 interconnects.

---

### PURPOSE OF VXLAN

VXLAN is not currently intended to enable vSphere clusters and vCloud implementations to span more than one physical datacenter. You cannot use VXLAN to support long-distance vMotion type activities. The primary use case for VXLAN is the extension of Layer 2 consumer networks outside a single datacenter, rather than the extension of management and replication connectivity across multiple sites.

---

Using VXLAN should result in fewer problems when you are extending datacenter networks between physical locations. The concerns voiced by most network engineers about the constraints of extending Layer 2 networks over extended distances and the risks posed by spanning tree protocols and convergence issues should lessen.

The network engineering team can build a stable Layer 3 network between sites using well-established tools and techniques. The server/virtualization team can then layer their own network on top of that, benefiting from failover and link resiliency provided by the underlying Layer 3 network. Figure 3.7 shows a provider WAN cloud (for example, MPLS) between datacenters with redundant routers and data paths all dealt with at Layer 3.

**FIGURE 3.7**
Using VXLAN to extend a layer 2 network over a layer 3 WAN using VTEPs

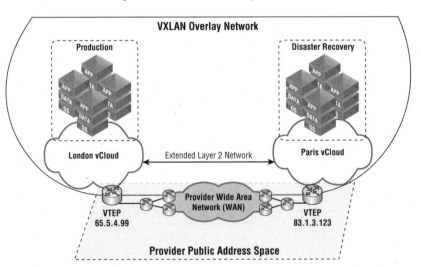

VXLAN functionality is provided by virtual tunnel endpoints (VTEPs), which act to encapsulate outbound traffic and de-encapsulate inbound traffic and insert it into the appropriate VLANs on local physical networks (see Figure 3.8).

**FIGURE 3.8**
VTEP encapsulating
Layer 2 networks
over a multicast
connection

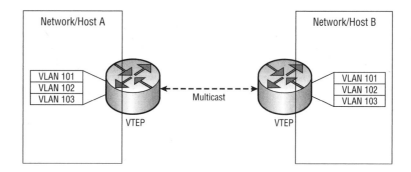

In vCloud Director, VXLAN VTEP functionality is provided by the vCNS Gateway appliance
and an agent running on each ESX host that is deployed by vCloud Director and controlled by
vCNS Manager. Some emerging physical switches that support the VXLAN standard, such as
the Cisco Nexus 5000/7000, can also act as VTEPs, thus allowing you to extend your vCloud
VXLAN network with a physical or non-vCloud network (see Figure 3.9). In addition, the Cisco
Nexus 1000V virtual switch supports VXLAN functionality and can act as a VTEP.

**FIGURE 3.9**
Using VXLAN to
extend Layer 2 net-
works from vCloud
to a vSphere plat-
form over a private
Layer 3 network
connection using a
mix of vCloud and
physical switch
VTEPs

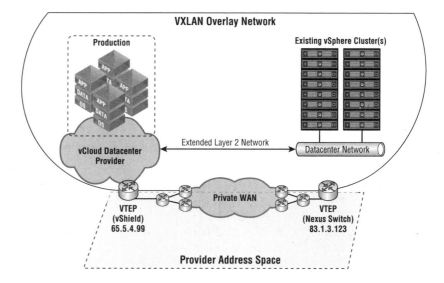

VXLAN is a MAC-in-UDP–based encapsulation technology that uses multicast as a transport between VTEPs. As such, it requires the traffic path between the VTEPs to have multicast
enabled and an MTU size of at 1600 bytes. Although VCNI requires its own MTU change for
hosts within a cluster, VXLAN by its very nature extends traffic outside of single clusters, so this
will require a higher level of involvement from your network and WAN team. The physical network must support the following features:

◆ Maximum Transmission Unit (MTU) of 1600 bytes is recommended.

◆ Internet Group Management Protocol (IGMP) snooping (IGMP querier).

◆ PIM for multicast routing.

◆ If VXLAN traffic will traverse routers, multicast routing must be enabled and configured for bidirectional mode rather than PIM sparse mode (PIM-SM).

Because of these configuration requirements, you can configure VXLAN only over a private type of WAN between your locations and won't be able to provide this level of functionality over the public Internet. If you find yourself with this sort of requirement, deploying vCloud Connector is a better solution since it can be used to deploy a site-to-site IPsec VPN.

VXLAN and VCNI can coexist on the same vCloud instance with traditional vSphere port groups, but they do not directly interoperate. However, you can route traffic between these networks at Layer 3 using vCNS Edge.

VXLAN is a logical successor to VCNI and allows for future integration with physical network devices and future installations spanning multiple datacenters. Both are currently supported in vCloud 5.1. VXLAN is based on a draft IETF standard, whereas VCNI, although proprietary, has been established and deployed since vCloud Director 1.0 and does not require any multicast configurations.

## Network Pools

Network pools are methods of allocating individual VLANs from a predefined range. There are four ways that network pools can be configured in vCloud Director. Each one instantiates virtual networks for your vApps at the vSphere layer in a different way.

**vSphere Port-Group Backed**   This is the least common way to deploy network pools but has the lowest software license requirement since it does not require an Enterprise Plus license for the distributed virtual switch (VDS) functionality.

A number of standard vSphere port groups must be created in vCenter. They must be consistent across all hosts within a cluster that will be used by vCloud Director. If you have to take this approach, Windows PowerShell would be an ideal tool to create and maintain them, or you can use the host profiles feature of Enterprise Plus licenses.

Because this method doesn't require the vSphere VDS, it's possible to implement it with lower editions of vSphere. But this method does have a large manual overhead in terms of configuration and management when compared to using the VDS.

**VLAN Backed**   In this type of pool, you configure vCloud Director with a pool of VLAN numbers. As vCloud networks are created, the matching port groups are created automatically in vCenter. Likewise, when vCloud networks and dependent vApps are removed from vCloud Director, the port groups are removed automatically.

This functionality requires vSphere hosts that are licensed for the VDS to function correctly.

**vCloud Network Isolation (VCNI)**   This is one of the most complex types of network pools in vCloud Director. It is a way of encapsulating multiple VLANs inside a single transit or carrier VLAN through MAC-in-MAC encapsulation to create an overlay network, a set of virtual networking carried inside a single logical network.

Because the vCloud Director architecture makes it easy to create multiple private and shared networks to isolate tenant platforms, you will find that you are deploying significantly more VLANs than would typically be required for a traditional virtualization platform. Most switching infrastructure has a technical limit of 4095 VLANs per switch. This can be a serious issue for service providers that have many enterprise customers looking to consume a public cloud service, so this ability to scale is important. Most enterprises are not likely to reach this level in normal operation, but there is a significant benefit in provisioning vCloud Director within your enterprise network using VCNI. You can request a single VLAN once from the networking team within your business and from then on you have nothing more to do with them as you scale out the platform.

Because all of the traffic on the same port group (and thus vCloud network) between hosts is tunneled over this transit VLAN, it needs to be accessible to the relevant VDS on each of your hosts. Any routing to and from the outside physical network is carried out by the vCNS Edge appliances that connect internal networks to real external networks.

Because of the effect this encapsulation has on network packets, you will need to increase the MTU value to at least 1600 bytes for all of the switches that carry this transit VLAN. Typically this would include just the switches that carry traffic between your vSphere hosts but not all of the switches out to your network edge.

VCNI is not a native feature of vSphere 4 or 5, and the functionality it provides is supplied by an add-in driver that is deployed to vSphere hosts when they are prepared for use by vCloud Director.

**VXLAN**    VXLAN allows your organization to extend an internal IP network range across multiple datacenters and can simplify scenarios in which you are building a hybrid cloud with an external or hosted vCloud Datacenter provider by allowing you to extend your internal network ranges outside your own datacenters over a private WAN connection.

This approach uses a transport VLAN in a manner similar to VCNI but requires multicast to be configured on the physical switches between the hosts.

**WARNING**    If you have a compliance or audit requirement to use packet-level network monitors like intrusion protection/detection systems on your networks, you will need to ensure that they can support VCNI or VXLAN. Otherwise the IPS/IDS systems may not be able to interpret the packet payload for inspection, if you have this requirement and they do not support VCNI/VXLAN you will need to use port group–backed network pools to allow physical inspection of vCloud Director traffic.

## vCloud Director Networks

vCloud Director provides several network abstractions to facilitate a number of different use cases. When combined with network pools, they hide the underlying complexities and processes of allocating VLANs, creating vSphere port groups, and attaching them to VMs. They provide a simple way for consumers to request virtual networks from a preallocated pool.

These are very powerful constructs; not only do they deal with provisioning, but when these network objects are no longer required they are automatically deleted and returned to the pool when all associated objects (VMs) are deleted so they can be reused by other consumers.

There are three fundamental network types, each with specific subtypes:

- External network

- Organization network

    - Direct (external organization direct)

    - Routed (external organization NAT-routed)

    - Isolated (internal organization)

- vApp network

    - Direct

    - Routed

### External Networks

This is a network available to vCloud Director that represents an external physical network, as shown in Figure 3.10. The External network object maps to a port group in vSphere and should have a dedicated port group with a VLAN attached to a vSwitch.

**FIGURE 3.10**
How an external network is physically connected

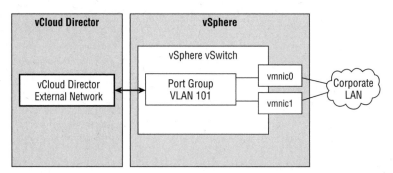

This type is typically used to connect to the Internet or a corporate LAN. It can also be used to provide access to physical appliances like network-attached storage or external hardware firewalls from vCloud-hosted VMs.

### Organization Networks

This is a network that exists inside an organization in vCloud and allows vApps to communicate with each other. These networks are created on the fly by vCloud Director from the defined network pools, which determine how they are created at the vSphere layer.

Organization networks can be connected to external networks to allow interaction with the outside world in the following ways:

**Direct (External Organization Direct)**   In this case vApps connected to this network attach to what is presented as an organization network object but are really bridged to an external network and can coexist on the physical network without a vCNS Edge appliance (see Figure 3.11).

**FIGURE 3.11**
How an external
organization direct
network is physi-
cally connected

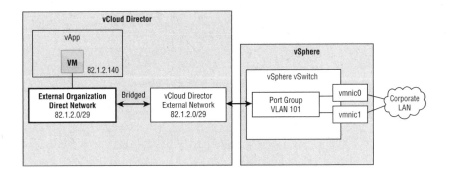

This method is the only way to "directly" attach a vApp to a corporate LAN without involving the vCNS Edge appliance or any sort of network or port address translation.

This obviously means that VMs attached to this network need to have a "real" IP address
configured by vCloud Director to enable them to communicate with external systems.

**Routed (External Organization NAT-Routed)**   This is an organization network connected
to an external network by a vCNS Gateway appliance. The private network has its own IP
addressing scheme—for example, 10.0.0.1 - 10.0.0.254 (Figure 3.12).

**FIGURE 3.12**
How an external
organization
NAT-routed net-
work is physically
connected

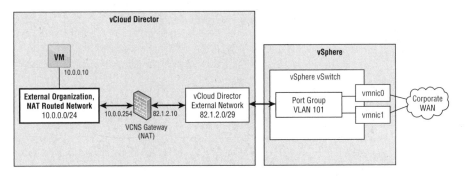

Although the name of the network includes the term *routed*, don't confuse this with
traditional network routing. The vCNS Edge cannot act as a default gateway from your
production network into the private network range. The vCNS Edge appliance performs
Network Address Translation (NAT) between "real" IP addresses allocated when it is
attached to the external network and private IP addresses allocated from the defined network
range of the private routed network object.

A simple analogy for a private routed network is a home network connected to the Internet
with a simple broadband router. Outbound the router acts as the default gateway for traffic
from the private network (10.0.0.x), but the "real" Internet traffic cannot route traffic destined
for 10.0.0.x addresses back to the router; instead, it deploys NAT to allow traffic to pass.

**Isolated (Internal Organization)**   An isolated network is just that: an internal network that
isn't connected to any sort of external network. You can use this approach to provide a backend network for applications to exchange data without it being exposed to the external world
(see Figure 3.13) or for a standalone application that can be accessed from the vCloud interface.

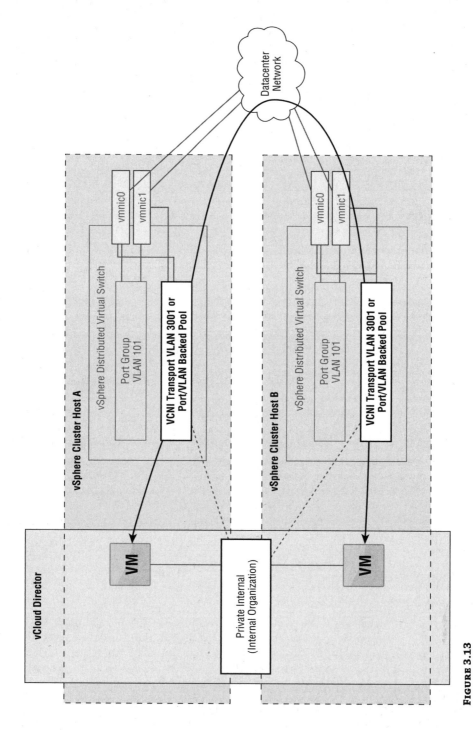

**FIGURE 3.13**
How traffic between VMs is carried in an isolated network using network pools

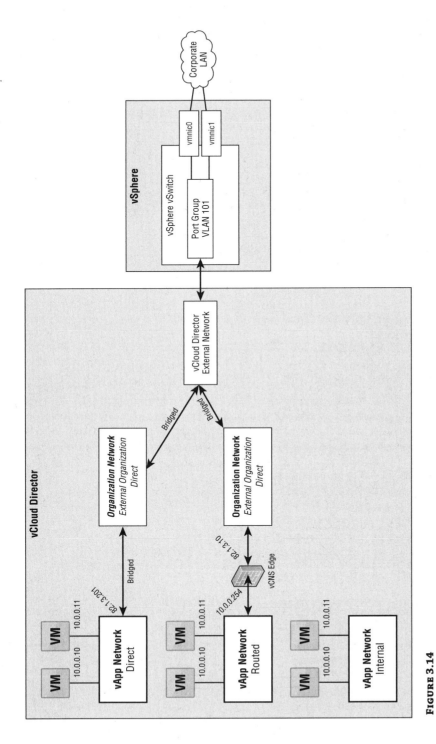

**FIGURE 3.14**

Joining vApp networks to the outside world (or not)

This is similar to defining a vSwitch in vSphere with no external uplink NICs, creating a port group and attaching virtual machines to it. In this instance, the virtual machines communicate with each other over a private network that only exists within the ESX host. In this example, traffic over this private network travels over a VLAN allocated from a network pool to enable VMs connected to that private network to communicate across a cluster (Provider vDC). In the case of a VCNI backed network pool, it travels between hosts over the transit VLAN and is encapsulated during transit.

### vApp Networks

vApp networks are entirely configured by the consumer and exist to provide network access for vApps. They are the same as private internal networks. Multiple vApps can communicate with each other by connecting to an organization network. Each vApp network consumes a VLAN from the network pool.

There are two ways to create a vApp network:

**Direct** A vApp network is connected directly (bridged) to an external organization network (public or private).

**Routed** A vApp network is private, behind a vCNS Edge appliance that performs NAT. The vCNS Edge appliance then connects the vApp network to an organization network, which in turn can be privately routed or directly routed (Figure 3.14).

## Summary

vCloud Director uses components of the vSphere product range in a modular manner, aggregating together the resources they manage into a single entity. The "brains" of vCloud Director are contained in one or more cell servers, which also provide the API and web user interface to both administrators and consumers. Cell servers control vCenter and vCNS Manager servers. Cell servers store their state and configuration in a database, which can be held on Oracle or Microsoft SQL. As of vCloud Director 5.1, Oracle RAC and Microsoft SQL Clustering are supported to provide high availability for those databases.

Other vSphere components, like Chargeback Manager 2.0, run on a Windows server, gathering utilization statistics via a series of data collection processes from vCenter, vCloud Director and vCNS Edge. There is no direct integration between the vCloud Director web interface and Chargeback Manager; they are managed and accessed separately.

A number of objects are defined within vCloud Director that abstract underlying vSphere resources, such as organizations, which represent security and authentication boundaries between tenant organizations.

A PvDC typically represents a physical vSphere cluster with HA/DRS enabled. Several clusters may be provided, each offering a different level of service in terms of host resilience or disk performance.

DRS is mandatory for vSphere clusters underpinning PvDCs. HA is recommended but is technically optional depending on your availability goals. VMware Fault Tolerance (FT) is not currently supported by vCloud Director.

An Org vDC represents an allocation of resources from a provider virtual datacenter. The resource allocation models include PAYG, allocation pools, and reservation pools.

vCNS Edge is deployed and managed by vCloud Director using a virtual appliance called vCNS Manager. vCNS Edge and vCNS Edge Gateway appliances are used to provide virtual firewalling between the various virtual networks.

You should now have a good understanding of how vCloud Director fits together and how it relates to the vSphere layer that you're already familiar with. This knowledge will enable you to start building and implementing your vCloud Director platform.

# Part II

# Designing Your Cloud Service

# Chapter 4

# Defining the Service Catalog

By this point you understand what cloud computing is and how you should set your strategy for success. You'll have used some of the approaches from Chapter 2, "Developing Your Strategy," to gather buy-in for your project and will be looking to define some of the products that you plan to offer from your private cloud.

In this chapter we'll take the product life cycle approach discussed in Chapter 2 and use it to examine your current environment and dependencies. You'll learn how to best take advantage of VMware vCloud Director.

Infrastructure as a service (IaaS) is only part of the puzzle. It's all very well delivering virtual (or even physical) machines to your users, but for your platform to be a success, you need to make it easy for users to consume it and to ultimately build their own products on top of it.

In this chapter, you will learn to:

◆   Understand the service catalog

◆   Gather requirements and design vCloud infrastructure to deliver availability and performance goals

◆   Understand how to track and allocate costs to your consumers for using your cloud service

## From Stability to Dynamic Change

Cloud computing is geared up for churn and change, whereas traditional corporate IT is intended for life cycle management of largely static servers. Servers are born, live in a generally static configuration, and eventually die. Cloud computing provides an agile environment—servers are created quickly, provide their service, and are then disposed of. They may provide a service for only a short period of time (hours vs. months and years), and they may be created and destroyed programmatically rather than by a human operator.

That's not to say cloud computing isn't suitable for corporate IT. Quite the opposite is true, because cloud computing helps you to better manage business issues like agility and cost. However, you need to factor in a number of design considerations when approaching a private cloud implementation.

One step in managing successful change is standardizing your deployments into building blocks as much as possible. That way, components can be swapped in and out of your services, causing as little friction as possible. As we discussed in Chapter 1, "What Makes a Private Cloud?" having an agreed point of demarcation between components—such as an API—makes this possible. Taking this concept a step further, you can build and manage those building blocks as discrete products within your cloud platform. Consumers can choose to deploy your building blocks as separate components and configure them to their requirements, adding extra software, code, components, and tools to deliver the desired service.

This approach leads to a catalog of services, a shopping list of basic building blocks. That's not to say a consumer can't create their own building blocks; indeed, one of the features of VMware vCloud Director is that it allows consumers to easily take prebuilt and tested virtual machines, or even groups of virtual machines, and upload them into a service catalog to share with other users, departments, or organizations. In a private cloud setting, this enables consumers to quickly reuse and customize standard components without having to request a special build from a centralized team. This reuse and customization may be less common in a public cloud setting because each organization typically represents different customers.

## Understanding the Service Catalog

Think of the service catalog as a shopping list of products that your consumers can choose to deploy, very much like shopping on the Apple online store for an iPod. You can select the type: the Nano, Touch, Shuffle, or Classic. Next you pick the most suitable capacity for the size of your portable music collection—1 GB, 8 GB, or 32 GB. You can then choose to personalize your iPod in some way—for example, by having it engraved with a message or specifying a color. Finally, you are presented with the total cost and you can decide to purchase or go back and change the options to make it better fit your budget. You can then choose to have it delivered to a specific address.

Apple's staff invests time in developing, marketing, and manufacturing the product. Internally they need to define its life cycle, occasionally releasing updated versions and issuing software updates for versions that are currently in use. Apple maintains an online catalog system that manages the products and their variants. Employees manage attributes for each product related to capacity, color, availability, and inventory. Apple also has interfaces to various other systems to authenticate consumers for purchases (Apple ID), it has a method to charge consumers for media they consume (Apple store, iTunes), and it has a delivery method (iTunes) to deliver content and products to the user.

While it's a simplistic example, there are a lot of similarities to the way the service catalog is implemented in a private cloud to provide a shopping list of items for consumers to choose from (see Figure 4.1) that they can then further customize for their own use by loading their own personal music collection.

### Existing Standard Builds

Many organizations maintain "standard builds." These are scripted operating system installations that apply a consistent configuration to meet security and operational policies. They often include standard management toolsets, backup agents, antivirus tools, and so forth.

Such builds are usually set up to cater to servers in a configuration that will remain static for a reasonably long period of time. Likewise, a lot of management toolsets such as antivirus, backup, and monitoring services maintain a static entry in their own inventories for those servers.

Through private cloud technology, you enable the consumer to provide servers and services. Using scripts that are part of the standard build, these services can automatically register their existence with the appropriate management toolset servers. However, if a server is removed by the consumer, it may not be removed from the inventories of the management servers.

And because those toolsets are intended to manage largely static inventories of servers, they don't generally have a built-in cleanup process to remove servers that haven't checked in for a while.

**FIGURE 4.1**
How standard components consumed from a service catalog are used to build products

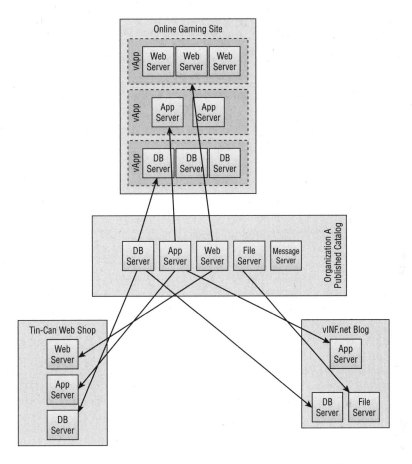

You can see where this is headed: If consumers can create and destroy machines at will, cleaning up the management tools, and in some instances reclaiming allocated but unused management and OS licenses that they leave behind, results in a management and licensing overhead.

There is a key decision point here: Do you treat machines in your private cloud in the same way you treat normal servers in your environment? Do you make them fully fledged corporate entities? The answer is that it depends on the following:

◆ The management toolsets and capabilities that you have in-house.

◆ The roles these servers will be performing:

  ◆ If the servers are stateless application servers, do you need to apply a backup agent? Assuming the data is held and protected elsewhere, a simpler and more efficient approach would be to destroy and re-create those servers to a known-good state by redeploying from the service catalog.

  ◆ If the servers are running complicated application workloads that are intended to be largely static and have a reasonably long life cycle and typical business SLA, they will likely need to be treated as normal corporate entities with the appropriate integration of management toolsets.

Such machines can still be deployed and managed within your private cloud, but if this is your goal, you will need to give careful consideration to how you are going to manage those machines.

## Sharing Service Catalogs

A powerful feature of vCloud Director is the ability to share a service catalog within an organization and publish it to other organizations. This way, consumers may have access to a wide library of prebuilt virtual machines but also have permission to upload new entries. When a catalog is published to another organization, it is accessible to its administrators and can be copied into their own catalog.

This strategy also allows the service provider to upload approved virtual machine builds for consumers to use to create virtual applications (vApps) and, in turn, enhance them and upload them back into the service catalog to share with other consumers (see Figure 4.2).

**FIGURE 4.2**
An example of a consumer deploying a vApp, enhancing it, and then uploading a copy to the service catalog for reuse by other consumers

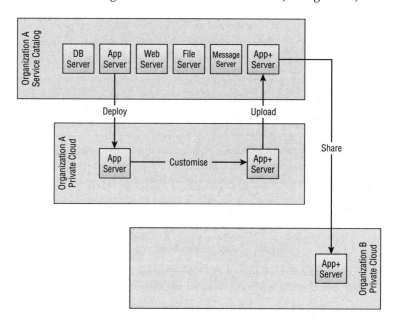

vCloud Director offers two mechanisms for distributing catalogs:

**Publishing**   The catalog is available to all organizations. This property is "on" or "off" with no granularity of permissions.

**Sharing**   The catalog is shared within an organization and access is assigned to specific vCloud users and groups.

It's important to understand that an organization is a logical and security boundary within vCloud Director—it doesn't necessarily refer to a different company or even a competitor. In a private cloud setting, an organization would usually map to a business unit or department.

We will discuss the concept of organizations within vCloud Director in more detail later in this book.

# The vApp

With vCloud Director, it's critical that you understand the concept of a vApp. A vApp is a logical construct that is a grouping of one or more virtual machines (VMs) and virtual networks, their requirements, and their interdependencies from an infrastructure point of view. Figure 4.3 shows examples of two vApps: a simple, single VM vApp connected to an external direct network, and a complex vApp with multiple VMs in an organization's internal network with a vCNS Edge firewall connecting it to an external routed network.

**FIGURE 4.3**
Examples of simple and complex vApps

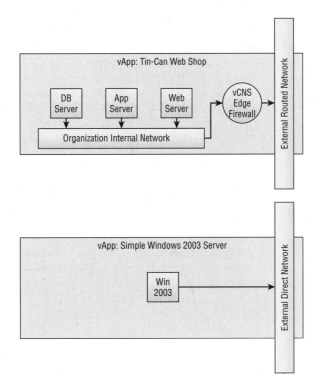

Do not confuse vCloud Director vApps with vSphere 4 and later vApps. They are similar in concept but are implemented using different technical approaches.

Think of a vApp as a discrete application stack—a self-contained web, application, and database stack of applications delivered, managed, and instantiated as a single entity.

A vApp has the following attributes:

◆ A set of VMs that in turn have CPU and memory allocations and virtual hardware (disks, network cards, and so forth)

◆ vApp networks and details of any connections to organization networks

- Storage resources

- Power actions and orders

- Resource allocation

A vApp is a unit of deployment within vCloud Director, and your consumers build and deploy vApps rather than individual VMs, although a vApp can contain just one VM.

## Examples of vApp Use Cases

Let's examine some common use cases of a vApp deployed within a private cloud. There are many more variations and this list is by no means exhaustive.

You should note that the external networks are denoted with public IP addresses, which doesn't necessarily denote a connection to the Internet. Many enterprise organizations use a public subnet for their internal IP address space rather than class C private IP address ranges (for example, 192.168.1.0). We have adopted this addressing to make it clear that the private address ranges are allocated and managed within vCloud Director, whereas "real" IP address ranges represent the typical corporate WAN on a routed network.

### SELF-CONTAINED LAMP STACK

Figure 4.4 shows an example of deploying a Linux, Apache, MySQL, PHP (LAMP) stack as a vApp. Note how it is isolated from the corporate network via a firewall and maintains its own internal IP addressing. vCloud Director automatically deploys the vCNS Edge appliance to isolate the vApp.

**FIGURE 4.4**
Example use case of a LAMP stack deployed as a single vApp

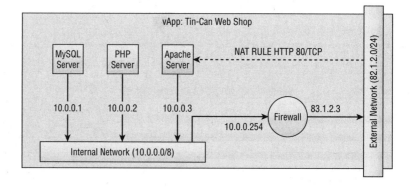

This LAMP stack can operate and be deployed independently from the rest of the corporate infrastructure. Network fencing can also be used to allow this configuration to be deployed multiple times while still using the same backend private IP addressing.

**NOTE** With network fencing, the vCNS Edge appliance provides network address translation (NAT) to hide backend addresses from the external network while still allowing access from the external network.

## PRODUCTION SQL SERVER

Figure 4.5 shows a Microsoft SQL database server deployed to an external corporate LAN, joining an external Active Directory and using an allocated IP address from the external network.

**FIGURE 4.5**

Example of a production SQL Server vApp, connected directly to an external network and joined to an Active Directory domain

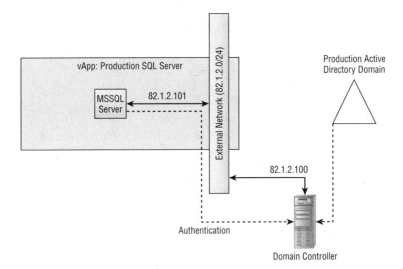

This vApp would typically be customized using Microsoft's System Preparation tool (Sysprep) to ensure a unique system ID (SID) is generated and allowing it to be joined to an Active Directory domain.

**WARNING**    We used the example of a SQL server to illustrate a common use case, but also to illustrate a common pitfall that we will cover later. If you deploy a Windows VM with SQL Server installed and then use Sysprep to make it unique, you might encounter issues within the configuration of SQL Server. Always keep in mind the impact of this process on the installed applications.

You can find more information about using Sysprep with Microsoft SQL Server here:

`http://msdn.microsoft.com/en-us/library/ee210754.aspx`

## TEST SQL SERVER

Similar to the previous example, the next use case shows a SQL server, but one that is deployed in a manner that isolates it from the external network and detaches it from the production Active Directory. The prebuilt image may also include a prepared database loaded with dummy or cleansed customer data ready for a developer to perform testing against.

Note that the vCNS Edge firewall is in place with NAT rules allowing Remote Desktop Protocol (RDP) (port 3389/TCP) and SQL Server (port 1433/TCP) traffic to be translated from the external IP address 82.1.2.3 to the internal, private IP address 10.0.0.1. Figure 4.6 shows the test SQL server connected to an internal network and then out to the external network via a NAT rule, allowing it to be isolated from the production network.

**FIGURE 4.6**
A test SQL server
connected to inter-
nal and external
networks

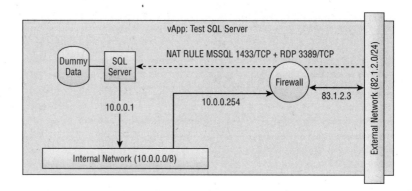

**FIGURE 4.6**
A test SQL server
connected to inter-
nal and external
networks

## ISOLATED SERVER SANDBOX

Our next use case contains a number of virtual machines built to a bare OS state and isolated
from the external network. RDP access is allowed from the external network to the internal network via a NAT configuration on the vCNS Edge firewall.

To conserve external IP addresses, the user can create a remote desktop connection to one
server within the sandbox, and then use it to "jump off" via RDP to other servers in the sandbox by running an RDP client from the desktop of the first server. Figure 4.7 shows an isolated
server sandbox deployed from vCloud Director; the user can make a remote desktop connection
into the sandbox, but the servers don't have access to the external network.

**FIGURE 4.7**
A server isolated
from the external
network

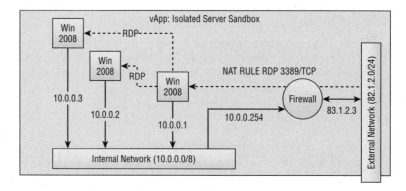

## CLONE OF PRODUCTION APPLICATION STACK

Our next use case is interesting; it has been built by taking a clone of a set of production servers. These production servers are then imported in a shutdown state into the vCloud Director
service catalog. They are then deployed in an isolated network configuration; this allows developers and system administrators to deploy and redeploy multiple instances of a complicated
production application, with all of its dependent services.

This use case is ideal for isolated testing of upgrade or patch processes. Because the application can be contained in a single vApp, you can treat it as a single entity from a deployment
point of view.

You can use the vCNS Edge virtual firewall to prevent the vApp from communicating with other production systems, thus ensuring the vApp can be worked on in total isolation. You can even deploy several instances of the vApp and make them available for independent groups or external suppliers (given appropriate network access) to test against in parallel.

This use case doesn't have to be limited to systems that are virtual in production. A creative use of VMware Convertor could also be implemented to perform physical-to-virtual (P2V) conversion of physical production systems into virtual machines that can be manipulated, imported, and redeployed within vCloud Director by importing a converted virtual machine from vSphere (VMware Convertor does not directly support vCloud Director as a target system) —a production test facility in a box!

## Operating System Templates

You can maintain a catalog of base operating systems for your consumers to deploy. Like traditional vSphere templates, base operating systems provide an easy way to give a consumer a "standard build" OS instance. This way, consumers don't need to boot a blank VM from a virtual CD or network PXE server and install, patch, and configure an operating system from scratch.

Some suggested vApp templates for your service catalog include the operating system variations commonly found in the enterprise:

◆　Windows 2003 R2 x86

◆　Windows 2008 R2 x64

◆　Windows 2008

◆　CentOS

◆　Red Hat Enterprise Linux (RHEL) 5.4 x64

You should adopt a uniform naming convention for these vApps, noting the product, version, edition (where applicable), and CPU architecture, for example:

Windows_2003_R2_Std_x86

or

RHEL_54_x64

Use the comment field to store specific details of the build, such as whether it contains patch-level or application components like .NET Framework 3.5 Service Pack 1.

## Media Files

The service catalog interface also allows consumers and providers to upload operating system and application installation media. It accepts files with the extensions .iso and .flp.

As of this writing, vCloud Director allows media files to be shared only within a single organization. So, at present it is not possible for the service provider to produce a single catalog of media files that can be shared with all organizations without manually creating and populating a separate instance per organization.

The virtual media can be used to install operating systems into a blank vApp if required, but this approach is not common in day to day build operations because it's easy to reuse a prebuilt operating system from the catalog. A more common use case is to transfer data or application code into a vApp with an isolated network configuration.

If, for security or operational issues a vApp from your private cloud isn't allowed to be connected to an external network, you can use virtual CD-burning software like Folder2ISO to create an ISO image of your files. Doing so is similar to burning those files to CD or DVD, except that the actual output is an ISO file rather than a physical CD. Folder2ISO is available at the following website: http://www.trustfm.net/divx/SoftwareFolder2Iso.php.

The consumer can then attach this virtual media file to a virtual machine via the vCloud Director interface. The ISO file emulates a CD/DVD being attached to the vApp. The consumer can then copy data into the virtual machine—test data, for example. This may seem to be a long-winded way of transferring such data, but this process may be required in regulated or highly secure environments where read/write network connections to VMs or external media are prohibited.

If you are working with Windows vApps and you have network access to the virtual machine, you'll be glad to know that mapping of remote client drives over RDP is supported. If allowed by your Group Policy, mapping can be a simpler way to get data to the virtual machine.

# What Is Your Current Environment?

An initial part of planning your service catalog is looking at your current application and operating system build method(s) to determine their suitability for deployment as part of your private cloud. This section describes the factors you need to take into account.

## Active Directory

Many organizations use Active Directory to authenticate users, and Windows is pretty ubiquitous in the enterprise space. However, in a Windows-centric world, there is behind-the-scenes authentication for machine accounts, and a server can only belong to a single Active Directory domain at a time. If you are creating and destroying significant numbers of virtual machines in a relatively short period of time (for example, via an application calling the vCloud Director API to create and destroy several hundred instances of a test server over the course of a week), you will need to consider the impact this could have on the Active Directory those machines will join.

Active Directory maintains its object database in a file called NTDS.DIT. It uses the Microsoft JET database format that is common with Exchange. Each server object that you create consumes a small portion of this file. The JET database format has a built-in process called *tombstoning* whereby space occupied by deleted machine or user accounts is not able to be reused for a period of 60–180 days (depending on the version in use) following deletion. So if you create a large number of machines and join them to your Active Directory, it will result in a net increase of the size of NTDS.DIT. If you then destroy those virtual machines, the machine accounts are not automatically cleaned up and will reside in Active Directory until you remove them manually.

Although each entry in Active Directory consumes a relatively small amount of disk space, you can see that over time this process of creating and destroying machines at scale on a regular basis could lead to significant growth of the Active Directory database if not carefully managed. Not only will this impact your domain controllers, it will also affect your network—these changes are replicated to all domain controllers within the same domain, and some attributes may go even wider in scope as part of the global catalog.

The amount of data required to store individual machine accounts in Active Directory is relatively small. But if you have a bandwidth-constrained network, you are creating the possibility for a consumer to inadvertently impact your Active Directory and network by increasing replication requirements.

If this sort of scale is likely to be a requirement, you'll need to check that your Active Directory design is suitable in terms of network and domain controller specification. Alternatively, consider using a separate Active Directory forest or domain to support cloud services. Microsoft offers a useful tool that you can use to size your domain controllers based on the expected load:

```
www.microsoft.com/download/en/details.aspx?id=10595
```

Some corporate Active Directories also have technical controls in place to limit the number of machines a user account can join to a domain. You'll need to check what policies are in force with your Active Directory administrators if this is your plan. The Microsoft KB article 243327 (`http://support.microsoft.com/kb/243327`) will help.

One approach to tackling this task is to create a resource forest for cloud-based resources with scripts to more aggressively police and remove stale machine accounts. Or you may even choose to not join such machines to your Active Directory and treat each as its own standalone workgroup. Figure 4.8 shows an example implementation of an Active Directory resource forest to manage private cloud resources. This is spilt into a resource forest to allow a more flexible but highly audited security policy and aggressive cleanup of machine accounts—while still permitting access to users from the corporate domains via means of an interforest trust without the need for duplicating logons for "cloud" resources.

**FIGURE 4.8**
A comparison of a cloud forest and a typical forest in an enterprise

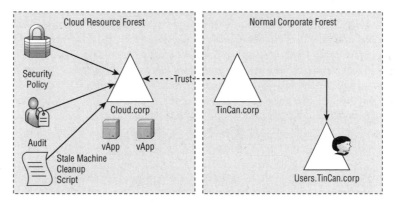

Depending on your environment, you may also choose to build service catalog entities that are entirely self-dependent, each with its own application stack and Active Directory domain controller. This is the simplest form of "build and forget" for your service catalog. You can deploy fenced networking to ensure that there are no IP addressing conflicts, but be sure to consider the wider impact. This standalone Active Directory has a unique SID, which is populated throughout the installation. When you import this virtual machine into a vApp and deploy instances of it, it is essentially cloned as an offline VM with the guest operating system in a shutdown state at the vSphere level. As a result you will have many instances of a domain controller, all with the same SID.

If these stacks never need to talk to each other, or use any services that rely on Windows-level Active Directory authentication or trusts outside of the vApp, then this generally isn't a problem. But if you do, you'll likely run into problems with authentication due to duplicate SIDs.

Networking and the built-in vCNS Edge firewall that ship with vCloud Director can also pose a problem for authenticating your vApps to an external Active Directory if you choose to implement the firewall services. Active Directory authentication relies on a number of TCP ports being open from the client to any domain controller belonging to the same domain—which is a lot of configuration to build and maintain. The Microsoft KB article at `http://support.microsoft .com/kb/832017` describes the TCP/IP ports required to successfully authenticate a domain member across a firewall if you find yourself in this situation. If you are considering deploying domain controllers inside a vApp and having them communicate with an external Active Directory via a trust relationship, check out Microsoft KB 978772 (`http://support.microsoft.com/kb/978772`) about using Active Directory across an interface that does NAT. We haven't experienced any serious issues with this sort of authentication across a NAT, but that's not to say they don't exist and you may find yourself in a difficult situation should you experience one.

## Backup/Restore

Do your vApps need to be backed up in the traditional sense? If you are creating stateless app servers from a template, arguably there are fewer reasons to do a traditional backup. If your application or operating system gets corrupted, you can probably redeploy it from the service catalog in less time than it would take to restore the virtual machine from a backup. Of course this will depend on your specific implementation.

Because of the way vCloud Director manages the underlying vSphere infrastructure, it maintains its own database of virtual machines that it manages.

Be certain that your VMware-aware backup tool is also compatible with vCloud Director. If not, you may be able to successfully back up a vCloud Director–created virtual machine from vSphere, but when you restore it from that backup, it will be missing critical metadata about the vCloud Director networks and services it is associated with. That means you won't be able to manipulate the virtual machine from vCloud Director.

## IP Addressing

There are a number of ways to assign IP addresses within a vApp. You can rely on an external Dynamic Host Configuration Protocol (DHCP) service (such as a physical network router or a dedicated corporate DHCP server). You can apply a static IP address from vCloud Director, or you can apply totally private, fenced networking where a vCNS Edge appliance is deployed to isolate the vApp network from the external, corporate network using NAT. In the traditional IT world, servers almost always have static IP addresses rather than DHCP-assigned ones.

For the best results with vCloud Director, we recommend that you get an IP address range and VLAN allocated by your network team for each external network you will be deploying. You can then use vCloud Director to assign and manage IP addresses for all the internal networks. vCloud Director has methods of assigning guests IP addresses, including its own DHCP server and automatic configuration via VMware Tools.

Using a mix of external and internal DHCP for your guests will overcomplicate your networking configuration and make it hard for vCloud Director to track and manage guests. If you do need to use your corporate DHCP server for vApps that will be connected to an external network, you should work with your DHCP administrator if you are planning to create and destroy virtual machines at scale for short periods of time. Ensure that you have enough IP addresses available and that leases are set to an appropriate length so that you can reclaim address leases at regular intervals to avoid running out.

## Management Agents and Firewalling

Where you are deploying vApps with management tools like backup programs, intrusion detection systems (IDSs)/intrusion prevention systems (IPSs), or antimalware agents, keep in mind these two factors: network fencing and vApp deployment with internal networks.

Deploying vApps in this manner puts a vCNS Edge firewall—possibly performing NAT in the network path—between the agent and its monitoring console. If, as part of its communication with the management console, the agent asks its operating system what its current IP address is, it will get a private IP address, whereas network communications from the vApp to the management console will appear to come from an external IP address.

This situation can result in issues for products that compare the two or that attempt to communicate from the management console to the guest agent. The application will have an internal IP address registered in its database, rather than the external IP address it is actually reachable on. The only way to work around this is to place such vApps on the external network, which works fine but will consume IP addresses more rapidly.

Use caution when you have requirements for third-party management agents. This issue is common with backup and anti-malware products in production vCloud Director installations.

## Legacy System Dependencies

Because vCloud Director can only manage vSphere resources, systems that are not able to be virtualized or are unsupported on vSphere are unsuitable for deployment in your private cloud. vCloud Director has a pretty exhaustive list of supported guest OSs, but there are some slight differences from the standard vSphere list. VMware KB article 2034491 provides the definitive list (kb.vmware.com/kb/2034491).

That's not to say that supported vApps cannot talk to legacy systems that are not supported over a network. Communication is limited to TCP/IP, which is commonplace today.

With the move to a less static list of servers and IP addresses, you may have issues with older systems that either authenticate or determine access permissions by IP or MAC address. You'll need to define a wide range of IP addresses for these systems to match what is available within your private cloud, or you can implement some kind of manual or scripted process to update such systems when machines are deployed that require access.

## Security Considerations

Consider how secure your servers are and how this security is applied. As previously mentioned, if you have a high dependency on Active Directory or management agents for application and compliance checking against a defined security policy, you must take the networking requirements into account. Depending on your organization's security policy, it may be acceptable to export the required profile and have it applied manually to a vApp catalog entry.

Many organizations' security policies prevent access to a virtual machine using the built-in vSphere remote client, which is the equivalent of console type access on a physical server. As with a physical deployment, if you don't connect a server to an external network in some way, either isolated by vCNS Edge or a NAT rule, you'll need to be able to provide access to the console to install software and maintain the server OS.

vCloud Director provides console access via a browser plug-in, so you may need to consider this in your security design.

## N-Tier Applications

Where applications have multiple tiers of servers—such as database, application, and web servers that are interdependent—how you deploy them will depend on the specific application. We suggest keeping applications tightly coupled in a single vApp rather than a single vApp per server tier; see Figure 4.9.

**FIGURE 4.9**
Tightly coupled vApp (left) vs. loosely coupled (right)

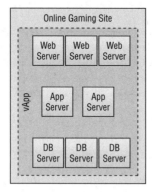 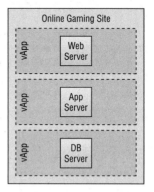

This way, you can control the sequence in which they start within the vApp administration user interface (UI) and treat the vApp and the virtual machines it contains as a single entity for patching, upgrades, and release management. You can deploy multiple instances of an entire application stack through development, testing, and production release processes using the same end-to-end configuration.

## End-to-End Automation

Automation is critical to delivering a cloud platform because it helps meet the definition for rapid provisioning. To make things simple for your consumers, you should strive to deliver a working vApp that is ready to use or customize. Most of the VMware toolsets are designed to deliver to the point of a configured OS—that is, installed and customized with a unique hostname, IP address, and SID.

Say you are delivering the production SQL server in our earlier example. You install the SQL Server application into your virtual machine; then there are a number of postdeployment steps you'll need to take to ensure that the installation of SQL Server is customized and ready for use.

Not all applications work well once the guest OS has been customized with a unique hostname and/or IP address. You should be aware of applications that maintain their own internal configuration files containing references to the server hostname or IP address.

In many cases, you may have to package a script that runs once the virtual machine has been customized to carry out this further customization. This builds on the production SQL server use case discussed earlier; Figure 4.10 shows an example of a vApp deployed from the service catalog. The guest OS is customized by the Microsoft Sysprep process and a user-defined post-deployment script makes further configurations.

**FIGURE 4.10**
Example deployment workflow for a SQL server vApp

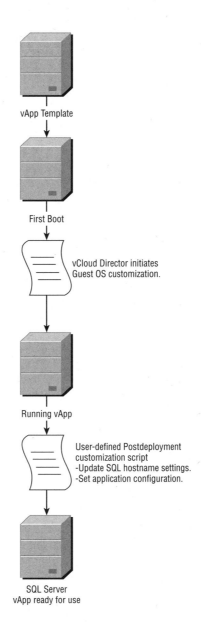

vApp Template

First Boot

vCloud Director initiates
Guest OS customization.

Running vApp

User-defined Postdeployment
customization script
-Update SQL hostname settings.
-Set application configuration.

SQL Server
vApp ready for use

# Summary

A service catalog functions as a place to store, share, and distribute building blocks for cloud services. It is a way of delivering application and operating system instances ready for your consumers to deploy, customize, and use.

A vApp is a discrete unit of deployment within vCloud Director. It consists of one or more virtual machines, clones of which are imported to and made available from the vCloud Director service catalog.

The service catalog provides a mechanism for your consumers to enhance your basic building blocks and share them with other consumers in the same organization. Or consumers may decide to store them with specific customizations for their own personal reuse.

When looking at how you should build and define your service catalog, you must take several factors into account. Many common operating systems and applications used in the enterprise need some special care when being deployed from a cloned virtual machine.

Windows is prevalent in most enterprises looking to deploy a private cloud, and while the Sysprep guest customization process is pretty well understood by most enterprise-scale businesses and can handle making installations unique, vCloud Director enables a number of deployment models—such as fenced/firewalled internal networks that have been less common in traditional corporate infrastructure to date.

As such, many of the common management toolsets for backup, monitoring, and antimalware protection assume full IP connectivity to managed guests and thus are not designed with this sort of network topology in mind. This can lead to complications when integrating vApps from your private cloud with traditional corporate management and authentication systems. There could be a mismatch in the IP address that management agents report back to a centralized management console.

The network fencing features of vCloud Director also make it possible for a consumer to deploy multiple instances of the same virtual machine template a number of times. Because of the fencing functionality, they can communicate with an external network; this means duplicate hostnames, IP addresses, and SIDs could be operational on your corporate network at the same times. This means careful design of management toolsets is necessary to avoid potential problems or confusion over the identity of machines on the network.

We've explored a number of approaches, but the key takeaway is that you'll need to make a careful assessment of the types of management toolsets you apply to your private cloud platform. You may decide they have less relevance in the virtual world and you want to investigate the problem from a different angle. You can then evaluate tools that interact with the vSphere and vCloud Director layers directly rather than with the guest itself via an agent.

# Chapter 5

# Platform Design for vCloud Director

In this chapter, you will determine your design goals for building a private cloud. Are you seeking to provide a low-cost offering for test and development activities, or do you want to provide an enterprise platform for production workloads—or a mix of the two? This chapter builds on the requirements you identified in Chapter 2, "Developing Your Strategy," and takes your MoSCoW (Must, Should, Could, Won't) classification into consideration when applying technical design decisions. We'll look at some common deployment models for vCloud and discuss the relative merits.

It's important to remember that, as we outlined in earlier chapters, vCloud is very much a management and orchestration layer that sits on top of a vSphere deployment. Design decisions that you make at the vSphere layer can impact the vCloud solution as it aggregates the discrete vSphere clusters together into an abstracted set of computer, storage, and network resources; therefore, it's important to understand the conceptual vSphere design and deployment. You don't necessarily need to have a detailed knowledge of each configuration setting; however, you do need an appreciation of the impact they have on performance, availability, and manageability.

In this chapter, you will learn to:

◆ Identify design goals

◆ Understand design constraints

◆ Design the management and resource pods

## Identifying Design Goals

As part of developing your strategy in Chapter 2, you worked to identify design goals and express them in MoSCoW notation. In this chapter, you will use these goals to build a consolidated list of requirements to inform your design; see Table 5.1.

**TABLE 5.1:** Requirements/implication matrix

| REFERENCE | REQUIREMENT | MoSCoW | IMPLICATION |
|---|---|---|---|
| R001 | Must achieve an availability metric of 99.9 percent within a single site, excluding planned maintenance with no degradation of performance. | M (Must) | N+1 cluster required, additional cost of $10,000 per resource node. |
| R002 | Must be able to provide enough CPU resource for a 72 GHz and 120 GB of RAM workload with no oversubscription. | M (Must) | Physical cluster needs to consist of at least 3 x Dual socket, Quad-Core 3GHz CPU hosts with 48 GB of RAM each, at a cost of $10,000 each. |
| R003 | Server hardware should not have a single point of failure within a single site. | S (Should) | Nonredundant model of chosen server hardware (power supplies, disks, fans) is $6,000 vs. $10,000 for the redundant model but introduces a single point of failure, mitigated by VMware HA resulting in a 15-minute outage. |

As you progress through the design, process and cost out elements of the infrastructure and service required to support requirements. You should be able to map the relative cost of each requirement to elements of infrastructure through this process.

For example, to support R001, a requirement that states that you "must achieve a 99.9 percent availability metric within a single site with no degradation in performance," you may have to purchase N+1 servers for your production workload cluster. If you are challenged on the cost of the solution, you can use this method to explain the relative saving of compromising on a requirement.

For example, it may cost $40,000 for a 3+1 cluster to support a 99.9 percent workload with no oversubscription. However, compromising by removing the "+1" node and accepting a 3-node cluster where CPU and memory resources are oversubscribed by 33 percent in the event of a single host failure could save $10,000 on the solution cost. The implication of this risk is that there would be reduced performance until the failed node was repaired and returned to service. This risk and implication can then clearly be communicated to the business in terms of a potential 33 percent reduction in performance until a failed server is replaced but mitigated by the fact that you have a third-party hardware maintenance contract that can accomplish this in 8 hours.

In this case, the relative cost of meeting this requirement is $10,000 and the relative saving of compromising the requirement by accepting reduced performance in the event of a failure is thus $10,000 of capital expenditure. This metric can be used by the business to determine whether the cost of reducing the availability requirement is less than the potential business impact of a 33 percent reduction in service for 8 hours.

Or you could compromise R003 by choosing four servers with nonresilient hardware and accepting that there would be a 15-minute outage in the event of a server component failure while vSphere HA restarted the workload on an alternative node in the cluster. This results in a net savings of $6,000 and means not compromising R001.

Where you have to convey such decisions to the business, you can present options as *decision points*. This approach not only helps you quantify the impact and risk of such decisions, but it also helps the business stakeholders understand the implication and risk of compromising requirements and aids their buy-in with design decision points. The following are examples of decision points:

**Option 1**  4 × resilient servers @$10,000 = $40,000 and no oversubscription in the event of a single server failure; meets R001, R002, and R003 but costs $10,000 more than option 2 and $16,000 more than option 3.

**Option 2**  3 × resilient servers @$10,000 = $30,000 and 33 percent oversubscription in the event of a single server failure; meets R002 and R003, compromises R001, but costs $10,000 less than option 1 and costs $6,000 more than option 3.

**Option 3**  4 × nonresilient servers @$6,000 = $24,000 and no oversubscription in the event of a single server failure; meets R001 and R002, but compromises R003. Costs $16,000 less than option 1 and $6,000 less than option 2.

This is a simple example, but it is a common situation you will encounter as an architect. As an architect you typically strive to deliver the best highly available infrastructures possible, but you should remember to be open to challenges by your customer (the business) as to the economics of your design and thus design to the requirements (unless there is a commercial case to design beyond them). Otherwise you are investing unnecessarily, and given that a key principle of private cloud is metered usage, these costs become much more transparent in a service provider–consumer relationship.

Your design goals should fall broadly into two categories:

**Provider Goals**  What are the design goals for you as the provider? What are the availability and performance requirements for you to manage, build, and scale the platform within the SLA you are planning to offer your consumers?

**Consumer Service Goals**  What SLAs are you going to offer to your consumers?

These goals are explained in detail in the following sections.

## Provider Design Goals

Sustained provider access to the vCloud is arguably more important than consumer access in terms of design goals. If there is a problem and you as the administrator are unable to access the platform to diagnose and resolve it, this will impact your consumer design goals. The minimum

SLA you can offer your consumers depends on your own capability to operate the platform within the agreed availability SLA.

How available do you need the management platform to be? What is the impact if your consumers are unable to access the vCloud portal?

How large do you want to scale the platform? The best approach to designing is in a modular fashion; rather than building a massive system, you can build discrete vSphere components and aggregate them together with vCloud Director. This way, you don't have to start with the largest storage arrays or servers that will allow significantly more CPU and RAM to be added because these systems typically require much more up-front investment. For example, purchasing one or more fully populated dual-socket, multicore CPU servers (horizontal scaling) is generally significantly cheaper than buying a server chassis that is capable of supporting eight or more CPU sockets and then adding CPUs later (and scaling vertically).

Another important design goal for the provider is the commercial aspect of the platform. You probably have a specific budget for building and operating your platform; this will likely impact your design decisions but will usually be treated as a design constraint. For example, you may have a capital budget of $60,000 to build the platform to support an initial workload of 500 virtual machines.

## Consumer Design Goals

Most common examples of defining service levels divide them into categories like bronze, silver, and gold. These definitions are totally flexible and are up to you to define as the service provider, depending on your design goals. Defining these services, even at a high level, allows you to design the appropriate vSphere and vCloud infrastructures to deliver them, factoring in quantity and type of servers, storage, and networking. For example, you may wish to offer the tiers of service focused on the capabilities of underlying infrastructure defined by performance and availability characteristics denoted as gold, silver, and bronze, as shown in Table 5.2.

**TABLE 5.2:**     Example service offerings (infrastructure focused)

| SERVICE DESCRIPTION | SERVICE LEVEL GOAL | PROVIDER vDC INFRASTRUCTURE REQUIREMENTS |
| --- | --- | --- |
| High performance: Gold | 99.9 percent availability<br>5 input/output operations per second (IOPS) per GB of storage<br>0 percent oversubscription of resources during routine maintenance or server failure | N+1 vSphere Cluster, resilient server hardware<br>Mixed SSD/Fibre Channel 15k disk, RAID 0+1 disk groups with array managed caching |

**TABLE 5.2:**     Example service offerings (infrastructure focused)  *(CONTINUED)*

| SERVICE DESCRIPTION | SERVICE LEVEL GOAL | PROVIDER vDC INFRASTRUCTURE REQUIREMENTS |
|---|---|---|
| Medium performance: Silver | 99.9 percent availability | N+0 vSphere Cluster, resilient hardware |
| | 2 IOPS per GB of storage | Fibre Channel 10k disk, RAID 6 disk groups |
| | 33 percent oversubscription in the event of single server failure or routine maintenance | |
| Low performance: Bronze | 0.1 IOPS per GB of storage | N+1 vSphere cluster, nonresilient hardware, SATA RAID 6 disk groups |
| | 0 percent oversubscription in the event of single server failure or maintenance | |

Alternatively it may be more suitable to adopt a business function–oriented view (Table 5.3), whereby consumers can choose which type of infrastructure to deploy their vApps into, depending on performance and availability targets that have been defined for various functional areas of the business.

**TABLE 5.3:**     Example service offerings (business function focused)

| SERVICE DESCRIPTION | SERVICE LEVEL GOAL | PROVIDER vDC INFRASTRUCTURE REQUIREMENTS |
|---|---|---|
| Financial trading apps | 99.9 percent availability 5 IOPS per GB of storage | N+2 vSphere Cluster, resilient server hardware |
| | 0 percent oversubscription of resources during routine maintenance or server failure | Mixed SSD/Fibre Channel 15k disk, RAID 0+1 disk groups with array managed caching |
| Back-office functionality | 99.9 percent availability | N+1 vSphere Cluster, resilient hardware |
| | 2 IOPS per GB of storage | Fibre Channel 10k disk, RAID 6 disk groups |
| | 0 percent oversubscription of resources during routine maintenance or server failure | |
| Archive/compliance services | 0.1 IOPS per GB of storage | N+1 vSphere cluster, nonresilient hardware, SATA RAID 6 disk groups |

In a regulated environment, it may make more sense to define a security-defined group set of services (Table 5.4), in which each service is hosted on infrastructure that has been designed specifically to meet security or compliance requirements. Likewise, defining a functionally focused service can create a clear demarcation for your consumers between infrastructures that are suitable for running regulated workloads and infrastructure that is not suitable at all for this sort of workload, for example, infrastructure that does not meet security requirements or PCI workloads.

**TABLE 5.4:** Example service offerings (security capability focused)

| SERVICE DESCRIPTION | SERVICE LEVEL GOAL | PROVIDER vDC INFRASTRUCTURE REQUIREMENTS |
| --- | --- | --- |
| PCI compliance<br><br>Services in scope of payment card industry (PCI) standards | 99.9 percent availability<br><br>5 IOPS per GB of storage<br><br>0 percent oversubscription of resources during routine maintenance or server failure | N+2 vSphere Cluster, resilient server hardware<br><br>Mixed SSD/Fibre Channel 15k disk, RAID 0+1 disk groups with array managed caching<br><br>Array-level disk encryption<br><br>Access to encrypted network links only |
| Web-facing services (non-PCI services) | 99.9 percent availability<br><br>5 IOPS per GB of storage<br><br>0 percent oversubscription of resources during routine maintenance or server failure | N+2 vSphere Cluster, resilient server hardware<br><br>Mixed SSD/Fibre Channel 15k disk, RAID 0+1 disk groups with array managed caching<br><br>No array-level disk encryption<br><br>Access to public Internet networks |
| Archive/compliance services | 0.1 IOPS per GB of storage | N+1 vSphere cluster, nonresilient hardware, SATA RAID 6 disk groups<br><br>No access to Internet |

When defining services along security and compliance lines, you should keep in mind that vCloud Director doesn't necessarily control what happens inside your vApps. vCloud Director is focused on controlling and orchestrating deployment of your vApps into VMware infrastructure.

It is up to your consumers to ensure that the operating systems, applications, and users that comprise your vApps are suitably designed and configured to provide such compliance and security. For example, operating system templates in a catalog must be configured with appropriate encryption levels and auditing settings. vCloud Director can help your consumers to deploy into correctly labeled services, but it cannot enforce what happens inside the vApps that your consumers deploy.

### LAYERED EXTERNAL SERVICES

Layered external service levels specify vCloud-specific design elements that translate to a level of performance and availability that can be allocated and controlled by vCloud Director. Although this is the main scope of providing an infrastructure as a service (IaaS) platform, many real-world business scenarios will require further services to be layered on to provide backup, management, and monitoring. This task is out of the scope of vCloud Director, but it's an important consideration for private cloud scenarios. Some common examples are shown in Figure 5.1, where backup, security, and management agents are "layered" into vApps either by a scripted build process or a centralized tool.

**FIGURE 5.1**
Layering external services on IaaS hosted application servers

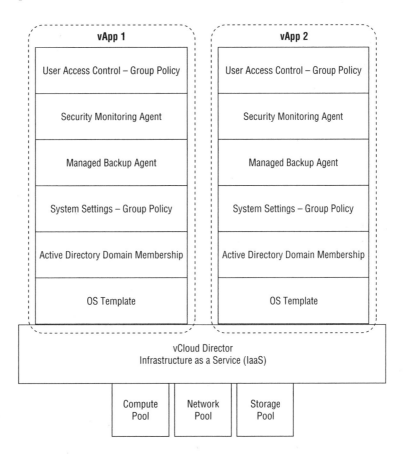

### Identifying Design Constraints

In the real world there are very few design projects that do not have any constraints placed on them. So it is important to identify and document constraints as part of your vCloud design.

Common design constraints follow, but you should also take care to document constraints that you assume are well known within your business:

**Budget**  As part of setting your strategy, you should have created an outline budget estimate; depending on how your organization handles this process, you may have a fixed maximum budget for your project. In that case, the budget imposes a constraint on the project and may impact your design decisions.

**Organizational**  Though not usually a technical constraint, the concept of sharing infrastructure between different business units may introduce some unexpected problems for your project. It may be that previously these business units had their own infrastructure under their sole control, and moving to a shared platform introduces some political sensitivity that could impose a design constraint where there is a technical preference or requirement for specific hardware solutions or services. This is where having good executive sponsorship for your project is critical to making progress.

**Existing Hardware Platform**  You may have an existing hardware platform that you need to reuse for your vCloud platform that dictates what hardware you have available and determines how you can deploy it.

As mentioned earlier in this book, vCloud Director isn't designed to share clusters it manages as Provider Virtual Datacenters (Provider VDC) with non–vCloud Director workloads, so you should always provide dedicated vSphere hosts and clusters for vCloud Director to use. But an existing hardware platform may impose some constraints in terms of the resources available (CPU, memory, and storage).

**Vendor Selection**  Your organization may have a single-supplier agreement with a hardware vendor; such an agreement will impose a constraint on your design as you will likely have to stay within the bounds of that agreement and work within the range of hardware that is available to you.

## Common Architecture Decisions

When working on any design, you must make a number of common architecture design decisions. In this section, you'll see how these decisions relate to vCloud Director.

### Conceptual Design

vCloud Director is designed to aggregate resources from a number of vCenter instances. This is how it is able to manage large numbers of virtual machines from a single interface. To accomplish this, a common design pattern is to define various "pods" of infrastructure; each pod will typically consist of management elements (such as vCenter) and resource elements (such as vSphere hosts). Multiple pods can then be managed from a single vCloud Director instance. Each pod can be independently scaled out to meet overall demand, and hosts can be reallocated between pods to balance demand for particular resource roles.

As you can imagine, controlling a large number of vSphere hosts can become complex. Such automation tools like automatic deployment and host profiles become more important than they typically are for smaller, static vSphere deployments. The vSphere product line is now quite broad and contains many solutions. Most of these solutions have a management element as well as a resource/workload element.

A vSphere cluster consists of one or more vSphere hosts. To manage these vSphere hosts, you need a vCenter server (or appliance), which in turn requires a database server (SQL, Oracle, or DB/2). You may also need an authentication service, DNS, and NTP time source. In larger environments, you may also have a requirement for VMware Update Manager, the vSphere Virtual Management Appliance (VMA) that provides command-line access to vSphere hosts.

When you deploy vCloud, you require further databases, cell servers, vCloud Networking and Security (vCNS) Manager Appliances, and chargeback servers. This all leads to a lot of "moving parts" that comprise the management elements of the platform that control the resource elements (such as vSphere hosts and vCNS Edge appliances).

In Information Technology Infrastructure Library (ITIL) terms, capacity planning is most important in resource pods whereas change management is most important in management pods, as you'll see in the following sections.

## Management Pod

Given that all of these vSphere and vCloud roles are typically deployed as virtual machines, an increasingly common deployment pattern is to deploy a dedicated management cluster, or *management pod*, as shown in Figure 5.2. The management pod is distinct from the vSphere hosts and clusters that run your virtual machines. It runs one or more vCenter instances and the backend databases and services such as VMware Update Manager and vSphere Virtual Management Appliances (VMAs).

**FIGURE 5.2**
Virtual machines in
a management pod
cluster

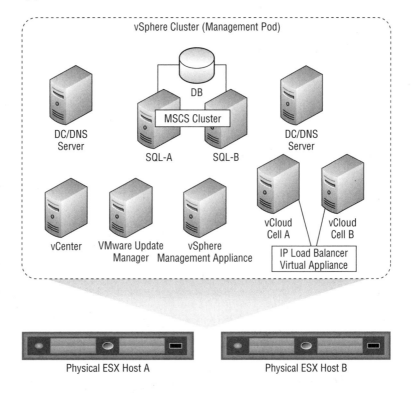

Depending on your resource and security requirements, you can then leverage a shared database for all of your management elements. You can possibly use a database cluster or other high-availability solution to increase availability for this critical element of the infrastructure.

With vCloud Director, this management/resource split makes a lot of sense and helps with partitioning security access. The provider has exclusive access to the management pod; from there they can control a number of *resource pods*, as shown in Figure 5.3.

If you are constrained by the amount of hardware that is available to deploy a dedicated management pod, a workable approach is to treat the management pod as a guest workload on an existing vSphere cluster and configure appropriate security permissions to restrict access to just vCloud administrators. These virtual machines then run the management roles for one or more vCloud resource pods. However, avoid running management workloads in vSphere clusters managed by vCloud Director (resource pods).

Your provider design goals may well be different from those of your consumers in terms of availability, security, and performance. A split management/resource "pod" architecture is generally suggested.

The management pod is generally considered static. Changes to its workload can occur, and it can come under tight security and change control processes. After all, this "pod" holds the keys to the rest of your infrastructure, so you want to ensure it is as well protected and controlled as possible.

## Resource Pod(s)

Once you've placed your management elements into a separate cluster, you are free to allocate hosts as resource pods. Each resource pod is a vSphere cluster of one or more hosts. Its associated vCenter and other supporting infrastructure runs from a small, controlled management cluster. This approach allows your resource pods to become more dynamic in their nature. The resource pods would generally fall under more relaxed change control processes that enable the provider to quickly move to meet consumer demand and respond to changing requirements.

When you are designing a vCloud platform, each resource pod is represented in vCloud as a provider virtual data center. It has a number of hosts of a determined configuration, storage of a particular tier and capacity assigned, and access to a number of external networks and vCloud internal network pools. In addition, hosts in your resource pod (vSphere cluster) are zoned to specific storage logical unit numbers (LUNs), or on access lists in the case of IP-based storage. You should not share storage targets between multiple resource pods.

Figure 5.4 shows some of the example service types we identified in the "Consumer Design Goals" section earlier.

Because your resource pod(s) may be quite flexible, it makes sense to use the configuration and automation features found within vSphere (or a third-party solution if you have it) to create an automated deployment and configuration of your vSphere hosts.

Autodeploy and host profiles are two excellent features that allow you to automatically deploy vSphere hosts from a predefined configuration template and join it to an appropriate cluster. These features apply only to vSphere-specific configuration, but if you use a hardware platform that uses converged I/O technologies like Cisco Unified Computing System (UCS) or HP Virtual Connect, it can make the other required tasks (such as mapping VLAN IDs and SAN zoning and masking) much simpler than traditional rack-mount and cabled servers.

You must enable Distributed Resource Scheduling (DRS) for each cluster that you are intending to use as a resource pod. Otherwise, CPU and memory resources will be imbalanced within each resource pod and vApp performance will be impacted. vSphere High Availability (HA) is technically optional, but if HA is not enabled vApps will not be automatically restarted by a consumer or a provider administrator in the event of a host failure.

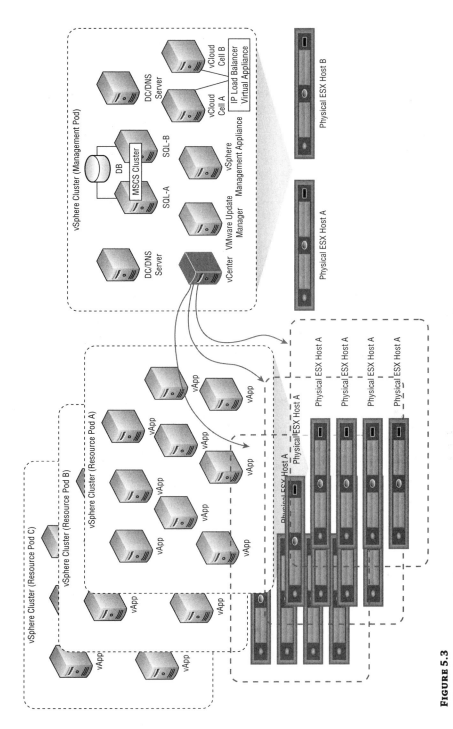

**FIGURE 5.3**

vCenter in management pod managing a resource pod and its own management pod

Resource pods inherit the same sizing constraints that apply to the underlying vSphere versions they are running, but vCloud Director also applies its own. vCloud can support up to 25 vCenter servers, but it can't support the combined resources that could be technically supported by 25 vCenter servers.

If you are running versions earlier than vSphere 5.0 or versions of VMFS older than 5, there is also a limit of eight hosts per cluster if you enable fast provisioning (linked clones).

**FIGURE 5.4**

A management pod and various resource pods

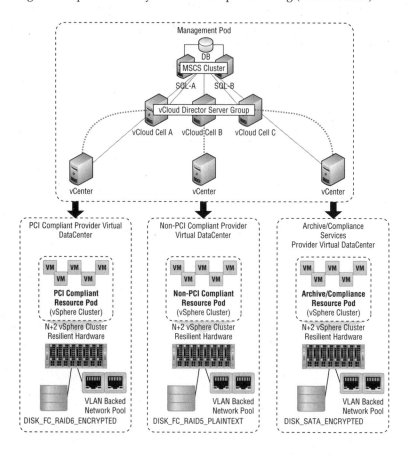

## Design for Failure

You may choose to use resilient hardware to provide protection against failure of individual components like disks, fans, and power supplies. Additionally, using native vSphere features like HA can prevent such hardware failures from seriously impacting your workload by recovering your workload to alternative physical servers from a failed server. But from time to time, servers, networks, and storage will fail, either due to multiple cascading hardware failures, power interruption, or some kind of software or firmware bug. In smaller systems, these incidents occur less frequently, but as you aggregate multiple resources together with vCloud Director, the likelihood of an individual failure increases.

It is important that you design to meet availability goals, which may involve adding capacity for failover. In terms of vCloud design, normal vSphere design principles apply when you are sizing your resource pods. But keep in mind that each vSphere host will need to be "prepared" for use with vCloud Director by having an agent installed. You can do so by using the vCloud Director user interface; this process can be automated if you are using Autodeploy.

**NOTE**   Cross-site and replicated storage scenarios are currently limited with vCloud Director 5.1. Learn more in Chapter 12, "Business Continuity."

You should teach your consumers who are building vApps how to design their applications to take advantage of vCloud. With the provided APIs, it is possible for consumers and their application code to autonomously request new instances of vApps from a catalog. Such capabilities are basic at present, but APIs are available for your consumers that allow them to configure the vCNS Edge Load Balancer via vCloud Director to automatically manage removing failed vApps and/or virtual machines from load balancers, while the vCloud platform deals with automatic restart of workloads on other functioning nodes in each resource pod.

## Design for Manageability

Another important design factor to consider is manageability. We highly recommend that you follow the management/resource pod architecture for your vCloud so that you can effectively isolate your management workload and access from the hosts that are serving your consumers.

Most elements of vCloud can be patched online if you deploy resilient roles. Unavailability of individual management components for a short time does not generally disrupt access by your consumers, although it may impact certain activities, such as deploying a vCNS Edge appliance if you take the vCNS Manager offline.

Within your business you should identify and design a specified maintenance window. This doesn't necessarily mean the platform will be unavailable during that period, but it may mean that resilience is reduced while patching is performed. So there is a slightly higher-than-usual risk of an outage during that window.

## Scaling Approaches

Horizontal scaling, such as adding more hosts to a cluster, is generally the preferred approach for scaling vCloud Director. Vertical scalability is also possible by putting a host into maintenance mode and then upgrading its hardware.

## Availability/Performance

Because a vCloud platform is essentially a collection of resources from a number of vSphere clusters, it enables you to have various service offerings in your portfolio. You may have one or more clusters with enterprise-grade hardware and multiple levels of resilience to support important production workloads. You may also have a cluster built on low-cost commodity server hardware to support less important workloads, or workloads where cost is important but higher levels of availability can be provided at a software level with the virtual machines running in the cluster. Likewise, you will probably have multiple tiers of disks, each with different performance (SSD, Fibre Channel, SATA) and availability levels (RAID type).

You use storage profiles, which are abstractions of vSphere clusters and vSphere datastores, to define units of consumption in vCloud Director. These units of storage are allocated to PvDCs as logical objects. Your consumers are then allocated Organization (Org) virtual datacenters, which exist in one (or more, in the case of an elastic PvDC) Provider Virtual Datacenter.

# Designing the Management Pod

Although not directly under the control of vCloud Director, the design of the management pod in your overall vCloud design is critical to successful management and provisioning within your environment. The management pod hosts the vCloud cell servers, vCenter, and their supporting databases as well as other ancillary functions like VMware vCloud Networking and Security (vCNS).

In this section we'll examine some of the key services that need to be available in your management pod and discuss design principles that ensure availability and supportability.

## vCloud Databases

Like most elements of the vCloud and vSphere suites, vCloud Director relies on a backend database to store its configuration. Therefore, availability of the database is critical to operations. Most implementations leverage some kind of application-level database high-availability technology. Official support has been patchy in previous versions of vCloud Director, but as a result of customer feedback in this area, VMware has clarified the support position of the following solutions as of vCloud Director 5.1:

- Microsoft SQL Clustering (Microsoft Clustering Services)
- Oracle Real Application Clusters (RAC)

**NOTE**    SQL log shipping and mirroring are not explicitly supported. But you can provide a method for data protection when you combine these features with a manual failover process. If you don't have suitable licenses for these features, you can rely on traditional SQL backup and restore processes. But be aware that if you have to roll back the database from a backup, any vApps created since the backup may remain on the storage and vSphere layer but vCloud Director will not be aware of them.

---

### OFFICIAL SUPPORT MATRIX

VMware, Microsoft, and Oracle revise these policies from time to time. The definitive current source is VMware Product Interoperability Matrixes, available at `http://partnerweb.vmware.com /comp_guide2/sim/interop_matrix.php?`.

---

If you chose to build your database clusters in the management pod, you should be aware that virtualized clusters are supported on vSphere but have some official support constraints that can limit your use of vMotion and DRS for your management cluster. You can work around this by using the DRS Groups feature in vSphere 5.0 and later for SQL cluster nodes. Virtualized clusters also require Raw Device Mapping (RDM) storage from a VMFS volume and as such do not support NFS presented datastores.

The official support statement for Microsoft clusters on vSphere can be found in KB article 1037959 at `http://kb.vmware.com/selfservice/microsites/search.do?language=en_US& cmd=displayKC&externalId=1037959`.

Because the vCloud Director database mainly stores metadata about vCloud Director–managed objects, it does not typically grow very large; 100 MB should provide ample headroom for most deployments.

You can use a single database cluster to host databases for a number of vCenter, vCloud, and chargeback installations, as shown in Figure 5.5, unless there are security boundaries that you need to enforce that would prevent this approach in your organization. If you are going to do this, we highly recommend that you adopt an easily understood naming convention to clearly identify which database belongs to which server/role and that you conduct regular backups and test restores.

**FIGURE 5.5**
Single database cluster supporting multiple server roles, vCenter, cell server, etc.

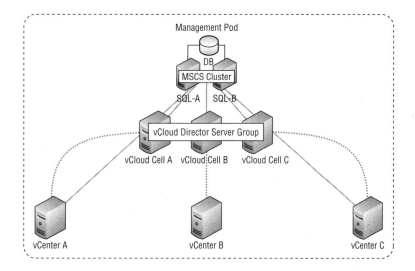

**WARNING**    vCloud Director does not support Windows Authentication when using SQL Server as its backend database; you need to use built-in SQL authentication only.

## vCloud Cell Servers

You'll need at least one cell server to run your vCloud platform. The cell server is a RedHat Enterprise Linux virtual machine. A virtual appliance–based version is available, but it is not supported for production.

The vCloud Director software is an installable package for Linux. Other than its basic system and package requirements, it does not have any special design requirements. It requires at least two IP addresses. It is technically possible to put multiple IP addresses on a single NIC, and given that cell servers are typically deployed as virtual machines, we recommend that you build this cell server by using separate virtual NICs. Doing so makes things easier to troubleshoot and to demonstrate network isolation to auditors.

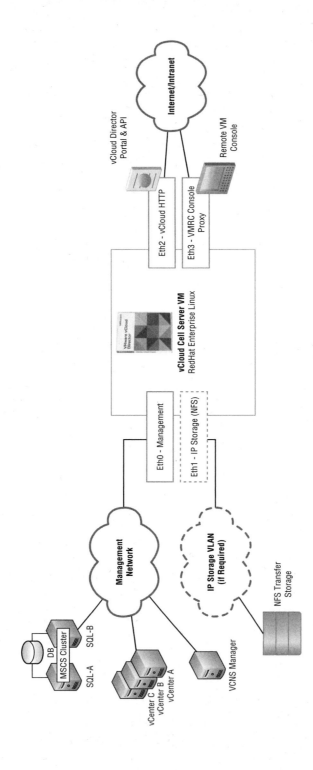

**FIGURE 5.6**
NIC usage in a vCloud Director cell server

In practice, most enterprise private cloud deployments will use three vNICs in a cell server as follows (a fourth may be required if a physical NFS device is used for the transfer storage, as shown in Figure 5.6):

**Management NIC**   Ensures private connectivity between the cell server and vCenter; if you are using a dedicated virtual appliance or another Linux host to provide NFS storage, this can also provide access to the NFS transfer location.

**HTTP NIC**   Provides an HTPPS service to serve the UI and REST API to consumer web browsers to the Internet or company WAN.

**Virtual Machine Remote Console (VMRC) Proxy NIC**   Proxies SSL requests for the virtual machine console from the consumer's web browser to vSphere.

The VMRC proxy allows your consumers to have direct access to the virtual machine console via the vCloud Director interface using a web browser. It is implemented as an Active X component for Internet Explorer and a plug-in for Mozilla Firefox, other browsers like Chrome and Safari do not support the VMRC plug-in. VMRC connections from consumer browsers are directed to the dedicated console proxy NIC via SSL; the VMRC proxy then proxies a connection to the vCenter Server, which in turn directs the VMRC to the vSphere server hosting the virtual machine and presents a VMware Remote Console to the consumer's browser over SSL.

Each cell server is a stateless web application that deals with servicing requests from consumers and handles orchestration to the various vCloud components like vCenter and vCNS Manager. Each cell server has an internal mechanism for managing internal cell health and availability as follows:

◆   One of the cell servers is designated as the master cell server and the remaining cells are designated as slave cells. The master cell server is responsible for ensuring that all critical services are running on all cell servers by monitoring the state of the services on each slave cell.

◆   Each cell server's service makes a regular heartbeat entry in the cell database. The master cell server uses this entry to determine whether each cell service is running and responding correctly; if it detects a service failure, the master cell server restarts the relevant service on the affected cell automatically.

◆   Slave cells likewise check that the master cell is updating its heartbeat monitor. If they detect it is not updating its heartbeat, they assume it has failed and they hold an election to appoint a new master cell server, which then resumes the role of master slave and restarts any failed cell services on slave nodes.

Adding more cells increases the possible number of concurrent operations and connected users and is how you can horizontally scale the vCloud Director cells. However, to achieve true availability you will need to deploy an IP load balancer solution in front of the cell server(s), as shown in Figure 5.7. You should configure your IP load balancer to query for responding HTTP services on each cell server by querying the following URLs every 5 seconds and route traffic appropriately:

◆   vCloud Portal UI: `https://<Cell_Hostname>/cloud/server_status`

◆   Console Proxy URL: `https://<Cell_Hostname>//sdk/vimServiceVersions.xml`

The load balancer you choose needs to support session persistence for SSL connections. Note that the VMRC console proxy does not support SSL offloading. Both need to be accessible from

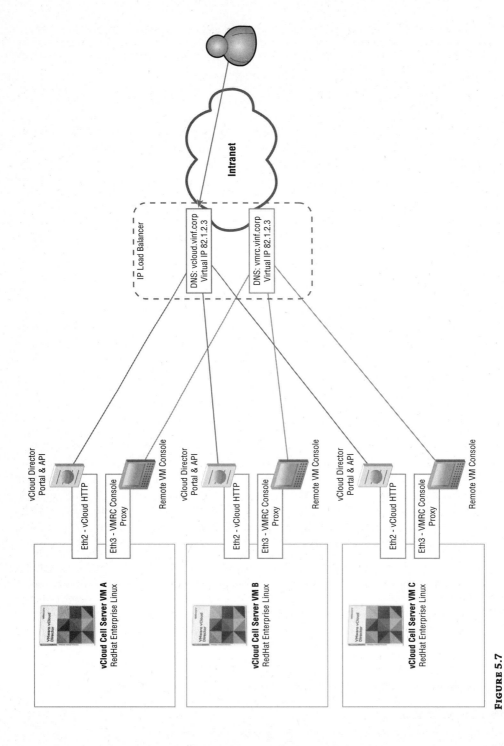

**FIGURE 5.7**

An IP load balancer distributing sessions to vCloud cell servers

the corporate WAN or intranet. If yours is purely an internal-only deployment, you should always use static IP addresses for these NICs. Bear in mind that the IP addresses you assign are configured within vCloud director as well as the operating system, and changing them will require you to take all vCloud Director cells offline.

If you do need to change them at some point in the future, you will need to follow the steps outlined in KB 1028657: `http://kb.vmware.com/selfservice/microsites/search.do?language=en_US&cmd=displayKC&externalId=1028657`.

From a security perspective, there is no way to isolate consumer and provider access to the UI. Both are routed via the same HTTP NIC. Your organization may have security policies that prohibit administrative-type access from external networks like the Internet or an intranet. In this case, you will need to deploy a web application firewall in front of the cell server(s) that can filter based on URL and specifically block access to `https://your.vcloud.org/cloud`.

This single root URL can be problematic for some web application firewalls because normal consumer access to vCloud is via `https://your.vcloud.org/org/YourOrgName/` and applying a block on `https://your.vcloud.org/cloud/*` would also block your consumers from connecting. Therefore, ensure that you block access to that specific URL from an external network but allow all other subsites.

If this use case applies to your private cloud, you should also consider that in order to provide this level of application inspection you will need to terminate the SSL connection on your web application firewall, inspect the payload, and re-encrypt to pass it on to the cell servers. This means you will require a more advanced web application firewall configuration. This type of configuration is common in public cloud scenarios where a provider needs to segregate access to provider and consumer infrastructures.

## Transfer Storage

Each vCloud Director installation needs shared storage as a mount point configured on each Linux cell server. This shared area of storage is used to temporarily store vApp, OVF, and media file (`.iso`, `.flp`) uploads from consumers via the vCloud Director UI. This location should be the maximum size of a single virtual machine that a user uploads in a given time multiplied by the number of consumers doing so. Its contents are entirely transient—that is, as soon as an upload from a consumer has completed, the file(s) are transferred to the vSphere datastores via the cell servers and vCenter, and the space becomes available again.

We suggest that you allocate 2 TB of storage for this location, because it potentially needs to be accessible from more than one cell server. This storage is typically provided over NFS, but other shared storage options can be used if they support multiple host access.

If you do not have network attached storage, you can configure another server within the management pod (or even one of the cell servers) to export an NFS mount, which is mounted on each of the other servers within the cell. Keep in mind that this approach creates a single point of failure, but since you are not storing significant long-term data, this is a manageable solution.

The transfer storage must be mounted in the following location on each cell server to function correctly:

```
$VCLOUD_HOME/data/transfer
```

which by default maps to

```
/opt/vmware/vcloud-director/data/transfer
```

## SSL Certificates

You can create self-signed SSL certificates or requests to be signed by an external certificate authority (CA) as part of the cell server installation process. However, all of the internal vSphere components (vCenter, vSphere, vCNS Manager, etc.) use self-signed SSL certificates as part of the default installation to secure their communication traffic.

It is technically possible to change all of these certificates to use SSL certificates signed by a public or internal CA, but doing so requires a significant manual effort. So unless you have a hard security requirement to do so, we suggest that you allow the internal vSphere communications to be carried out using self-signed certificates but protect the external-facing vCloud Director portal and VMRC SSL interfaces with publicly signed SSL certificates.

The risk of using self-signed certificates is that they could be open to a man-in-the-middle attack. That risk is somewhat mitigated by the fact that all the internal communications are over internal datacenter networks and that you are using SSL certificates and an external firewall to protect externally facing elements of your vCloud Director instance.

Figure 5.8 shows how use of public SSL certificates is also a good example of how you can differentiate between various PvDCs at a security level in order to comply with regulations. You may choose to invest the effort to change to public CA SSL certificates for one or more clusters and vCenters within your vCloud Director platform.

**FIGURE 5.8**
Differentiating between self-signed and publicly signed SSL certificate PvDCs

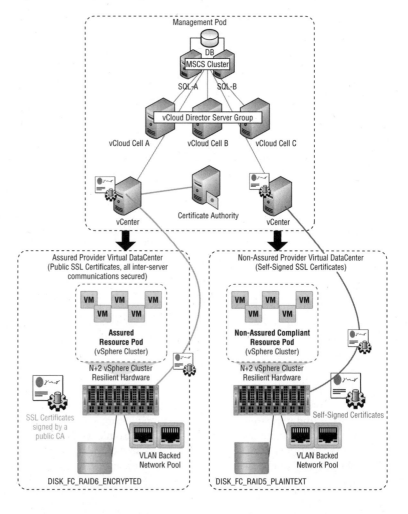

At present, the supported method to change vSphere SSL certificates is covered here:

www.vmware.com/resources/techresources/10318

Changing vSphere SSL certificates is a mostly manual and time-consuming process at present, although VMware has indicated that it's an area of focus for future releases. A commercial product called vCert Manager from Virtual System Solutions is in development that promises to automate much of this process. As of this writing, vCert Manager is available in beta form and looks to address many of these pain points. You can read more about it here:

www.vsslabs.com/vCert.html

## vCNS Manager

vCNS Manager is the new name (as of vCloud 5.1) for vCNS Manager. One vCNS Manager appliance is deployed at build time for each vCenter managing resource pod. It is responsible for deployment and configuration of VCNS gateway appliances within your vCloud. The appliance is deployed from an OVF package, and all it requires is a static IP address as well as network access and authentication details to connect to your vCenter server as well as access to DNS and an accurate Network Time Protocol (NTP) time source.

vCNS Manager has no built-in high-availability features but can be protected using VMware High Availability to ensure an automated restart if a host fails. VM Monitoring can be used to detect a problem within the virtual appliance and automate a restart. In either case, a failure of the host or appliance will result in a cold reboot of the virtual appliance. During this time consumers will not be able to create new vCNS gateway appliances, although currently deployed vCNS gateway appliances will continue to function as normal.

---

### CAN I USE VSPHERE FAULT TOLERANCE FOR VCNS MANAGER?

In versions of vCloud prior to 5.1, vShield Manager was often protected using VMware Fault Tolerance (FT) functionality, but because of the increased scale and functionality of the vCNS Manager appliance, it now uses two vCPUs, which makes it incompatible with the FT feature.

---

# Resource Pod Design

Now that you understand the design considerations for the management elements of the platform, let's take a look at the design considerations for the infrastructure that will be running your consumers' workload.

## Compute

In vCloud vSphere, clusters are abstracted and dealt with as PvDCs, but other than that the underlying vSphere cluster design principles, maximums, and calculations still apply. Some additional constrains come into play; for example, vCloud can support 25 vCenter servers, but it cannot support the total supported workload of 25 vCenter servers. vCloud Director automates the creation of resource pools on the clusters to create Org vDCs.

Your design decisions as to which servers to use to provide your computing "horsepower" depend on the requirements you have captured and any constraints at play within your environment.

---

**CONFIGURATION MAXIMUMS**

The "Configuration Maximums" document is one of the most important that VMware publishes. You can use it to check the supported sizing boundaries of the vCloud and vSphere suites—for example, the maximum number of hosts in a vSphere cluster, or the maximum number of vCenter Server instances supported by vCloud Director.

The document can be found here:

    www.vmware.com/pdf/vsphere5/r51/vsphere-51-configuration-maximums.pdf

---

When working at scale, as you are likely to do with a private cloud implementation, strongly consider standardization of your server hardware models and purchasing groups of servers together. Not only does this approach guarantee you'll have compatible CPU generations and identical hardware, it makes your deployment process simpler. You can use tools like Autodeploy and host profiles to deploy and redeploy your servers. Likewise, using DHCP rather than static IP addressing schemes for vSphere servers becomes more appealing. vSphere 5.1 with Autodeploy also allows you to deploy stateless vSphere hosts, where each node is booted from the network using a Trivial File Transfer Protocol (TFTP) server. The host downloads the vSphere hypervisor at boot-time and runs it in RAM; then it downloads its configuration from the Autodeploy server.

You can further customize this process to deploy the vCloud agent and join the host to a cluster as part of the Autodeploy configuration, which means the host automatically becomes part of the PvDC you specify.

Blade servers also become more suitable for cloud deployments. You can leverage many of the converged I/O technologies to allow for rapid redeployment of server hardware and drastically simplified cabling; you essentially wire a blade chassis once and everything from there is logical configuration (such as tagging VLANs and SAN zoning). Where you deploy converged I/O technologies, you may also want to consider storage and network I/O control functionality in vSphere. You can configure this functionality at the vSphere layer and it is independent of vCloud Director.

You should map out your design in terms of each PvDC. Each will have its own requirements for performance, security, and availability that define the SLA that you are able to offer.

## Networking

As with computing design, the network design of vCloud Director and the way it is delivered to individual hosts follows standard vSphere design principles, thus separating management, vMotion, and storage traffic from virtual machine workload. With vCloud Director, the virtual machine workload port groups can be managed, created, and deleted entirely by vCloud Director automatically.

vSphere design principles for NIC redundancy, traffic management, and failover still apply to vCloud. However, you will need specific maximum transmission unit (MTU) settings for NICs that are carrying the vCloud Director Network Isolation (VCNI) and Virtual Extensible LAN (VXLAN) transport VLAN, so you will want to isolate them to their own physical NICs.

Many organizations deploy management interfaces on standard vSwitches and use the distributed virtual switch for virtual machine workload if they have suitable vSphere licensing. This is also a common model for vCloud Director, and in fact the more advanced types of port group require distributed vSwitches to function.

One of the primary design decisions for vCloud networking is what network pool type(s) you will support. It is possible to specify a different network pool type for each PvDC in your platform, but unless you have specific requirements to do so, your main choice will be which type of network pool you will be using. Table 5.5 illustrates the options, typical deployment reasons, and the technical implications.

**TABLE 5.5:**     Network pool design criteria

| NETWORK POOL TYPE | TYPICAL REASON FOR CHOOSING | IMPLICATION |
|---|---|---|
| Port group backed | No license for vSphere distributed vSwitch or NX1000V available | Can use standard or distributed vSwitches<br><br>Administrator needs to manually create port groups on all hosts in a cluster |
| VLAN backed | Cannot make advanced network configurations to support VXLAN or VCNI | Requires distributed vSwitch |
| VCNI backed | Need large scalability to support a significant number of VLANs; a large enterprise or where you have a limited number of physical VLANs available to use | Requires distributed vSwitch<br><br>Needs dedicated transport VLAN between all hosts in cluster; vSwitch and physical switch MTU of at least 1,600 required to prevent fragmentation and poor performance |
| VXLAN backed | Need to extend virtual layer 2 networks across sites and across an existing layer 3 network<br><br>Hybrid cloud scenario with public provider or physical network devices that can support VXLAN<br><br>Need large scalability to support significant number of virtual networks | Requires distributed vSwitch or NX1000V<br><br>Needs dedicated transport VLAN between all hosts in cluster; vSwitch and physical switch MTU of at least 1,600 required to prevent fragmentation and poor performance<br><br>Requires multicast support on the physical network between sites<br><br>Requires nondefault settings on all network devices in the data path between sites, which will need to be approved and configured by your network administrator |

External networks in vCloud Director are physical VLANs that, for example, provide access to a corporate WAN or an Internet connection. These are configured in vSphere as port groups and then allocated in vCloud Director to an organization.

## vCNS Gateway

The vCNS gateway appliance is deployed, managed, and configured by the vCNS Manager. There are no real design considerations for the provider at this stage, but the consumer can choose to deploy the vCNS gateway appliance in one of two modes:

**Compact**    Basic vCNS gateway appliance

**Full**        Higher throughput appliance; can be deployed in high availability mode as an active/passive clustered pair of virtual appliances (host affinity is configured by vCloud to keep the appliances on separate vSphere hosts)

## Storage

Good storage design has always been critical with vSphere, and the same design principles apply to a vCloud Director installation. You should leverage appropriate connections to ensure redundant paths and sufficient bandwidth for all your hosts as well as at the array controller and disk levels.

Because you are providing general pools of storage for vCloud Director to consume, a good approach to defining your storage tiers is to define them along the following lines. Averaging the number of IOPS per GB is a reasonable way to represent the amount of performance you can get from a specified disk type.

Actual figures will vary depending on the array and disk access pattern (Table 5.6). Your vendor should be able to provide you with some figures; there are also some excellent free resources on the Internet such as those provided by Marek Wolynko at www.wmarow.com/strcalc/, who offers a number of calculators that estimate IOPS for various disks and RAID configurations and disk types.

**TABLE 5.6:**      IOPS for various disk types and RAID configurations

| DISK TYPE | RAID LEVEL | AVERAGE IOPS/GB | ARRAY ENCRYPTION |
|---|---|---|---|
| Enterprise SSD (Gold) | 1+0 | 7.52 IOPS/GB | No |
| 15k RPM FC SCSI (Silver) | 1+0 | 1.49 IOPS/GB | No |
| Enterprise SATA (Bronze) | 6 | 0.03 IOPS/GB | No |
| Consumer SATA (Protected Archive Only) | 5 | 0.01 IOPS/GB | Yes |
| 15k RPM FC SCSI (PCI Compliant) | 1+0 | 1.49 IOPS/GB | Yes |

To validate these numbers, you can then estimate or measure an average number of I/O operations per second that the datastore can deliver per second, known as an IOPS.

**MEASURING I/O PERFORMANCE**

As part of your deployment plan, you can use open source tools like IOmeter (http://sourceforge
.net/projects/iometer/) to test the number of IOPS per datastore by placing a test probe onto
the datastore inside a virtual machine and using IOmeter to simulate disk activity. You can gradually increase the number of IOPS until you see a reduction in performance. Doing so should give you
a reasonable estimate of the maximum I/O operations per second, commonly abbreviated to IOPS.

As part of your service description, you can give these disk tiers a name such as gold, silver,
or bronze, or you can denote some sort of security or capacity characteristic. It's important to
note that in this example the encryption is being performed at the array level. Neither vSphere
nor vCloud has this capability today.

vSphere 5.0 and later introduced the concept of storage profiles. You create storage profiles at
the vSphere layer, and they are allocated to a PvDC. You can create storage profiles along these
lines within vSphere by assigning a datastore a "user-defined storage capability" (Figure 5.9).

**FIGURE 5.9**

Creating a user-
defined storage
capability attribute

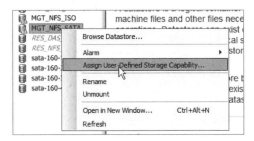

You then give your capability a name and enter some descriptive text to describe it
(Figure 5.10).

**FIGURE 5.10**

Describing a user-
defined storage
capability

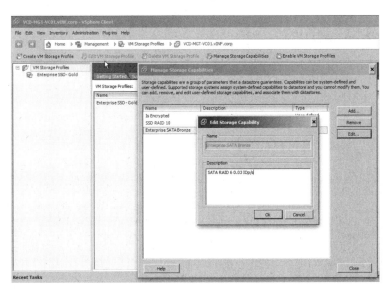

You can then assign the storage capability attribute to a datastore, as shown in Figure 5.11.

**FIGURE 5.11**
Assigning a user-
defined storage
capability to a
datastore

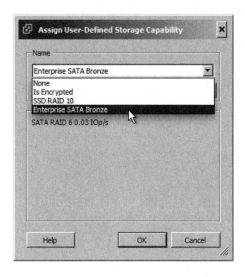

You can define a storage profile for an Org vDC. It will then place vApps onto an appropriate datastore that meets the defined profile.

As with vSphere, when you create your cluster you need to zone the storage LUNs to the hosts within your cluster. That way, only those hosts have access to the LUNs you have created for them.

Storage DRS is supported if you are using vSphere 5.1 hosts in your provider VDC. Storage DRS is configured independently of vCloud Director at the vSphere layer.

## Summary

The first part of your design for vCloud is to define your requirements. MoSCoW (Must, Should, Could, Would) notation is useful to capture and refine the requirements to determine their relative cost.

As you progress through your design, you can make comparisons for relative cost to deliver each requirement. Where you are challenged on cost or have budgetary constraints, you can analyze the relative differences to determine which requirements have to be compromised to meet a financial or design constraint. This is a useful technique for explaining the implication of technical and commercial decisions to a nontechnical audience and allowing stakeholders to make an informed decision.

A pod-based architecture is highly recommended for vCloud Director. Hosting the management elements in a dedicated management pod isolates the infrastructure and software delivering the vCloud service from the consumer workloads. The management pod then manages one or more resource pods, which are provider virtual datacenters in vCloud and are used to host organization virtual datacenters for consumers. Pods can be scaled out by adding further hosts to the cluster or adding further datastores.

When designing your resource pods (provider virtual datacenters), normal vSphere design principles and best practices apply. DRS must always be enabled for resource clusters. HA is highly recommended but it's optional. vCloud Director aggregates these discrete clusters and vCenters into a single point of management.

# Chapter 6

# Building a Cost Model

Cloud computing is about moving IT to a utility model, where you pay for the services you consume on a usage or rental basis. Nicholas Carr makes a great analogy in his book *The Big Switch: Rewiring the World, from Edison to Google* (W. W. Norton & Company, 2009) whereby he contrasts the technology industry (and thus the provision of computing resources) to the way electricity was originally delivered in the early days of electrification.

In short, when companies first started to realize the benefits that electrification could bring to their manufacturing operations, there was no utility supply; if a company wanted to use electricity, they had to generate it. This meant significant investment in electricity-generating equipment and the staff to operate and maintain it. Because of those capital and operational costs, only the larger organizations could afford to fund it. Manual labor was cheaper than power-generating infrastructure unless you achieved a critical mass of scale in your manufacturing operation where it was cheaper to purchase and run an electrical plant and machines than employ large numbers of cheap laborers to do the manual assembly work.

As time went on, more and more organizations developed their own generating capacity, often running at customized levels of voltage so that equipment had to be specifically designed to run on that voltage standard. The result was less standardization and more operating cost. To make matters worse, generating capacity had to be designed to meet the peak workload expected to deliver the required level of service (sound familiar?), meaning that for nonpeak hours of the day, equipment was idle or underutilized. Some factories operated only during daytime hours, whereas other industries operated overnight production runs but were quiet during the daylight hours.

As the requirement for electrical power became increasingly commonplace, companies that were colocated in city blocks joined forces to generate and sell electrical capacity, moving from the in-house generation model (with the required capital and operational costs) to a shared model. In this model, electricity-generating companies supplied power on demand to a number of organizations and charged each for a share of the cost (plus the profit) of building and operating the necessary equipment. This model was only possible once a critical mass of consumers was willing to pay for consumption on demand of electrical power and was willing to adopt a standardized model of usage (standard voltage).

This parallels the IT industry: If you equate the private cloud to an organization generating electricity in-house, there are a number of providers offering shared, multitenant cloud solutions on a pay-per-use model that are akin to the electricity-generating utility companies.

Many of the arguments we hear today about the move from private to public and hybrid cloud are common to discussions in the early days of electrification: "What if the utility company goes bankrupt and stops my supply?" "My competitors also use the same utility company;

what if they draw all the power and I don't get any?" Or worse: "What if my competitors negoti-ate an exclusive deal that precludes the utility company from supplying me?"

Many of these arguments have been made before, and they will be made again. Critical mass is the lever in this case. The supply of electricity simply became cheaper, ubiquitous, and easier to consume from the electrical utility companies than building and managing your own gener-ating capacity.

The comparison with electrical generation is obviously a simplistic one. For example, people can't steal your customer's personal financial data from the electrical supply for profit, but they could impact your ability to produce products and operate your business.

We're not saying that a private cloud is a dead-end and that the public cloud is the only stra-tegic choice. For some organizations, getting out of the IT business and focusing on their prod-ucts is the desired goal. But consider how many of those businesses may hedge their bets by taking services from more than one cloud provider, or continue to host critical services in-house, like many large enterprises (and even service providers) that maintain and operate their own backup electrical generators to provide business continuity in the event that the utility power supply fails.

Now that you have a firm grasp of what you need to be offering with your proposed cloud platform, it's important to understand how to charge for it.

In this chapter, you will learn to:

◆ Build a cost matrix to better understand the components required to build and operate your cloud

◆ Standardize units of resource consumption to allow you to apportion cost against them

◆ Understand constraints in-place for building true pay-as-you-go cloud environments with current software vendor licensing

## Economics of Cloud

The traditional model of procuring IT services, where software and hardware are procured up front and in capacities sufficient to meet maximum demand, is very different from one of the attributes of cloud computing: *measured service.*

For example, in the traditional IT procurement model, if designers of a solution overesti-mated the resource required to service maximum demand for the solution, that resource would typically go to waste over the lifetime of the solution. Or where a solution is heavily used for relatively short periods of time but remains largely idle for the remainder of the year, that resource typically goes to waste since it is "owned" by the solution or project.

Measured service introduces a different model, whereby the consumer offsets the risk and cost of equipment procurement by focusing merely on requesting and consuming resources from a potentially infinite pool of resources owned by a provider. The provider in turn charges the consumer for the amount of resources actually consumed.

Nobody wants to be "that guy" who underestimated how much RAM or CPU or disk space the product would consume and must take the blame for poor performance or user experience. So, it's human nature, given that compute resource is relatively cheap, that people give generous estimates of minimum system requirements when asked. Often this isn't so bad for individual products, but when you multiply this excess capacity across an enterprise, it can become a significant waste. Measured service allows consumers to adopt a flexible approach to allocation of resources, and the on-demand self-service attributes of cloud computing make it feasible to conduct prototyping and load-testing activities on a solution before committing to a significant infrastructure spend, as would happen in the traditional IT procurement.

The benefit of measured service to the consumer is obvious. It streamlines costs and minimizes waste, but it does present a problem for the would-be cloud provider. In order to build a platform that you can share among your various consumers, you must procure hardware in the traditional up-front way. Most hardware vendors are not geared up to sell hardware in a "cloudy" way yet; they still sell servers, storage, and so forth regardless of how much of it you actually use.

Some hardware vendors will allow gradual scale-out of your environment, so though there is some initial capital investment, if your platform is successful the cost to scale it out to accommodate more consumers is incremental. Be sure to investigate these deals carefully; many are "dressed-up" finance agreements with minimum expansion and significant penalty and exit clauses on top of heavily marked-up prices over the contractual term.

In a private cloud model, you rely on the multitenancy of your cloud to increase overall utilization to make the most of the investment. You remove traditional silos through virtualization but have a much tighter handle on actual resource consumption that you can reflect in your billing (or at least cost attribution) to your consumers.

For your consumer the appeal of moving to your private cloud is a switch from capital expenditure (CAPEX) to an operational expenditure (OPEX) model, based on actual usage rather than a fixed or projected usage (although less popular, these models can also be accommodated). Much like the way you pay for utilities like electricity, water, and gas, your consumption of the resources is metered and technical toolsets are used to present your consumer with a bill.

vCenter Chargeback has a flexible architecture to allow for integrated metering and reporting. The focus of this chapter is on the concepts of building a cost model that you will need to understand before implementing.

## Building a Cost Matrix

To grasp what it will cost you to build and operate a cloud computing platform, you need to determine all the component costs, capital, operational, and people costs to build and operate the platform (Figure 6.1).

**FIGURE 6.2**
The component parts that can make up a cost model and how they are split between CAPEX and OPEX type costs

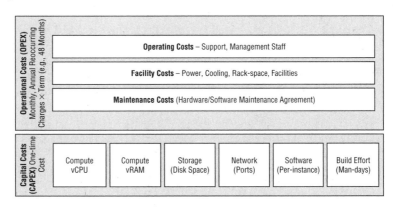

Cloud computing is geared toward consuming standard items from the service catalog rather than facilitating truly customized configurations. There are a number of reasons for this, but at the heart of the issue is preserving the abstraction of the underlying platform complexity and thus cost. The more customized the implementation, the less a common build, resource consumption, and operating model can be used. This drives up cost since there is less sharing of common configuration, processes, and resources; it could also potentially reduce portability of the solutions you build as a consumer between different providers of vCloud implementations.

To better understand your cost of operation, you can build a model or matrix. In its simplest form, this is best implemented as a spreadsheet.

## Table of Costs

You should build a cost table that encompasses all of the capital and operational costs involved with your platform, along the lines of Table 6.1.

**TABLE 6.1:** An example of a cost table

| ITEM | UNIT CAPITAL COST (CAPEX) | POWER + COOL/ MONTH | MAINTENANCE + 24×7 4-HOUR RESPONSE | NOTES |
|---|---|---|---|---|
| Server blade | $8,750 | $300 | $250 | HP BL460c, 2 × CPU, 8 GB of RAM, 2 × SAS hard disk space |
| Server network connection | $1,500 | $5 | $50 | 2 × 1 Gb from core 6509 switches + 100 Mb/s or Integrated Lights-Out (iLO) from out-of-band network |
| 1 TB of usable tier 3 SAN storage | $400 | $8 | $10 | Hewlett Packard Enterprise Virtual Array (HP-EVA) array 1, RAID 5 volume of 10 disks with 1 × hot spare |
| 300 GB of usable SAN disk | $800 | $9 | $10 | HP-EVA array 1, RAID 0/1 volume of 20 disks with 2 × hot spare |
| Firewall port | $4,000 | $200 | $200 | 1 port from large (16 port) Checkpoint firewall |

Where you have items like network ports that are from a switch containing multiple ports, you should try to attribute the cost to individual units of consumption. In many cases, this will be a server connection. If you have a redundant switching infrastructure, this may equate to two switch ports (from different switches) per server, then a further connection for an out-of-band (OOB) management network. It makes sense to treat these as a whole, rather than breaking out each item individually unless you are planning to offer entirely customized configurations.

We also recommend that you maintain a notes field in your cost table so you can document how individual unit costs were determined should they need to be changed in the future. In complex environments, it's wise to maintain a specific document formally detailing pricing calculations and historical changes.

For an operational cost, where the line item incurs a periodic charge such as the cost of power it consumes over a month, take care to ensure the periods you use are consistent. For example, if you pay for power per watt per month, ensure you match up that monthly period with other operational items like maintenance, which may be priced on an annual basis. In that example, it's simply a case of dividing the annual cost by 12 to reflect a monthly cost.

Where possible, you should standardize your units of consumption, particularly when it comes to disk space. As we'll discuss in later design chapters, it's sensible to carve up storage into standard units of allocation based on its performance and availability characteristics. This is when you'll see it gets more complex to accommodate customized configurations because you need to apportion a large number of elements.

You can then use the data you have captured in this table to start to build your cost model. A spreadsheet is a great tool for this sort of cost modeling. In Figure 6.2, notice the tabs across the bottom; each worksheet includes the calculations that derive the unit price denoted on the summary page. Large service providers build entire IT systems around this sort of tool, but for most private cloud implementations a well-thought-out spreadsheet is flexible enough to meet your needs.

**FIGURE 6.2**

An example of a cost model spreadsheet

| Item | Monthly cost | Notes |
|---|---|---|
| Compute cost VM type 1 | $ 15.00 | 1 vCPU, 2Gb RAM |
| Compute cost VM type 2 | $ 30.00 | 2 vCPU, 4Gb RAM |
| Compute cost VM type 3 | $ 45.00 | 4 vCPU, 8Gb RAM |
| Compute cost VM type 4 | $ 80.00 | 4 vCPU, 32Gb RAM |
| Compute cost VM type 5 | $ 150.00 | 8 vCPU, 64Gb RAM |
| Tier 1 storage per GB | $ 10.00 | RAID 0+1 SAN storage |
| Tier 2 storage per GB | $ 3.00 | SATA storage |
| Backup cost per GB | $ 0.40 | including backup software license |
| Network cost per VM | $ 80.00 | share of 10Gb link, 16:1 contention |
| Gold Management SLA per VM | $ 200.00 | 24x7 4hr fix |
| Silver Management SLA per VM | $ 100.00 | 24x7 12hr fix |
| Bronze Management SLA per VM | $ 50.00 | 9-5 support |
| Power per VM | $ 5.00 | contribution towards power/cool/facilities |
| Software pack per VM | $ 30.00 | Windows 2008 R2 Ent SPLA license, VSPP vSphere license |

Per-VM Cost Calculator | **Summary** | Compute | Storage | Network | Software | Management | Build-out

You have a front sheet showing a summary of costs, including base platform run cost and capacity, to keep things simple. We suggest using a separate tab for each functional area of your platform, organized along the following lines, covering the procurement costs of each item (you can focus on depreciation and other accounting functions once you understand the total costs):

**Computing**  Cost for servers, blades, etc.

**Network**  Cost for switches, firewalls, etc.

**Storage**  Cost for disks, SAN/NAS, fiber-channel switching

**Software**  Operating system licenses (such as Windows 2008 R2x64 Standard Edition)

**Management**  Cost for management toolsets (monitoring, alerting, etc.)

**Operations**  Cost for staff/resources to manage the platform

**Build**  Cost for staff/resources to design and build the platform

**Power/Cool/Facilities**  Cost for the power and cooling of the platform, as well as datacenter facilities (this may be a share of an existing DC, or space charged on a per-rack or per-kilowatt/month basis)

**Products**  Definition of the unit cost of each product; made up of its constituent parts, share of platform, software licenses, etc.

Using this method, you can construct a cost calculator (Figure 6.3) that takes the raw numbers and applies them to a per-VM cost. We will be discussing VMware vCloud Director later in this book, but in the meantime this is a useful tool for planning your private cloud for vCenter Chargeback.

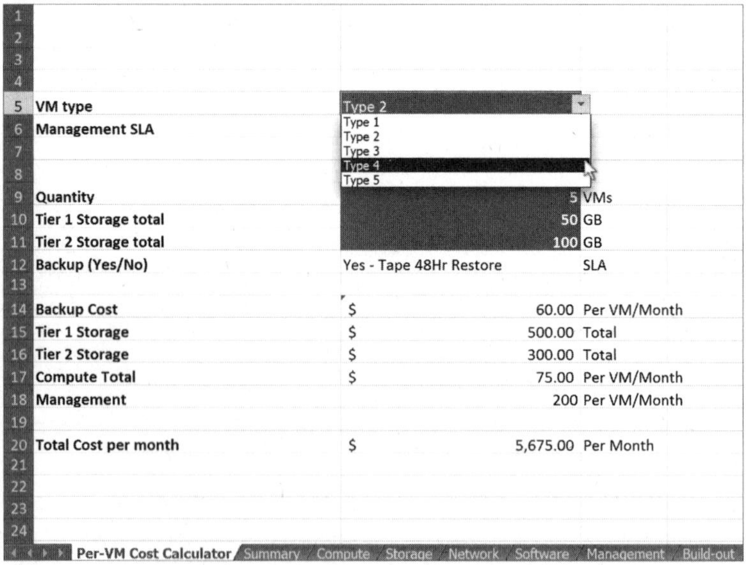

**FIGURE 6.3**

An example of per-VM cost calculator sheet in the cost model

You'll also need a good understanding of where there are price breaks and step changes in those costs and how and when you will attempt to recover those costs.

## Price Breaks

Price breaks come when you achieve a certain critical mass of infrastructure or software with a particular vendor's product (Figure 6.4). For example, there may be additional discount tiers available from an OS license if you commit to purchasing over a certain amount over a term of years.

**FIGURE 6.4**
Price breaks in unit price reduction as quantities of purchase increase

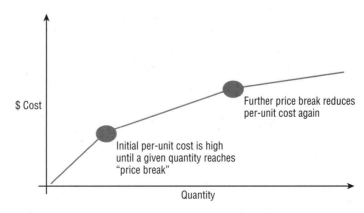

$ Cost

Initial per-unit cost is high until a given quantity reaches "price break"

Further price break reduces per-unit cost again

Quantity

## Step Changes

A step change in price typically relates to physical infrastructure that is scaled horizontally (Figure 6.5)—hardware, for example. When a blade chassis runs out of slots for more blades, a further chassis needs to be added to host the additional blades. Such items typically reflect large items of capital expenditure; though the blades themselves may be cheap, the costs of high-tech power supplies, cooling, and I/O modules are offset into the chassis.

**FIGURE 6.5**
The effect of step changes on hardware spend for a blade implementation

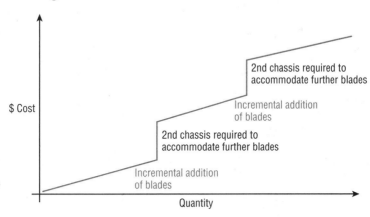

$ Cost

2nd chassis required to accommodate further blades

Incremental addition of blades

2nd chassis required to accommodate further blades

Incremental addition of blades

Quantity

For example, let's consider a Hewlett-Packard C-class blade chassis. When fully configured with interconnect bay modules and fans it could cost $60,000, whereas the blades you use to incrementally scale out the computing capacity only cost about $5,000. If the chassis in question has 16 slots, then the actual unit cost of a blade is no longer $5,000—it is $5,000 + 1/16th of $60,000, or $8,750.

Or consider a storage array. The incremental units of scale-out are individual disks worth $1,000, whereas a new storage frame to accommodate them once full is about $50,000.

All of these costs should be reflected in your cost model, even if it's just for your own use in understanding the cost of running a service. This is especially important if you are looking to recoup revenue or even make a profit on its provision as would typically be the case within a commercial service provider.

Companies generally understand this concept, which is sometimes referred to as "contribution to finite capacity." Per-unit costs are loaded to reflect each unit's contribution to the point at which the next major item will be required.

It's all about understanding production and operating cost over a period for a product or service, but this knowledge rarely feeds into IT operations. When moving to become a cloud provider, even in a purely internal private cloud delivery model, you must determine what makes up your cost of operation to avoid any expensive surprises.

## Cost vs. Price

At this early stage, it's important to clarify the terminology:

**Cost**  The actual cost to you (as the provider) to purchase or run something

**Price**  What you would sell that same service for to the consumer

If you have worked things out correctly, then the difference between the two is actually *profit*. It's up to your organization whether you intend to make a profit from the service you are offering or are willing to offer it at cost. The concept of profit is less common in the private cloud sense than it would be in a public cloud provider, but you should view it as money to reinvest in developing the service, or you could return a share of it to the consumers.

Depending on how you do your accounting, that cost (or indeed price) may also include some factor of contingency—that is, how you protect yourself from the cost of that entity unexpectedly increasing in cost during the life cycle of your service. Likewise, some costs are back-loaded, whereby the provider can offer a lower up-front price, making little or no "profit" in the early days of the service because they anticipate a particular component's price will decrease over time. This often happens with storage; as larger drives become the norm, the per-gigabyte price decreases.

## Cost of Operation

In our experience, IT projects spend a lot of time focusing on the acquisition cost of software and hardware to deliver a planned service. However, they often miss the fact that these costs are relatively small over the life cycle of a service when you compare them to the actual cost of operating the service.

Even if you are delivering an entirely black-box, self-managing, self-commissioning system, you must account for human costs. Staff is going to be the most significant cost because you'll need people to support, troubleshoot, and maintain the system. If you need to deliver a 24/7 service and are bound by a service level agreement (SLA) to your consumers, this cost can triple as you have to resource your team around shifts.

For example, to cover a 24/7 requirement you'd need three 8-hour shifts. If you operate in a global setting where you are supporting multiple time zones, this cost can triple because you may need to provide multiple shifts and increased pay for those working the needed hours. You'll also have to factor in that those staff will want to take vacations. To keep on top of those requirements, you'll also need to have someone to manage the staff, ensure they are delivering, and help them to develop their careers and keep on top of the scheduling.

Standby/on-call is a cheaper approach, whereby you have a rotating member of the team to take and respond to calls out of normal business hours. This is a workable approach when there are no massive time zone differences between your consumers, but consider that anything more than +/– 4 hours from your own time zone will put 50 percent of those customers' business day outside of your own.

On-call support is a double-edged sword. If you are only dealing with consumers in similar time zones, then it's workable, as long as your consumers can accept that out-of-hours support response is going to be slower and possibly more limited than in-business hours. But you also have to consider that in the event of a major problem, the staff member on-call may end up being awake all night working on a problem before they can hand the issue over to support for the normal business hours. At that point the individual is unlikely to be available during their normal working hours as they recover, so though you've responded to a problem out of hours, you're a person short during your normal business hours (when you would expect the team to be most busy).

Staff costs are also not just about their salaries. If you employ permanent staff (that is, employees), you will also need to cover their retirement, healthcare, and other benefits—and that's before you factor in the cost to give them a PC, software licenses, a desk, a phone, and a user account on your corporate IT systems.

Many organizations use concept of "landed cost," which is a per-head or per–pay grade cost of employing someone that reflects all the ancillary costs such as benefits, office space, and equipment. If you have access to this number when designing your cost model, you should definitely use it.

## Standardizing Units of Consumption

To help you develop your cost model and plan, it's useful to standardize the units of consumption as much as possible. In the private cloud setting, a unit of consumption is typically a virtual application (vApp) (consisting of one or more virtual machines) to allow for flexibility and to provide flexibility for your consumers. It makes sense to treat one vCPU (virtual CPU) or 1 GB of vRAM (virtual RAM) or disk space as a unit of consumption and assign a unit cost to each. You can then calculate its monthly (or whatever period you decide is most appropriate) cost across its intended life cycle. This approach lets you define the cost of a vApp based on the quantity of those units that it consumes in a given period.

The self-service attribute of cloud computing goes some way to reducing the impact on (and thus cost of) operations for day-to-day provisioning tasks. For example, if you build your cloud correctly, a consumer no longer has to log a service request for a new virtual machine to be provisioned and built. They simply request it from a portal and then work with it. As you learned in Chapter 3, "Introduction to vCloud Director," your consumers are also able to import their own virtual machines that they manage and work with or chose from pre-built offerings that the provider supplies.

So as a provider you are less concerned with maintaining standard builds for consumption. Your role is reduced to just providing infrastructure on demand—in line with the IaaS definition.

But from a cost model point of view, it makes sense to standardize on units of consumption. It's much easier to apportion cost to something of a known size and quantity.

Different components of the infrastructure will have differing life cycles. For example, network equipment may be deployed for 5-plus years before it is refreshed, whereas servers are refreshed at just 18 months to benefit from Moore's law (http://en.wikipedia.org/wiki/Moores_law), which represents the long-standing industry trend for computing density increasing every 18 months—which typically has the effect of reducing power/cooling footprint (Figure 6.6).

**FIGURE 6.6**

Calculating unit
cost for resource

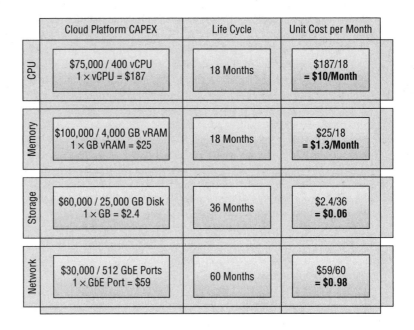

| | Cloud Platform CAPEX | Life Cycle | Unit Cost per Month |
|---|---|---|---|
| **CPU** | $75,000 / 400 vCPU<br>1 × vCPU = $187 | 18 Months | $187/18<br>= **$10/Month** |
| **Memory** | $100,000 / 4,000 GB vRAM<br>1 × GB vRAM = $25 | 18 Months | $25/18<br>= **$1.3/Month** |
| **Storage** | $60,000 / 25,000 GB Disk<br>1 × GB = $2.4 | 36 Months | $2.4/36<br>= **$0.06** |
| **Network** | $30,000 / 512 GbE Ports<br>1 × GbE Port = $59 | 60 Months | $59/60<br>= **$0.98** |

Using these metrics, you can apportion costs within vCloud Director and set the correct cost metrics when using the various resource allocation models it offers (such as dedicated, allocation, or pay as you go).

### Custom Configurations

All this talk of standardization isn't to say you can't accommodate a custom requirement for an application in your private cloud, such as an extra network connection between hosts for an application cluster heartbeat. Indeed, this area is where private cloud implementations have significant advantages over pure public cloud services, which do not allow you to deviate from the off-the-shelf products they offer. Because you own the underlying methods of delivering and managing services, you have the flexibility to do something nonstandard. However, you should do so with a full understanding of the impact to the operating and commercial models and ensure that you charge (or proportion cost) appropriately.

## Software Licensing for the Cloud

Software licensing is one of the biggest issues on the economic side of cloud computing today. Software is complex, time consuming, and risky to develop, and it needs to be maintained to ensure it is compatible with changes to the underlying operating systems and platforms.

The entire software industry has largely been built on the principle that company X spots a gap in the market and spends time developing functional (what it should do) and nonfunctional (how it should do it) specifications for a software product. They then have developers write code to meet those specifications; the code is then tested for reliability and conformance to the specifications. Despite huge advancements in high-level languages and automated testing suites, human labor is needed to devise, craft, and maintain the code, and that's not cheap labor in the current market. Good developers are very expensive and they want high salaries, benefits, and perks in exchange for their labor.

It's also a risky business; a large amount of intellectual property is built in the development of a software solution, and it's not unheard of for companies to seek to hire resources away from their competitors to gain access to that bank of already solved problems and potentially great ideas. Companies spend a lot of effort in the legal and contractual space to prevent this IP leakage, but it still happens. It poses a risk to any company that is invested in bringing a software solution to market because, while the company is dealing with the problem, a competitor could leap-frog them and become more successful.

When they invest in development and time in bringing a software solution to market, companies understandably want to recover that development investment in bringing a product to market as quickly as possible. They have traditionally done so by charging a license fee to anyone who wants to use the software solution.

Almost all enterprise software is licensed on a perpetual basis, whereby you are given a license to use the provided version of the software solution until you decide you no longer need it. Many vendors then charge an additional annual maintenance fee that entitles the customer to receive minor enhancements and bug fixes. Sometimes it also entitles them to subsequent major releases of the software product.

The perpetual license cost contributes to allowing the vendor to recoup the cost of developing the software and a slice of profit.

The maintenance fee helps the vendor to cover the cost of teams to maintain the product on an ongoing basis, providing technical support, feature enhancements, and bug fixes as required.

Enterprise software licenses have traditionally been tied to a physical entity, such as a site, end user, discrete server, or an individual CPU. With the advent of cloud computing, whereby the physical resources and indeed locations are abstracted away and shared between multiple end users, this approach becomes problematic.

If you review the licensing agreements for many major software packages, you'll see that they explicitly prevent the resale, rental, or time-sharing of the perpetual license you have purchased. Most also explicitly prevent the transfer of "title" to the license outside of the organization that purchased it.

Legally this is murky water when you are moving into a cloud computing model. You'll need to work with your vendors to determine what is allowable or seek a special dispensation if your organization carries sufficient commercial weight with a particular vendor.

The legal side of this is more problematic in the public cloud space, where you don't own the infrastructure that the service is running on, and it is potentially shared with other customers. In the private cloud space, the commercial aspects of perpetual licensing start to impact you more significantly; elasticity and perpetual licensing aren't really all that compatible.

Suppose you have to provide a middleware application for a peaky workload, such as the Christmas sales period. You may need to license that software solution for an increased number of servers for a relatively short period of time, from December to February. For software that is perpetually licensed, it means you are paying license and maintenance fees for the peak level of licensing that you require but are never realizing any cost saving for the period of lower usage from March to November.

It is uncommon for major vendors of enterprise software to license their software on a pay-per-use model. The software business is built on the perpetual plus maintenance model. Salespeople and the distribution channel and supply chain that supports them are typically compensated on the basis of units sold. The business, compensation, and reward model is geared toward returning maximum revenue to the developer as soon as possible, essentially seeking the shortest return on investment (ROI), whereas cloud licensing necessitates a steady trickle of incremental revenue.

Very few vendors take the long view that they will gather more users over time that will lead to a longer ROI but deliver a more flexible pay-per-use licensing model (Figure 6.7) that will allow customers to adopt their products more rapidly. To do this, they must be able to deal with peaks and troughs of demand; current business models do not cater well to those troughs of demand.

**FIGURE 6.7**

Revenue from traditional perpetual software licensing vs. pay-per-use licensing for the cloud

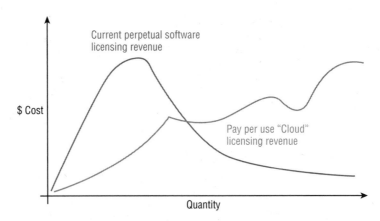

Large up-front investment requirements can make it harder for a company to justify purchase of a software solution, but a lower cost of entry with an incremental increase in licensing cost as requirements grow or shrink may capture a wider market.

Vendors are waking up to the pay-per-use model, but to be fair, it does take time to change how products are licensed and sold as they have a downstream chain of distribution, resellers, and partners that have built businesses on this model. Change of this sort takes time, but we are starting to see a critical mass of cloud computing adoption (both public and private). Even major enterprise software vendors are starting to react to changing customer demands or risk being outmaneuvered by smaller, more agile companies that can.

The open source community is leading in this space, because they are less dependent on perpetual license models and commercial implementations often instead relying on paid-for support services for their products. This, combined with the continuing maturity and commercialization of open source software, poses a significant risk for traditional enterprise software vendors and so is forcing change.

Longer term, this shift to service- or consumption-based pricing may lead to licensing models that are more in line with the elasticity attributes of the NIST definition of cloud computing and will deliver a more cost-effective solution for your consumers.

## Service Provider Licensing

For some time, service providers have had access to special licensing models, whereby they license on a cloud-compatible model, per-user, per-CPU, or per-server, but pay on a monthly basis without a long-term lock-in.

Service provider licensing is essentially a rental agreement with minimal commitment. The big advantage to a service provider is that in exchange for a slightly higher unit cost, they are able to build a service and take on customers with a lower up-front commitment to cover licensing.

The service provider benefits in a simpler model to pass through license costs to the customer, by allowing a much more granular unit of allocation in a multitenant environment (user or CPU) or even by licensing an individual node for an unlimited number of instances of a particular product.

**NOTE** This type of licensing will generally be unavailable to you if you own the underlying infrastructure or host it internally in your own datacenter. But as high-speed network communications are becoming increasingly common, many organizations are moving away from building internal datacenters, instead choosing to host with a service provider. If you contract with that service provider for them to operate your private cloud as a managed or hosted service, you could gain access to more flexible software licensing for your private cloud. You should apply pressure to your software vendors for these sorts of licensing models for your private cloud scenario. Vendors are unlikely to adopt such changes without significant pressure from customers.

## Microsoft SPLA

Microsoft has had its Service Provider Licensing Agreement (SPLA) model for a number of years. SPLA is ideal for varying or transient workloads because it is based on monthly charges rather than traditional perpetual licensing.

However, for servers that have a fixed configuration and aren't likely to change, traditional licensing may work out to be more cost-effective over a number of years. Unfortunately, if your requirements for your static server are modified, you cannot simply change between the two. So it's important that you make the right choices up front.

For example, you may flex up the platform to provide extra Windows or SQL servers for a couple of months. The net cost to you is a per-month charge per OS/application instance, using the retailer example from earlier in this chapter. You only pay for the extra OS/SQL instances for the December–February period (3 months) rather than perpetual licenses and capacity that isn't required for the rest of the year.

SPLA won't be an option for your enterprise unless you are planning to take a managed service from a service provider because there are a number of complex stipulations in the agreement over who owns the infrastructure and where it is located. There is a complex document called the Service Provider Usage Rights (SPUR) that details the specific use cases and required licenses for each product.

Because the document is so complex, Microsoft offers a tool to help you interpret it and extract the relevant section for your own solution. You can learn about the Service Provider Usage Rights Tool here:

```
www.microsoft.com/licensing/spur/products.aspx
```

You can't host services on an SPLA basis when they are hosted on your own premises, so you'll need to work with a service provider to build a managed service if you are looking for this sort of licensing model for Microsoft software. The Windows datacenter licenses may be an appropriate middle-ground model for your private cloud. Although they are still purchased up front and licensed on a perpetual basis, they can enable you to run an unlimited number of Windows instances per licensed physical CPU socket. Similar models are available for Microsoft SQL Server and a few other server products.

**NOTE**   We hope that in the future Microsoft will adopt options for SPLA-type models in their enterprise license agreements, allowing those organizations to take advantage of a much more flexible licensing model. Given the dependence of many enterprises on Microsoft products, a more flexible, consumption based licensing model would certainly help Microsoft maintain use of its products in a private cloud setting, especially when you consider the advances that the open source movement has made in gaining enterprise traction.

### VMware Service Provider Program

In a manner similar to Microsoft's, VMware offers the VMware Service Provider Program (VSPP) program, which has been gradually gaining popularity with service providers and managed service companies for a number of years. VSPP provides licensing purely on a per-VM, and, more recently, vRAM consumption basis, rather than the traditional per-CPU model. This program has allowed service providers to build VMware vSphere environments without making a large up-front commitment to licensing each host; they can incrementally grow the service.

When the program was first launched, it had a limited numbers of products that could be licensed under it. View and SRM, for example, couldn't originally be licensed under VSPP but were added due to customer demand. As the program gained traction among the service provider community, they added more and more products from the overall portfolio to VSPP. However, equivalent licensing models are not generally available to enterprise organizations for internal use.

## Summary

Cloud computing is based on the ability to turn expensive and traditionally siloed infrastructure into a commoditized resource by sharing it among many consumers. This approach isn't a new idea, and it parallels how, in the early years, electric companies moved from the need to build and maintain in-house generating capacity to simply subscribe to companies that sought to share those investments in electricity-generating infrastructure and charge consumers on the basis of the amount of resources they consume.

The adoption of cloud computing in small companies has led to a wide range of consumers with different load profiles. This diversity means that the overall load averages out, allowing the provider to maintain less overall headroom to deal with peak demands.

It's useful to build a cost matrix that apportions costs of major components of infrastructure down to an individual unit of consumption like a switch port or a share of a CPU. A spreadsheet is a useful tool for analyzing such costs, building example costs, and modeling various scenarios.

Traditional software and hardware sales models aren't yet fully geared up for the elasticity of the cloud era. They are based on up-front sale of a product that is licensed on a perpetual basis. You'll need to carefully model your planned environment and determine how you'll scale it out to support your consumers' demands, particularly as there is little scope to scale down if you find demand reduces.

If you choose to host your private cloud as a managed service with an official Microsoft or VMware partner, some further software licensing options may be available to you that can help you keep control of your costs, especially where you have a varying demand from consumers.

So, though you're likely to be able to realize infrastructure and operational savings, increased agility, and speed to market by building a private cloud, software and hardware vendors have a way to go before allowing you to realize significant savings in the procurement of the underpinning technologies in a similar manner, and you need to understand this as part of your planning.

# Part III

# Building the Cloud

## Chapter 7

# Installing VMware vCloud Director

By this point you should have a good appreciation of what a private cloud is, what vCloud Director can help you achieve, and how you should make your cloud ready to offer services to your consumers. This chapter is about planning and implementing vCloud Director.

As you'll have seen from earlier chapters, vCloud Director is essentially an abstraction layer on top of a vSphere-managed physical infrastructure. In order for it to function correctly, it is vital that you have a good foundational layer in terms of network, storage, and computing infrastructure.

You'll recall from Chapter 5, "Platform Design for vCloud Director," that because of the number of management components required, a management pod is a recommended design practice for vCloud Director platforms. This chapter assumes that the vSphere cluster that will become your management pod is already built and is ready to accept management virtual machines like vCloud Director cell servers and vShield Manager appliances.

In this chapter,you will learn to:

◆ Create a database for use with vCloud Director

◆ Create self-signed or CA-signed SSL certificates

◆ Install and configure one or more vCloud Director cell servers in a server group

◆ Complete the first-time configuration of vCloud Director

## Obtaining the Media

As with most VMware products, you download the installation media for your product from the VMware site. You will need an active licensing agreement to do so; if you don't have one, you can download the binaries by registering for a trial, but be warned that the trial license keys will expire.

To install vCloud Director, you must obtain the following binaries:

**vCloud Director (.bin) file**   This is a binary package and installation package, ready to be installed into your RedHat Enterprise Linux cell server(s). Note you cannot mount this file into your guest via the vSphere client as you would with an ISO file.

You will have to use Secure Copy Program (SCP)/File Transfer Protocol (FTP) to move the file into the Linux cell server; mount it over a (NFS) share like the transfer location; or create an ISO file containing the bin file and present it to the cell server VM using the vSphere client.

**vShield Manager (.ovf) file**   This is a packaged virtual appliance using OVF (Open Virtualization Format). You can import this virtual appliance directly into vCenter 4.0 and later using the OVF import feature.

**Adobe Flash**    To access the vCloud Director web portal, you will need an administrative machine with a supported browser and the Adobe Flash plug-in installed. If you have a locked-down environment, you may need to have this machine prepared in advance.

The latest list of supported browsers can be found here:

`kb.vmware.com/kb/2034554`

Note that although the article mentions support for 64-bit *operating systems*, the 64-bit *browsers* they contain are not supported and you should use the 32-bit version of browsers on such platforms. For example, you should use the 32-bit version of Internet Explorer 8.0 or later when running the Windows 7 64-bit operating system.

**License Key**    You will be able to base install your vCloud Director system without license keys; Microsoft Windows 2008 and vSphere will give you a 60-day trial installation before you require paid-for licensing.

You will also be able to install the vCloud Director binaries without a license key, but you will need a key to configure the product for the first time and will not be able to proceed without it. A 60-day evaluation license is available from the VMware website, and the license key can easily be changed from a trial to a production license key postinstallation.

**NOTE**    Most trial licenses for vCloud Director are limited to a limited number of virtual machines during the trial period.

## Preparing the Management Pod

For your vCloud Director platform, your management pod should be ready to support the virtual machines described in this section. Your management pod could consist of resources allocated from an existing vSphere cluster within your enterprise, provided it supports the minimum requirements of the appliances. For example, vShield Manager requires your virtual hardware to be at least version 7. In larger environments, you could use a dedicated cluster for management, but it is important that you do not share vCenter installations with non–vCloud Director–integrated installations, as shown in Figure 7.1.

This separation allows you to keep a clear boundary between vCenters that are managed by vCloud and those that are not. In this way, you avoid situations where vSphere administrators make changes that could impact objects under the control of vCloud Director. If you are planning to implement disaster recovery capabilities like those discussed in Chapter 12, "Business Continuity," then this separation is especially important because you need to recover management pods as separate entities from resource pods.

vSphere High Availability (HA) and Distributed Resource Scheduling (DRS) should be configured for this cluster as good practice, although doing so is not mandatory. If your cluster hardware is capable of supporting VMware Fault Tolerance (FT), then you can use FT to protect some of the services. However, note that most of the appliances and virtual machines required by vCloud recommend at least two virtual CPUs, which is not supported by FT.

The following list of virtual machines would typically be deployed in a vCloud Director management pod depending on the components you are planning to use:

- vCenter, to support the management cluster (if you are using a dedicated management cluster)

- One or more vCenter servers, to manage resource pod(s)

**FIGURE 7.1**
A dedicated management cluster (pod) vs. a management pod created from an existing cluster; in both instances there is still a dedicated resource cluster (pod).

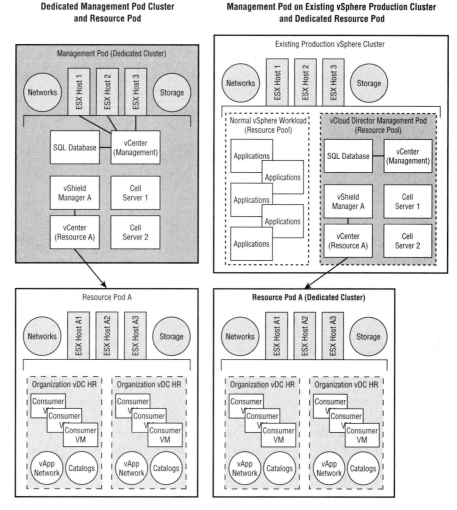

- vCloud Director cell server(s) (one or more RedHat Enterprise Linux [RHEL] virtual machines)

- The IP Load Balancing virtual appliance (if you are planning to host resilient cell servers using a software-based load balancer rather than a physical IP load balancer)

- vCenter Chargeback Server (Windows 2003 or later)

- vCloud Director database (supported Oracle/SQL version)

- vCenter Chargeback database (supported Oracle/SQL version)

- vShield Manager, virtual appliance, one per vCenter instance supporting resource clusters

- Cisco Nexus 1000V Virtual Supervisor Modules (VSMs) if you are deploying the Nexus 1000V in your resource clusters

- vSphere management appliance (VMA) for command-line access to your vSphere hosts

◆   vSphere Update Manager (VUM) Server to patch vSphere hosts

◆   AMQP (RabbitMQ) broker server if you are using advanced automation functionality

◆   vCenter Orchestrator

Now that you have an understanding of the role of the management pod and its contents, we will look at the steps required to configure the critical roles and appliances within it to use vCloud Director.

## DNS Configuration

DNS resolution is critical to the function of vCloud Director and its supporting elements. You should take some time to ensure that you have both forward (A) and reverse (PTR) entries defined in your DNS server for all elements of your infrastructure.

Certificates rely on authenticating the connection from your consumer's browser to the cell server(s). Therefore, if you plan to use an IP load balancer to distribute connections across more than one cell server for resilience, you'll need to ensure that the first and last name properties in the certificate match the DNS entry for this certificate.

If you are planning to make your vCloud platform available on the Internet you will have to use a publicly accessible DNS name. If you use a private DNS namespace like .corp internally you may have to implement a split-horizon DNS or route traffic to your internal DNS via a Virtual Private Network (VPN) because a cell server can only have its HTTP service associated with a single fully qualified domain name (FQDN).

In this example you'll be using an internal namespace (`vinf.corp`) signifying that this is a private cloud on the internal network, any external access will be over a VPN connection and thus will use the corporate DNS servers (see Figure 7.2).

## vCenter Server

vCloud Director requires at least one dedicated vCenter Server installation, which in turn manages your resource pods. The requirements for installing vCenter Server for vCloud Director are similar to those for a standard vSphere installation, but we strongly recommend that your vCenter installation should not be deployed on vSphere resources managed by vCloud Director as resource pods.

The vCenter appliance that shipped with vSphere 5.0 is supported by vCloud Director if you are not running the Windows version of vCenter. However, bear in mind that if you use the built-in appliance database rather than an external database server, Chargeback Manager will not be able to query the database for statistics.

## Deploying vShield Manager

vShield Manager is distributed as a virtual appliance, which means it must run as a VM on a vSphere cluster somewhere, ideally within your management pod. It is responsible for managing the configuration of the various vShield Edge appliances that are deployed and managed by vCloud Director.

**NOTE**   vShield Manager runs in the management cluster, whereas vShield Edge virtual appliances run on the various resource pods alongside the vApp networks they protect and interconnect.

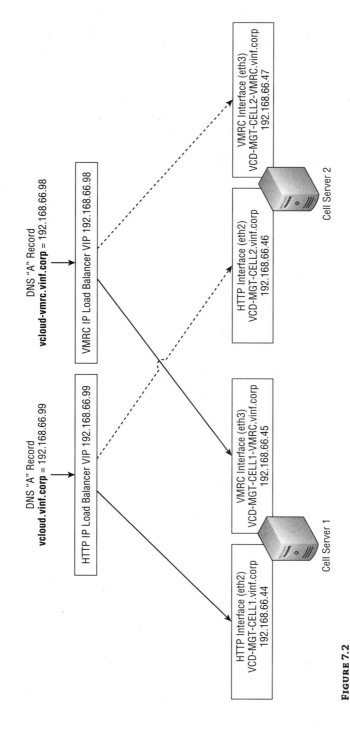

**FIGURE 7.2**
DNS mapping to vCloud cell server and its relationship to hostnames specified in SSL certificates

Connect your vSphere client to your management vCenter with administrator credentials. Then deploy the OVF file into your management pod.

When this process has completed, power on the vShield Appliance and open the console. You should see a Linux-like operating system booting (see Figure 7.3); the vShield appliance is based on BSD Linux.

**FIGURE 7.3**
vShield Manager
appliance booting

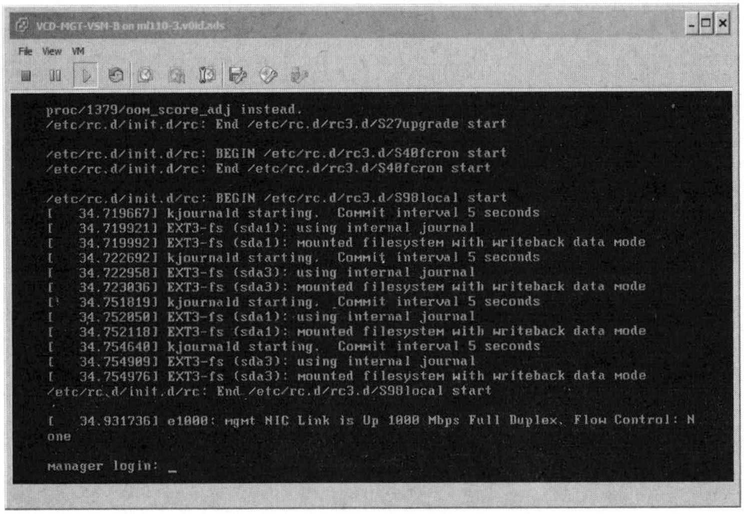

Note at this stage you haven't allocated an IP address to the vShield Manager appliance. Therefore, your only access is via the vSphere client's remote console feature.

When the operating system has booted, you will be presented with a logon prompt asking for the manager login. The default manager username is **admin** and the default password is **default**. Use these credentials to log on at the console.

The vShield Manager appliance adopts a Cisco-like convention: to enter configuration mode, type **en** (for enable) and enter the default password, which is also **default**. Then, to configure the vShield Manager appliance with an IP address, type **setup** to start the setup script. Follow the prompts to enter the relevant IP address details for your environment, as shown in Figure 7.4. Type **y** to accept.

**FIGURE 7.4**
Configuring the
vShield Manager
with an IP address

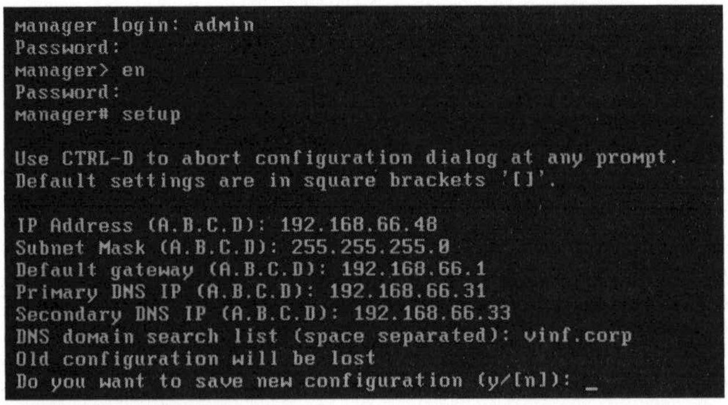

Type **exit** to exit the console and log in again. You should wait approximately 5 minutes for the configuration to apply and for services to start. You can then verify connectivity by pinging the vShield Manager appliance from your vCenter host.

The vShield Manager console supports basic IP testing tools like `ping` and `traceroute`. Type a question mark (**?**) or type **list** to be shown basic online help. You can see subcommands and some further help by typing a question mark after a command name—for example, **ping ?**.

**WARNING** If you cannot connect between the vShield Manager appliance and the vCenter server, then you should troubleshoot and resolve network connectivity because it will be required for the next steps.

At this point the vShield Manager is base configured. You should change the password from the default by navigating to the vShield Manager appliance's IP address with a web browser. You will get a warning that the appliance uses a self-signed certificate, as shown in Figure 7.5; click Continue To The Website.

**FIGURE 7.5**
vShield Manager
certificate warning

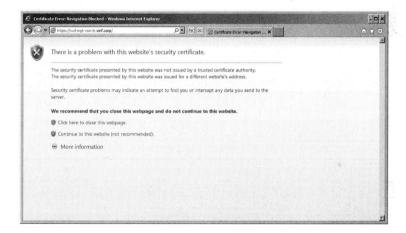

Once you have clicked past the warning, you will see the logon page for vShield Manager (see Figure 7.6). Enter the default credentials again (username **admin**, password **default**).

**WARNING** Confusingly, there are two accounts named admin: one is the login for the web interface, and the other is for command-line access at the console. There is a separate privileged (enable) mode password. You cannot change the password of the command-line admin or privileged account from the web interface, but you can delete and re-create it with a different password using the console command line.

When you see the home page, click the Change Password link at the top (see Figure 7.7) to change the web interface admin password from the default.

Reenter the current admin password of **default** and then enter and confirm the password of your choice. Remember this password applies only to the web interface for vShield Manager and is the password you will use later to connect it with vCenter.

**FIGURE 7.6**
vShield Manager
appliance login with
default credentials

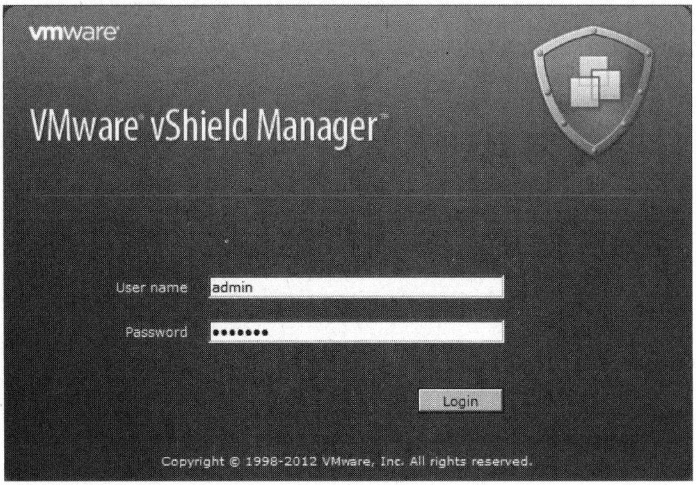

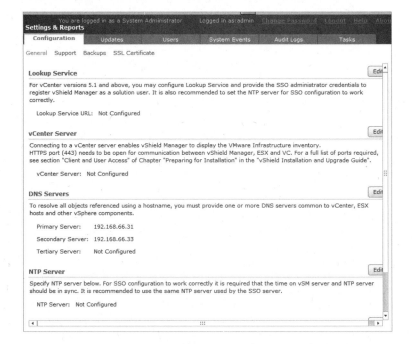

**FIGURE 7.7**
You should change
the vShield Web UI
password

The command-line admin account is only accessible by people accessing the physical console via the vSphere client and is not available over the network using SSH or something similar. If your security policy dictates that the command-line admin password also needs to change, the simplest way to do this is to follow the process outlined in KB article 1012479, which is available here:

```
http://kb.vmware.com/kb/1012479
```

You should log out and log in again with the new password and set the NTP server of your preference. This step is important to ensure logging and other functions operate correctly with the rest of the infrastructure. You do not need to configure any of the other settings to use vShield Manager with vCloud Director; they are intended mainly for use if you want to manage vShield Manager from vCenter in a traditional vSphere environment.

We also recommend that you configure the vShield Manager to back up its configuration to a location on your network. FTP or SFTP are the only supported methods of doing so, and you can schedule a regular backup job. Figure 7.8 shows how to schedule a backup of the configuration daily at 1a.m. to an FTP server in a specific folder and to prefix all files with the DNS name of the vShield Manager to aid identification.

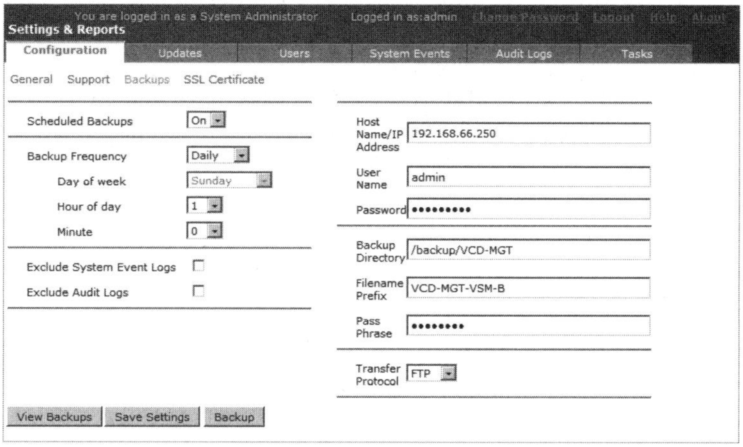

**FIGURE 7.8**
Scheduling a backup of the vShield Manager appliance

Once you have completed these steps, your vShield Manager appliance is ready for use with vCloud Director.

## vCloud Director Database

vCloud Director 5.1 supports SQL and Oracle databases for its own management information. This list is periodically updated, and if you want to find the most current compatibility information, the following web tool is very simple to use:

    http://partnerweb.vmware.com/comp_guide/sim/interop_matrix.php

Simply select the Solution/Database Interoperability radio button, as shown in Figure 7.9, to see the list of specifically supported versions.

If you are using Microsoft SQL, the database server needs to be in SQL Server And Windows Authentication Mode (known as mixed authentication mode) because Windows Authentication is not supported by vCloud Director (see Figure 7.10). If you don't configure this setting properly, you won't be able to establish a connection from the vCloud Director software running on the cell server to the database hosted on Microsoft SQL.

**NOTE**    If you use an Oracle database solution, the process is similar and the specific steps are documented in the VMware installation guide, which you can find at http://pubs.vmware .com/vcd-51/topic/com.vmware.ICbase/PDF/vcd_51_install.pdf.

You or your database administrator should pre-create the SQL database on a supported SQL server and assign permissions. The installation program does not do so automatically. To do this on SQL Server 2008 R2, you can carry out the following steps or ask your organization's DBA to do this task on your behalf:

**FIGURE 7.9**
VMware Product
Interoperability
Matrix

1. Run SQL Server Management Studio and select New Query (Figure 7.11).

   An editor opens where you can enter SQL commands to execute against your database server. Or you can cut, paste, and edit the relevant SQL commands from the VMware installation guide located here:

   `http://pubs.vmware.com/vcd-51/topic/com.vmware.ICbase/PDF/vcd_51_install.pdf`

FIGURE 7.10

**FIGURE 7.10**

Selecting SQL
Server And
Windows
Authentication
Mode (Mixed Mode)

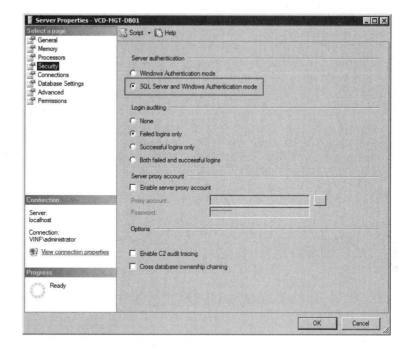

**FIGURE 7.11**

Click New Query
in SQL Server
Management
Studio

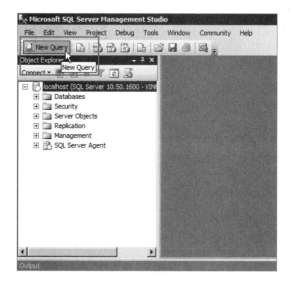

**2.** Use the following set of commands to create a database:

```
USE [master]
GO
```

```
CREATE DATABASE [vcloud-production] ON PRIMARY
(NAME = N'vcloud-production', ↵
FILENAME = N'C:\database\vcloud-production.mdf', ↵
SIZE = 100MB, FILEGROWTH = 10% )
LOG ON
(NAME = N'vcloud-production_log', ↵
FILENAME = N'C:\database\vcloud-production.ldf', ↵
SIZE = 1MB, FILEGROWTH = 10%)
COLLATE Latin1_General_CS_AS
GO
```

You'll notice that the query editor color-codes some fields in red. You should pay attention to these fields because they are user-adjustable parameters. As shown in Figure 7.12, in this example c:\databases\vcloud-production.mdf is specified as the path for the database and c:\databases\vcloud-production.ldf is specified as the path for the log file that you will be creating.

You can specify whatever you like for the database name, as long as you ensure the name is used consistently throughout the scripts.

**FIGURE 7.12**
Use the SQL query editor to create the vCloud Director database

3. Click Execute to run the SQL query against the SQL server.

Once the query runs, you should see "Command(s) completed successfully" in the Messages window, as shown in Figure 7.13. If not, check that the paths exist and that the database name you specified is consistent throughout the script. In this example, we are using vcloud-production.

**FIGURE 7.13**
The database was created successfully.

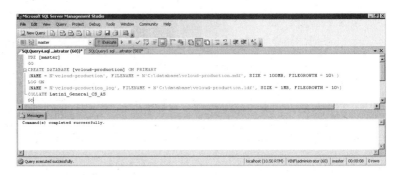

The next task is to set the database properties, specifying the various modes the database needs to operate in.

**4.** Paste the following script into a new SQL query window (Figure 7.14). Be sure you use the database name you specified when it was created. In this example we are using a database called vcloud-production.

```
USE [vcloud-production]
GO
ALTER DATABASE [vcloud-production] SET SINGLE_USER WITH ROLLBACK IMMEDIATE;
ALTER DATABASE [vcloud-production] SET ALLOW_SNAPSHOT_ISOLATION ON;
ALTER DATABASE [vcloud-production] SET READ_COMMITTED_SNAPSHOT ↵
ON WITH NO_WAIT;
ALTER DATABASE [vcloud-production] SET MULTI_USER;
GO
```

**FIGURE 7.14**
Setting vCloud
Director database
properties

**5.** Click Execute to carry out the database configuration on the database you created in the previous step.

**6.** Create a SQL user account and assign it permissions (Figure 7.15). You can specify your own password; likewise, the username can be anything you specify. In this example we're using vcloud-production.

```
USE [vcloud-production]
GO
CREATE LOGIN [vcloud-production] WITH PASSWORD = 'aLongPassword123!', ↵
DEFAULT_DATABASE =[vcloud-production], ↵
DEFAULT_LANGUAGE =[us_english], CHECK_POLICY=OFF
GO
CREATE USER [vcloud-production] for LOGIN [vcloud-production]
GO
```

**NOTE**    You'll recall from Chapter 5 that Windows Authentication is not supported by vCloud Director when using Microsoft SQL Server, so Active Directory accounts cannot be used for authentication.

**FIGURE 7.15**
Creating the SQL user account for the vCloud Director database

7. Grant permissions to the SQL user account (Figure 7.16) you created in the previous step (vcloud-production) in the vcloud-production database, using the following script:

```
USE [vcloud-production]
GO
sp_addrolemember [db_owner], [vcloud-production]
GO
```

**FIGURE 7.16**
Assigning permissions to the vcloud-production user in the vcloud-production database

Once this command completes, the database is ready for use by vCloud Director. The vCloud Director installer will create the database structure and contents as part of its installation process.

**NOTE** You'll notice that the sample SQL script noted in the VMware installation guide references database and log files in c:\. If you have a Windows 2008 R2 server, this path won't work due to file permissions. You or your organization's DBA should specify an appropriate path for your environment; in this example, the SQL script uses c:\database.

Now, the database is configured and ready to have items loaded into it by the vCloud Director installer.

## Preparing the Cell Servers

The cell server is the core of the functionality of vCloud Director: it consists of some VMware software that installs on a RedHat Enterprise Linux (RHEL) server. It can exist on a physical server but is typically deployed as a virtual machine within the management pod. It is possible to install vCloud Director on CentOS and similar generic Linux systems, but because RHEL is the only supported version, you should only consider RHEL for production systems.

You will need one or more cell servers for vCloud Director running one of the following supported RHELversions:

- RHEL 5 (64-bit) Update 4 (known as 5.4)

- RHEL 5 (64-bit) Update 5 (known as 5.5)

- RHEL 5 (64-bit) Update 6 (known as 5.6)

- RHEL 5 (64-bit) Update 8 (known as 5.8)

- RHEL 6 (64-bit) Update 1 (known as 6.1)

- RHEL 6 (64-bit) Update 1 (known as 6.2)

The cell server will need at least two network interfaces, as illustrated in Figure 7.17, to support management and client connectivity. Two IP addresses on the same physical interface are supported, but given that most implementations will deploy cell servers as virtual machines, it makes for a much simpler architecture to have multiple virtual NICs in a cell server. If you have a policy that dictates NFS and management traffic have to be on separate networks, you may have to add further NICs to carry this traffic in isolation.

**FIGURE 7.17**
Cell server NIC
assignment

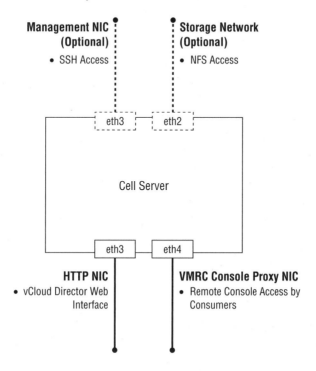

vCloud Director supports multiple cell servers for resilience. The first server installation populates database entries, whereas subsequent cell servers can be installed based on a response file generated during installation that connects them to an already "live" vCloud Director database.

You should perform a typical installation of a RHEL server. If you have in-house build standards, you can typically follow them, but review the security settings applied.

You will need to install the following packages on the cell server if they are not present in your standard RHEL build:

- `alsa-lib libICE module-init-tools`
- `bash libSM net-tools`
- `chkconfig libstdc pciutils`
- `coreutils libX11 procps`
- `findutils libXau redhat-lsb`
- `glibc libXdmcp sed`
- `grep libXext tar`
- `initscripts libXi which`
- `krb5-libs libXt`
- `libgcc libXtst`

Most modern RHEL builds have most of these packages in place, but you should issue the following command as root on your cell servers to ensure they are installed and to update to the current versions. You will be prompted to download any packages that are not already installed from a repository. To do this, your cell server will need to have Internet access or access to an internal repository.

```
Yum install alsa-lib libICE module-init-tools bash libSM net-tools chkconfig ↵
libstdc pciutils coreutils libX11 procps findutils libXau redhat-lsb ↵
glibc libXdmcp sed grep libXext tar initscripts libXi which krb5-libs libXt ↵
libgcc libXtst
```

The yum tool will check dependencies (Figure 7.18) and ask if it's okay to install the packages. Choose Yes.

**FIGURE 7.18**
Updating and installing RHEL packages as part of vCloud Director prerequisites

```
[root@VCD-MGT-CELLB1 test]# yum install alsa-lib libICE module-init-tools bash libSM net-tools chkconfig libstdc pciutils coreutils libX11
  procps findutils libXau redhat-lsb glibc libXdmcp sed grep libXext tar initscripts libXi which krb5-libs libXt libgcc libXtst
Loaded plugins: product-id, refresh-packagekit, rhnplugin, security, subscription-manager
Updating certificate-based repositories.
Unable to read consumer identity
Setting up Install Process
Package alsa-lib-1.0.22-3.el6.x86_64 already installed and latest version
Package libICE-1.0.6-1.el6.x86_64 already installed and latest version
Package module-init-tools-3.9-20.el6.x86_64 already installed and latest version
Package bash-4.1.2-9.el6_2.x86_64 already installed and latest version
Package libSM-1.1.0-7.1.el6.x86_64 already installed and latest version
Package net-tools-1.60-110.el6_2.x86_64 already installed and latest version
Package chkconfig-1.3.49.3-2.el6.x86_64 already installed and latest version
No package libstdc available.
Package pciutils-3.1.4-11.el6.x86_64 already installed and latest version
Package coreutils-8.4-19.el6.x86_64 already installed and latest version
Package libX11-1.3-2.el6.x86_64 already installed and latest version
Package procps-3.2.8-23.el6.x86_64 already installed and latest version
Package 1:findutils-4.4.2-6.el6.x86_64 already installed and latest version
Package libXau-1.0.5-1.el6.x86_64 already installed and latest version
Package redhat-lsb-4.0-3.el6.x86_64 already installed and latest version
Package libXdmcp-1.0.3-1.el6.x86_64 already installed and latest version
Package sed-4.2.1-10.el6.x86_64 already installed and latest version
Package grep-2.6.3-3.el6.x86_64 already installed and latest version
Package libXext-1.1-3.el6.x86_64 already installed and latest version
Package 2:tar-1.23-7.el6.x86_64 already installed and latest version
Package initscripts-9.03.31-2.el6_3.1.x86_64 already installed and latest version
Package libXi-1.3-3.el6.x86_64 already installed and latest version
Package which-2.19-6.el6.x86_64 already installed and latest version
Package krb5-libs-1.9-33.el6_3.3.x86_64 already installed and latest version
Package libXt-1.0.7-1.el6.x86_64 already installed and latest version
Package libgcc-4.4.6-4.el6.x86_64 already installed and latest version
Package libXtst-1.0.99.2-3.el6.x86_64 already installed and latest version
Resolving Dependencies
--> Running transaction check
---> Package glibc.x86_64 0:2.12-1.80.el6_3.6 will be updated
--> Processing Dependency: glibc = 2.12-1.80.el6_3.6 for package: glibc-common-2.12-1.80.el6_3.6.x86_64
---> Package glibc.x86_64 0:2.12-1.80.el6_3.7 will be an update
--> Running transaction check
---> Package glibc-common.x86_64 0:2.12-1.80.el6_3.6 will be updated
---> Package glibc-common.x86_64 0:2.12-1.80.el6_3.7 will be an update
--> Finished Dependency Resolution

Dependencies Resolved

================================================================================
 Package          Arch         Version                  Repository         Size
================================================================================
Updating:
 glibc            x86_64       2.12-1.80.el6_3.7        rhel-x86_64-server-6   3.8 M
Updating for dependencies:
 glibc-common     x86_64       2.12-1.80.el6_3.7        rhel-x86_64-server-6   14 M

Transaction Summary
================================================================================
Upgrade       2 Package(s)

Total download size: 18 M
Is this ok [y/N]: 
```

# Configuring the Management Pod

Now that the foundations for your management pod have been prepared it's time to install vCloud Director and configure the management layer for vCloud Director; this pod will coordinate the various resource pods that will run your consumer workloads.

## Installing vCloud Director

Now you're ready to install the vCloud Director binaries on your first cell server. Before starting the installer, verify that you can ping the SQL server that will be hosting the vCloud Director databases and that it is accepting connections on the relevant TCP/IP port (see Figure 7.19).

For example, you want to make sure a firewall is not blocking communications. The easiest way to verify this is by using Telnet on each cell server.

**FIGURE 7.19**

Testing connection to a SQL server on 1433. This proves DNS resolution and that it is listening on port 1433; if it were not listening, you would get a "connection refused" message.

```
[root@VCD-MGT-CELLB1 /]# telnet vcd-mgt-db01.vinf.corp 1433
Trying 192.168.66.37...
Connected to vcd-mgt-db01.vinf.corp.
Escape character is '^]'.
```

**NOTE** By default Microsoft SQL Server uses port 1433/TCP and Oracle uses port 1521/TCP to aid future troubleshooting; you should use these ports unless you have a corporate policy that requires them to be changed.

The product is distributed as an installable bin file that you downloaded and copied across to the cell server earlier. Perform the following steps:

1. Locate the bin file.

2. Log on to the cell server as root.

3. By default the bin file is not executable; in order to make it so, type **chmod +x** *\<filename\>* where *\<filename\>* is the bin file you downloaded; the default filename is typically vmware-vcloud-director-5.1.1-868405.bin.

**NOTE** The long suffix number—for example, 868405—denotes the build number, which may vary if you have downloaded a more recent build from the VMware site.

4. Run the installer (Figure 7.20). The installer extracts an RPM package containing the vCloud Director binaries and installs them to the local file system.

5. Once the installer has completed, you will be prompted to run the configuration script. Choose N for No—there are some further steps you need to complete before progressing to configuration.

## Configuring the Transfer Location

If you plan on having more than one vCloud Director cell server for resilience or performance reasons, then you'll need a shared area of storage presented via NFS or some other form of shared storage that is accessible from all of the cell servers with the root account having write permissions.

The transfer location is used to store virtual machines and media files that are being uploaded to the vCloud UI. It only stores transient data and so doesn't necessarily need to be backed up. But you should size it to be able to cope with the largest number of concurrent upload activities you plan for your environment.

**FIGURE 7.20**
Running the vCloud
Director installer

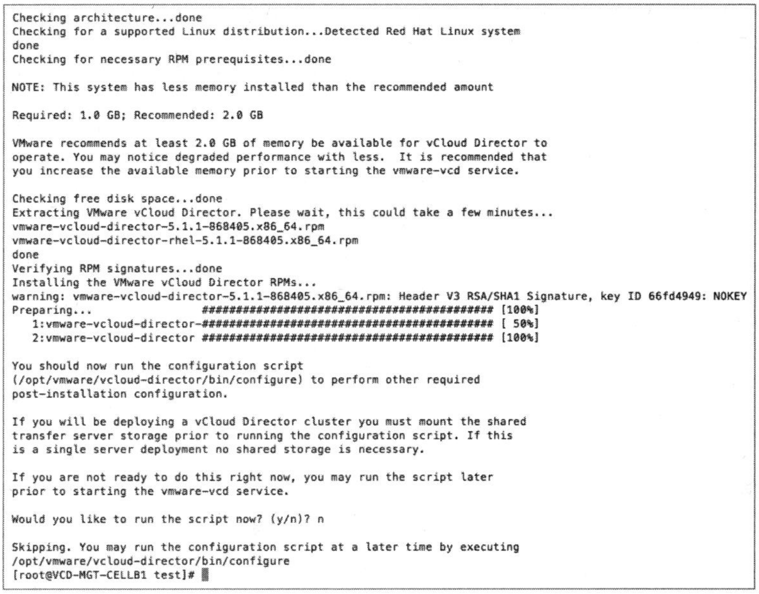

```
Checking architecture...done
Checking for a supported Linux distribution...Detected Red Hat Linux system
done
Checking for necessary RPM prerequisites...done

NOTE: This system has less memory installed than the recommended amount

Required: 1.0 GB; Recommended: 2.0 GB

VMware recommends at least 2.0 GB of memory be available for vCloud Director to
operate. You may notice degraded performance with less.  It is recommended that
you increase the available memory prior to starting the vmware-vcd service.

Checking free disk space...done
Extracting VMware vCloud Director. Please wait, this could take a few minutes...
vmware-vcloud-director-5.1.1-868405.x86_64.rpm
vmware-vcloud-director-rhel-5.1.1-868405.x86_64.rpm
done
Verifying RPM signatures...done
Installing the VMware vCloud Director RPMs...
warning: vmware-vcloud-director-5.1.1-868405.x86_64.rpm: Header V3 RSA/SHA1 Signature, key ID 66fd4949: NOKEY
Preparing...                ########################################### [100%]
   1:vmware-vcloud-director-###########################################  [ 50%]
   2:vmware-vcloud-director ########################################### [100%]

You should now run the configuration script
(/opt/vmware/vcloud-director/bin/configure) to perform other required
post-installation configuration.

If you will be deploying a vCloud Director cluster you must mount the shared
transfer server storage prior to running the configuration script. If this
is a single server deployment no shared storage is necessary.

If you are not ready to do this right now, you may run the script later
prior to starting the vmware-vcd service.

Would you like to run the script now? (y/n)? n

Skipping. You may run the configuration script at a later time by executing
/opt/vmware/vcloud-director/bin/configure
[root@VCD-MGT-CELLB1 test]#
```

In high-traffic environments or those with a policy that requires any IP storage to be isolated to a separate network, you may need a separate NIC for your cell server to carry such traffic to and from your shared storage. All cell servers need to mount the transfer location specified in an environment variable to be recognized by vCloud Director:

```
$VCLOUD_HOME/data/transfer
```

The default mount point for this example is

```
/opt/vmware/vcloud-director/data/transfer
```

You need to mount the transfer storage using the following command to test it (substitute your own values for server name and path):

```
mount 192.168.66.250:/nfs/VCD-MGT-TRANSFER1 ↵
/opt/vmware/vcloud-director/data/transfer/
```

If it mounts correctly, then you should make this a persistent mount on every reboot. You do this by editing the /etc/fstab file. Figure 7.21 shows an example. Be careful to validate the paths for your own implementation.

## Creating SSL Certificates

vCloud Director requires a number of certificates to secure communications between various components and your consumers. You can use certificates trusted by a public certification authority (CA) like VeriSign or Thawte, or you can use an internal CA or self-signed certificate.

The choice depends on your use case. Certificates from major public CAs are trusted on most computer browsers by default. You'll need to pay the CA to validate and sign your certificate; this can cost up to several hundred dollars, but is generally advisable if you are publishing services to a third party or to the Internet. If you have an internal CA as part of a Private Key Infrastructure (PKI) implementation, it may make more sense to use it, assuming your internal machines trust your internal root CA or are able to grant an exception in their browsers.

**FIGURE 7.21**
Permanently mounting the NFS transfer location by editing the /etc/ fstab file

```
[root@VCD-MGT-CELLB1 /]# cat /etc/fstab
#
# /etc/fstab
# Created by anaconda on Thu Feb 16 23:30:07 2012
#
# Accessible filesystems, by reference, are maintained under '/dev/disk'
# See man pages fstab(5), findfs(8), mount(8) and/or blkid(8) for more info
#
/dev/mapper/VolGroup-lv_root /                       ext4    defaults        1 1
UUID=7a477c67-92d5-4096-a741-83d17a50b04f /boot                ext4    defaults        1 2
/dev/mapper/VolGroup-lv_home /home                   ext4    defaults        1 2
/dev/mapper/VolGroup-lv_swap swap                    swap    defaults        0 0
tmpfs                   /dev/shm                tmpfs   defaults        0 0
devpts                  /dev/pts                devpts  gid=5,mode=620  0 0
sysfs                   /sys                    sysfs   defaults        0 0
proc                    /proc                   proc    defaults        0 0
192.168.66.250:/nfs/VCD-MGT-TRANSFER1   /opt/vmware/vcloud-director/data/transfer     nfs     rw      0 0

[root@VCD-MGT-CELLB1 /]#
```

Self-signed certificates are free and are generally suitable for small or test deployments. However, a self-signed certificate will display a warning to your end users noting that it is a nontrusted certificate. This is mainly a cosmetic issue unless you have specific regulatory or policy requirements that prevent the use of self-signed certificates.

---

### WHICH VERSION OF KEYTOOL SHOULD YOU USE?

It's important to use the version of Keytool that ships with vCloud Director to avoid any compatibility issues. We recommend that you create the certificates after installing the binaries to a cell server and specifically call Keytool from the location vCloud Director installs it to.

The vCloud version of Keytool can be located on the local filesystem at /opt/vmware/ vcloud-director/jre/bin/keytool.

---

### GENERATING A SELF-SIGNED SSL CERTIFICATE

The steps to generate a self-signed certificate are as follows:

1. Generate the HTTP certificate. This certificate will be presented to your consumers (and administrators) who access the vCloud Director web interface. Note the vCerts.ks file marked in bold—this is where you will be storing your certificates. You also need to specify a password to protect this key store file as specified with the storepass parameter, where the value of YourPassword is a password of your choosing. You'll need this password in subsequent steps to add further certificates to this file and import them for use with vCloud Director.

   ```
   /opt/vmware/vcloud-director/jre/bin/keytool -keystore vCerts.ks ↵
   -storetype JCEKS -storepass YourPassword -genkey -keyalg RSA ↵
   -keysize 2048 -alias http-validity 365
   ```

**KEYTOOL PARAMETERS**

The keytool command supports a -validity option, whereby you can specify the number of days the certificate is valid for. The default is 90 days.

If you are planning to use self-signed certificates, you'll want to specify something like -validity 365 (days) unless you want to change the certificate every 90 days.

The -alias parameter specifies how vCloud Director will identify this certificate. You should not change the -alias http and -alias consoleproxy parameters for the certificates you are generating. Otherwise, vCloud Director will fail to install correctly.

The -keysize parameter is used to specify how many bits you should use in generating encryption details for the certificate. Unless you have a specific policy in this area, -keysize 2048 would be a reasonable option for generating secure keys and does not add any practical overhead.

The key size of your SSL certificate determines how large it is, and how long it could potentially take to compromise through brute-force methods, as analysis shows:

*Using 2048 bit keys does not add a practical overhead to your environment and as of 2003 RSA Security claims that 1024-bit RSA keys are equivalent in strength to 80-bit symmetric keys, 2048-bit RSA keys to 112-bit symmetric keys and 3072-bit RSA keys to 128-bit symmetric keys. RSA claims that 1024-bit keys are likely to become crackable some time between 2006 and 2010 and that 2048-bit keys are sufficient until 2030.*

*Source: http://en.wikipedia.org/wiki/Key_size*

2. Answer the questions, as shown in Figure 7.22, entering relevant information for your organization.

When you are prompted for first and last name, enter the fully qualified domain name you wish to use to identify your vCloud installation. If you are planning to use a DNS alias or Virtual IP (VIP) to load-balance across multiple cells, this field should be the fully qualified domain name (FQDN) that your users will be using to access the vCloud UI from their web browsers. You can reuse the password you specify in the command-line parameters by pressing Enter when prompted. We recommend you do so to avoid confusion unless you have specific security requirements.

**FIGURE 7.22**
Using the keytool command line

```
[root@VCD-MGT-CELLB1 /]#    /opt/vmware/vcloud-director/jre/bin/keytool -keystore vCerts.ks -storetype JCEKS -storepass YourPassword -genk
ey -keyalg RSA -keysize 2048 -alias http -validity 365
What is your first and last name?
  [Unknown]:  vcloud.vinf.corp
What is the name of your organizational unit?
  [Unknown]:  IT Services
What is the name of your organization?
  [Unknown]:  vINF Inc.
What is the name of your City or Locality?
  [Unknown]:  Mayfair
What is the name of your State or Province?
  [Unknown]:  London
What is the two-letter country code for this unit?
  [Unknown]:  GB
Is CN=vcloud.vinf.corp, OU=IT Services, O=vINF Inc., L=Mayfair, ST=London, C=GB correct?
  [no]:  y

Enter key password for <http>
        (RETURN if same as keystore password):
Re-enter new password:
[root@VCD-MGT-CELLB1 /]# █
```

**NOTE**   The password input does not echo to the screen.

**3.** Generate an untrusted certificate.

For the console proxy service, this certificate is used to secure console sessions to vCloud Director–hosted virtual machines. You should not change the -alias parameter. The product relies on -alias being set to consoleproxy for validation. Figure 7.23 shows the example vcloud-vmrc.vinf.corp FQDN specified for first and last name in the certificate, which is the DNS alias specified in Figure 7.2.

You can generate the certificate using the following command. (Note that we are using the vCerts.ks key store file as noted in bold—this adds further certificates to that key store file. Also note that you specify the same password for the key store that you specified in step 1.)

```
/opt/vmware/vcloud-director/jre/bin/keytool -keystore vCerts.ks ↵
-storetype JCEKS -storepass YourPassword -genkey -keyalg RSA ↵
-keysize 2048 -alias consoleproxy -validity 365
```

**FIGURE 7.23**
Generating the consoleproxy certificate

```
[root@VCD-MGT-CELLB1 /]# /opt/vmware/vcloud-director/jre/bin/keytool -keystore vCerts.ks -storetype JCEKS -storepass YourPassword -genkey
-keyalg RSA -keysize 2048 -alias consoleproxy -validity 365
What is your first and last name?
  [Unknown]:  vcloud-vmrc.vinf.corp
What is the name of your organizational unit?
  [Unknown]:  IT Services
What is the name of your organization?
  [Unknown]:  vINF Inc.
What is the name of your City or Locality?
  [Unknown]:  Mayfair
What is the name of your State or Province?
  [Unknown]:  London
What is the two-letter country code for this unit?
  [Unknown]:  GB
Is CN=vcloud-vmrc.vinf.corp, OU=IT Services, O=vINF Inc., L=Mayfair, ST=London, C=GB correct?
  [no]:  y

Enter key password for <consoleproxy>
        (RETURN if same as keystore password):
[root@VCD-MGT-CELLB1 /]# █
```

---

### THE KEYSTORE FILE

The -storepass parameter denotes the password to your keystore file (which has a .ks extension). You created this file in the first step. Be sure you specify the same password on the command line.

The keystore file is a container that holds multiple SSL certificates. You'll be asked to supply the path to this file when you configure vCloud Director.

The password you enter in the setup script at the "Enter key password for" prompt can be the same as the key store password, or it can be a separate password for each certificate depending on your security requirements. The password you enter when Keytool prompts is the password that sets the private key for the certificate itself and is used when exporting or importing the certificate in the future, so make sure you know the password or store it securely.

If you deploy multiple cell servers, you'll need to make this file containing the certificates accessible to them in order to configure vCloud Director. During installation, the transfer location is a useful place to put the file. The installer will copy the file to /opt/vmware/vcloud-director/etc/certificates on the vCloud Director cell during configuration. Don't forget to remove it from the shared storage and store it securely once you've finished configuring your cell servers.

If you are using a load balancer, you may also need to import these certificates on your load balancer. Consult the manufacturer of your load balancer for the required steps.

You can view the contents of the vCerts.ks file using the keytool command (Figure 7.24):

```
keytool -storetype JCEKS -storepass YourPassword -keystore vCerts.ks -list
```

Verify that the file contains both the http and consoleproxy certificates.

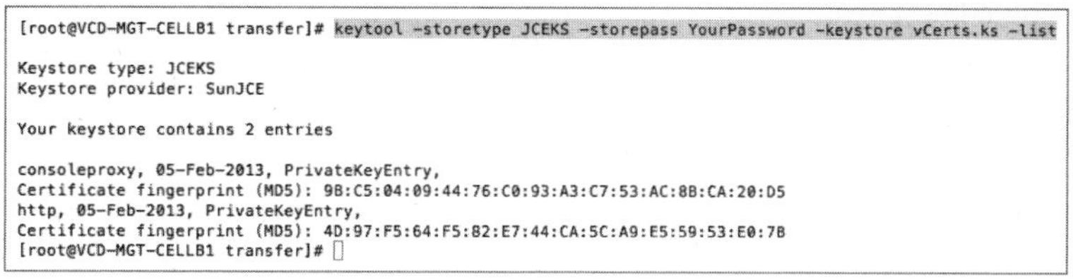

**FIGURE 7.24**
Examining the contents of the vCerts.ks file using keytool

```
[root@VCD-MGT-CELLB1 transfer]# keytool -storetype JCEKS -storepass YourPassword -keystore vCerts.ks -list

Keystore type: JCEKS
Keystore provider: SunJCE

Your keystore contains 2 entries

consoleproxy, 05-Feb-2013, PrivateKeyEntry,
Certificate fingerprint (MD5): 9B:C5:04:09:44:76:C0:93:A3:C7:53:AC:8B:CA:20:D5
http, 05-Feb-2013, PrivateKeyEntry,
Certificate fingerprint (MD5): 4D:97:F5:64:F5:82:E7:44:CA:5C:A9:E5:59:53:E0:7B
[root@VCD-MGT-CELLB1 transfer]# 
```

**NOTE**   Certificate fingerprints will be unique in each environment.

### USING A SSL CERTIFICATE SIGNED BY A PUBLIC OR INTERNAL AUTHORITY

The steps to generate a certificate signing request (CSR) for a public CA are similar to those for a self-signed certificate, but the process is a bit more involved. You'll need to check with your public CA as to what key length and validity periods they support if you want to use the -keysize and -validity parameters.

#### Generating a Certificate Signing Request

The steps to generate the requests are as follows:

**1.** Generate an untrusted certificate for the HTTP service:

```
/opt/vmware/vcloud-director/jre/bin/keytool -keystore vCerts.ks ↵
 -storetype JCEKS -storepass YourPassword -genkey -keyalg RSA -alias http
```

**2.** Create a certificate signing request (CSR file) for this certificate:

```
/opt/vmware/vcloud-director/jre/bin/keytool -keystore vCerts.ks ↵
-storetype JCEKS -storepass YourPassword ↵
-certreq -alias http -file http.csr
```

**3.** Create an unsigned certificate for the console proxy service:

```
/opt/vmware/vcloud-director/jre/bin/keytool -keystore vCerts.ks ↵
-storetype JCEKS -storepass YourPassword -genkey ↵
-keyalg RSA -alias consoleproxy
```

**4.** Create a CSR for this certificate:

```
/opt/vmware/vcloud-director/jre/bin/keytool -keystore vCerts.ks ↵
-storetype JCEKS -storepass YourPassword ↵
-certreq -alias consoleproxy -file consoleproxy.csr
```

You'll now need to take these CSR file contents to your public CA or corporate PKI service for them to sign and issue a valid certificate. This process varies depending on your CA of choice, but it typically involves uploading the CSR file or pasting its contents into a section of your CA's website.

Some CAs can take a couple of days to issue a certificate, so be sure to understand their process and factor it into your project. You'll need the certificates to be available before you can install vCloud Director or be prepared to change them afterward.

### Importing Your CA-Signed SSL Certificate

When the SSL certificate request has been completed by your CA, you will receive the signed CSR request as a binary format CER file (or you may have to paste some encoded text into a text file yourself). You should keep these files securely and use the following steps to import the signed SSL certificate.

1. Obtain a copy of the root certificate from your CA and import it into your certificate keystore; if you fail to do so, the cell won't automatically trust your root CA and vCloud Director will issue warnings during installation. The code for importing the root CA certificate is as follows (adjust the path to the vCerts.ks and root.cer files and keystore password as appropriate for your environment):

   ```
   /opt/vmware/vcloud-director/jre/bin/keytool -storetype JCEKS -storepass YourPassword ↵
   -keystore vCerts.ks -import -alias root -file root.cer
   ```

2. Import the signed certificate for the HTTP service as follows (adjust the path to the vCerts.ks and http.cer files and keystore password as appropriate for your environment):

   ```
   /opt/vmware/vcloud-director/jre/bin/keytool -storetype JCEKS -storepass YourPassword ↵
   -keystore vCerts.ks -import -alias http  -file http.cer
   ```

3. Import the signed certificate for the console proxy service as follows (adjust the path to the vCerts.ks and consoleproxy.cer files and keystore password as appropriate for your environment):

   ```
   /opt/vmware/vcloud-director/jre/bin/keytool -storetype JCEKS -storepass YourPassword ↵
   -keystore vCerts.ks -import -alias consoleproxy -file consoleproxy.cer
   ```

4. Check that the certificates have been correctly imported to your certificates file as follows:

   ```
   /opt/vmware/vcloud-director/jre/bin/keytool -storetype JCEKS -storepass YourPassword ↵
   -keystore vCerts.ks -list
   ```

## Configuring the First Cell Server

By this point, everything should be in place to allow you to configure your first cell server. Follow these steps:

1. Begin by logging onto the cell server as root and invoking the script located at /opt/vmware/vcloud-director/bin/configure. When you run the script, you'll be asked which IP address will service the HTTP traffic as shown in Figure 7.25. This is where your end users will point their web browsers to access vCloud.

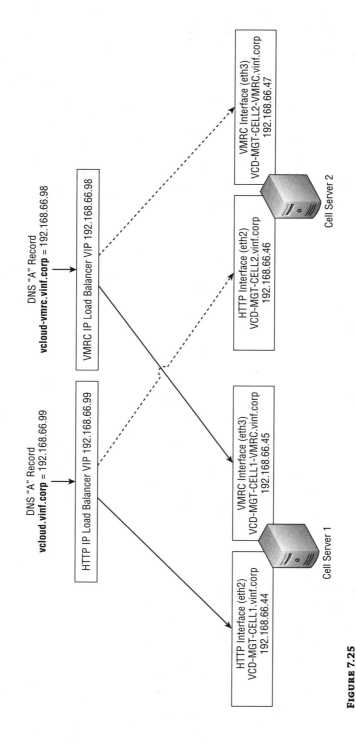

**FIGURE 7.25**
vCloud Director cell server NIC assignment

If you are using an IP load balancer, use the IP address that is behind the virtual IP address (VIP: 192.168.66.99, as shown in Figure 7.25) you configured. In this example the NIC with 192.168.66.44 is used to serve HTTP requests on the first cell server and is chosen, as shown in Figure 7.26.

**FIGURE 7.26**
Selecting the HTTP
service IP address

```
[root@VCD-MGT-CELLB1 transfer]# /opt/vmware/vcloud-director/bin/configure
Welcome to the vCloud Director configuration utility.

You will be prompted to enter a number of parameters that are necessary to
configure and start the vCloud Director service.

Please indicate which IP address available on this machine should be used for
the HTTP service and which IP address should be used for the remote console proxy.

The HTTP service IP address is used for accessing the user interface and the
REST API. The remote console proxy IP address is used for all remote console (VMRC)
connections and traffic.

Please enter your choice for the HTTP service IP address:
        1. 192.168.66.44
        2. 192.168.66.45
Choice [default=1]: 1█
```

2. Select the IP address that will be servicing remote console proxy traffic; in this example, choose 192.168.66.45, as shown in Figure 7.27.

**FIGURE 7.27**
Selecting the
remote console
proxy IP address

```
Please enter your choice for the remote console proxy IP address:
        1. 192.168.66.45
Choice [default=1]: 1█
```

3. Next you will be asked for the location of the keystore file containing the SSL certificates and keys that you generated in the previous step. Enter the path to the location of that file.

   In this example the file has been temporarily copied to the vCloud transfer location, so it will be accessible on all cells for the installation process. But if you have different security requirements this could be any local or network location as long as it is the same on all cell servers.

4. You will then be prompted for the password to this file (Figure 7.28). This is the password you specified on the command line in the earlier steps (in the previous example, we used YourPassword). Note there is no input displayed on the screen when entering passwords.

**FIGURE 7.28**
Entering the path
to the keystore file
generated in the
previous step

```
Please enter the path to the Java keystore containing your SSL certificates and
private keys: /opt/vmware/vcloud-director/data/transfer/vCerts.ks
Please enter the password for the keystore: █
```

5. If you have a syslog server in your environment, you can enter its hostname and port to allow messages to be sent to it by vCloud Director. Doing so is optional but recommended (Figure 7.29).

**FIGURE 7.29**
Syslog settings

```
Syslog host name or IP address [press Enter to skip]: syslog.vinf.corp
What UDP port is the remote syslog server listening on? The standard syslog
port is 514. [default=514]:
Using default value "514" for syslog port.
```

**6.** Enter the details of the database server hosting the vCloud Director database that you configured earlier in this chapter (Figure 7.30). In this example we'll be using Microsoft SQL, but the steps are similar for an Oracle database.

Make sure you specify the FQDN—you previously validated that you could connect to it—and the appropriate username/password. You'll recall that vCloud Director only supports SQL authentication and is unable to use Windows Authentication for this connection.

**FIGURE 7.30**
Entering SQL database connection information

```
The following database types are supported:
        1. Oracle
        2. Microsoft SQL Server
Enter the database type [default=1]: 2
Enter the host (or IP address) for the database: vcd-mgt-db01.vinf.corp
Enter the database port [default=1433]:
Using default value "1433" for port.

Enter the database name [default=vcloud]: vcloud-production
Enter the database instance [Press enter to use the server's default instance]:
Using server's default instance name.

Enter the database username: vcloud-production
Enter the database password:
Connecting to the database: jdbc:jtds:sqlserver://vcd-mgt-db01.vinf.corp:1433/vcloud-production;socketTimeout=90
```

If the connection is successful, the install script will start populating the SQL database with vCloud Director data, as shown in Figure 7.31.

**WARNING** If you get an error, check DNS resolution and that the database name, username, and password settings match those configured in SQL Server.

**FIGURE 7.31**
The vCloud Director installer populates the database

```
Connecting to the database: jdbc:jtds:sqlserver://vcd-mgt-db01.vinf.corp:1433/vcloud-production;socketTimeout=90
loading /opt/vmware/vcloud-director/db/mssql/NewInstall_PreInit.sql
[4 statements]
....[4]

loading /opt/vmware/vcloud-director/db/mssql/NewInstall_System.sql
[103 statements]
........................................................................................[100]
...[103]

loading /opt/vmware/vcloud-director/db/mssql/NewInstall_Deprecated.sql
[39 statements]
...............................[39]

loading /opt/vmware/vcloud-director/db/mssql/NewInstall_System_Public.sql
[20 statements]
..................[20]

loading /opt/vmware/vcloud-director/db/mssql/NewInstall_System_Data.sql
[16 statements]
...............[16]

loading /opt/vmware/vcloud-director/db/mssql/NewInstall_Inventory.sql
[145 statements]
........................................................................................[100]
.............................................[145]

loading /opt/vmware/vcloud-director/db/mssql/NewInstall_Inventory_Public.sql
[23 statements]
.....................[23]

loading /opt/vmware/vcloud-director/db/mssql/NewInstall_Inventory_Data.sql
[1 statements]
.[1]

loading /opt/vmware/vcloud-director/db/mssql/NewInstall_Storage.sql
[96 statements]
...................................................................[96]

loading /opt/vmware/vcloud-director/db/mssql/NewInstall_Storage_Public.sql
[38 statements]
.................................[38]

loading /opt/vmware/vcloud-director/db/mssql/NewInstall_Storage_Data.sql
[5 statements]
```

Once the database is populated, you'll be shown a message that vCloud Director configuration is complete, as shown in Figure 7.32. You are given the option to start the vCloud Director service on the cell server.

**FIGURE 7.32**
The vCloud Director configuration is complete.

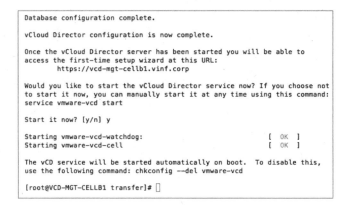

```
Database configuration complete.

vCloud Director configuration is now complete.

Once the vCloud Director server has been started you will be able to
access the first-time setup wizard at this URL:
          https://vcd-mgt-cellb1.vinf.corp

Would you like to start the vCloud Director service now? If you choose not
to start it now, you can manually start it at any time using this command:
service vmware-vcd start

Start it now? [y/n] y

Starting vmware-vcd-watchdog:                                    [  OK  ]
Starting vmware-vcd-cell                                         [  OK  ]

The vCD service will be started automatically on boot.  To disable this,
use the following command: chkconfig --del vmware-vcd

[root@VCD-MGT-CELLB1 transfer]# □
```

This completes the installation and configuration of vCloud Director on the first cell server.

Although the vCloud cell service has started, a number of background activities are going on to complete cell service startup. Therefore, you may not be able to connect to the cell server URL for a couple of minutes.

If you want to check on the status, you can monitor the cell.log file, which is located at /opt/vmware/vcloud-director/logs/cell.log. This file shows the progress of the background activities associated with starting the cell service; you can see an example of the log file in Figure 7.33.

Once the log file confirms the application has initialized, you should check that you can connect to the web server via HTTPS using a web browser by going to the FQDN of the cell server—in this example, https://vcloud.vinf.corp.

**TIP**  If you are unable to access the web UI in your browser after the service has started, check that you can Telnet to the cell server on port 443. This will prove whether the web server providing the vCloud Director interface has started or if there is a firewall or network condition preventing access. If you are unable to connect, you may have the host firewall enabled on the cell server.

## Configuring the RHEL Firewall for vCloud

The default configuration for RHEL has the host firewall enabled on all interfaces. This firewall configuration will not cause an error when you install vCloud Director on the cell, although the installer does not automatically create a rule to allow access. If you need to have the host firewall enabled and are unable to connect to the cell server after configuration, you will need to manually create a rule to allow access to the web server on the cell server from your network(s).

You can check the status of the firewall by issuing this command:

```
/etc/init.d/iptables status
```

**FIGURE 7.33**
The cell.log file
showing the vCloud
Director cell service
startup

```
Application Initialization: 5% complete. Subsystem 'com.vmware.vcloud.common-util' started
Application Initialization: 11% complete. Subsystem 'com.vmware.vcloud.api-framework' started
Successfully bound network port: 443 on host address: 192.168.66.45
Application Initialization: 17% complete. Subsystem 'com.vmware.vcloud.consoleproxy' started
Application Initialization: 23% complete. Subsystem 'com.vmware.vcloud.common-vmomi' started
Application Initialization: 29% complete. Subsystem 'com.vmware.vcloud.jax-rs-activator' started
Application Initialization: 35% complete. Subsystem 'com.vmware.pbm.placementengine' started
Application Initialization: 41% complete. Subsystem 'com.vmware.vcloud.vim-proxy' started
Application Initialization: 47% complete. Subsystem 'com.vmware.vcloud.fabric.foundation' started
Application Initialization: 52% complete. Subsystem 'com.vmware.vcloud.fabric.storage' started
Application Initialization: 58% complete. Subsystem 'com.vmware.vcloud.fabric.compute' started
Application Initialization: 64% complete. Subsystem 'com.vmware.vcloud.fabric.net' started
Successfully verified transfer spooling area: /opt/vmware/vcloud-director/data/transfer
Application Initialization: 70% complete. Subsystem 'com.vmware.vcloud.backend-core' started
Application Initialization: 76% complete. Subsystem 'com.vmware.vcloud.ui.configuration' started
Application Initialization: 82% complete. Subsystem 'com.vmware.vcloud.imagetransfer-server' started
Application Initialization: 88% complete. Subsystem 'com.vmware.vcloud.rest-api-handlers' started
Application Initialization: 94% complete. Subsystem 'com.vmware.vcloud.jax-rs-servlet' started
Application initialization detailed status report: 94% complete
    com.vmware.vcloud.common-util                   Subsystem Status: [COMPLETE]
    com.vmware.vcloud.api-framework                 Subsystem Status: [COMPLETE]
    com.vmware.vcloud.consoleproxy                  Subsystem Status: [COMPLETE]
    com.vmware.vcloud.common-vmomi                  Subsystem Status: [COMPLETE]
    com.vmware.vcloud.jax-rs-activator              Subsystem Status: [COMPLETE]
    com.vmware.pbm.placementengine                  Subsystem Status: [COMPLETE]
    com.vmware.vcloud.vim-proxy                      Subsystem Status: [COMPLETE]
    com.vmware.vcloud.fabric.foundation             Subsystem Status: [COMPLETE]
    com.vmware.vcloud.fabric.storage                Subsystem Status: [COMPLETE]
    com.vmware.vcloud.fabric.compute                Subsystem Status: [COMPLETE]
    com.vmware.vcloud.fabric.net                    Subsystem Status: [COMPLETE]
    com.vmware.vcloud.backend-core                  Subsystem Status: [COMPLETE]
    com.vmware.vcloud.ui.configuration              Subsystem Status: [COMPLETE]
    com.vmware.vcloud.imagetransfer-server          Subsystem Status: [COMPLETE]
    com.vmware.vcloud.rest-api-handlers             Subsystem Status: [COMPLETE]
    com.vmware.vcloud.jax-rs-servlet                Subsystem Status: [COMPLETE]
    com.vmware.vcloud.ui-vcloud-webapp              Subsystem Status: [WAITING]

Application Initialization: 100% complete. Subsystem 'com.vmware.vcloud.ui-vcloud-webapp' started
Application Initialization: Complete. Server is ready in 2:04 (minutes:seconds)
Successfully initialized ConfigurationService session factory
Successfully posted pending audit events: com/vmware/vcloud/event/cell/start
Successfully started scheduler
Successfully started remote JMX connector on port 8999
```

If the firewall is enabled, it will provide a printout of the firewall rules currently in force as shown in Figure 7.34.

**FIGURE 7.34**
The default RHEL
host firewall rules;
no inbound SSL is
allowed

```
[root@VCD-MGT-CELLB1 transfer]# /etc/init.d/iptables status
Table: filter
Chain INPUT (policy ACCEPT)
num target     prot opt source               destination
1   ACCEPT     all  --  0.0.0.0/0            0.0.0.0/0            state RELATED,ESTABLISHED
2   ACCEPT     icmp --  0.0.0.0/0            0.0.0.0/0
3   ACCEPT     all  --  0.0.0.0/0            0.0.0.0/0
4   ACCEPT     tcp  --  0.0.0.0/0            0.0.0.0/0            state NEW tcp dpt:22
5   REJECT     all  --  0.0.0.0/0            0.0.0.0/0            reject-with icmp-host-prohibited
6   ACCEPT     tcp  --  0.0.0.0/0            0.0.0.0/0            tcp dpt:22

Chain FORWARD (policy ACCEPT)
num target     prot opt source               destination
1   REJECT     all  --  0.0.0.0/0            0.0.0.0/0            reject-with icmp-host-prohibited

Chain OUTPUT (policy ACCEPT)
num target     prot opt source               destination
1   ACCEPT     udp  --  0.0.0.0/0            0.0.0.0/0            udp spt:22

[root@VCD-MGT-CELLB1 transfer]#
```

You can quickly eliminate the firewall as the cause of connectivity issues by temporarily stopping it using this command:

```
/etc/init/d/iptables stop
```

If you retry connecting to the portal and are successful, then it's clear that the firewall was blocking the connection and that temporarily disabling the firewall has allowed access.

vCloud Director needs a number of outbound firewall ports to access the infrastructure. The default iptables rules allow this access, but the cell requires at least HTTPS 443/TCP inbound to function, although SSH 22/TCP and HTTP 80/TCP are also useful for troubleshooting and administration. Full and current details of firewall port requirements for vCloud Director are maintained in a support article on the VMware website at kb.vmware.com/kb/2034426.

To create a rule that allows HTTPS traffic to the vCloud Director service through the default iptables firewall, issue the following commands:

```
iptables -I INPUT -p tcp --dport 443 -j ACCEPT
iptables -I OUTPUT -p udp --sport 443 -j ACCEPT
```

Be careful to specify -I (for insert) rather than -A (for append) because one of the last rules in the firewall is to reject all traffic that hasn't been specifically allowed by an earlier rule; therefore, your new rule will need to precede this one.

To make these rules persist after a reboot, save them to the configuration file by issuing this command:

```
/etc/init.d/iptables save
```

The HTTPS firewall rules you specified will now persist if the cell server is rebooted.

## Securing the Configuration Files

Installing your first cell server automatically created an answer file that can be used to automate installation of subsequent cell servers. The file is created in /opt/vmware/vcloud-director/etc/responses.properties.

Although the file does not contain plain-text passwords, it does contain connection details for your environment. Therefore, it is a sensitive file and should be removed or protected once you have finished working with it—especially if you move it to a shared location for installing subsequent cell servers.

If you look at the response file, you'll see the contents shown in Figure 7.35.

**FIGURE 7.35**
The responses
.properties file

```
[root@VCD-MGT-CELLB1 /]# cat /opt/vmware/vcloud-director/etc/responses.properties
user.keystore.path = \/opt\/vmware\/vcloud-director\/data\/transfer\/vCerts.ks
user.keystore.password = t\/\/bBxTJCamFFcg9t65aJlCRcqArKgsZY+At9eXbQ9lxvhcQsop1dh1eiwQnZN0w
database.jdbcUrl = jdbc:jtds:sqlserver:\/\/vcd-mgt-db01.vinf.corp:1433\/vcloud-production;socketTimeout=90
database.username = vcloud-production
database.password = +uHUT1WEPnNbmsVn7vbYD\/\v8UZ+m6u5cHdFbr1XryuKn0MaLy2K9ubRCU4SbCT96
system.info = pzIz\/8qsK50p1y3yu25hNQ==
system.version = 2
audit.syslog.host = syslog.vinf.corp
audit.syslog.port = 514
[root@VCD-MGT-CELLB1 /]# 
```

If you plan to copy this file to a shared location to deploy additional cell servers, you will need to ensure that the owner of the file is vcloud.vcloud after you have copied it. vcloud.vcloud is a user created by the vCloud installer on your cell server.

You can verify the current owner of the file you have copied to a shared location by looking at the output of the `ls -l` command (Figure 7.36). Note the `root root` entry, specifying that the owner is the root account that was used to copy the file to the shared location.

**FIGURE 7.36**
Verifying the current owner of the file

```
[root@VCD-MGT-CELLB2 mnt]# ls -l responses.properties
-rw-------. 1 root root 522 Feb  5  2013 responses.properties
```

To change the owner of this file to `vcloud.vcloud`, execute the following command on the file from your first cell server (Figure 7.37):

```
chown vcloud.vcloud responses.properties
```

**FIGURE 7.37**
The responses
.properties
owner set to
vcloud.vcloud

```
[root@VCD-MGT-CELLB2 mnt]# ls -l responses.properties
-rw-------. 1 vcloud vcloud 522 Feb  5 18:14 responses.properties
```

If you do not change the owner of the file, the installer will fail when you try to run it on additional cells. This is because it will not be able to access the response file as it does not run as a privileged user.

Also note that the certificate location you specified during the software installation is hard-coded in the `user.keystore.path` variable in this file. This example points to the keystore file on the transfer location as it is being used to install multiple cell servers.

Once you have installed all of your cell servers, you can remove both the `vCert.ks` and `responses.properties` files from the shared location and store them in a secure location.

The `responses.properties` file is required only if you need to install another cell server and want to automate the installation. The certificate keystore file (`vCert.ks`) is copied locally to the cell server during installation so the copy on shared storage is thus redundant for day-to-day operations.

## Creating Sysprep Packages

Unless you plan to exclusively support non-Windows installations or Windows 2008 and later for your cloud, we recommend that you create the Microsoft Sysprep deployment packages. Sysprep is required to be able to customize Windows XP and Windows 2003 guest operating systems. Windows 2008 and later have the Sysprep binaries included in the default operating system installation.

This is a simple task that must be performed on each cell server you build. You'll need to download the Sysprep binary packages from the following locations to a workstation:

**Windows 2000** http://download.microsoft.com/download/D/2/C/D2CBC4DA-5F0D
-435F-AE2C-FE9FCB6BDA8E/sp4DeployTools.exe

**Windows 2003 (32-bit)** www.microsoft.com/downloads/details
.aspx?FamilyID=93f20bb1-97aa-4356-8b43-9584b7e72556&displaylang=en

**Windows 2003 (64-bit)** www.microsoft.com/downloads/details
.aspx?FamilyID=c2684c95-6864-4091-bc9a-52aec5491af7&displaylang=en

**Windows XP (32-bit)** www.microsoft.com/downloads/details
.aspx?FamilyId=3E90DC91-AC56-4665-949B-BEDA3080E0F6&displaylang=en

**Windows XP (64-bit)** www.microsoft.com/downloads/details
.aspx?familyid=C2684C95-6864-4091-BC9A-52AEC5491AF7&displaylang=en

Once you've downloaded the Sysprep binary packages (Figure 7.38), extract the contents of
the downloaded files into the folder structure shown in Table 7.1.

**TABLE 7.1:** Folder structures for Windows OSs

| OS | FOLDERS |
| --- | --- |
| Windows 2000 | sysprep\win2000 |
| Windows 2003 (32-bit) | sysprep\win2k3 |
| Windows 2003 (64-bit) | sysprep\win2k3_64 |
| Windows XP (32-bit) | sysprep\winxp |
| Windows XP (64-bit) | sysprep\winxp_64 |

**FIGURE 7.38**
Extracting Sysprep
binaries

You should have the folder structure shown in Figure 7.39. In this example we are not providing the Sysprep binaries for Windows XP because we have only server operating systems in our
sample private cloud.

**FIGURE 7.39**
Extracted deploy
.cab files
organized per
operating system

Now, extract the contents of each `deploy.cab` file in each subfolder (Windows Explorer can open CAB files directly) and copy the root of the per-operating system subdirectory (Figure 7.40).

**FIGURE 7.40**
Extracting the `deploy.cab` files back to the per-operating system subdirectory

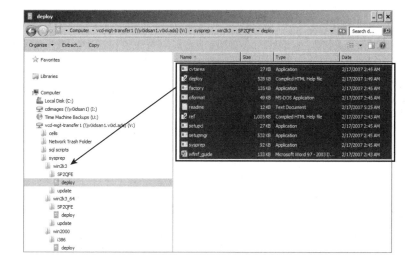

You can delete the remaining files and subdirectories since they are not required. You should be left with a folder structure like the one seen in Figure 7.41, with a single directory per operating system containing the contents of the `deploy.cab` file.

**FIGURE 7.41**
Extracted contents of `deploy.cab` file

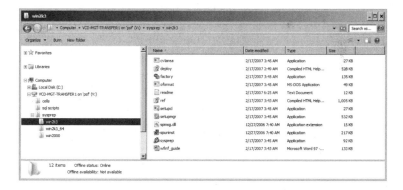

In this example the folder structure has been placed on the cell server transfer location, which is an NFS share on the network. The transfer location is a convenient place to place these files; they will be required in this format to setup all subsequent cell servers. If this is not possible in your environment, you can secure copy or FTP the files and folder structures to a temporary location directly on your cell server(s).

Now you will need to run a script on the cell server to take the Microsoft binaries that you have extracted and bundle them ready for use by vCloud Director. To do so, log on to your cell server as root and issue the following command, replacing *<path to files>* with the location to which you copied your Sysprep packages:

```
/opt/vmware/vcloud-director/deploymentPackageCreator/ ↵
createSysprepPackage.sh <path to files>
```

For example:

```
/opt/vmware/vcloud-director/deploymentPackageCreator/ ↵
createSysprepPackage.sh /opt/vmware/vcloud-director/data/transfer/sysprep
```

You will see the output shown in Figure 7.42 if it was successful. Note in this platform we are not providing Windows XP resources, which explains the errors recorded on the console.

**FIGURE 7.42**

The Sysprep package was successfully created, except for the Windows XP–based operating systems

```
[root@VCD-MGT-CELLB1 sysprep]# /opt/vmware/vcloud-director/deploymentPackageCreator/createSysprepPackage.sh /opt/vmware/vcl
oud-director/data/transfer/sysprep
Warning! Did not find 'sysprep.exe' for 'Windows XP 32 bit' in '/opt/vmware/vcloud-director/data/transfer/sysprep/winxp'
    Check folder name mactches 'winxp' exactly and sysprep binaries are copied.
    Ignoring this warning will cause failure of guest customization on 'Windows XP 32 bit' guest VMs

Warning! Did not find 'sysprep.exe' for 'Windows XP 64 bit' in '/opt/vmware/vcloud-director/data/transfer/sysprep/winxp_64'
    Check folder name mactches 'winxp_64' exactly and sysprep binaries are copied.
    Ignoring this warning will cause failure of guest customization on 'Windows XP 64 bit' guest VMs

Sysprep deployment package successfully created at /opt/vmware/vcloud-director/guestcustomization/windows_deployment_packag
e_sysprep.cab
Log writen to system log. Use 'grep createSysprepPackage /var/log/messages' to view log
[root@VCD-MGT-CELLB1 sysprep]# []
```

**NOTE** The path to the Sysprep binaries should not have a /character at the end because the script appends subfolders to the end of the path.

If you examine the /opt/vmware/vcloud-director/guestcustomization/vcloud_ sysprep.properties file (Figure 7.43), you will see which operating systems now have a Sysprep package available, as denoted by the =1 value.

**FIGURE 7.43**

The contents of the vcloud_ sysprep.proper- ties file denoting the Sysprep pack- ages ready for use by vCloud Director

```
[root@VCD-MGT-CELLB1 guestcustomization]# cat /opt/vmware/vcloud-director/guestcustomization/vcloud_sysprep.properties
#Do not modify this file manually. It can result in failures in VM deployments
win2000=1
win2k3=1
win2k3_64=1
winxp=0
winxp_64=0
[root@VCD-MGT-CELLB1 guestcustomization]# []
```

## vCloud Director Setup Wizard

Now that you have your first cell server installed and you can connect to it, you should carry out initial configuration of vCloud Director before proceeding any further. To accomplish this, you use the Adobe Flash–based web interface.

**1.** Connect directly to the cell server using a web browser.

**NOTE** If you are deploying a load balancer, you should still connect directly to the cell server to do the first-time configuration of the vCloud Director software—in this example, https:// vcd-mgt-cellb1.vinf.corp. Once you've built the subsequent cell servers, you can configure the load balancer and access the vCloud interface through it.

If you used a self-signed SSL certificate for your cell server rather than a public CA, you will see the warning shown in Figure 7.44. In this example,this warning appears for two reasons:

♦ The certificate is self-signed; thus the browser does not have a root certificate installed.

♦ You are accessing the cell server directly and you may recall in this example we configured the certificates with the `vcloud.vinf.corp` name rather than the cell server name because we eventually intend to use this service behind a load balancer.

**FIGURE 7.44**
Certificate warning
at first use

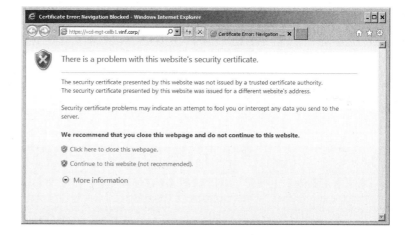

2. When you click Continue (or a similar button if you are using a different browser), you should see the vCloud Director Setup wizard screen shown in Figure 7.45.

**FIGURE 7.45**
vCloud Director
Setup wizard

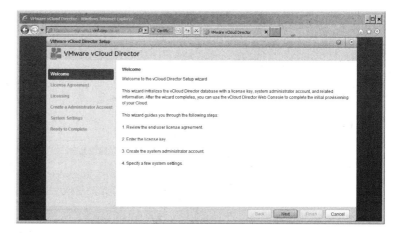

This wizard will step you through the process of configuring vCloud Director for administrative access. At this point you don't have any access configured for your consumers; you will do that in Chapter 8, "Delivering Services."

**3.** Click Next to start the Setup wizard and accept the end-user license agreement (EULA) for the vCloud Director software (Figure 7.46).

**FIGURE 7.46**
EULA screen

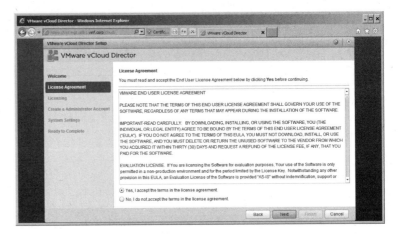

**4.** Enter the license key you have for vCloud Director (Figure 7.47).

This key will be required to continue any further. If you haven't purchased your final licenses and been allocated product keys, you can use an evaluation license to proceed. You can change the license key at a later date if you have to follow this route.

**FIGURE 7.47**
License key

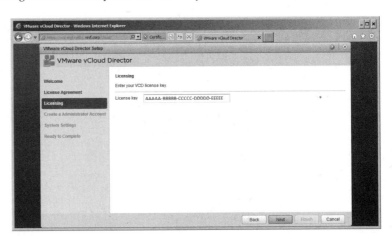

**5.** You will be prompted to create an initial administrator account (Figure 7.48). This is an account internal to vCloud Director, and you will use it to do initial configuration and create subsequent administrators (or link to an external directory source).

**FIGURE 7.48**
Creating the initial administrator account

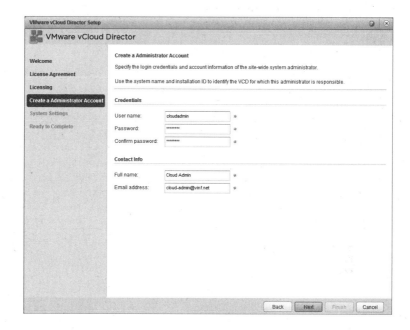

**6.** Provide a system name and installation ID (Figure 7.49).

**WARNING** Ensure that the system name and installation ID are unique—especially the installation ID since it is used to generate MAC addresses and you need to ensure that it does not conflict with any other vCloud Director installations within your organization.

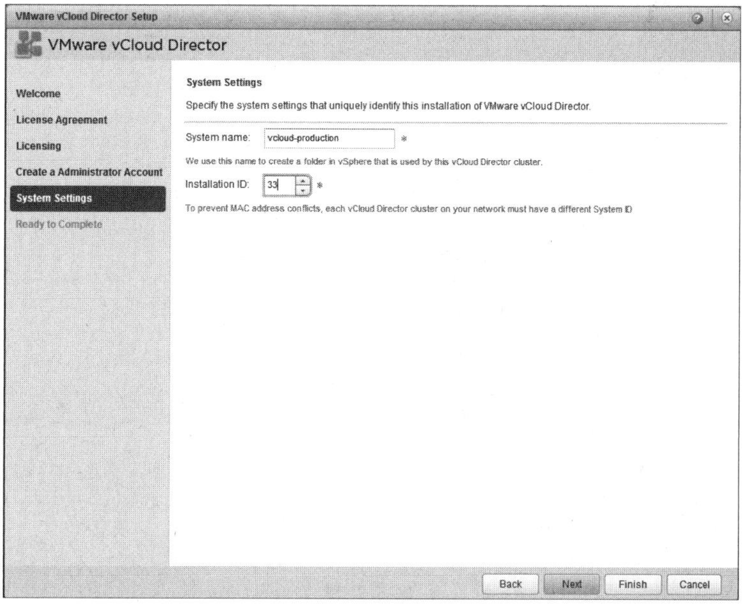

**FIGURE 7.49**
vCloud Director system settings

**7.** Click Next and you will be shown a summary screen. Click Finish and after a short wait you will see the default vCloud Director logon screen.

Once this process has completed (it can take a couple of minutes to initialize all settings), you'll be redirected to the vCloud Director logon page (Figure 7.50) and the basic installation is completed.

**FIGURE 7.50**
Congratulations, you made it! The default logon screen for a vCloud Director cell server

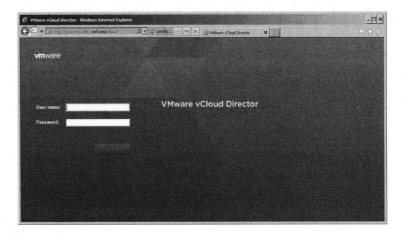

## Installing Additional Cell Servers

If you plan to implement multiple cell servers for resilience or performance reasons, you can use the `responses.properties` file that was created when you installed the first cell server to semi-automate the process. Doing so is advisable because it will ensure you have known-good vCloud Director settings on your cell server. Follow these steps:

**1.** Ensure your subsequent cell servers are prepared in the same way as the first, ensuring DNS configurations are correct and that NIC/IP assignments are known.

**2.** Install the system packages as specified earlier in this chapter.

**3.** Install the vCloud binaries, but do not select Yes to run the configuration script. You need to carry out some configuration after the installation is complete before this is possible:

```
vmware-vcloud-director-5.1.1-868405.bin
```

The installer extracts the package and begins to install to your new cell server, as shown in Figure 7.51.

**4.** Mount the transfer location on your new cell server. Doing so will allow you to access the certificate and response file (you were not able to mount this earlier until the vCloud Director installer created the `/opt/vmware/vcloud-director` directory structure for you):

```
mount 192.168.66.250:/nfs/VCD-MGT-TRANSFER1 ↵
/opt/vmware/vcloud-director/data/transfer/
```

**FIGURE 7.51**
vCloud Director
installer

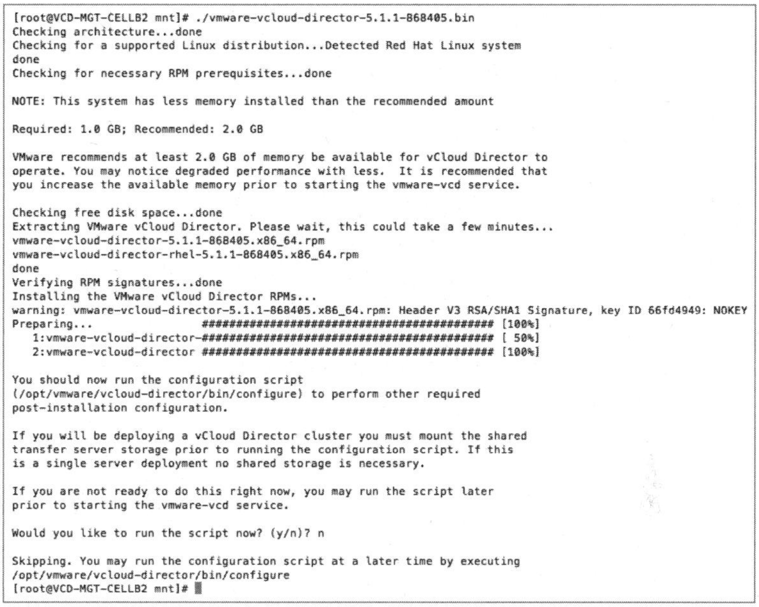

```
[root@VCD-MGT-CELLB2 mnt]# ./vmware-vcloud-director-5.1.1-868405.bin
Checking architecture...done
Checking for a supported Linux distribution...Detected Red Hat Linux system
done
Checking for necessary RPM prerequisites...done

NOTE: This system has less memory installed than the recommended amount

Required: 1.0 GB; Recommended: 2.0 GB

VMware recommends at least 2.0 GB of memory be available for vCloud Director to
operate. You may notice degraded performance with less.  It is recommended that
you increase the available memory prior to starting the vmware-vcd service.

Checking free disk space...done
Extracting VMware vCloud Director. Please wait, this could take a few minutes...
vmware-vcloud-director-5.1.1-868405.x86_64.rpm
vmware-vcloud-director-rhel-5.1.1-868405.x86_64.rpm
done
Verifying RPM signatures...done
Installing the VMware vCloud Director RPMs...
warning: vmware-vcloud-director-5.1.1-868405.x86_64.rpm: Header V3 RSA/SHA1 Signature, key ID 66fd4949: NOKEY
Preparing...               ########################################### [100%]
   1:vmware-vcloud-director########################################### [ 50%]
   2:vmware-vcloud-director########################################### [100%]

You should now run the configuration script
(/opt/vmware/vcloud-director/bin/configure) to perform other required
post-installation configuration.

If you will be deploying a vCloud Director cluster you must mount the shared
transfer server storage prior to running the configuration script. If this
is a single server deployment no shared storage is necessary.

If you are not ready to do this right now, you may run the script later
prior to starting the vmware-vcd service.

Would you like to run the script now? (y/n)? n

Skipping. You may run the configuration script at a later time by executing
/opt/vmware/vcloud-director/bin/configure
[root@VCD-MGT-CELLB2 mnt]#
```

5. Once the transfer location is successfully mounted, you can run the configuration script with the following parameter to reuse the information provided in the `responses` `.properties` file (in this example a response file is held on the transfer location):

   /opt/vmware/vcloud-director/bin/configure -r /opt/vmware/ ↵
   vcloud-director/data/transfer/responses.properties

6. The configure script will now execute (Figure 7.52). You are prompted only for the IP address you want to use for the HTTP and console proxy services. The script takes all the other configuration information, such as the database, username, password, and keystore file, from the response file.

**FIGURE 7.52**
Automated installation of an additional cell server using a response file

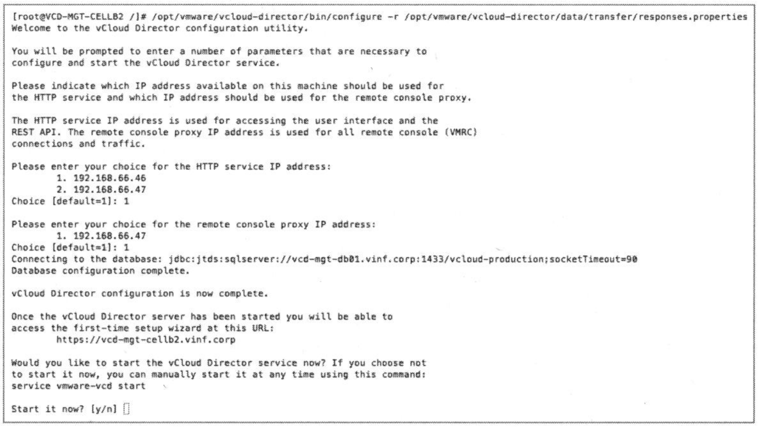

```
[root@VCD-MGT-CELLB2 /]# /opt/vmware/vcloud-director/bin/configure -r /opt/vmware/vcloud-director/data/transfer/responses.properties
Welcome to the vCloud Director configuration utility.

You will be prompted to enter a number of parameters that are necessary to
configure and start the vCloud Director service.

Please indicate which IP address available on this machine should be used for
the HTTP service and which IP address should be used for the remote console proxy.

The HTTP service IP address is used for accessing the user interface and the
REST API. The remote console proxy IP address is used for all remote console (VMRC)
connections and traffic.

Please enter your choice for the HTTP service IP address:
        1. 192.168.66.46
        2. 192.168.66.47
Choice [default=1]: 1

Please enter your choice for the remote console proxy IP address:
        1. 192.168.66.47
Choice [default=1]: 1
Connecting to the database: jdbc:jtds:sqlserver://vcd-mgt-db01.vinf.corp:1433/vcloud-production;socketTimeout=90
Database configuration complete.

vCloud Director configuration is now complete.

Once the vCloud Director server has been started you will be able to
access the first-time setup wizard at this URL:
        https://vcd-mgt-cellb2.vinf.corp

Would you like to start the vCloud Director service now? If you choose not
to start it now, you can manually start it at any time using this command:
service vmware-vcd start

Start it now? [y/n]
```

7. If you want to start using the new cell server immediately, enter Y for yes when asked if you want to start the vCloud service.

   You'll now find that your second cell server is functional. You should follow this same process for any further cell servers you intend to deploy.

If you are planning to use an IP load balancer, you'll need to add the new cell server into the load-balancing configuration in order to use it that way.

---

**MICROSOFT SYSPREP PACKAGES ON ADDITIONAL CELL SERVERS**

If you intend to support deploying Microsoft operating systems, you'll also need to run the same script to package Microsoft Sysprep packages on this cell server as you did in an earlier step on the first cell server. However, you can reuse the file structure you downloaded and created multiple times.

---

To verify the configuration, do the following:

1. Use your web browser to connect to any of the cell servers.

2. Logon using the cloudadmin user account created during the Setup wizard the first time.

3. Navigate to the Manage & Monitor tab and click Cloud Cells.

   You should see the screen shown in Figure 7.53, which in this example shows the first cell server VCD-MGT-CELLB1 and the additional cell server VCD-MGT-CELLB2 with a status of Connected.

**FIGURE 7.53**
An example of vCloud Director cell servers connected following automated installation of second server

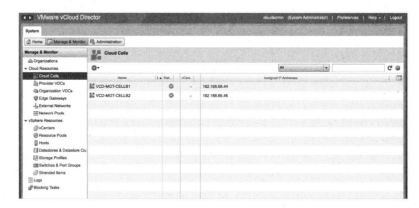

# Summary

vCloud Director requires a number of virtual machines and databases to support its various management roles. At present this is a mix of applications running on RedHat Linux, Microsoft Windows, and dedicated virtual appliances, typically referred to as a "management pod."

The management pod is hosted on either a self-contained vSphere cluster or a cluster that is not already managed by vCloud Director.

You must gather various media files before you install services into your management pod. Adobe Flash is a commonly overlooked requirement that will need to be installed on workstations from which you plan to administer vCloud Director.

A number of certificates are required to secure SSL communications between consumers and vCloud Director. Self-signed certificates are acceptable but will trigger warnings in your consumers' browser sessions. As such, certificates signed by a public or internal certificate authority are recommended for anything other than small internal or test installations.

You need to build a number of databases on a Microsoft or Oracle database server. Microsoft SQL Server is a popular and low-cost choice for most enterprises, but vCloud Director does not support Windows Authentication for its database. Therefore, you can only use SQL authentication for this component. These databases are critical to the function of vCloud Director; if they fail the vApps will continue to run, but administrative access to the vCloud Director portal and statistic gathering for billing will be unavailable.

vCloud Director requires one or more vCenter Server installations to manage the resource pods allocated to it: a standard vCenter server installation. We strongly recommended that you host the vCenter Server database on a database server, rather than using the built-in SQL express database because it can cause complications for vCenter Chargeback Manager and won't scale appropriately with your cloud.

vShield Manager is required to manage the deployment of the various firewall instances for your resource pods and is simply a matter of importing a virtual appliance in OVF format into vCenter and configuring it with an IP address (although the process to change the default password is somewhat convoluted).

A vCloud Director installation consists of one or more cell servers. A cell server is essentially the vCloud Director software, which is installed on a RedHat Enterprise Linux server that provides the web interface and orchestration of the constituent components of vCloud Director. If you wish to install multiple cell servers for performance and high availability, you can use the responses.properties file that is automatically generated the first time you run the setup script on a cell server to duplicate the configuration on further hosts.

# Chapter 8

# Delivering Services

Now that you have a vCloud Director management pod, this chapter focuses on how you, as the system administrator, use that environment to build service offerings ready for your consumers to use.

We will cover the steps you'll take to create Provider Virtual Data Center (PvDC) to deliver tiers of service. You'll define organizations within your vCloud Director platform and nominate administrators for the various organizations. You'll create Organization vDCs (Org vDCs), which are allocations of resources from PvDCs, each with its own model for resource allocation and connections to various logical cloud networks.

In this chapter, you will learn to:

◆ Create PvDCs

◆ Create organizations and configure LDAP authentication

◆ Allocate resources to an organization

◆ Connect an organization to the corporate datacenter network

◆ Create and publish a basic service catalog to other organizations

## Laying the Foundation: Building the Resource Pod

You will first explore the steps required to add the first vCenter server and the set of clusters that it controls. These will become PvDCs in vCloud Director, and from there you'll build Org vDCs.

You need to provide vCloud Director with at least one PvDC, which it will use to host Org vDCs. This chapter assumes that you have one or more vSphere clusters ready to use as PvDCs with vCloud Director, as described in Chapter 5, "Platform Design for vCloud Director," and that you have deployed a vCNS Manager appliance in your management pod for the resource pod vCenter, as described in Chapter 7, "Installing VMware vCloud Director."

A PvDC typically maps 1 to 1 with a vSphere cluster. Each cluster is differentiated by the tiers of service they are able to offer. For example, you may have a cluster that offers a gold-level service level agreement (SLA), with fast disks and redundant hardware. You may also have a lower-tier SLA cluster that offers slower disks and less resilient hardware or clusters that provide specific business or security-driven functionality such as encryption or increased security and auditing.

It is technically possible to map PvDCs to resource pools at the vSphere level. However, we strongly discourage you from doing so unless you have a comprehensive understanding of vSphere resource pools and a well-thought-out design. Such an approach can compromise vCloud Director's ability to effectively control the levels of resource allocation if they are not carefully implemented. This is especially true if you are planning to mix allocation models in a single PvDC; it limits vCloud Director's control of physical resource utilization because the various resource settings deployed by each allocation model can overlap. If you are considering this use case, check out the VMware white paper illustrating the impact of these scenarios here:

```
http://www.vmware.com/files/pdf/techpaper/vCloud_Director_Resource_
Allocation-USLET.pdf
```

## Building an Example Resource Pod

In this section, you will build on the management pod you created in Chapter 7 by adding an example resource pod design. The goal is to build a private cloud like that shown in Figure 8.1. The Human Resources (HR) and Research and Development (R&D) departments in this organization are bound by a security and regulatory policy that dictates they have a separate set of physical hosts, storage, and networks for their workload with specific security policy settings.

The IT, finance, and sales organizations can share common computing, storage, and network infrastructure. They can choose from two service tiers: Bronze and Silver. The R&D and HR organizations can consume resources from a single secure service tier.

The sales organization has a data analytics application that requires 100 percent dedicated performance at all times. Therefore, their production Org vDC is configured with the Reservation Pool allocation model to ensure they always have dedicated computing resources available.

In terms of the vSphere configuration, each cluster has a specific host profile attached to it. This host profile ensures that the appropriate storage is mounted on each host and is consistent across the cluster.

Each datastore has a set of defined capabilities that are mapped into storage profiles. In this example you will use user-defined capabilities, but if you have a storage array that supports the vSphere API for Array Integration (VAAI) and vStorage APIs for Storage Awareness (VASA) extensions, then you can also create storage profiles based on attributes they expose.

Each cluster is configured in a specific manner to deliver three service tiers to our consumers in vINF Enterprises, our example company:

**Gold** Provides a "gold" level 99.9 percent service to our consumers, with DRS and HA functionality and N+1 resilience. It only uses Tier 1 disk storage but offers Tier 3 disk storage for temporary storage.

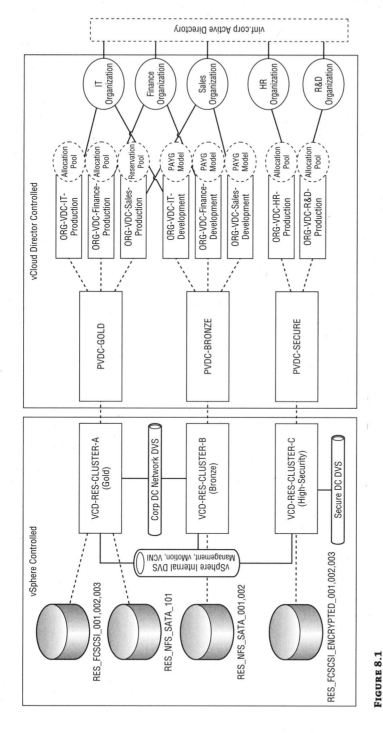

**FIGURE 8.1**

Mapping physical infrastructure to logical service tiers and organizational entities

**Bronze**    Provides a "bronze" level service, using only DRS functionality on the physical cluster and offering N+0 resilience (which means that in the event of a hardware failure, the hardware will be oversubscribed). Only Tier 3 disk storage (SATA) is available to this cluster.

**High-Security**    Provides a physically separate set of storage, computing, and network resources to meet a regulatory constraint and has array-level storage encryption to protect virtual machines (VMs). This solution is still able to be administered by vCloud Director administrators and uses a common vCloud infrastructure, but consumer workloads can run only within an isolated set of infrastructure within this cluster.

This high-security example is provided to illustrate a non-performance-driven capability provided by the underlying storage and computing infrastructure. Neither vSphere nor vCloud provides native filesystem encryption or other types of security enforcement. In this example, you should assume that this storage is supplied by a physically separate storage array that provides such functionality at the hardware level.

Each cluster is connected to a management network on a distributed virtual switch (DVS) that supports management traffic like vCenter, SSH, and vMotion. To support VM workload traffic, each cluster is connected to either the corporate datacenter network or a high-security network. Both networks are connected by means of a DVS and dedicated uplinks to the physical network on each vSphere host.

The logical diagram shown in Figure 8.1 represents a series of PvDCs that are created and mapped to vSphere clusters. For example, the VCD-RES-CLUSTER-A (Gold) cluster provides resources for the PvDC-Gold PvDC.

Each PvDC provides resources to one or more Org vDCs. Each Org vDC has an allocation model that is one of the following types:

◆ Allocation Pool

◆ Pay-As-You-Go

◆ Reservation Pool

Each Org vDC is "owned" by an organization, which is an administrative and authentication boundary for a department or business unit within your private cloud. Each Org vDC has an associated authentication source—in this case, the vinf.corp Active Directory.

Figure 8.2 shows that the VCD-MGT-VC03 server is a dedicated vCenter for Resource Pod A. Resource Pod A is a logical grouping of vSphere clusters managed by a single vCenter server. Each service tier maps to a vSphere cluster, and each vSphere cluster has access to different sets of physical infrastructure (storage, networks) and logical configuration (DRS/HA) to build up the service offering.

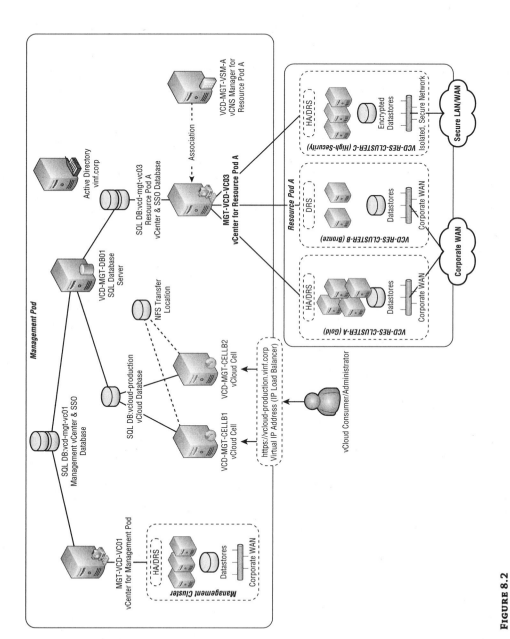

**FIGURE 8.2**
Resource pod design for vINF Enterprises Inc.

At a physical level we have three clusters configured and ready to use in this resource pod. Figure 8.3 shows a view of the clusters from the vSphere client.

**FIGURE 8.3**
vSphere client view of resource pod containing three clusters ready for consumption by vCloud Director

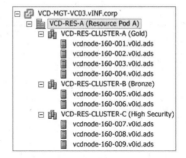

## Associating vCNS Manager with Your Resource Pod

In Chapter 2, "Developing Your Strategy," you deployed a vCNS Manager appliance in the management pod, VCD-MGT-VSM-A. You must associate this appliance with the resource pod you are building by connecting it to the vCenter server, as shown in Figure 8.4.

**FIGURE 8.4**
The relationship between vCNS Manager and vCenter within a resource pod

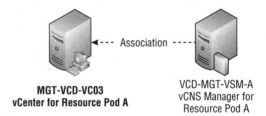

This is a simple process; you use a web browser to connect to the web server running on the vCNS Manager appliance and log on using the credentials you set in Chapter 7. Click on the Settings & Reports item in the left-hand navigation tree; then use the interface shown in Figure 8.5 to complete the association with vCenter Server.

**FIGURE 8.5**
vCNS Manager interface accessed by web browser

Enter credentials for your vCenter server, as shown in Figure 8.6, by clicking the Edit button next to the vCenter Server entry.

**FIGURE 8.6**
vCNS Manager credentials to attach to vCenter Server

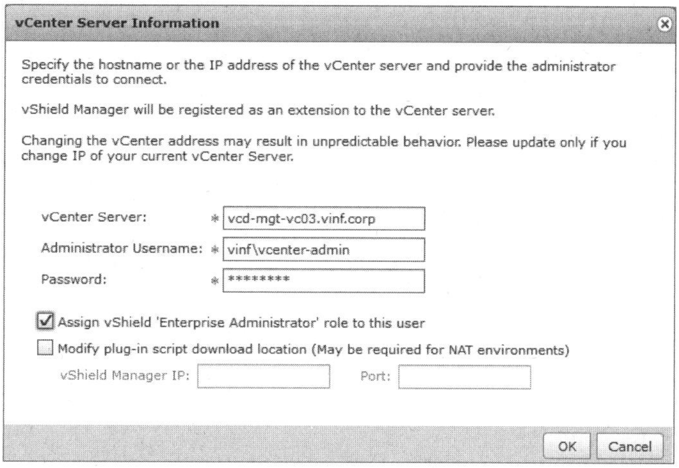

You may get a warning about an unrecognized thumbprint. Choose to import it, and when it's completed you'll see that vCNS Manager can connect and inventory the vCenter server, as shown in Figure 8.7.

**FIGURE 8.7**
vCNS Manager connected to vCenter

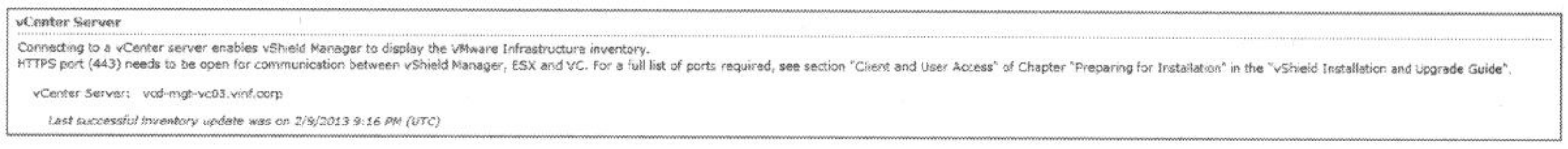

If you get an error, you should verify name resolution between your vCNS Manager appliance and your vCenter. You can log on to the console of the vCNS Manager from the vSphere client and access the basic tools (like ping) that are available in its console.

## Licensing vCloud Networking and Security

vCNS has its own license. You need to license it before you can use it fully. By default, vCNS installs using an evaluation license that expires approximately 90 days from installation.

You configure this license using the vSphere client. To begin, connect to the vCenter server that you set up in the previous section. On the Home screen, click Licensing, as shown in Figure 8.8.

Locate the vCloud Networking And Security entry in the asset list. Right-click and choose Change License Key, as shown in Figure 8.9.

**FIGURE 8.8**
Click Licensing

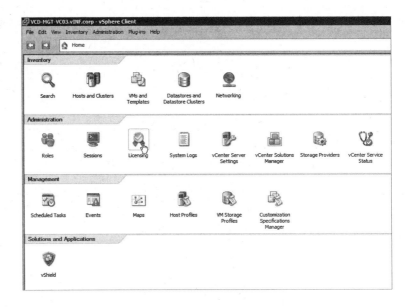

**FIGURE 8.9**
Choose Change
License Key

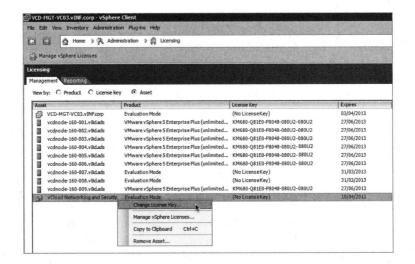

Choose Assign A New License Key To This Solution and enter your license key, as shown in
Figure 8.10.

FIGURE 8.10

Entering a license
key for vCNS
Manager

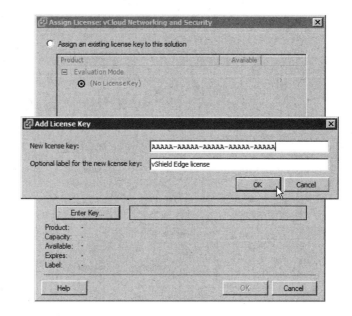

Once you complete these steps, your vCNS solution is licensed.

## Configuring LDAP Authentication

Before your consumers can use LDAP authentication in your vCloud, you need to configure
vCloud Director to communicate with your corporate Active Directory (or other LDAP-based
directory).

If you want any of your consumers to be able to use LDAP or to authenticate to a separate
Active Directory, you'll also need to configure the system with a default LDAP server. Your
consumers can later override this setting to use their own server when they configure their
Org vDCs.

This is a simple process and it's done from the Administration tab of the vCloud Director
interface. If you click on LDAP, you can enter the name of a single domain controller you want to
communicate with for authentication.

As shown in Figure 8.11, you can specify the base distinguished name for your directory.
In this example you are connecting to your corporate Active Directory (vinf.corp) by specifying **dc=vinf,dc=corp**. You need to enter a user account and a static password. This user
can be a standard user account; it does not require administrative access as it simply queries
Active Directory for account names to authenticate against rather than requiring any write
permissions.

**FIGURE 8.11**
Configuring LDAP
server details

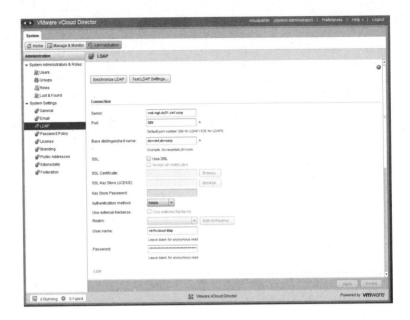

Click the Test LDAP Settings button to search for a user account and validate that the communications are successful.

---

### CELL SERVER ACCESS TO LDAP SOURCE

This authentication originated from the vCloud Director cell servers, so you will need to ensure that the cell servers can communicate with the LDAP sources you specify on whatever port you configure (the default is 389). This is a consideration in more secure deployments where you may have firewalls between your vCloud environment and corporate systems or with a public service provider where vCloud cell servers will almost certainly be in a restricted DMZ network.

---

In our example organization, there is a group in Active Directory called vCloudAdministrators. This means vinf.corp users can log on to vCloud Director using their Active Directory account to administer vCloud. This approach is desirable for larger environments and to ensure there is an audit trail to changes made.

To allow an Active Directory (or any LDAP source) group access to vCloud Director, navigate to the Groups section of the vCloud Director interface under the Administration tab, as shown in Figure 8.12.

Click the Import Groups button and enter a search string (in this case, **vcloud**). You will see a list of matching groups from your LDAP source. You want to make the vCloud Administrators Active Directory group a member of the vCloud system administrator role, so click Add and then click OK to make the change (Figure 8.13).

**FIGURE 8.12**
Importing groups
from an LDAP
source

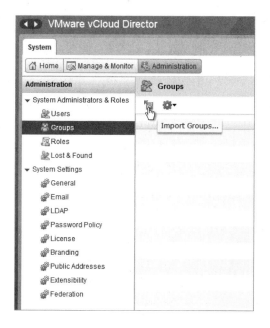

**FIGURE 8.13**
Selecting an LDAP
group from a search

All members of the vCloud Administrators Active Directory group can now log on to the vCloud Director interface using their Active Directory credentials, as shown at the top of Figure 8.14.

**FIGURE 8.14**
Logged on using
LDAP credentials

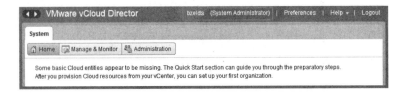

## Setting the SMTP Server

vCloud Director can use an SMTP server to send notifications to administrators and consumers. You can configure this on the Administration tab of the vCloud Director interface. Under System Settings click Email to see the options shown in Figure 8.15.

**FIGURE 8.15**
SMTP server
settings

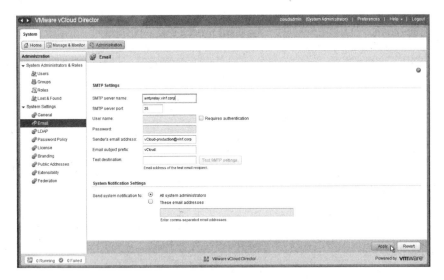

As with the LDAP configuration, bear in mind that the communication is initiated from the cell server(s), so your network should allow SMTP traffic (port 25, TCP) from the cell server to your SMTP relay. If your SMTP relay requires authentication, you can specify it on this page. When you create organizations, they have the option of using the system default SMTP server or specifying their own. Again, if you have a segregated environment, your consumers will need to ensure that their own SMTP relay server can receive SMTP traffic from the cell servers and that appropriate authentication is configured on both sides.

## Attaching a vCenter Server to Your Resource Pod

When you log on to vCloud Director as the cloud administrator account (cloudadmin) that you created in Chapter 7, you'll see a familiar wizard/checklist type interface, as shown in Figure 8.16.

**FIGURE 8.16**
Logging on to
vCloud Director

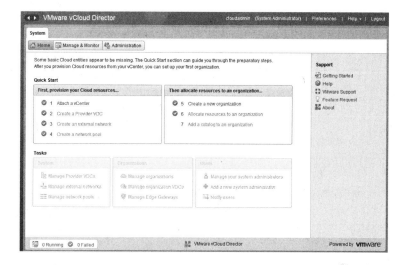

You'll notice that the wizard shows the next required step as a clickable option. The steps you cannot yet complete because they are dependent on the first are grayed out.

The first task is Attach A vCenter. Click the link and you are prompted for the details of the vCenter server you are connecting to. Enter the details of VCD-MGT-VC03, which will be controlling Resource Pod A and the three initial clusters that it contains, as shown in Figure 8.17.

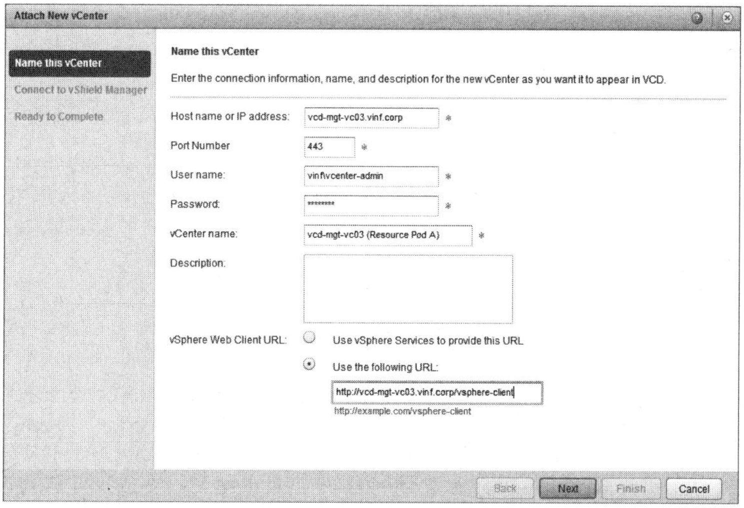

**FIGURE 8.17**
Attaching a vCenter
server to vCloud
Director to
create the first
resource pod

The account you specify must have administrative permissions to the vCenter server. You can enter the vSphere web client URL manually. This allows administrators to right-click objects in the vCloud Director interface and browse to the underlying object in the vSphere web client if you have it installed on your vCenter server.

Click Next and you'll be prompted for vCNS Manager connection details, as shown in Figure 8.18.

**FIGURE 8.18**
Entering creden-
tials to connect to
vCNS Manager

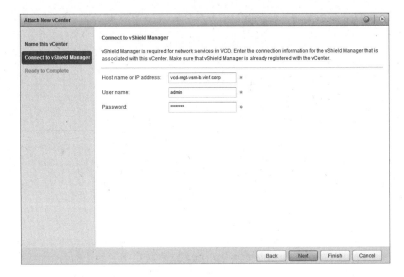

You'll recall that you associate one vCNS Manager with every vCenter you deploy as part of a resource pod in your cloud. In this case you are going to associate your resource pod with VCD-MGT-VSM-B and provide the FQDN and credentials to connect to it.

**NOTE**   The credentials you enter are the same ones you used to log on to the web interface of the vCNS Manager in Chapter 7. If you changed the password as part of your installation process, be sure you supply the updated password.

If you have to change the vCNS Manager password after making this connection, you can edit the password within vCloud Director and reconnect it.

Your resource pod is now ready to be mapped to PvDCs in vCloud Director.

## Creating PvDCs

In this step you will be creating the Gold PvDC for our example deployment. This configuration is carried out from within vCloud Director, and assuming your vSphere layer has been appropriatley prepared with storage profiles and clusters, you do not have to configure anything else in vCenter.

Figure 8.19 shows that the Gold PvDC is made up of specific storage (as grouped together via a storage profile), a cluster, and an external network. In the following steps you'll group all these resources together into the first PvDC.

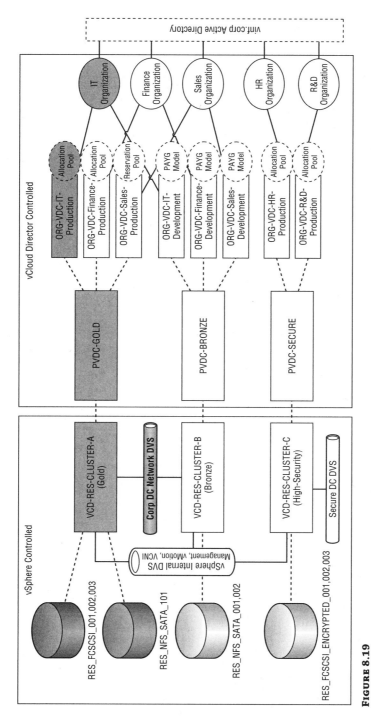

**Figure 8.19**
Resources mapped to the Gold PvDC

Connect to your vCloud Director interface—in this example, https://vcloud.vinf.corp. You'll notice that the root URL automatically redirects you to /cloud/; this is the logon page for cloud administrators.

Log on using the cloudadmin account that was created when you installed vCloud Director, as shown in Figure 8.20. Only the system administrator can create PvDCs.

**FIGURE 8.20**
Logging on as the system administrator (cloudadmin)

As shown in Figure 8.21, click Create A Provider VDC. A wizard launches that lets you create a PvDC. Enter descriptive information about the PvDC you are creating. In this example, you will be creating a PvDC that is capable of delivering a Gold level of service.

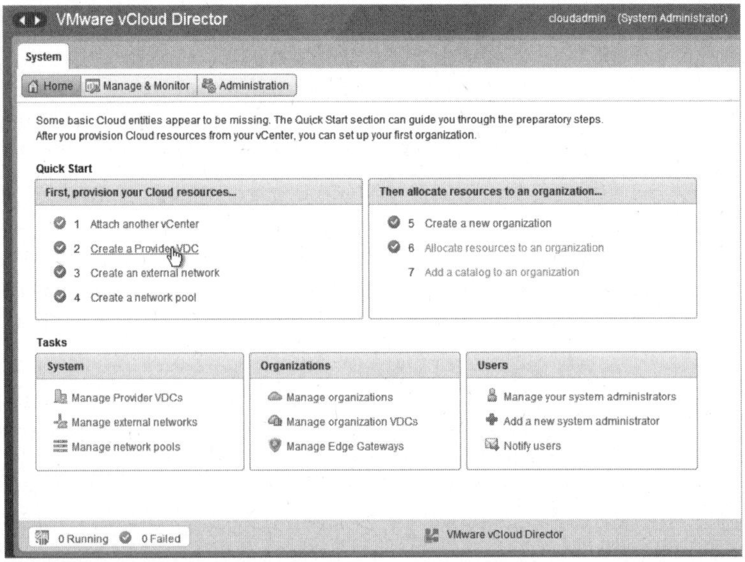

**FIGURE 8.21**
Click Create A Provider VDC to launch the wizard

The description field can be used to give the consumer and organization administrators a better idea of what facilities are available. In this case, the Gold PvDC consists of a cluster with N+1 resilience and is built on Tier 1 15K Fibre Channel SCSI storage. As such, this is a tier of service that may be well suited to production or high-performance activites in your organization.

You'll notice in Figure 8.22 that you can set the highest supported hardware version. This is an important consideration if you have a platform that mixes older versions of vSphere like 4.x in a cluster with 5.x hosts, which do not support Hardware Version 8. Mixing host versions in a cluster is not generally a good practice, but you may find yourself in this situation if you are in the process of a version upgrade. In this example, our hosts are all running vSphere 5.1, so you can support the latest virtual hardware version (which is 9).

**FIGURE 8.22**
Naming the PvCD and examining supported virtual hardware versions

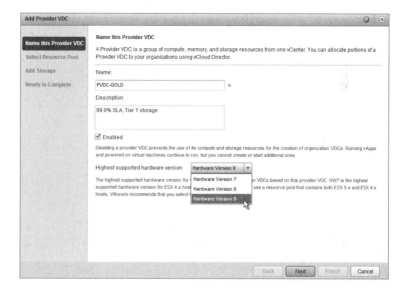

The wizard asks you to select a resource pool, as shown in Figure 8.23. For our example, choose a cluster from our vCenter called VCD-RES-CLUSTER-A (Gold). Doing so allocates the resources of the entire cluster to the Gold Provider vDC you are creating, and as such you will not be able to create any further provider vDCs that use the resources from this cluster. This step allocates the cluster as a resource available to vCloud Director and will make it unavailable for any other PvDCs.

**NOTE**  It is possible to select vSphere-defined resource pools at this step, but this is not a recommended practice in a production vCloud Director environment. Additional resource pools can be included later if you are using an Org vDC with the Allocation Pool or Pay-As-You-Go allocation model with the elastic vDC functionality enabled.

As shown in Figure 8.24, you are prompted to choose the storage profiles that are availabe to this PvDC. For this example you are presenting two tiers of storage to the Gold PvDC, Tier 1 and Tier 3. Select each storage profile and click Add.

**FIGURE 8.23**
Select Resource
Pool page

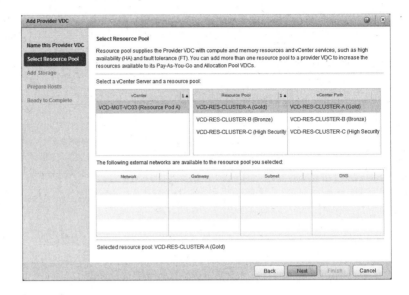

**FIGURE 8.24**
Selecting storage
profiles for our
PvDC

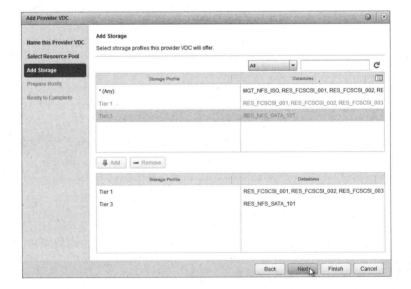

## VISIBLE STORAGE PROFILES

You are shown only the storage profiles that are available to the cluster you selected for this PvDC on the previous screen. If you are not seeing the storage profiles you are expecting, then check to see which datastores are presented to the hosts that you have in this cluster at the vSphere layer (for example, check SAN zoning/masking or NFS mount configurations on each host).

vCloud Director needs to install its agent to a host to enable it to function with vCloud Director, and you must provide root credentials for each host. As shown in Figure 8.25, if you have the same root credentials for each host, you can choose to use one set of credentials or enter a password individually for each host.

**FIGURE 8.25**
Providing credentials on the Prepare Hosts page

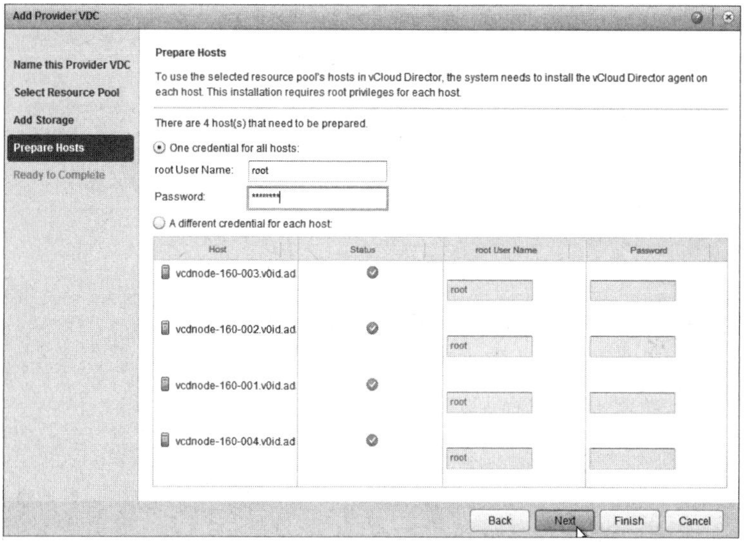

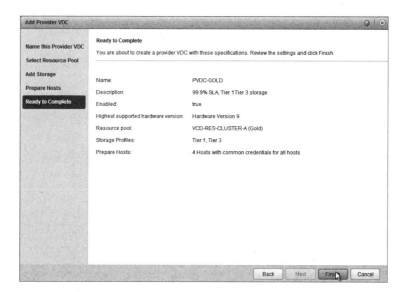

You are shown a summary screen (see Figure 8.26). This page summarizes the details you have just entered. Click Finish to complete the wizard and create the PvDC.

**FIGURE 8.26**
Summary screen

You can check the status of the PvDC creation by clicking at the bottom left of the screen, where in Figure 8.27 it says "2 Running." This will show you the status of the agent installation task(s). This task will automatically put each vSphere host into Maintenance Mode, install the agent, and then exit Maintenance Mode. This process does not require a reboot of each host or any manual intervention.

**FIGURE 8.27**
Host preparation
job progress screen

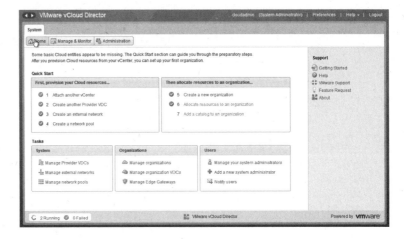

You can verify that the task has completed sucessfully by selecting the Manage & Monitor tab at the top of the vCloud Director interface and then clicking in the Provider vDCs section and selecting the PvDC. You should see your hosts on the Hosts tab, as shown in Figure 8.28. A green check mark indicates they are ready for use. Any errors will be flagged by a red circle with a line through it. You can click on each for troubleshooting details.

**FIGURE 8.28**
Hosts prepared and
ready for use with
vCloud Director

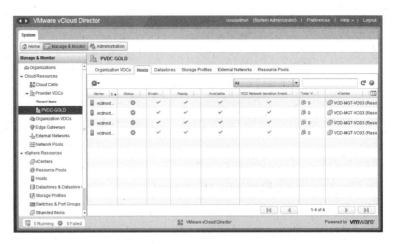

Once the task has completed successfully, you'll notice that you have a new System vDC object created in vCenter, as shown in Figure 8.29. This demonstrates that vCloud Director is in control of the vSphere cluster, and it will use this newly created resource pool to house system resources like vCNS Edge appliances.

**FIGURE 8.29**
vSphere objects
created by vCloud
Director

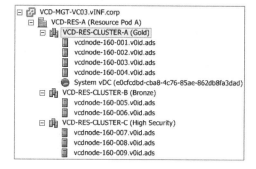

You now have created your first PvDC. The process is the same for the remaining PvDCs in our example (PvDC-Bronze and PvDC-Secure); you select different clusters and storage profiles when prompted. Figure 8.30 shows the settings applied to the PvDC-Secure PvDC.

**FIGURE 8.30**
Creation of the
PvDC-Secure PvDC

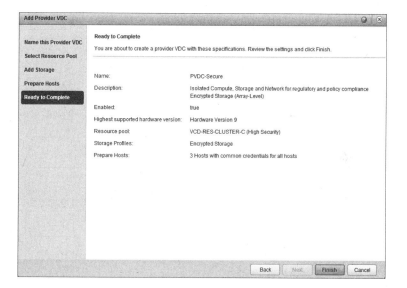

## Creating an External Network

Now that you've created your first PvDC, you'll notice that the wizard on the home page changes. The next step is to allocate an *external network* to your PvDC. You should think of an external network as a datacenter network. There may be several available for PvDCs within a resource pod to connect to. In most private cloud deployments, the external network will be one or more physical datacenter VLANs and associated IP subnets that are accessible from the corporate datacenter LAN and then out to the corporate WAN (depending on your network topology).

The external network acts as an interchange point of traffic between organization and internal networks. This is where vCNS Edge plays an important role by providing Network Address Translation (NAT) for organization networks to do the following:

◆ Reduce the number of IP addresses required in the corporate datacenter

◆ Allow fencing to support creation of multiple instances of the same vApp and IP address ranges

In this example, you will create an external network to represent our corporate datacenter network, which you can use to allow organizations running services in the Gold and Bronze PvDCs to connect to the corporate network. Click Create An External Network to begin the process (Figure 8.31).

**FIGURE 8.31**
Click Create An External Network

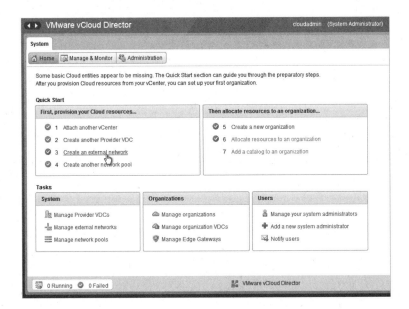

You will see the wizard shown in Figure 8.32. Select the vCenter controlling this resource pod—in this instance, VCD-MGT-VC03, which is controlling Resource Pod A. You are going to add the CorpDatacenterNetwork to our cloud to allow our consumers to make connections to the corporate network.

As shown in Figure 8.32, vCloud Director automatically detects that PvDC-Gold and PvDC-Bronze have access to it. vCloud Director knows this because if you refer to Figure 8.1 only those clusters are attached to the CorpDatacenterNetwork distributed virtual switch (DVS).

Likewise, as Figure 8.33 shows, the HighSecurityNetwork is only available to the secure PvDC because the vSphere cluster underpinning PvDC-Secure is the only one attached to the HighSecurityNetwork DVS.

The external network that is attached to it is shown. In this simple example the VM Network vSphere network is a port group with access to the corporate datacenter LAN.

On the next step in the wizard, shown in Figure 8.34, click Add to add a subnet to this external network. You should think of this as entering the subnet details that have been allocated to you by your corporate datacenter network administrators. In this example you have been allocated 75 IP addresses from the datacenter range of 192.168.66.0/24. Each device that is connected to the external network—for example, a vCNS Edge appliance—will be allocated an IP address from this static IP pool.

**FIGURE 8.32**

External networks available from Gold and Bronze PvDCs

**FIGURE 8.33**

Differences in available external networks between PvDCs due to different underlying vSphere configurations

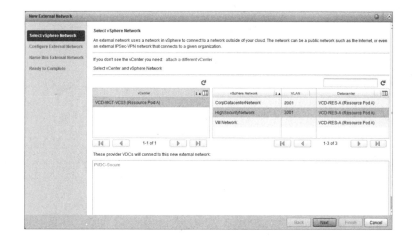

**FIGURE 8.34**

Entering IP
subnet details
for our external
network

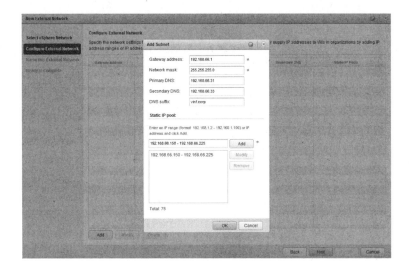

vCloud Director uses this information to act as an IP address management tool for the virtual networks you define. But it's not only capable of allocating IP addresses from the static IP pool; it can also configure vApps under its control with the relevant IP address information from this pool. This is the reason you specify DNS server and suffix details as they are automatically configured inside the VM by vCloud Director if you enable guest customization.

You'll be asked to give the network a name; then you are shown a summary screen (Figure 8.35). Click Finish to complete the wizard and create the external network.

**FIGURE 8.35**

Ready to create an
external network to
connect to the cor-
porate datacenter
network

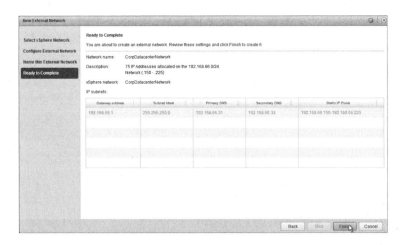

Your resource pod now has a logical connection to the corporate datacenter network with a pool of 75 IP addresses from the 192.168.66.0/24 range. This connection is available to the PvDC-Gold and PvDC-Bronze PvDCs you created earlier.

If you navigate to the Manage & Monitor tab of the vCloud Director interface, as shown in Figure 8.36, and look under Cloud Resources at External Networks, you'll see the external network object. You can see that it has picked up the VLAN ID associated with this vSphere network (2001). You can also see the percentage of IP addresses in use from the pool of 75 IP addresses that we defined in the previous step.

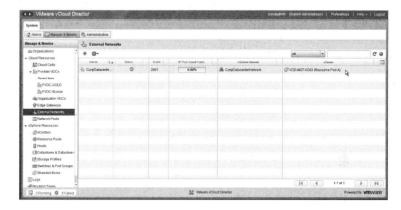

**FIGURE 8.36**
External network showing the IP address pool

## Creating a Network Pool

Now that you have defined an external network, you'll need to create a *network pool*. You'll create a pool of virtual networks that can be created and deleted on demand by vCloud Director for networks required to support vApp and organization networks.

On the Home screen, click the Create Another Network Pool task, as shown in Figure 8.37. In this example environment, previous network pools have been created prior to this step.

**FIGURE 8.37**
Click the Create Another Network Pool task

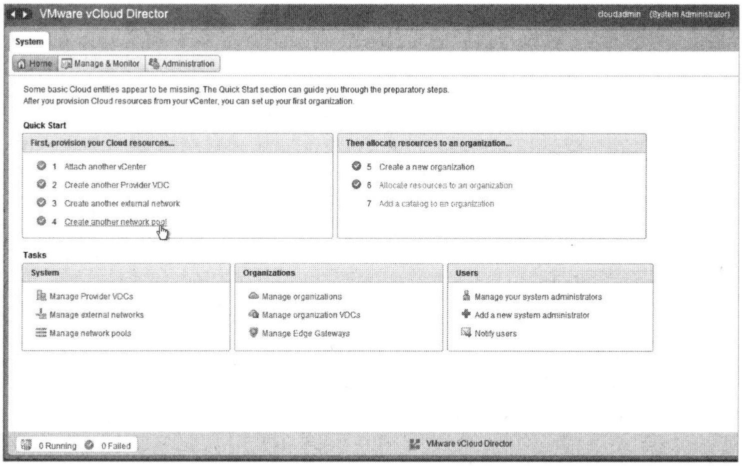

You need to specify how the network pool will be created on the vSphere layer. For the most appropriate choice here, refer to Chapter 5 for the various options and criteria. The three options are shown in Figure 8.38.

**FIGURE 8.38**
Network pool types

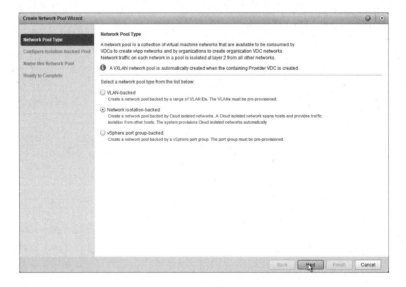

In this example, you are going to create a vCloud Director Network Isolation (VCNI)-backed network pool, a pool of virtualized and isolated Layer 2 networks that are encapsulated inside a physical transport VLAN between vSphere hosts in your PvDCs.

You will need a dvSwitch to use this setting. In our example resource pod shown in Figure 8.1, you have all the vSphere internal communications (HA, vCenter, vMotion traffic, etc.) going through a separate DVS with its own physical uplinks called vSphereInternal.

**NOTE**    This is a separate DVS from the one that carried virtual machine traffic to and from the datacenter (CorpDatacenterNetwork) and secure networks (HighSecurityNetwork).

You'll create a pool of 500 vCloud Director networks, all of which will be encapsulated inside a single physical VLAN. You'll recall from Chapter 5 that this process has some physical network requirements. You must increase the MTU size for all uplink ports attached to the vSphereInternal DVS and ensure that the transport VLAN you specify in Figure 8.39 is valid and configured on the physical switch interfaces to all hosts in your cluster. Otherwise, cross-host communications using VCNI will fail.

You'll appreciate that the ability to create 500 (and up to 1000 per VCNI pool) isolated Layer 2 networks, and only having to ask your networks team for a single physical VLAN is a powerful feature.

You're asked to give the network pool a name. To simplify troubleshooting and maintenance, it's advisable to specify the VLAN ID in the name. Click Next and you are shown a summary screen (Figure 8.40). Click Finish to complete the wizard.

Now this task is complete. You'll see that the first part of the wizard is done. You now have a single PvDC with a connection to the corporate datacenter network, as well as a pool of virtual networks ready to be allocated.

**FIGURE 8.39**
Configuring the quantity of vCloud isolated networks and specifying the transport VLAN ID

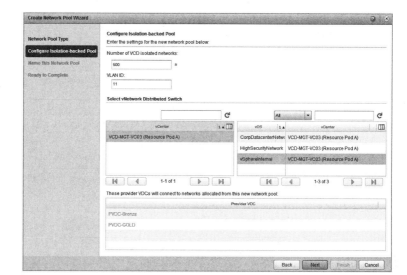

**FIGURE 8.40**
Creating VCNI network pool summary screen

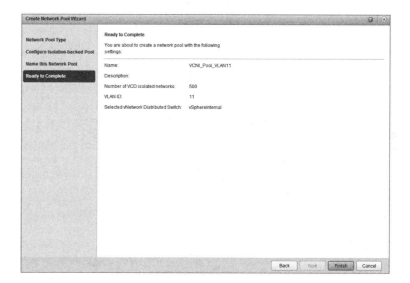

# Creating an Organization

In a private cloud setting, an organization is likely to map to a business unit, department, or division. Each organization has its own suballocation of resources from one or more PvDCs, which are known as Org vDCs.

An organization is an authentication boundary for your consumers. Each organization can have individual settings for authentication and authorization.

In addition to providing a standalone list of users, an organization in vCloud Director can be configured to integrate with an LDAP directory like Microsoft Active Directory to use a common authentication source for your consumers. You cannot create a hierarchy of organizations in vCloud Director—they are all equal—but you can apply roles and permissions to user accounts and groups associated with an organization.

Only the system administrator can create organizations, but during creation a user is nominated to be the administrator of each organization (known as an organization administrator). They can subsequently create further user accounts or reconfigure authentication.

In this example, you'll create an organization called IT. It will own and share various template and master image vApps for other organizations to consume as well as run its own production vApps. You can create this organization from the Home screen on the vCloud Director interface, as shown in Figure 8.41.

**FIGURE 8.41**
Choose Create A
New Organization

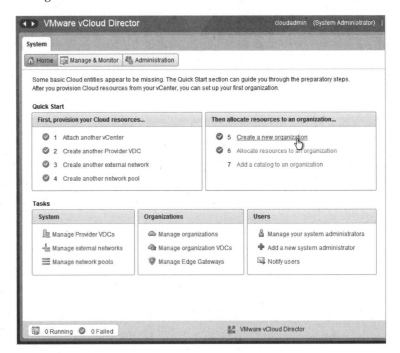

When prompted, enter some descriptive information for your new organization. You cannot use a space or nonalphanumeric character in the organization name, but you can in the organization full name (which equates to a display name).

Some security-conscious organizations prefer to specify a number or something that isn't obviously guessable for the organization name. This would result in an ambiguous URL like `https://vcloud.vinf.net/cloud/org/9022145X`. As there is no way of obtaining a master list of configured organizations available unless you are logged on as a system administrator, this makes it harder for attackers to guess default logon URLs.

**NOTE**    The default organization URL is derived from the organization name you enter. Your consumers will use this to log on to the vCloud Director interface. You cannot change the organization name after the organization has been created. The organization URL cannot be customized after the vCloud FQDN and will always be in this form: `https://<vCloud FQDN>/cloud/org/<Organization Name>`.

Naming the department IT results in the settings shown in Figure 8.42. Click Next to continue.

**FIGURE 8.42**
Naming an
organization

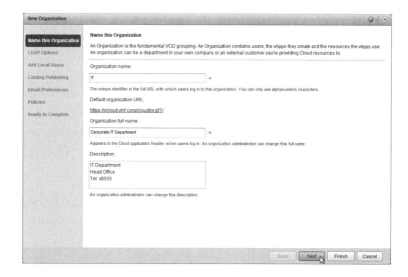

In this example, you'll point this organization at Active Directory for authentication and provide a distinguished name (DN) that maps to an OU in the vinf.corp Active Directory, as shown in Figure 8.43.

**FIGURE 8.43**
Object location in
Active Directory

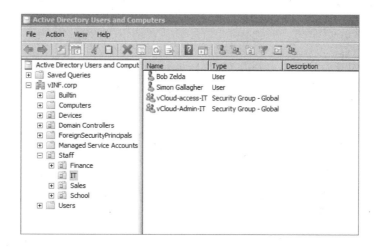

You'll recall that you configured the system LDAP service to point at the vinf.corp Active Directory. You now need to specify which organizational unit (OU) in the directory contains users and groups that are associated with this new vCloud organization. In this example, you specify the DN of the IT OU in Active Directory, as shown in Figure 8.44.

**FIGURE 8.44**
Configuring LDAP
options

You are advised to create at least one local user. In practice this is a private cloud implementation and isn't generally required. The system administrator will still be able to log on if Active Directory is unavailable and so could potentially override such settings if required due to a long-term Active Directory failure. Therefore, you can skip this step.

In our example organization, the IT department will be providing standard operating system install media and VM builds for use by consumers. So you can select the Allow Publishing Catalogs To All Organizations option, as shown in Figure 8.45. For most other organizations in our private cloud, this isn't likely to be required and can be left at the default; the setting can be changed by the system administrator if required at a later date.

**FIGURE 8.45**
Catalog publishing
options for a new
organization

You next see a set of email preferences, as shown in Figure 8.46. Enter SMTP server details for email notifications from vCloud Director if they differ from the system settings, but bear in mind that the communication is initiated from the vCloud Director cell servers to the SMTP relay you specify. That means you need to ensure there is a network path through any firewalls or routers and that authentication is correctly configured on both ends.

**FIGURE 8.46**
Setting email preferences

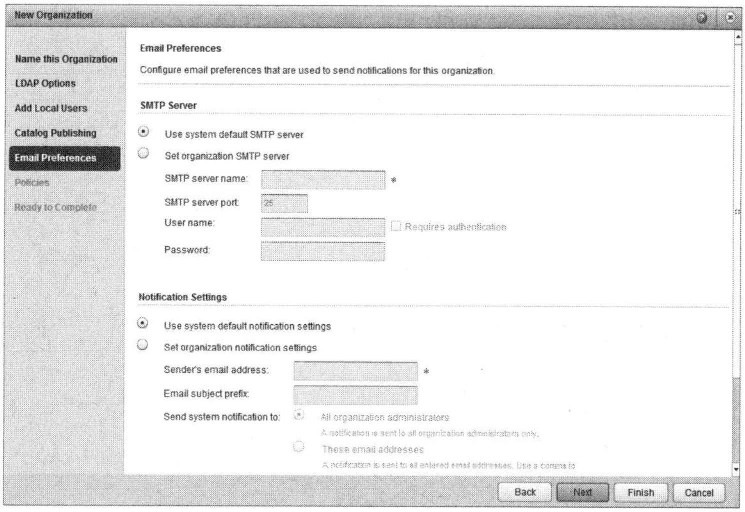

In this example, the IT department is part of the vinf.corp Active Directory, so you will use the system default SMTP server, which will accept email for @vinf.corp email addresses.

Next, you are prompted to set policy information for the organization that you are creating, relating to how long consumers within this organization are allowed to consume resources. This is known as a *lease*.

You can set appropriate options for this organization by choosing from the list. The system defaults are sensible for most use cases (Figure 8.47).

**FIGURE 8.47**
Specifying policies for the new organization

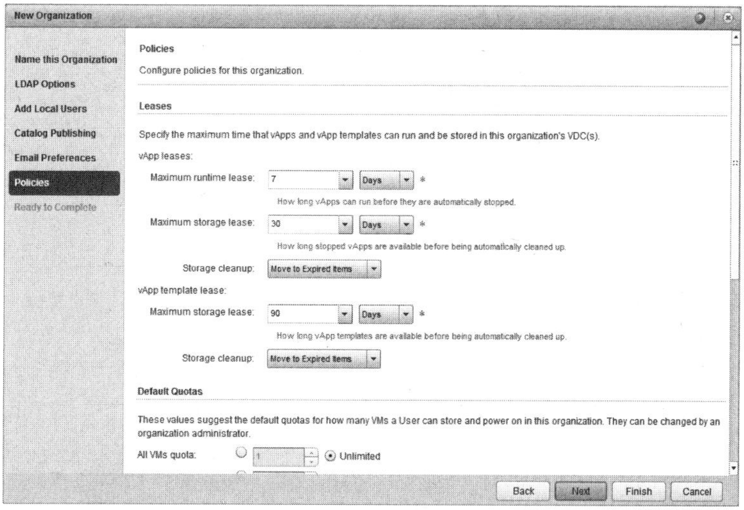

A number of policy settings are available on a per-user basis. You'll typically have to scroll down to see all of them, as shown in Figure 8.48.

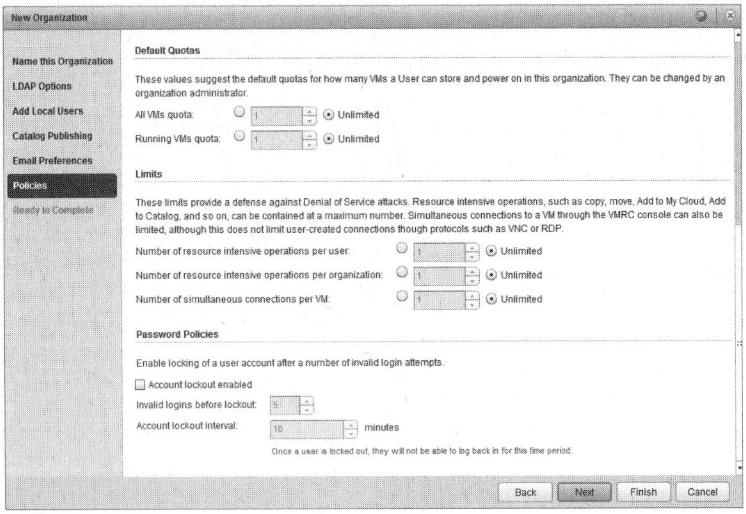

**FIGURE 8.48**
Organization
policies: quotas and
limits

Although leases control the duration for which resources can be consumed, quotas and limits are useful settings to control the amount of resources individual consumers can use at a given point in time.

The password policies apply only to vCloud Director authentication. If you are using an external LDAP source, the settings should be those enforced by the external LDAP source.

You are shown a summary screen (Figure 8.49). Once you click Finish, the organization will be created and ready for use.

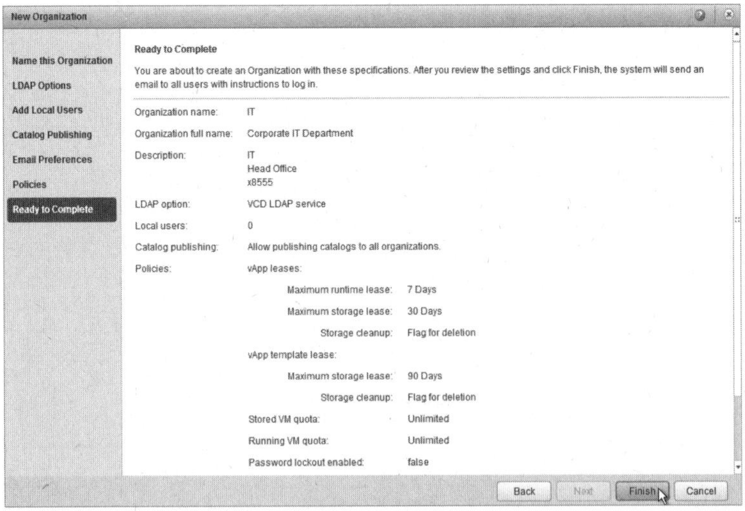

**FIGURE 8.49**
You're ready to
create the IT
organization

Once the organization is created in this way, only the system administrator will be able to log on. Although the LDAP source was configured, the wizard does not allow any users to use vCloud Director by default. To allow this, you must navigate to the organization in the vCloud Director interface by clicking Manage Organizations on the Home screen or by using the Manage & Monitor tab and selecting Organizations.

Once you have opened the IT organization (as denoted by the new IT tab at the top of the screen), navigate to Members, select Groups, and then click Import Groups, as shown in Figure 8.50.

**FIGURE 8.50**
Importing an LDAP group to an organization after creation

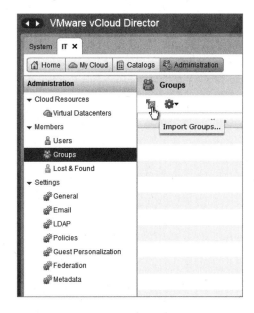

In this example, you'll enable a group called vCloud-admin-IT for organization administrators in vCloud, as shown in Figure 8.51.

**FIGURE 8.51**
Importing an LDAP group for an organization

Using groups is the most efficient approach for managing access to vCloud resources. As part of normal Active Directory management, you can add and remove users from groups, rather than directly configuring vCloud Director.

You can follow the same process to enable other users and groups to use this vCloud organization.

## Creating an Organization Virtual Datacenter

Each organization is configured with one or more Org vDCs. Each Org vDC has an allocation model, which determines how it can consume resources from the underlying PvDCs it is configured to use.

In this example, you're going to create the first of several Org vDCs to represent different levels of service that you are making available to each organization in our example vCloud implementation.

**Production**   Resources in the Gold service tier are consumed and allocated using the Allocation Pool model within vCloud Director. Each Org vDC is given a fixed allocation of CPU and memory with a minimum percentage of those resources being guaranteed. They have the ability to consume extra resources from the cluster up to the allocation if they are available (commonly known as bursting).

**Development**   Resources in the Bronze service tier are consumed on a Pay-As-You-Go allocation model. The primary use case here is test and development, so a low resource guarantee is given and resources are allocated on a first-come, first-served basis until they are exhausted or further capacity is added.

**High-Security**   Like the Gold service tier, the Secure service tier is intended for production services and is configured for the Allocation Pool model within vCloud Director, but it runs on isolated computing and network resources and dedicated storage with array-level encryption.

The sales organization is an exception to this convention and has a single Org vDC configured to use the reservation pool model for its production workload.

In the previous step, you created the first organization to represent the IT department, and you are ready to allocate resources to it. This allocation of resources creates the Org vDC. As shown in Figure 8.52, click Allocate Resources To An Organization.

Select the organization you are going to be adding resources to. In this example we have a single organization, IT, as shown in Figure 8.53.

Figure 8.54 shows how you choose where these resources will be allocated from. In this example, you'll be allocating resources from the PvDC-Gold PvDC that we created earlier. Notice that if you hover your mouse over each PvDC you'll see a note showing the description of each PvDC as a reminder of what has been set.

**FIGURE 8.52**
Allocating resources

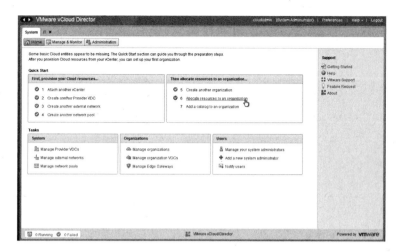

**FIGURE 8.53**
Choosing the
organization

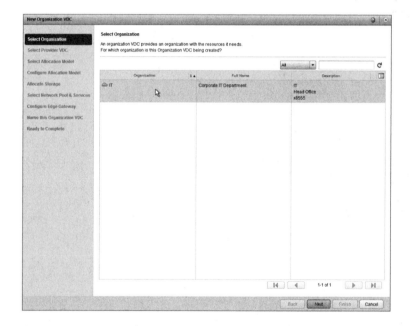

**FIGURE 8.54**

Selecting the PvDC to allocate resources from

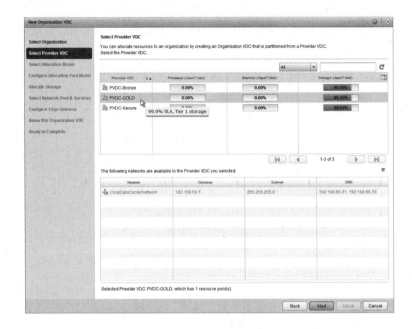

## CONFIGURING THE RESOURCE MODEL

Each Org vDC that you deploy can be configured with one of three allocation models. Each allocation model determines how resources are allocated from the PvDC. Settings within an allocation model can be adjusted by the system administrator. An Org vDC cannot be changed to a different allocation model once the Org vDC has been created. If you need to change the model, the only option is to delete and re-create it.

Only the system administrator can configure the allocation model settings for an Org vDC. Organization administrators can only work with what they have been granted.

In the following examples you'll learn how to configure each of the three allocation models and Org vDCs. See the following mapping of resource models to the Org vDCs.

| Organization vDC | Allocation model in use |
| --- | --- |
| ORG-vDC-IT-Production | Allocation Pool |
| ORG-vDC-IT-Development | Pay-As-You-Go |
| ORG-vDC-Sales-Production | Reservation Pool |

The overall service level on offer to consumers is determined by the PvDC, which defines base performance, availability, and capacity characteristics, and by the Org vDC, which defines how much of that resource is guaranteed from the PvDC (see Figure 8.55).

**FIGURE 8.55**
How provider and Org vDCs define a service level to consumers

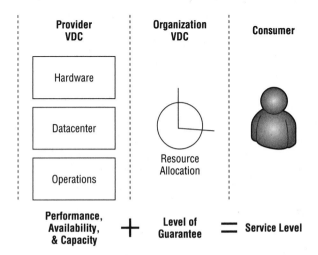

The allocation model you configure determines the level of resource oversubscription that will apply to vApps deployed into this Org vDC. As such, you are defining the last part of the performance service level for consumer vApps that are deployed into this Org vDC.

### Configuring the Allocation Pool Model

In this example you'll deploy our PvDC using the Allocation Pool allocation model for the Org vDC called ORG-vDC-IT-Production. Your choice here will depend on your specific solution design and service offering.

Figure 8.56 shows the elements involved in building the ORG-vDC-IT-Production Org vDC. The Internal DVS is part of the back-end transport for VCNI and underlying cluster functionality like vMotion and management. Thus it is not specifically highlighted as part of Figure 8.56.

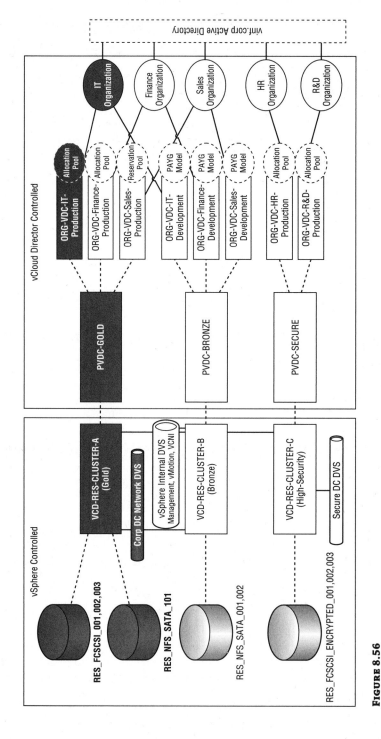

**Figure 8.56**

ORG-vDC-IT-Production elements

When prompted, choose the Allocation Pool allocation model, as shown in Figure 8.57.

**FIGURE 8.57**

Choosing an allocation model

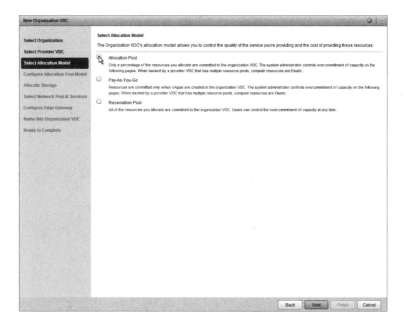

Use vSphere Client to look at the physical properties of the cluster that the PvDC-Gold object represents, as shown in Figure 8.58. Note that there are resources consisting of 16 GHz of CPU and 64 GB of RAM provided from four hosts that comprise the VCD-RES-CLUSTER-A (Gold) cluster in vSphere.

**FIGURE 8.58**

Physical properties of the cluster that backs PvDC-Gold PvDC: 16 GHz of CPU and 64 GB of RAM (1 failover host)

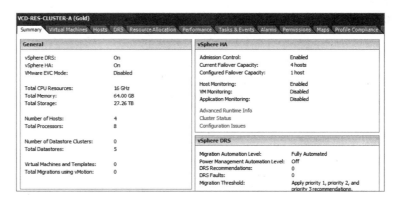

But on the Resource Allocation tab shown in Figure 8.59, you can see that slightly fewer resources are available to vCloud Director. This is because of the one dedicated failover (N+1) host setting that has been configured for HA in this cluster. This leaves fewer overall resources available for consumption.

**FIGURE 8.59**

Cluster resource allocation, factoring in HA overhead

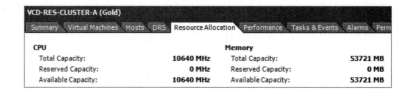

You are prompted to configure the Allocation Pool model for this Org vDC, as shown in Figure 8.60. The Allocation Pool model is most commonly found in production environments, where it provides a minimum guaranteed level of service with some "burst" capability.

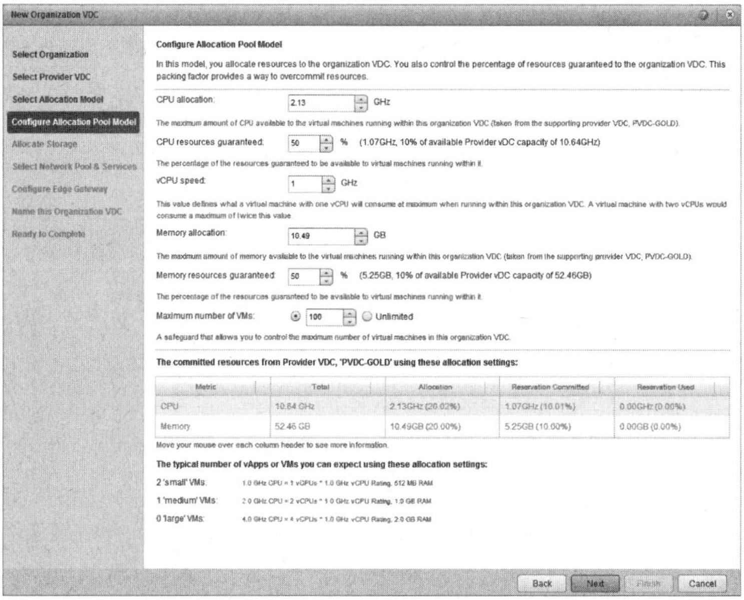

**FIGURE 8.60**

Options available when configuring an Org vDC with the Allocation Pool model

In this example you have a small PvDC from which to allocate resources. The default options reserve a large amount of infrastructure.

The CPU Allocation value specifies how many CPU resources (expressed in GHz) from the PvDC are to be allocated to this Org vDC.

In the example shown in Figure 8.61, you'll specify that you want to allocate 8 GHz for VMs to the IT department's Production Org vDC. The IT department needs only low-usage VMs for running domain controllers and DNS servers. You'll then define what percentage of this maximum CPU allocation is to be guaranteed to those VMs. Prior to vCloud Director 5.1 this percentage was the amount of CPU reserved on the resource pool. However, as of vCloud Director 5.1 that's no longer the case. The amount is still reserved on the resource pool, but it is calculated based on the VM vCPU Count, vCPU Speed, and Reservation settings. A cumulative total for all VMs is then used to define the resource pool reservation.

In this example, you know the IT department production workload is low usage, so you'll set a low resource guaranteee of 20 percent and define a vCPU speed of 1 GHz.

You'll notice that the dialog box automatically calculates how much physical resource this allocation will consume from the PvDC. You are going to allocate 15 percent of the overall available CPU capacity on the PvDC for this Org vDC, leaving 85 percent available for other Org vDCs or as capacity for the IT department to consume if needed.

**FIGURE 8.61**
CPU allocation
settings

| | |
|---|---|
| CPU allocation: | 8 GHz |
| *The maximum amount of CPU available to the virtual machines running within this organization VDC (taken from the supporting provider VDC, PVDC-GOLD).* | |
| CPU resources guaranteed: | 20 % (1.60GHz, 15% of available Provider vDC capacity of 10.64GHz) |
| *The percentage of the resources guaranteed to be available to virtual machines running within it.* | |
| vCPU speed: | 1 GHz |
| *This value defines what a virtual machine with one vCPU will consume at maximum when running within this organization VDC. A virtual machine with two vCPUs would consume a maximum of twice this value.* | |

Likewise, in Figure 8.62 you set similar values for the Memory allocation in the IT department production Org vDC. You allocate the IT department a maximum "pool" of 10 GB of RAM for its VMs, but you guarantee that only 40 percent is allocated for its exclusive use.

**FIGURE 8.62**
Memory allocation
values in an
Org vDC

| | |
|---|---|
| Memory allocation: | 10 GB |
| *The maximum amount of memory available to the virtual machines running within this organization VDC (taken from the supporting provider VDC, PVDC-GOLD).* | |
| Memory resources guaranteed: | 40 % (4.00GB, 8% of available Provider vDC capacity of 52.46GB) |
| *The percentage of the resources guaranteed to be available to virtual machines running within it.* | |

In the Allocation Pool model, everything over the guarantee values is unreserved capacity, which can be used to "burst" but is shared with other consumers. This allows you to provide a guaranteed minimum level of service in terms of memory availability while allowing consumers to use additional resources if they are available in the PvDC. This configuration results in an estimate at the bottom of the dialog box that shows how many typical vApps or VMs your consumers will be able to create inside this Org vDC (Figure 8.63).

**FIGURE 8.63**
Burst capacity
provided in the
Allocation Pool
model

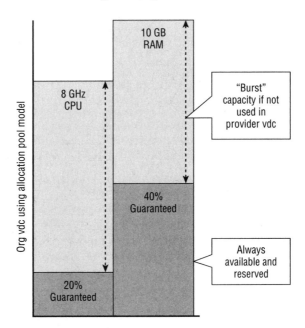

Note that from a total pool of 10.64 GHz of CPU and 52.46 GB of RAM, 8 GHz of CPU is allocated from the PvDC (which represents 75.19 percent of the overall physical capacity), but only 15.04 percent of that is reserved and thus guaranteed for consumers.

Likewise, you see that 19.06 percent of physical memory resources in the PvDC are allocated to this Org vDC, but only 4 GB (7.62 percent) of those physical resources are guaranteed.

Finally, Figure 8.64 shows that you can configure a maximum number of VMs that can be deployed into this Org vDC. This setting isn't commonly used in the Allocation Pool model; you are providing an allocation of resources for your consumers, and generally the amount of available resources is the controlling factor in determining how many VMs can be deployed. However, it may make sense to do so in other allocation models.

**FIGURE 8.64**

Controlling the maximum number of VMs allowed in an Org vDC

> Maximum number of VMs: ⦿ 100 ⬍ ◯ Unlimited
>
> A safeguard that allows you to control the maximum number of virtual machines in this organization VDC.

A summary (see Figure 8.65) is provided at the bottom of the page, which shows how many resources are allocated vs. the amount reserved for your consumer workloads. It provides an estimate of the number of typical vApps or VMs that you will be able to run within your Org vDC using the configured settings. These values are calculated dynamically as you adjust the settings so that you can see the impact of specific settings before committing to them.

**FIGURE 8.65**

Committed resources from PvDC-Gold, showing how much is reserved and allocated

The committed resources from Provider VDC, 'PVDC-GOLD' using these allocation settings:

| Metric | Total | Allocation | Reservation Committed | Reservation Used |
| --- | --- | --- | --- | --- |
| CPU | 10.64 GHz | 8.00GHz (75.19%) | 1.60GHz (15.04%) | 0.00GHz (0.00%) |
| Memory | 52.46 GB | 10.00GB (19.06%) | 4.00GB (7.62%) | 0.00GB (0.00%) |

Move your mouse over each column header to see more information.

The typical number of vApps or VMs you can expect using these allocation settings:

| 8 'small' VMs: | 1.0 GHz CPU = 1 vCPUs * 1.0 GHz vCPU Rating, 512 MB RAM |
| 4 'medium' VMs: | 2.0 GHz CPU = 2 vCPUs * 1.0 GHz vCPU Rating, 1.0 GB RAM |
| 2 'large' VMs: | 4.0 GHz CPU = 4 vCPUs * 1.0 GHz vCPU Rating, 2.0 GB RAM |

This example is representative of a workload that can benefit from occasionally consuming a lot of CPU resource if it is available but does not rely on it for day-to-day functionality. It is likely to consume little of the physical resource on a day-to-day basis, so you can be comfortable in oversubscribing the CPU resources heavily in this manner.

This demonstrates how you can define this level of oversubscription when allocating resources to an organization, but the organization administrator does not have control of this in the Allocation Pool model.

### Configuring the Org vDC for the Pay-As-You-Go Model

In this example you will be looking at the settings required to use the Pay-As-You-Go allocation model. In our sample vCloud Director environment, this allocation model will be used by the ORG-vDC-IT-Development Org vDC, which consumes the physical resources shown in Figure 8.66.

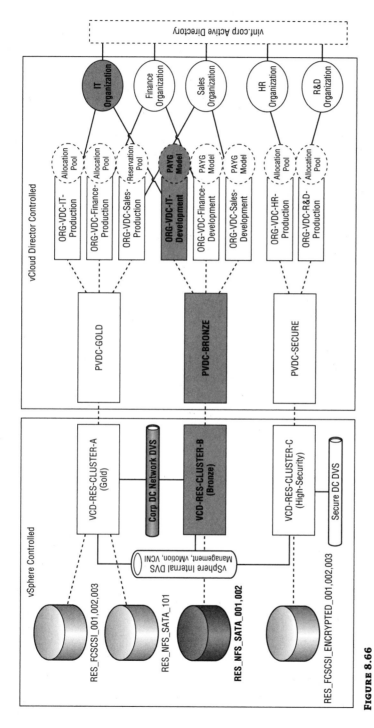

**FIGURE 8.66**

Resources consumed by the ORG-vDC-IT-Development Org vDC

Follow the same process to create another Org vDC, but when prompted to choose the allocation model, select Pay-As-You-Go, as shown in Figure 8.67.

**FIGURE 8.67**

Selecting the Pay-As-You-Go allocation model

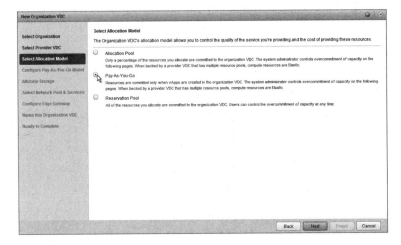

Next, you are shown the various options for configuring how resources are allocated in the Pay-As-You-Go allocation model, as illustrated in Figure 8.68.

**FIGURE 8.68**

Pay-As-You-Go allocation model options

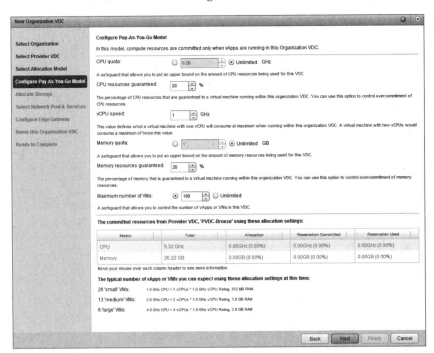

Pay-As-You-Go operates on a per-VM basis. Rather than creating a pool of finite capacity as in the Allocation and Reservation Pool models, it creates a resource pool whose size is derived from a cumulative total of VM resources.

Resources are committed in the Org vDC only when the vApp is started. As such it is treated as an infinite pool of resources to your consumers, while still being constrained by the limits of the resources available in the underlying PvDC.

CPU Quota, Memory Quota, and Maximum Number Of VMs settings can be applied to control the maximum amount of resources that this Org vDC consumes before it runs out of resources, or they can be set to unlimited. If they are set to unlimited, consumers can create vApps until the resources are physically exhausted. Pay careful attention to the amount of resources consumed to ensure there is sufficient capacity provided to meet demand. However, each organization does have to be configured with an allocation of resources (which they may or may not use). Pay-As-You-Go is most commonly found in development or hybrid/auto-scaling environments, where there are highly variable numbers of VMs on a day-to-day basis.

The Pay-As-You-Go model allows you to define a standard unit of computing in terms of a maximum CPU speed, expressed in GHz per vCPU with a level of resources guarantee. For example, Figure 8.69 shows a standard maximum unit of allocation of 1 GHz per vCPU with 20 percent guaranteed (0.2 GHz). This setting allows for fairly high levels of overcommitment of CPU resources. Likewise, similar settings can be applied for memory (Figure 8.70).

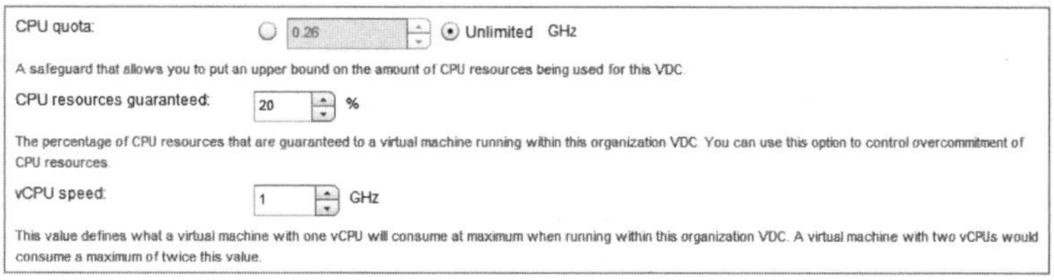

**FIGURE 8.69**
CPU settings in Pay-As-You-Go model

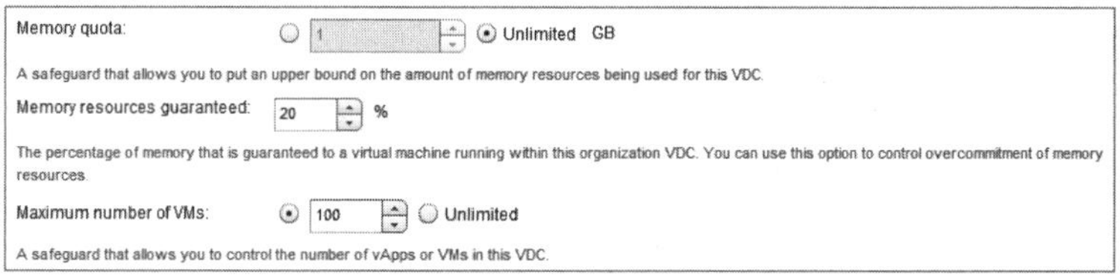

**FIGURE 8.70**
Memory settings in Pay-As-You-Go model

The wizard computes the typical number of VMs that could be deployed if you use this allocation model (Figure 8.71).

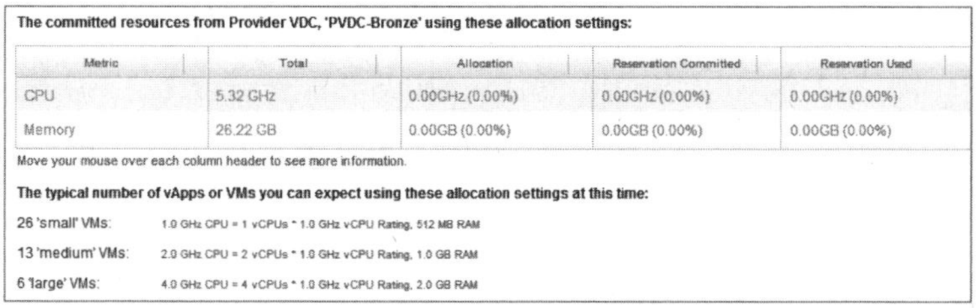

**FIGURE 8.71**
Committed resources in Pay-As-You-Go model

The committed resources from Provider VDC, 'PVDC-Bronze' using these allocation settings:

| Metric | Total | Allocation | Reservation Committed | Reservation Used |
|---|---|---|---|---|
| CPU | 5.32 GHz | 0.00GHz (0.00%) | 0.00GHz (0.00%) | 0.00GHz (0.00%) |
| Memory | 26.22 GB | 0.00GB (0.00%) | 0.00GB (0.00%) | 0.00GB (0.00%) |

Move your mouse over each column header to see more information.

The typical number of vApps or VMs you can expect using these allocation settings at this time:

26 'small' VMs:     1.0 GHz CPU = 1 vCPUs * 1.0 GHz vCPU Rating, 512 MB RAM

13 'medium' VMs:    2.0 GHz CPU = 2 vCPUs * 1.0 GHz vCPU Rating, 1.0 GB RAM

6 'large' VMs:      4.0 GHz CPU = 4 vCPUs * 1.0 GHz vCPU Rating, 2.0 GB RAM

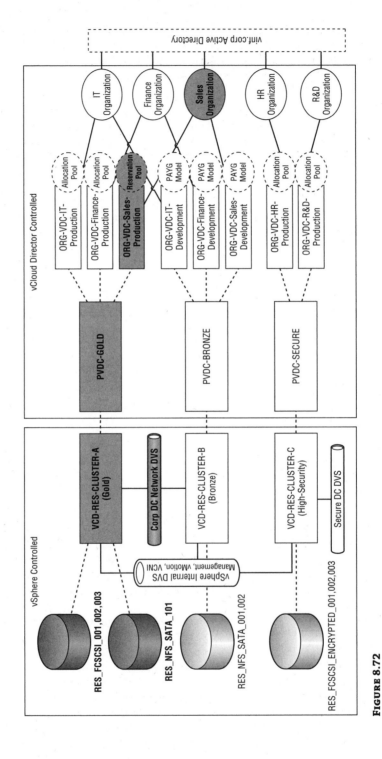

**FIGURE 8.72**

Resources that comprise the ORG-vDC-Sales-Production Org vDC

You'll notice in Figure 8.68 that unlike the Allocation and Reservation Pool models there is no allocation for the Pay-As-You-Go Org vDC. This is because resources from the PvDC are committed only when vApps are started and continue until resources are exhausted, at which point consumers will be prevented from starting further vApps.

### Configuring the Org vDC for the Reservation Pool Model

In this example you will be using the Reservation Pool allocation model for the ORG-vDC-Sales-Production Org vDC. This example Org vDC is designed to support workloads that require 100 percent guaranteed resources and the ability for individual consumers to control resource allocations for individual VMs. The Org vDC is constructed from the elements highlighted in Figure 8.72.

Follow the same process as in the previous examples to add another Org vDC. However, when prompted for the allocation model choose the Reservation Pool model, as shown in Figure 8.73.

**FIGURE 8.73**
Selecting the
Reservation Pool
allocation model

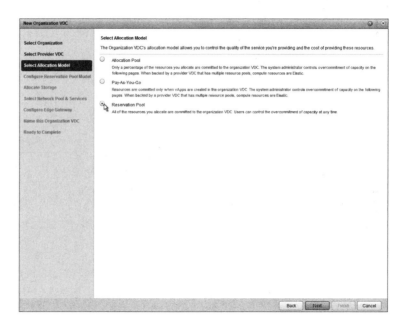

In this model, the Org vDC is allocated a fixed number of resources from the underlying PvDC. In the example shown in Figure 8.74, you'll allocate 8 GHz of CPU and 16 GB of RAM from the Gold PvDC.

This model is similar to the Allocation Pool model, except it enables the consumer to control commitment on a per-VM basis. If you look at the properties of a VM that resides in an Org vDC using the Reservation Pool model, as shown in Figure 8.75, you can see that the consumer can set the appropriate resource reservations for their own VMs. This option is not available for VMs running in Org vDCs using the Allocation Pool or Pay-As-You-Go allocation models.

There is no need for you to define a reservation level for the resources allocated to the Org vDC—all resources are 100 percent reserved in this model.

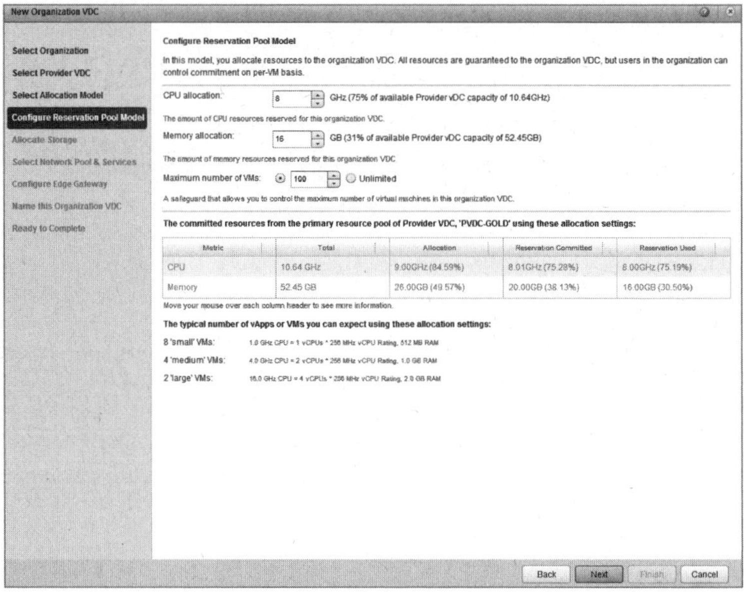

**FIGURE 8.74**
Reservation Pool
settings

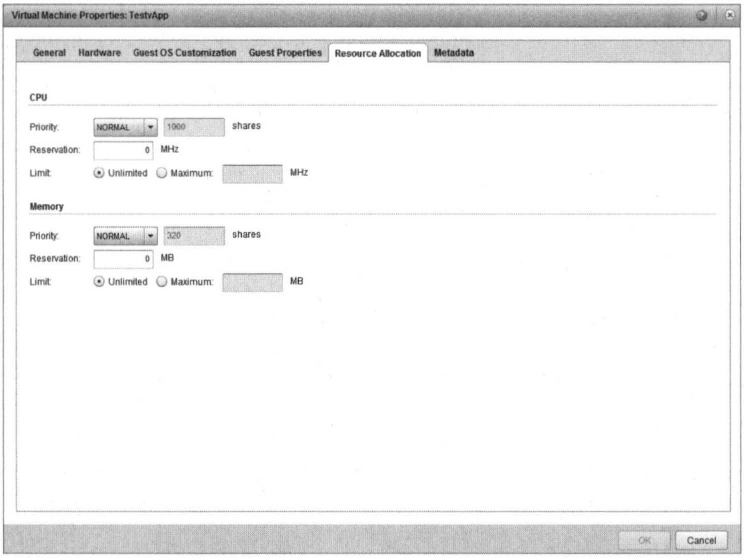

**FIGURE 8.75**
Setting individual
VM resource alloca-
tions when using
the Reservation
Pool model

The Reservation Pool model is one of the more expensive allocation models in vCloud Director because it dedicates physical resources to an Org vDC when it is created. This means those resources are not available to other organizations using the same underlying PvDC even if they are not being used.

The Reservation Pool model always guarantees resource availability to its consumers but allows the resource allocation of individual VMs to be delegated to consumers rather than being set at an Org vDC level.

## ALLOCATING STORAGE

Once you have configured your allocation model, you have a choice of how much storage you wish to allocate to your Org vDC and how it will be provisioned. This builds on the work you did earlier to define storage tiers using storage profiles and maps them to PvDCs.

In this example our Org vDC will be consuming Tier 1 storage that is presented to the PvDC-Gold PvDC. It is also possible to consume Tier 3 storage, but given that this Org vDC is intended for service production workloads, we will enable it to work only with Tier 1 storage.

As shown in Figure 8.76, a limit of 1 TB (1,000 GB) is set for this Org vDC. Thin-provisioning and fast-provisioning are also enabled.

**FIGURE 8.76**

Allocating storage to an Org vDC and setting a quota of 1000 GB

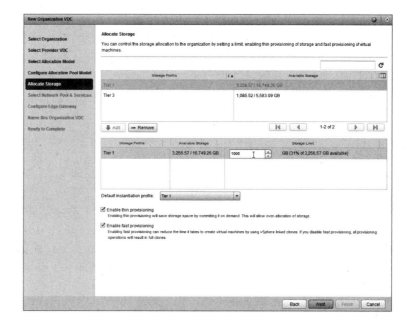

## ALLOCATING NETWORKS

The next step in the wizard allocates networks to your Org vDC. You are prompted to choose a network pool from which organization and vApp networks will be created. In this example you are using VCNI rather than VXLAN because the physical network does not yet support the system requirements of VXLAN. You must select the appropriate network pool from the drop-down box, as shown in Figure 8.77.

**FIGURE 8.77**

Selecting the network pool

You can specify a quota, as shown in Figure 8.78, which determines how many networks this organization is allowed to deploy from the pool. This will dictate the maximum number of Organization and vApp networks that can be configured in this Org vDC.

**FIGURE 8.78**

Specifying a
network quota

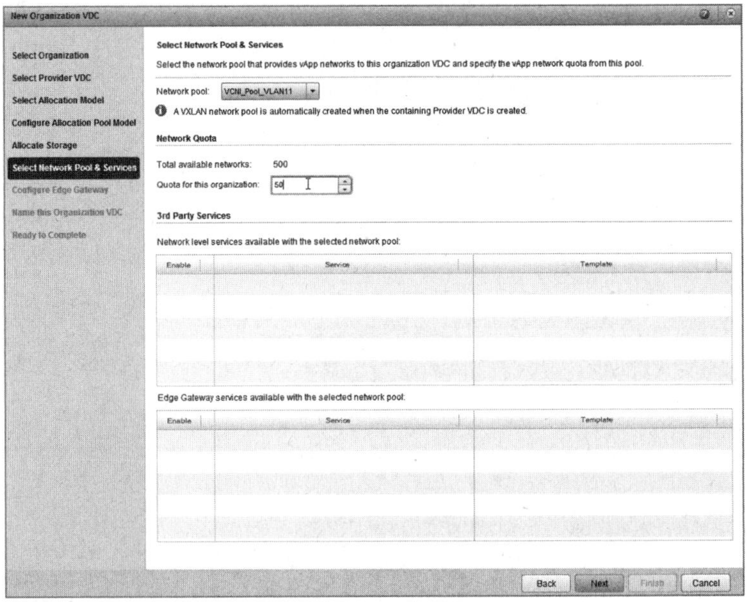

In this example you'll allocate a quota of 50 networks from this network pool. That means this organization can deploy up to 50 networks, which are allocated from the cloud-wide network pool of a possible 500.

In the next step, you are prompted to create a vCNS Edge Gateway. In this example the IT department vApps will be directly connected to the corporate WAN. We will look at the vCNS Edge Gateway later in this chapter; for now, choose to skip creating it at this time, as shown in Figure 8.79.

You are prompted to enter a name for the Org vDC you have just created. As shown in Figure 8.80, you are going to call it ORG-vDC-IT-Production, denoting that this is a virtual datacenter allocated to the IT organization that is capable of supporting production workloads.

**FIGURE 8.79**
Skip creating a
vCNS Edge Gateway
at this stage.

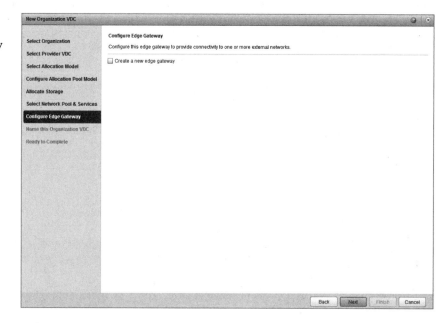

**FIGURE 8.80**
Naming the new
Org vDC

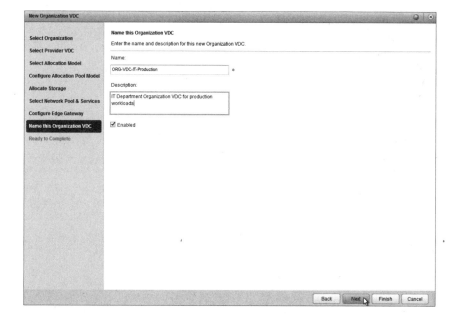

Using an easy-to-understand and consistent naming approach makes it easier for your consumers to determine the most appropriate place to deploy their workloads.

You can deselect the Enabled check box to configure the Org vDC without making it available to your consumers. This prevents your consumers from deploying workloads before the environment is fully configured.

Once you've checked all the details you have entered, click Finish to create the Org vDC in vCloud Director.

If you use the vSphere client to inspect the clusters that underpin the PvDC-Gold PvDC, you'll see that a resource pool object has been provisioned to represent the Org vDC you've created, as shown in Figure 8.81.

**FIGURE 8.81**
Newly created Org vDC as shown from vSphere Client

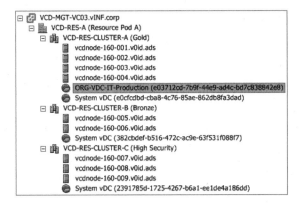

You have now created an organization that is a logical authentication and administrative boundary. You have also allocated and created an Org vDC that represents an allocation of physical computing, storage, and network resources from a PvDC.

## Connecting an Org vDC to the External Network

Now that you have created an Org vDC for the IT department, you need to provide a method of connecting to the corporate datacenter network. You can do so in one of two ways:

◆ Connect with an vCNS Edge Gateway

◆ Connect directly to an external network

As shown in Figure 8.82, you will be connecting the IT department directly to the external network. This is known as a direct Org vDC network. Later examples will show how the vCNS Edge Gateway can be used.

As the system administrator, you need to connect the Org vDC directly to the corporate datacenter network. This will allow the IT department to set up various shared services within the vCloud environment such as Active Directory and antimalware services.

From the Tasks section on the Home screen, click Manage Organization VDCs to browse the list of Org vDCs, as shown in Figure 8.83.

**FIGURE 8.82**
Direct Org vDC network

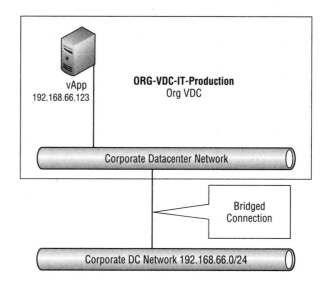

**FIGURE 8.83**
Choosing Manage Organization VDCs

Double-click on the ORG-vDC-IT-Production Org vDC you created in the previous step (Figure 8.84).

**FIGURE 8.84**
Administering Org vDCs

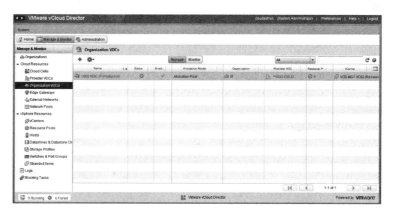

Select the Org vDC Networks tab. You'll note in Figure 8.84 that none have been defined yet. Click the green + symbol shown in Figure 8.85 to add a network. You are going to create an organization network that is directly connected to the CorpDatacenterNetwork.

**FIGURE 8.85**

Creating an external network

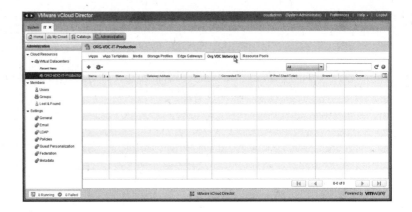

In this example we are going to create an external network that is directly connected (bridged) to the datacenter network. To do so, select Connect Directly To An External Network, as shown in Figure 8.86.

**FIGURE 8.86**

Creating a directly connected Org vDC network

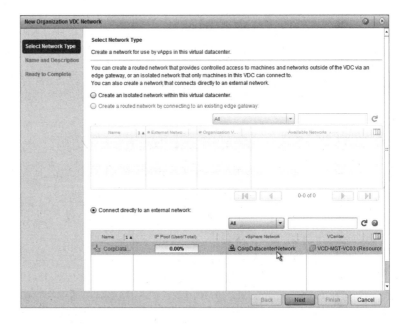

Enter a name for this organization network, as shown in Figure 8.87, and choose to share it with other Org vDCs that are created in the IT organization.

**FIGURE 8.87**
Naming the Org
vDC network

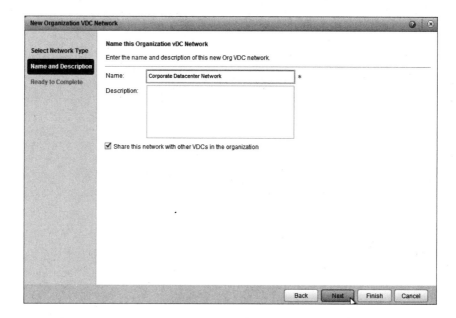

When you click Next, you are shown a summary screen (Figure 8.88) confirming that we are creating a direct Org vDC network connected to the CorpDatacenterNetwork external network. Click Finish to create the network. You'll then be able to review that the ORG-vDC-IT-Production Org vDC has a new Org vDC network added to it.

**FIGURE 8.88**
Direct Org vDC net-
work created within
the IT department
Org vDC

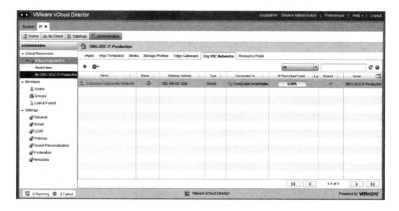

Our IT department now has a way of connecting vApps directly to the external corporate datacenter network so that vCloud-hosted vApps can participate directly on the corporate WAN.

## Creating a vCNS Edge Gateway

The previous example connected the Org vDC directly to the corporate datacenter network. This is fine for use cases where you want your vApps to be directly on the corporate network(s); however, one of the most powerful features of vCloud Director is its ability to create isolated vCloud networks. These can be used to provide isolated network segments, or network segments that have limited access to the corporate WAN, either to isolate particular traffic or as part of a strategy to reduce the number of IP addresses consumed on the corporate WAN.

Next you'll use a wizard that will allow our ORG-vDC-IT-Production Org vDC to connect to the external network via an vCNS Edge Gateway, as illustrated in Figure 8.89. At this stage the edge network is all you'll be configuring, but in Chapter 9, "Consuming Services," you'll create internal networks that use our vCNS Edge Gateway to connect to the corporate DC network.

**FIGURE 8.89**

vCNS Edge Gateway attached to our Org vDC

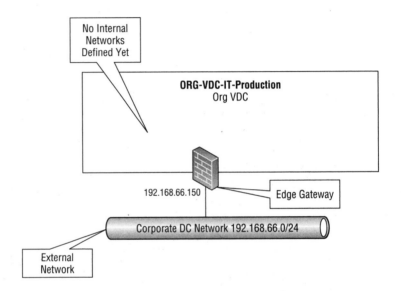

To enable the connectivity shown in Figure 8.89, you need to create an vCNS Edge Gateway. You do this for each Org vDC or external network that you are connecting to. You can create more than one vCNS Edge Gateway for an Org vDC if required.

As the system administrator, navigate to the Manage & Monitor tab, as shown in Figure 8.90, and open an Org vDC. In this example we will be adding a vCNS Edge Gateway to ORG-vDC-IT-Production.

Navigate to the vCNS Edge Gateways tab and click the green plus symbol to add a new vCNS Edge Gateway, as shown in Figure 8.91.

**FIGURE 8.90**
Opening the
Org vDC

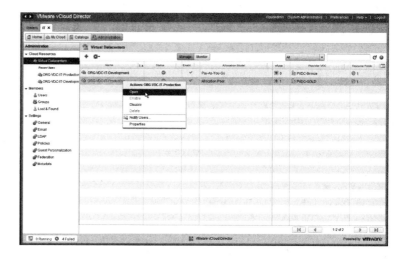

**FIGURE 8.91**
Adding a vCNS
Edge Gateway to an
Org vDC

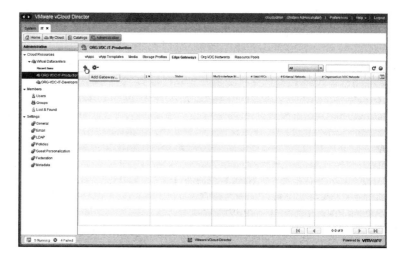

You'll be presented with a wizard, as shown in Figure 8.92. In this example you are building an vCNS Edge Gateway for a production Org vDC, so choose the Compact and Enable High Availability options. You will have the vCNS Edge Gateway's IP address assigned from the network pool, so leave Configure IP Settings unchecked. The remaining two options are not required to deploy the vCNS Edge Gateway and can be configured later if required.

**FIGURE 8.92**
vCNS Edge Gateway
configuration
settings

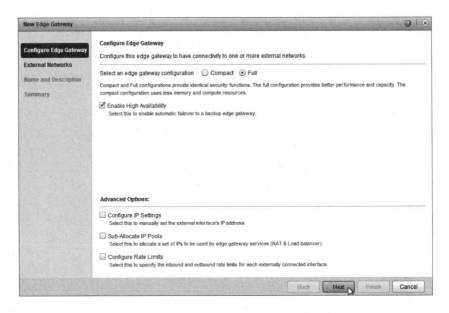

The wizard prompts for details of the external networks that this vCNS Edge Gateway will connect to. You will be connecting it to the CorpDatacenterNetwork, as shown in Figure 8.93, and using it to provide private network options within the Org vDC. One of the major new features of the vCNS Edge Gateway in vCloud Director 5.1 is its ability to support more than one network, which is a significant improvement over previous versions (which supported only two networks).

**FIGURE 8.93**
Configuring an
external network

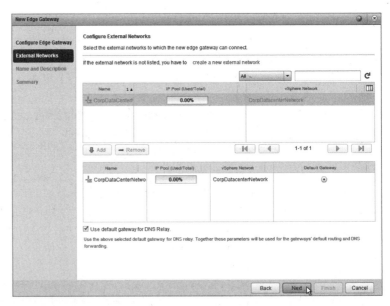

In this example, you'll be using the vCNS Edge Gateway to relay DNS requests to the corporate DNS servers that were configured as part of creating the external network earlier in this chapter. Enter a name and description for the vCNS Edge Gateway, as shown in Figure 8.94. Again, keeping a consistent naming scheme helps administrators and consumers understand what elements are connected to what.

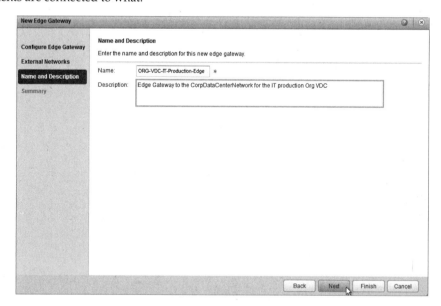

When you click Finish to complete the configuration, vCloud Director communicates with the vCNS Manager to deploy a vCNS Edge Gateway appliance and configure it with connections to the appropriate networks. You can see the IP address that it has been allocated by browsing the properties of the vCNS Edge Gateway and looking at the Configure IP settings tab.

The default configuration has the vCNS Edge Gateway firewall configured to drop all traffic. If you want to test connectivity by pinging it, you'll need to create a firewall rule via the Firewall tab to enable this traffic, as shown in Figure 8.95.

Browse to the Firewall tab and click Add to create a new firewall rule to allow ICMP traffic (Figure 8.96).

**FIGURE 8.95**

Choosing vCNS
Edge Gateway
Services

**FIGURE 8.96**
Adding a rule to
allow ICMP ping
traffic to the vCNS
Edge Gateway

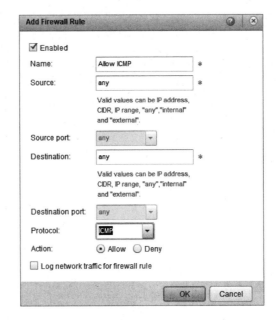

## Creating an Initial Service Catalog

By this point, as the cloud administrator, you have completed the base build tasks of the vCloud platform. You've allocated resources, connected them to external networks, and created one or more organizations to represent your consumers.

At this stage your initial consumers are likely to be the organization administrators of the various organizations you've implemented in your vCloud platform. Because of the way control is delegated to these organization administrators, they can then configure who is able to access each organization and create whatever catalogs, templates, and configurations they require.

Now it's time to let them use the service. One of the key attributes of cloud computing is self-service, so in that spirit you can provide the URL to each organization and they should be able to log on using the directory source (which you defined earlier) to authenticate. From there, your consumers can create vApps, catalogs, and so on, and can deploy services.

### Creating a Public Catalog

Our IT organization will be maintaining a number of standard operating system images and installation media for use and customization by consumers within other organizations such as sales and finance. In this section you'll import installation media in the form of ISO files. You'll also import existing VMs from vCenter Server in OVF format. To do so, you'll create a catalog owned by IT but published to other organizations in your vCloud Director deployment.

If other organizations wish to use items published in a public catalog, the organization administrators of each respective organization can copy the items to a local catalog and allow consumers to deploy from there. Consumers are unable to deploy directly from a public catalog.

You should note that media files are also associated with a particular Org vDC. Although you can copy media from a public catalog to a local catalog in order to mount those media files from VMs in an Org vDC, you need to copy them to each Org vDC.

To achieve this, you'll log on to the vCloud Director portal as the IT organization (itadmin), rather than the system administrator account (cloudadmin), as shown in Figure 8.97. To do so, you must use an organization-specific URL that was generated when the organization was created—in this case, `https://vcloud.vinf.corp/cloud/org/IT/`.

**FIGURE 8.97**
Log on to vCloud
Director as itadmin

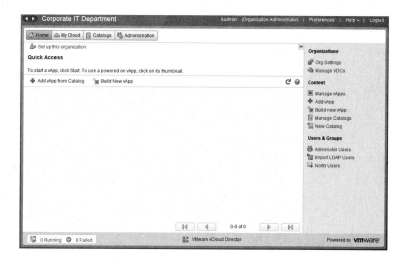

**NOTE**    The last part of the URL is the organization name. If you are unsure what this should be, you can define it as part of the creation of the organization.

Your first task for the IT organization will be to create a catalog that you can publish as a public catalog that other organizations in our company can download from. Select the Catalogs tab and then click the green plus button to add a catlog, as shown in Figure 8.98.

**FIGURE 8.98**
Creating a
catalog in the IT
organization

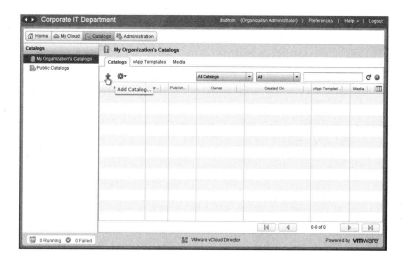

As shown in Figure 8.99, a wizard launches that lets you create a new catalog. Name the catalog **IT Department Standard Builds** and provide a description for consumers when they are browsing this catalog.

**FIGURE 8.99**
Naming a catalog

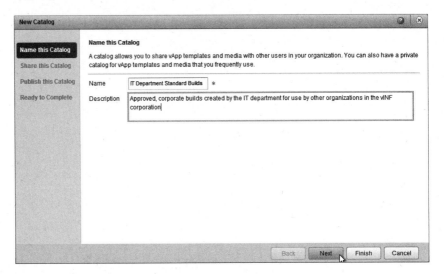

Next you must select who you want to share this catalog with. You want to create a public catalog that will be accessible to all organizations, but you want only members of the IT department to be able to create and delete catalog entries. Therefore, click Add Members and choose to share with everyone in the organization (in this case, the IT organization) with Read/Write access, as shown in Figure 8.100.

Next you are given the option to publish the catalog with other organizations. Your intention is to create a public catalog, so choose Publish To All Organizations, as shown in Figure 8.101.This is a binary setting so you can only make the catalog available to all organizations or none.

**NOTE**  This screen will not be shown if you did not grant permissions to publish catalogs when you created the organization.

You should now see the IT Department Standard Builds catalog in your list of catalogs (see Figure 8.102). Other organizations will be able to see it as a public catalog (see Figure 8.103).

**FIGURE 8.100**
Granting all members of the IT organization full control of the new catalog

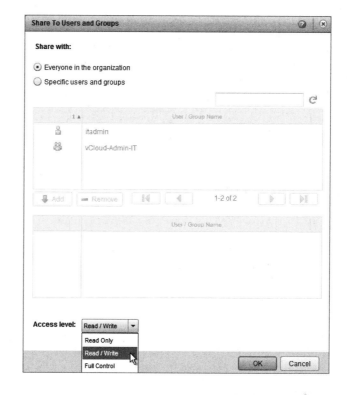

**FIGURE 8.101**
Publishing a catalog to all organizations in vCloud Director

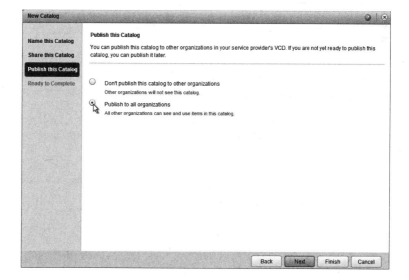

**FIGURE 8.102**
Catalog view within the IT organization

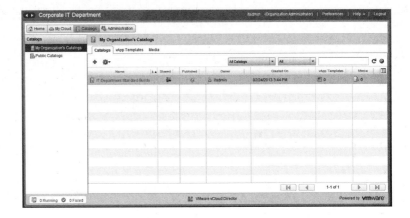

**FIGURE 8.103**
Public catalog created by the IT organization as viewed from the sales organization

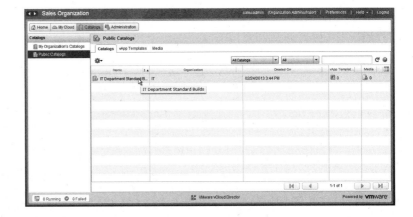

Your IT department has now defined a public catalog that is visible from other organizations within your vCloud Director platform. The next step is to populate that catalog with media and VMs.

## Uploading Media to vCloud Director

First, you'll import operating system installation media in ISO format. This allows the IT team to easily mount an installation disc image to an existing VM within the vCloud Director interface.

As the system administrator, you can also build VMs in vCenter and then import them into vCloud Director, but organization administrators cannot.

Select the Media tab to view the media section of the catalog. Then click the Upload icon, as shown in Figure 8.104.

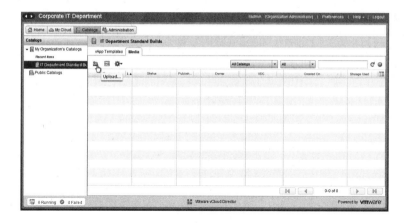

The file upload feature uses a Java applet. If you get the error shown in Figure 8.105, you do not have an appropriate Java Runtime Environment (JRE) on your administrative workstation, and you'll need to download and install one before you can proceed.

If you click on the blue text, you'll be redirected to download an appropriate Java Runtime Environment (JRE) from the Oracle website, which you should install to continue.

Next, in the Upload Media window, you'll select the ISO file you want to upload by clicking the Browse button, as shown in Figure 8.106. You'll be uploading a Windows 2003 R2 ISO file from a network share into vCloud via our administrative workstation by navigating to the file, as shown in Figure 8.107.

**FIGURE 8.107**
Selecting an ISO file
to upload

Enter some relevant information (Figure 8.108) about the ISO file you are uploading. It's a good idea to include some information about the CPU architecture and edition that the ISO file contains. The original filename won't be visible once it has been imported into vCloud Director, and using a structured naming convention makes it easier to search for.

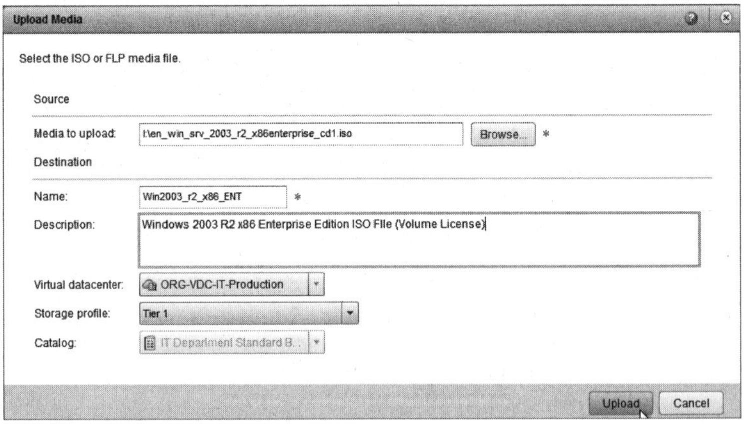

**FIGURE 8.108**
Entering descrip-
tive text for a
media file

**NOTE**  You can also choose which Org vDC and storage tier will house this virtual media file. Media files do not consume computing resources from your Org vDC, but they will obviously consume storage from the allocated quota.

Click Upload to start the process. You'll see a window shown in Figure 8.109.

**FIGURE 8.109**
Upload progress

If you are using self-signed certificates for your cell servers, you may also see the confirmation window shown in Figure 8.110. Click Yes to add the exception for this session.

**FIGURE 8.110**
Self-signed certificate warning

**NOTE** Some browser and JRE combinations seem to get the window ordering incorrect and the prompt boxes pop up behind other windows. So if it seems that your transfer is not starting, check behind the windows.

Depending on the size of your ISO file and the speed of the connection between your workstation and the cell server, this upload may take a while. When it has completed, in the vCloud Director interface the Status column will read Stopped, as shown in Figure 8.111.

**FIGURE 8.111**
Media file uploaded
and ready to use

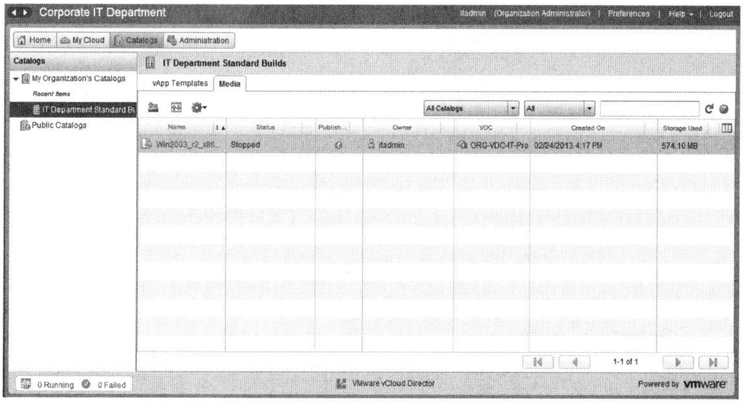

The ISO file you uploaded is now ready for use by other organizations. They can browse the public catalog you've just created and copy the media file to their own catalog files by right-clicking and choosing Copy To Catalog, as shown in Figure 8.112.

**FIGURE 8.112**
The media file is visible from the public catalog in the sales organization

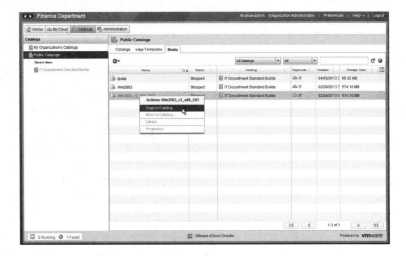

## Exporting a VM from vCenter for Use with vCloud Director in OVF Format

vCloud Director allows consumers to import their own VMs from other VMware platforms that support the Open Virtualization Format (OVF) standard. You can also download prebuilt and ready-to-use VMs as OVF files from many sources on the Internet. VMware maintains a marketplace for such virtual appliances from third-party vendors and community projects in the Marketplace section of their website:

```
https://solutionexchange.vmware.com
```

Alternatively, consumers can export an existing vCenter managed VM or template in OVF format and use it in vCloud Director.

vCloud Connector 2.0 can also be used to perform this export/import activity in a more streamlined manner if you have a large number of VMs to import.

This section assumes you have a VM ready to use in an existing (non-vCloud) vCenter installation. For example, you may have a standard vSphere template that you want to import for use with vCloud Director.

You can export the vSphere VM template to OVF format to a network share or portable drive using the VMware OVF Tool command-line utility or vSphere Client, as shown in Figure 8.113. You then reimport the template into vCloud Director from the catalog interface using a process similar to uploading media files.

**FIGURE 8.113**
Exporting a VM as
an OVF file from
vSphere Client

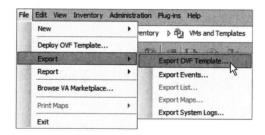

**NOTE**   vCloud Director only supports OVF format, not OVA (single file).

You can then upload the OVF template into vCloud Director via the web interface by clicking the Upload icon in the vApp section of the catalog, as shown in Figure 8.114.

**FIGURE 8.114**
Click the vApp OVF
Upload icon.

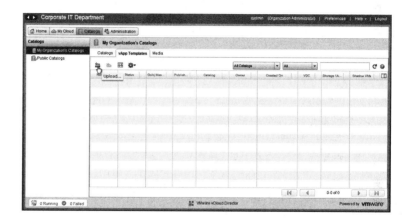

As you did in the previous task, enter some descriptive information, as shown in Figure 8.115. Then browse to the location of the OVF file that you wish to import and upload it into the vCloud Director catalog using the Java upload applet.

**NOTE**   The cloud administrator has an extra option to import directly from vCenter into a vCloud Director catalog, but organization administrators and consumers are restricted to the import OVF method only.

**NOTE**   In the catalog, the vApp template is listed by the entry you assigned in the Name field, so again be sure to make it as descriptive as possible to simplify searching since the original filename will be lost once the upload is completed.

Once the upload has completed, you'll see that the upload is being finalized within the catalog. When that process finishes, the template will be available to other organizations with access to the public catalog.

**FIGURE 8.115**
Enter descriptive text for the template that you are importing and assign it to an Org vDC and storage profile.

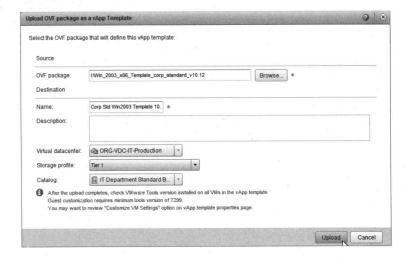

## Handing Over Access to Your Consumers

Once you have uploaded any required images for your vCloud public catalog, you have completed the main platform build tasks. You have defined a number of PvDCs, organizations, and Org vDCs in vCloud Director, and you are ready to hand over access to vCloud to your consumers so that they can start to build, upload, and configure their workloads. You've defined a framework in vCloud to marshal and control access to computing resources and provide a self-service interface that your consumers can interact with. The vCloud Director interface is self-explanatory, and its typical audience is system administrators rather than business end users.

In most organizations, you'll need to provide some basic training to your consumers—even to the more experienced system administrators, so that they can understand the logical abstractions you've created in vCloud Director. Ensuring you have logical naming conventions and completed description fields will pay dividends in consumer experience.

## Summary

Once the vCloud Director management platform has been built, you follow a process of defining a group of physical computing, network, and storage resources into a PvDC. You can define several organizations within vCloud Director. An organization acts as an authentication and administrative boundary and, in a private cloud scenario, typically maps to a department, business unit, or subsidiary company. In a public cloud scenario, an organization typically represents a customer.

Each organization contains a number of consumers. These consumers can be identified and authenticated using a local user or linked to an external directory service, such as Active

Directory or other LDAP authentication source. Each organization is configured for a specific authentication source, but it is possible to modify it after creation to use a different method—for example, moving from built-in user accounts to an external LDAP directory.

Using an external directory source requires an appropriate network communication path between your cell server(s) and the target directory. Ensuring this may involve firewall or VPN configuration if these services are in a highly secure or remote location.

Network resources are added to each PvDC and defined as external or internal networks. Internal network resources are allocated from a preconfigured network pool—a pool of VLANs that can be allocated, provisioned, and deprovisioned on behalf of consumerns by vCloud Director—to quickly deliver complicated network topologies to support vApps.

A number of networks are built as default object types within vCloud Director. As you build organizations and allocate resources to them, you'll define a number of logical organization internal and external networks, which in turn are connected to vSphere port groups and physical uplinks from PvDCs to the corporate datacenter.

As the system administrator, you can create one or more Org vDCs that represent allocations of resources from PvDCs. You must configure an allocation model for each Org vDC, choosing from three types: Allocation Pool, Pay-As-You-Go, and Reservation Pool.

Catalogs can be created to hold vApps (groups of VMs) and disc image media like ISO and FLP files. Organizations can be configured to allow them to publish catalogs of vApps and media with all other organizations in vCloud Director. A published catalog is known as a public catalog. If other organizations want to use components from the public catalog, they must copy them to their own catalog, from which they can be deployed. Apps are built from groups of VMs, which can be imported directly from a vCenter server or uploaded directly in OVF format by consumers. Consumers can build new vApps or choose VMs from the catalog to build their own vApps.

In the next chapter you'll build on our example design and look at how consumers from the HR, sales, and finance organizations can use the capacity you've provided to build, customize, and deploy vApps.

# Chapter 9

# Consuming Services

Up to now most of the focus of this book has been from the perspective of the provider whose role is building infrastructure and services. In a private cloud, the role of provider is typically filled by the corporate IT department or a shared service team. This chapter will focus on common ways consumers will use the capacity provided to build, customize, and deploy vApps. We will use the example of a typical finance department and how its administrators deploy applications as vApps in a number of different use cases.

A key concept to understand is that from this point on the consumer can operate independently of the provider. They have access to configure and manage everything they create and can consume as many resources as they are allocated by the provider.

Typically the only interaction between consumer and provider from this point forward is to request more or less capacity (CPU, RAM, networks, storage) to be provisioned for their use. Self-service enables consumers to be autonomous in how they deploy their solutions inside their vCloud organization.

In this chapter, you will learn to:

- Create a catalog and work with published catalogs

- Create a basic vApp

- Copy a vApp to a catalog

- Deploy a vApp to an organization network

- Deploy a vApp with a vApp network and manipulate vCNS Edge firewall rules

- Deploy a vApp with an IP load balancer and provide a resilient web service

## Example Configuration for This Chapter

This chapter builds on the platform you designed and built in Chapters 5–8. The finance department is represented by an organization in vCloud Director and has two Org VDCs allocated to it:

**ORG-VDC-FINANCE-Production**   This Org VDC is configured as part of the Gold SLA PvDC and has access to the highest Tier 1 disk storage as well as lower (Tier 3) storage, which can be leveraged for archival or backup purposes.

**ORG-VDC-FINANCE-Development**   This Org VDC is part of the Bronze PvDC and has access to lower-tier storage.

Figure 9.1 shows the elements that make up the two Finance Org vDCs.

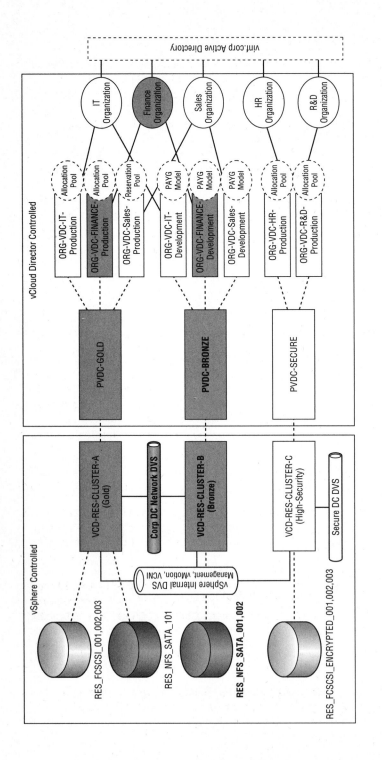

**FIGURE 9.1**

Infrastructure elements that the Finance organization consumes

# Creating Your First vApp as a Consumer

Up to this point you've spent most of your time in the provider role, building and provisioning services. Now you're going to take on the role of a consumer, as a developer in a finance department. You are going to build and use a simple vApp to provide front-end web servers for a finance application.

For this example, you'll assume the various roles of the administrator (finance-admin), a developer (finance-developer) and a consumer (finance-user). These users reside within the Finance organization, which has recently been added to our vCloud Director installation by the system administrator. These users are authenticated via LDAP using the corporate Active Directory, as shown in Chapter 8, "Delivering Services."

You will be carrying out the following tasks to build a vApp for a finance application that can be redeployed a number of times by other finance consumers leveraging catalog functionality:

◆ Create a vApp containing two IT-supplied standard build VM templates as building blocks

◆ Deploy the new vApp with the standard OS images and verify guest customization has completed

◆ Install the finance application into the VMs in the vApp

◆ Copy the two-VM vApp back into the catalog as a service catalog entry for other developers and consumers to deploy

## Creating an Organization Catalog

You'll recall that in Chapter 8 you assumed the role of the IT organization and published a catalog of IT standard builds in vCloud. The intention is that these can be used as building blocks by other organizations to build vApps and to use as the basis for their own standard builds. Follow these steps to create an organization catalog to copy the IT standard builds into so they can be modified to suit the requirements of the finance organization.

**1.** Log on to the vCloud Director interface as the Finance organization administrator; you'll notice the username and assigned role are shown in the top right of the interface.

**NOTE**  By default only users that have been assigned the Organization Administrator role in vCloud Director can access published catalogs. They can select items from these published catalogs to copy to catalogs they create within their own organization or deploy directly from the published catalog.

As the organization administrator of the Finance organization, your first task will be to create a Finance organization shared catalog and populate it with the items you require from the published IT-Standard Builds catalog, which includes VM templates and media (ISO) files.

**2.** Browse to the Catalogs tab in the interface as shown in Figure 9.2 and click on the green plus to add a catalog.

You'll also notice the Public Catalogs entry in the left-hand pane; this is where you can browse any catalogs that are published to the Finance organization by other organizations.

**FIGURE 9.2**

Adding a catalog

**FIGURE 9.2**

Adding a catalog

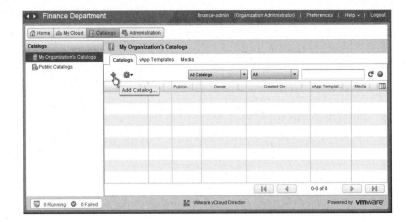

To create the organization catalog, you follow the same process that was outlined for the IT department in Chapter 8. Depending on your requirements, it's less likely that a finance department will choose to publish its catalog to other organizations in your vCloud.

**3.** When prompted, select what levels of access you'll provide to users in the Finance organization and configure for the catalog.

In this example you intend the finance-admin user to be able to fully control the catalog and its contents (Figure 9.3). The finance-developer user will be able to read/write catalog entries, such as uploading new vApps and changing existing vApps. Finally, finance-user has read-only access to catalog entries.

**FIGURE 9.3**

Sharing a catalog with varying levels of permissions

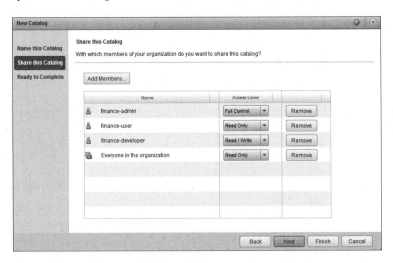

Clicking Next and then Finish creates a Finance Catalog object, which is then accessible to all users within the Finance organization.

**4.** Populate your catalog with items from one or more of the public catalogs or create new items from scratch.

In this example, you'll copy some standard builds provided by the IT organization to the Finance organization catalog.

## ORGANIZATION ADMINISTRATOR ROLE

Organization administrators can copy a vApp from a published catalog into their own organization's shared catalog, but vApp authors and lower roles cannot do this directly because they do not have visibility of catalogs from other organizations that have not been published.

This means the organization administrator is responsible for reviewing and importing vApps from a published catalog for consumption within their own organization. They can do so by right-clicking on a published catalog entry and choosing Copy To Catalog, as shown here:

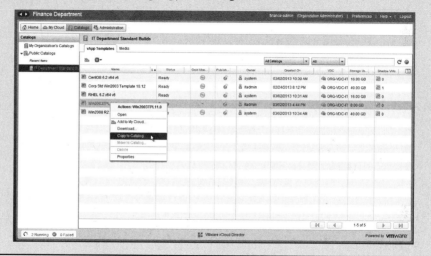

**5.** When prompted, enter some descriptive information for the vApp template, as shown in Figure 9.4, and select the catalog and Org vDC it will be stored within.

In this example, you are storing it in the Finance catalog and assigning it to the development Org vDC on Tier 3 storage.

**6.** Click OK and The vApp template will then be copied into the Finance catalog.

As the administrator of the Finance organization, you have imported a copy of the standard Windows 2003 build provided by the IT department. Any user with permissions to create a vApp can create a new vApp from it by browsing the Finance catalog, deploying a copy, and modifying it to meet their needs.

Provided that consumer has write permissions to the shared catalog, they can then, in turn upload their customized version back into the catalog to share with other Finance consumers. In this example, the finance-developer and finance-admin users have sufficient permissions to do so.

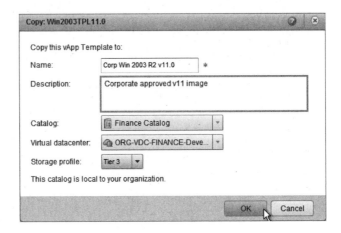

**FIGURE 9.4**
Naming the catalog
and specifying the
storage location

## Creating a Simple vApp from a Shared Catalog

Next you'll log on as a developer in the Finance organization and build a new vApp by taking
an existing standard build and deploying your Finance application within it. You'll then save it
back to the catalog for reuse by other consumers in the Finance organization. The example vApp
will be deployed in a network topology that keeps it segregated from the main corporate network, as shown in Figure 9.5.

**FIGURE 9.5**
Proposed network
topology for this
example

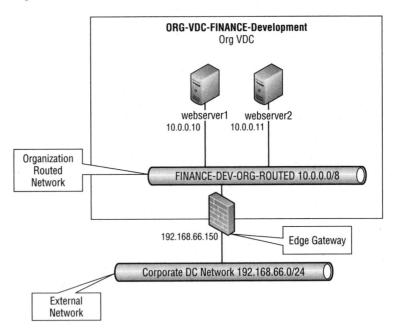

In these steps you'll create a front-end web server vApp for a Finance time-recording application:

**1.** Click the Build New vApp link on the Home screen, as shown in Figure 9.6.

**FIGURE 9.6**
Click Build New vApp.

**2.** A wizard launches and you are prompted to enter details for the new vApp, as shown in Figure 9.7.

**FIGURE 9.7**
Naming the new vApp

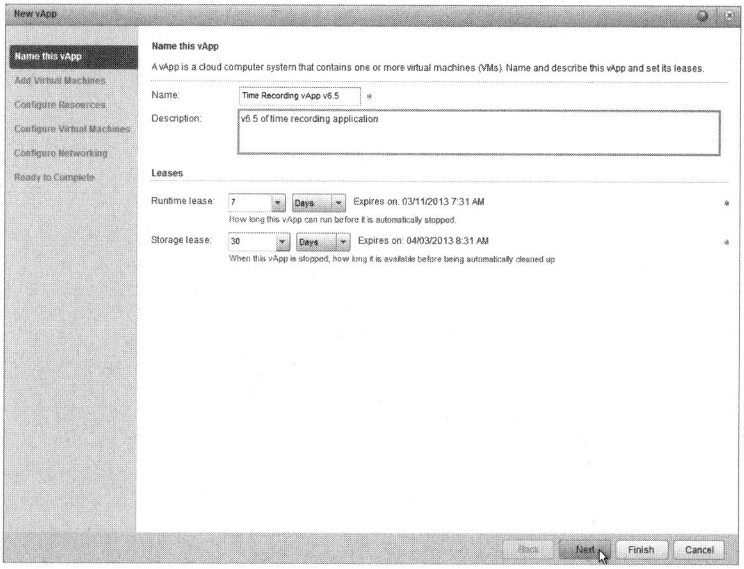

**3.** Name the vApp and specify the lease information.

You'll notice that by default there is no unlimited lease option for this vApp. This is because of the policy that is set for the organization. This can be changed by the system administrator.

Because this application server will be relatively stateless, it won't hold any data. Thus if it is removed, you don't care if the VM is removed quickly from the datastore once the vApp is stopped, so choose a short storage lease.

4. You are prompted to add VMs to the vApp. Click Add twice to add two instances of the Windows 2003 R2x86 VM to your new vApp.

   You'll notice that the VM templates that are available are the ones you imported into the Finance catalog (Figure 9.8) earlier from the IT standard build catalog.

**FIGURE 9.8**
Selecting VMs from the catalog

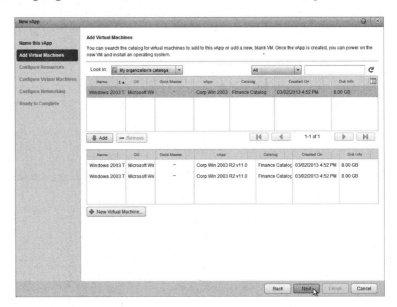

### BUILDING A NEW VM

You also have the option to build a new VM rather than deploy one from a prebuilt template. You are shown a familiar-looking wizard to do so, but bear in mind that if you do take this approach, you'll be installing the operating system from scratch and applying updates. Additionally, the VM you build will not have VMware Tools installed when it first boots and so will not be automatically configured with any vCloud Director–assigned IP address or hostname information. To resolve this, you need to install VMware Tools inside the guest, and then shut it down, right-click the VM, and choose Force Customization Process for the VM, which will bring it under vCloud Director's control.

You are prompted to select which vDC you want to deploy this vApp into. If you have more than one Org VDC, you can select which one to use by clicking on the drop-down box shown in Figure 9.9. In this case you'll be deploying your vApp in to the Finance-Development Org VDC.

Because it is still being built and is not yet in production, you'll also notice that you are shown the miniumum hardware version each Org VDC can support (this is also dictated by the under-lying PvDC).

**FIGURE 9.9**
Choosing the target
Org vDC, essentially
choosing a service
level for this vApp

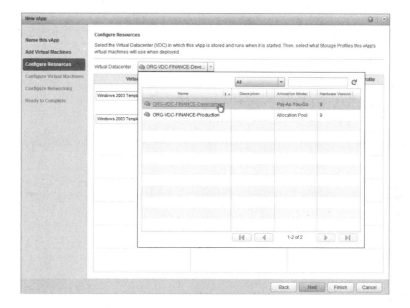

5. When prompted, enter the names for the VM. The name is the display name shown in vCloud Director, not the actual hostname that will be assigned to the VM.

You'll notice in Figure 9.10 that there is only one storage profile available. If you refer to Figure 9.1, you'll see that the ORG-VDC-FINANCE-Development Org VDC that this vApp is being created in has access only to Tier 3 storage as defined by a storage profile.

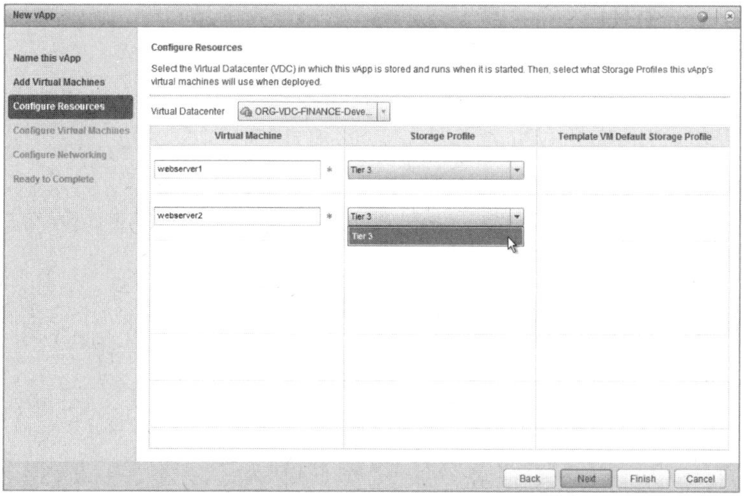

**FIGURE 9.10**
Selecting a storage
profile

**6.** Enter the computer name for each VM in the vApp.

By default, the VM uses the computer name set in the template you are deploying from and appends a numerical suffix as required to keep them unique. In this example, set the computer name manually, for example, by typing **webserver1 and webserver 2** in the Computer Name field or whatever names match your corporate naming standard.

**WARNING**  Be careful here: The computer name (called a hostname in some guest OS types) does not automatically match the VM name and so may lead to confusion when a machine is labeled as one thing in the vCloud Director interface and another in the guest OS. To aid trouble-shooting and management later and to reduce possible confusion, use the same name or include the computer name in the VM name. The Virtual Machine Name field is much less restrictive in terms of length, whereas most computer names are limited by the guest OS to 14 characters. For example, you may have a VM name of **Application Y Web server1 (UKLONAPP01)**.

You are going to attach this vApp to the development organization network, which connects to the corporate network via a vCNS Edge Gateway (Figure 9.11).

**FIGURE 9.11**
Selecting the
network

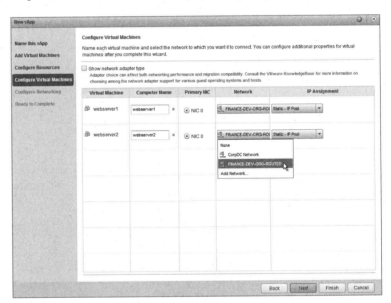

**7.** Select the appropriate network from the Network drop-down box.

You'll notice in Figure 9.12 that you have three options for configuring the IP address for your VMs:

◆  Static - IP Pool

◆  Static - Manual

◆  DHCP

**FIGURE 9.12**
Specifying the IP
assignment method

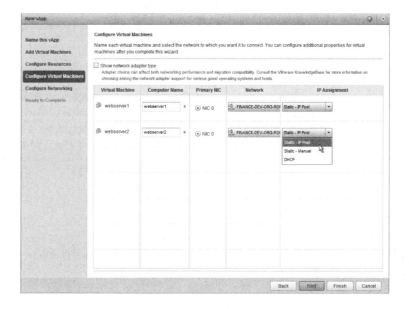

8. In this example, you want vCloud Director to allocate the IP address from the pool that is associated with the FINANCE-DEV-ORG-ROUTED network and have it configure the guest OS automatically through the guest customization process. So choose Static - IP Pool.

9. Finally you are given further options to customize the vApp networking, as shown in Figure 9.13. You have the option to fence the vApp, which would deploy another vCNS Edge appliance, as shown in Figure 9.14. In this example you will not be using a fenced vApp; instead, connect directly to the FINANCE-DEV-ORG-ROUTED network, as shown in Figure 9.15.

**FIGURE 9.13**
Fencing option

10. Click Finish to complete the wizard.

You'll see on the vCloud interface Home screen that a new vApp is being created (Figure 9.16).

**FIGURE 9.14**
Fenced vApp

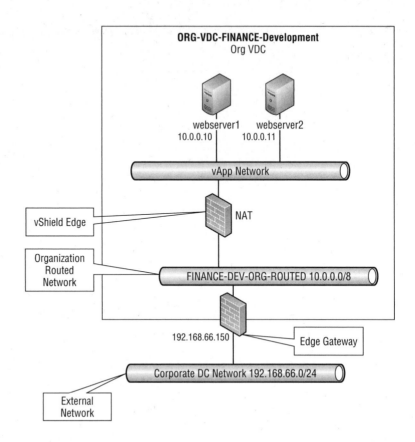

**FIGURE 9.15**
Configuring
Networking,
nonfenced

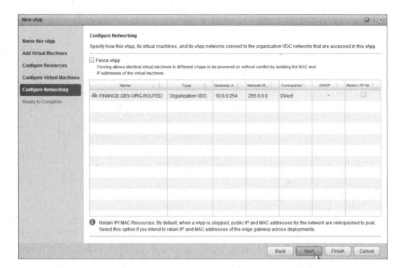

**FIGURE 9.16**
vCloud Director is
creating the vApp.

This process creates a clone of the VM template you chose. If you have fast provisioning enabled for the Org vDC, the wizard creates a linked clone of the base template VM; otherwise, it does a full copy.

Once the deployment has completed, the vApp object will show a status of Stopped in the bottom left.

If you have access to the vCenter Server that manages your resource pod (for example, the system administrator within the IT department, the provider), you'll see that the VMs have been created under a resource pool that represents your Org vDC, which in turn resides in a cluster (VCD-RES-CLUSTER-B) that represents the PVDC-Bronze PvDC (Figure 9.17).

**FIGURE 9.17**
Your vApp viewed
from vCenter

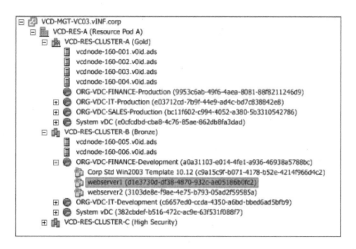

If you click the vApp to open it, you'll see a new multi-tabbed interface that allows you to inspect the configuration of the vApp and interact with it. Right-clicking on each VM brings up a context menu that allows you to manipulate individual VM settings. The vApp Diagram tab (Figure 9.18) also shows the virtual NIC(s) in each VM and the network it is attached to.

**FIGURE 9.18**

vApp Diagram tab

Notice that a 10.0.0.x IP address has been assigned. These IP addresses were chosen from the static IP pool configured by the system administrator when the FINANCE-DEV-ORG-ROUTED network was created, as shown in Figure 9.19.

**FIGURE 9.19**

Network
Specification tab

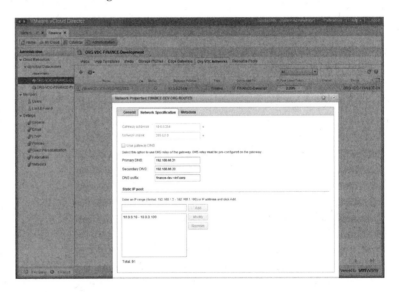

If you browse the Virtual Machines tab, you'll see that IP addresses have already been allocated for the VMs (Figure 9.20). This tab also provides details of each VM contained inside the vApp, such as its operating system type and the IP address that has been allocated by vCloud Director.

Because in this example you are using existing VM templates as building blocks to create a new vApp, you need to configure vCloud Director to have each VM perform customization activities at startup. You only need to perform this task when you are using the Build New vApp and Add VM links in the interface; otherwise, the setting shown in Figure 9.21 will take care of this for you.

**FIGURE 9.20**
Allocated IP addresses for VMs in a vApp

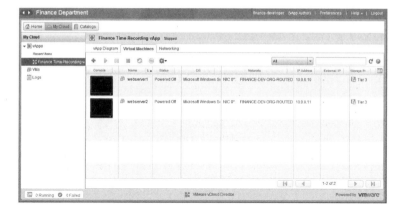

**FIGURE 9.21**
Application of guest customization settings is dependent on the method used to deploy the vApp.

Right-click on each VM and view its properties; then navigate to the Guest OS Customization tab (Figure 9.22).

You need each machine to have a unique Windows Security Identifier SID, and you want to specify a local administrator password. The servers are going to be in a routed network and not part of the main corporate domain, but if you were providing this vApp with network connectivity, you could enable it to join your Active Directory domain by clicking the Enable This VM To Join A Domain check box, as well as enable firewall rules (which will be covered later).

This process needs to be completed one time for each new VM in your vApp. There is no way to multiselect VMs in the interface, although you could consider using a script if you have a large number of VMs in a new vApp to configure.

If you now power on the vApp, you'll be able to see the individual VMs power on and boot their operating systems, in this case Windows 2003. Because you are building a new vApp from building blocks, you'll notice that the Starting And Stopping VMs tab in the vApp properties screen shown in Figure 9.23 displays the default settings, which are to power off the VMs rather than execute a guest OS shutdown. Change the default action to Shut Down to ensure that the VMs are cleanly shut down before being powered off.

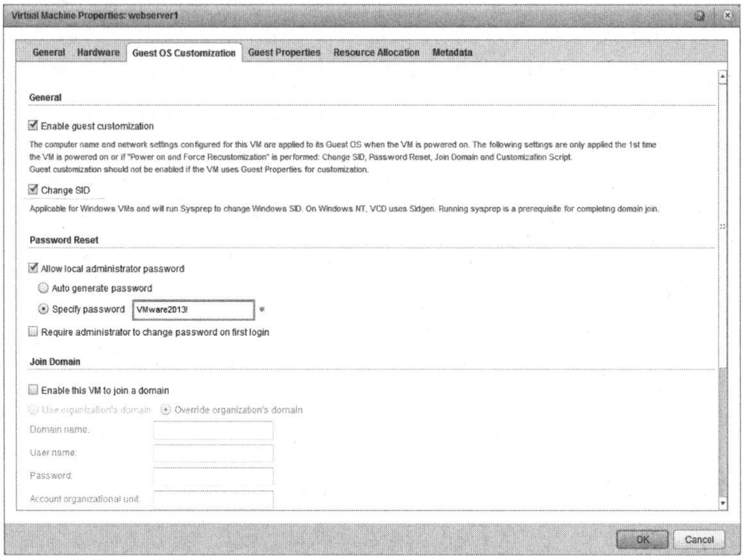

**FIGURE 9.22**
Guest OS
Customization tab

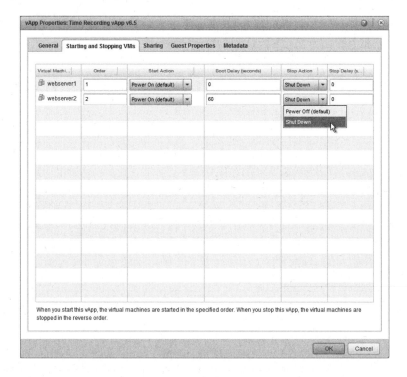

**FIGURE 9.23**
Setting vApp start/
stop actions

**NOTE** Powering on individual VMs is also possible by opening the vApp, right-clicking each VM, and choosing PowerOn from the context menu. However, as you'll recall, a vApp is a logical grouping of one or more VMs that are usually dependent on each other, so you should use the Starting And Stopping VMs tab of the vApp properties screen to define startup order and delay settings, as shown in Figure 9.23.

Now you will launch the vApp by clicking the Start icon in the vApp Diagram tab, as shown in Figure 9.24. The VMs will start in the sequence you specified in Figure 9.23.

**FIGURE 9.24**

Starting a vApp from the vApp Diagram tab

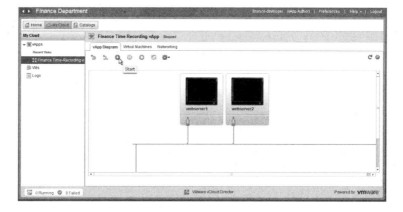

You can also start the vApp from the Home screen, as shown in Figure 9.25. When viewing the vApp in the Org vDC, both methods accomplish the same task. You are able to see a thumbnail image of the VMs starting up within the vApp.

**FIGURE 9.25**

Starting a vApp from the Home screen

Once the vApp has started, you can click on each of the VMs to open a remote console to it and watch the boot process. Because you chose to customize the guest and change the SID, the vApp runs through the Microsoft Sysprep process. (You'll recall that as part of the installation process detailed in Chapter 7, "Installing VMware vCloud Director," you downloaded and imported the Sysprep binaries from Microsoft; this is where they are used, as shown in Figure 9.26.)

**FIGURE 9.26**
Sysprep in action
on a newly
deployed vApp

If you are deploying operating systems based on Windows 2008 or Windows Vista, you won't see this process—it happens transparently as part of the boot process.

## INTERNET EXPLORER PROTECTED MODE AND VM REMOTE CONSOLE

If you are using Internet Explorer with Protected Mode enabled, you may encounter issues connecting to the VM console. The console window will launch but will only show a status of "connecting..." and will not show the remote console.

To resolve this, you can add your vCloud URL to the trusted sites list, as shown in the following graphic, or you can disable IE Protected Mode entirely.

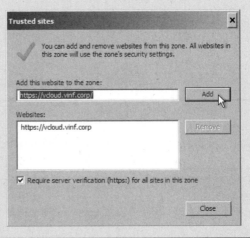

When the operating systems have completed their boot process, they should be attached to your chosen network with an IP address configured. You can verify this by logging on to the console and checking the configuration that has been applied.

If you chose to have guest customization, set the local administrator password, as shown in Figure 9.22. This is the password that will have been set in the guest and will be required for you to log on to the console. If you need to look it up, right-click the VM and view the password that was either specified or autogenerated. Note that this field is now grayed out and read-only; this is because the guest customization process has already been completed.

If you subsequently want to change this password (or other guest customization settings), you'll need to power off the VM, edit the settings, and then right-click and choose the Power On And Force Recustomization option, as shown in Figure 9.27.

**FIGURE 9.27**

Choose the Power On And Force Recustomization option to change guest customization settings applied to already deployed VMs.

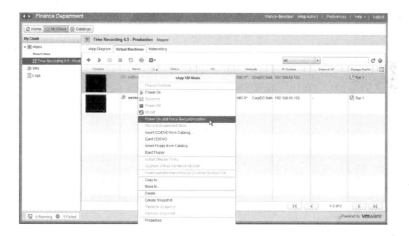

Now your first vApp is ready to customize.

## Customizing a vApp

Now that you have a basic vApp built, you need to install the applications and services you require inside it. This process will depend on your individual application requirements, but it could typically include steps like installing software and application code, enabling the web server, or applying an organization- or role-specific security configuration.

You should check that your application can tolerate changes that will subsequently be applied by the guest customization process when your vApp is deployed from the catalog in the future. For example, check that it doesn't have any license keys that are bound to VM-specific attributes like hostnames or MAC addresses. If this is the case, a more appropriate method would be to use the scripting section to automate an installation of your application after the vApp is deployed rather than including the application and guest customization settings in the vApp template itself, as shown in Figure 9.28.

In our example you'll enable IIS, populate the vApp with a dummy web page, install corporate monitoring agents, and configure accounts and permissions in the operating system.

Once these tasks have been completed, and you've tested your vApp, you need to shut it down in order to copy it to the catalog.

**FIGURE 9.28**
Guest OS customization settings

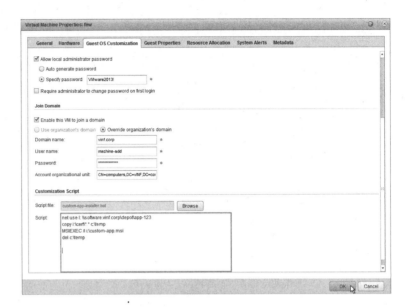

To do so, click the stop button on the vApp screen (Figure 9.29); this will then execute the shutdown process via VMware Tools using the sequence you defined in Figure 9.23. Note that the Power On button is also available from the same interface.

**FIGURE 9.29**
Stopping a vApp from the Home screen

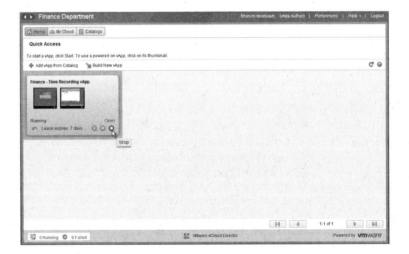

## Uploading Your vApp to a Catalog

Now that the example vApp has been customized with settings and software and has been shut down, do the following:

**1.** Right-click on the vApp and choose Add To Catalog, as shown in Figure 9.30.

**FIGURE 9.30**
Uploading a vApp to
the catalog

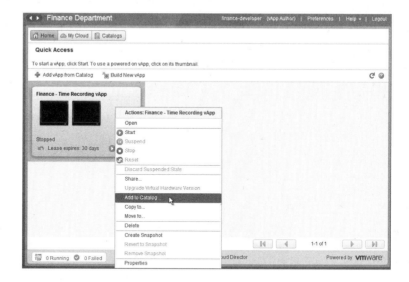

**FIGURE 9.30**
Uploading a vApp to
the catalog

**2.** When prompted, enter details of the vApp that will be recorded in the catalog
(Figure 9.31), as well as where you want it to go.

**FIGURE 9.31**
Choosing the
catalog and
enabling Customize
VM Settings

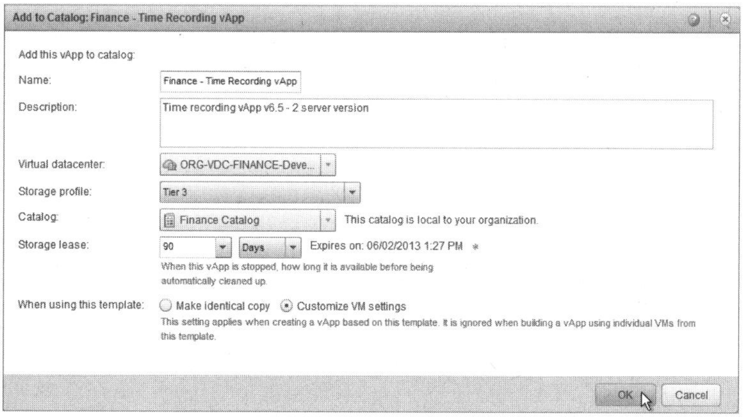

In this example you'll add it to the development Org vDC (ORG-VDC-FINANCE-
Development) and store it on Tier 3 storage. The default lease is inherited from the catalog
settings and describes how long the vApp can be deployed but switched off—in this case,
90 days.

**3.** You want each instance of the VMs contained inside this vApp to have their own SID, hostname, and IP address generated when they are deployed; therefore, enable the Customize VM Settings option.

If this option is not enabled, copies of the vApp are deployed with the same SID, hostname, and IP address.

**4.** Click OK.

vCloud Director clones the vApp into the catalog, and once completed, it will be available for other consumers to deploy.

You can view the vApp you've put into the catalog, as shown in Figure 9.32.

**FIGURE 9.32**
The vApp has been uploaded to the catalog.

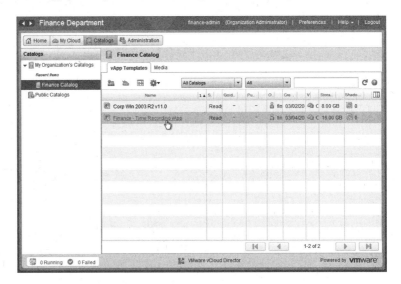

## Deploying a vApp from a Template

As a result of the previous step, you now have an example vApp stored in your catalog. Multiple developers can deploy instances of this application and have them automatically deployed with unique SIDs, hostnames, and IP addresses.

Next you'll assume the role of a consumer (finance-user). The consumer may be from the IT team within the Finance organization or a third party responsible for maintaining that application on behalf of the Finance organization. They are tasked with deploying the vApp for end users to use in production.

You'll note that for this example you're logged into the vCloud Director interface as the finance-user account. This is the first vApp you are deploying, so you do not have other vApps on your Home screen.

Our example vApp will be deployed directly to the corporate datacenter network, as shown in Figure 9.33.

**FIGURE 9.33**
Simple vApp
deployment direct
to the corporate DC
network

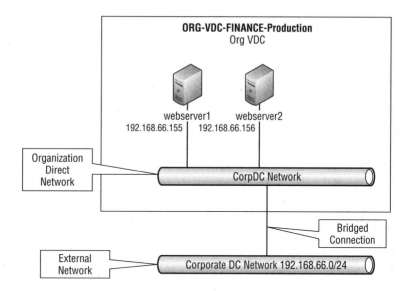

**1.** Click Add vApp From Catalog on the Home screen (Figure 9.34).

**FIGURE 9.34**
Adding the vApp
from a catalog

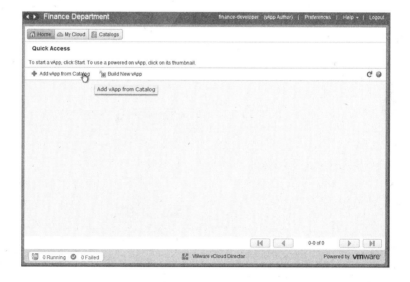

**2.** Select the vApp template you created in the previous step (Figure 9.35) and click Next.

**3.** Provide a name and description for the new vApp—in this instance, **Time Recording 6.5 - Production**, as shown in Figure 9.36.

**FIGURE 9.35**
Selecting the vApp
template

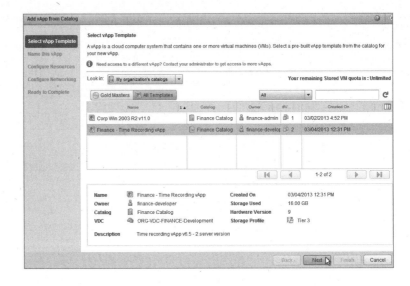

**FIGURE 9.36**
Name this instance
of the vApp being
deployed from the
catalog.

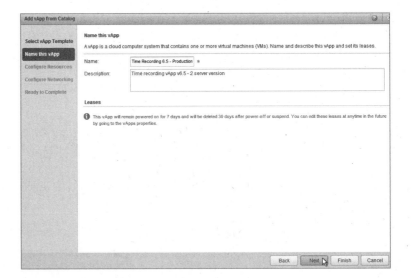

**4.** Choose to deploy to the ORG-VDC-FINANCE-Production Org vDC from the Virtual
Datacenter drop-down box, as shown in Figure 9.37.

The VM name is configured with a "p" suffix to denote production.

**5.** The ORG-VDC-FINANCE-Production Org vDC has a choice of Tier 1 and Tier 3 storage
(Figure 9.38). You need maximum performance, so choose to deploy the vApp to Tier 1
storage and click Next.

**FIGURE 9.37**
Selecting the target
Org vDC

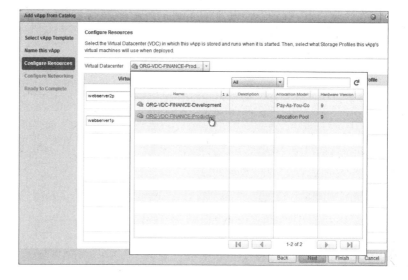

**FIGURE 9.38**
Selecting a storage
profile for this vApp

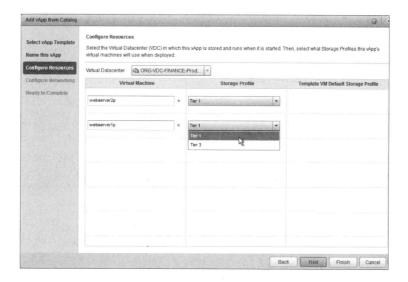

6. You are asked to configure the networking. Enter the computer name, which is the same as the VM name.

7. You are given two networking choices:

- Deploying the vApp to a set of private networks behind an Edge Gateway
- Directly attaching the vApp to the corporate DC network

Select the Switch To The Advanced Networking Workflow check box, as shown in Figure 9.39.

**FIGURE 9.39**
Selecting which
network to attach
your vApp to

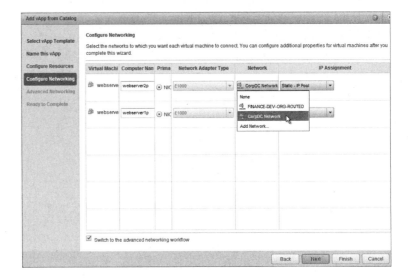

8. Deploy these vApps directly to the corporate DC network, and choose to have the IP address set as a static IP address in the guest, allocated from a pool configured within vCloud Director.

---

### VIRTUAL MACHINE NAME, COMPUTER NAME

The computer name is not automatically set to the same as the VM name, and there is no option in the interface to make these identical as there is with guest customization in vSphere. Therefore, you'll need to do this manually for each vApp you deploy.

---

9. Click Next. The Advanced Networking screen appears.

   You can skip this step as you are not using the more advanced network scenarios in this example.

10. When the Summary screen appears, click Finish. The vApp will be deployed and visible from the Home screen of the vCloud Director interface.

This exercise will result in a two-VM vApp being deployed to the production Org vDC in the Finance organization. When the vApp is started, the VMs will boot, generate a unique SID, and have their hostname and IP address configured automatically by vCloud Director.

If you click on the vApp Diagram tab within the vApp you deployed, you'll see an automatically generated diagram of the two VMs directly attached to the corporate DC network. If you hover your mouse over the virtual NIC, you'll see the IP address it is configured with, as shown in Figure 9.40.

**FIGURE 9.40**
Hover your mouse over the virtual NIC to see the IP address it is configured with.

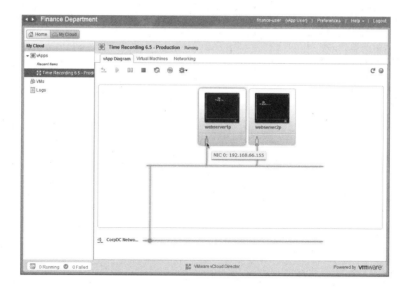

If you connect to the VM's remote console, you'll see that it has been assigned a new hostname and static IP address (Figure 9.41).

**FIGURE 9.41**
Results of guest customization, hostname, and static IP address set by vCloud Director

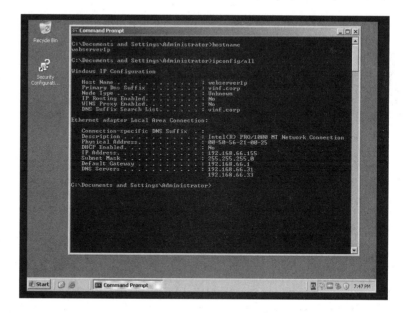

In this example, the vApp is connected directly to the corporate DC network (Figure 9.42) and so it is accessible on the IP address set by vCloud Director from any machine on the corporate network.

**FIGURE 9.42**
Connecting to
application hosted
in the vApp from
the corporate
network

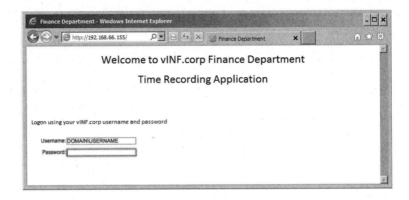

Of course, joining a vApp directly to the corporate network with a single vNIC is a simple use case, but it is a useful example of how vApps are built and deployed from catalogs from building blocks. In this example, where you have a Windows vApp directly attached to an external network, it can be useful to access the VM using the Remote Desktop functionality built into Windows. If you right-click on a VM in the vCloud Director interface, you can download a Remote Desktop shortcut. This shortcut can be opened with the Remote Desktop client on a Windows machine. Assuming Remote Desktop is enabled on your VMs, you can then make a direct connection to it over the external network.

One of the most powerful features of vCloud Director is its flexible and on-demand network provisioning. Next we'll look at some of those use cases by expanding your simple time recording vApp.

## Deploying a vApp on a vApp Network

Deploying a vApp on a vApp network is a common use case, especially for test and development activities. This process will deploy a vApp with its own vCNS Edge firewall that can perform Network Address Translation (NAT) and basic firewall functionality.

In our example, a private vApp network has been created for this vApp that is provided from the network pool specified and attached to the underlying Org vDC, which in turn is connected to the corporate DC network. This example will deploy your time recording application for user acceptance testing (UAT) in the topology shown in Figure 9.43.

1. Deploy the vApp as in the previous example, but choose to switch to the advanced networking workflow in the configure networking step, as shown in Figure 9.44.

2. Choose Add Network from the Network drop-down list for both VMs in the vApp.

3. When prompted, create a vApp network, as shown in Figure 9.45.

   An IP subnet is allocated for you, but you can enter any values you like here as it will be internal to the vApp and isolated from the main network by the vCNS Edge appliance performing NAT.

4. Select the IP assignment method for your VMs; for this example, use Static - IP Pool.

   Because you chose the advanced networking workflow, you are shown a screen where you can specify advanced network settings.

**FIGURE 9.43**
The vApp network
with a vCNS Edge
appliance
providing NAT

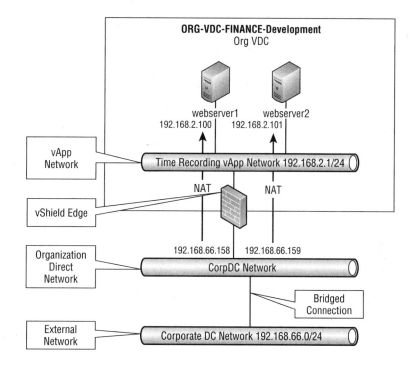

**FIGURE 9.44**
Adding a vApp
network at
deployment time

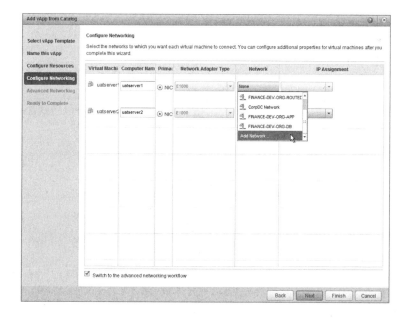

**FIGURE 9.45**
Entering network details for the new vApp network

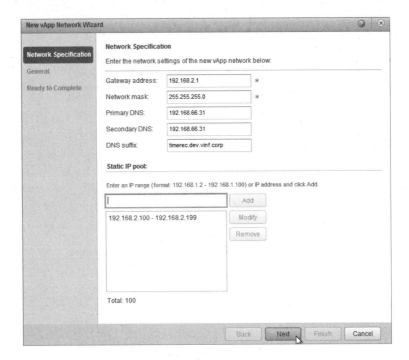

5. Select the CorpDC network from the Connection drop-down box (Figure 9.46).

**FIGURE 9.46**
Selecting the network to route the vApp network to via a vCNS Edge appliance using NAT

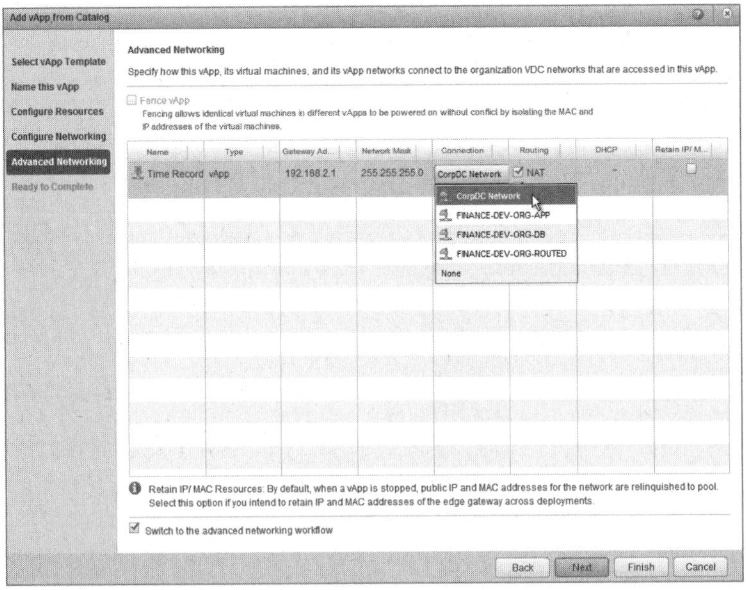

Leave the NAT and Firewall options checked. Once completed, this step will result in the vApp template being deployed in the topology shown in Figure 9.47.

**FIGURE 9.47**
The vApp network
routed to the
CorpDC network
via vCNS Edge

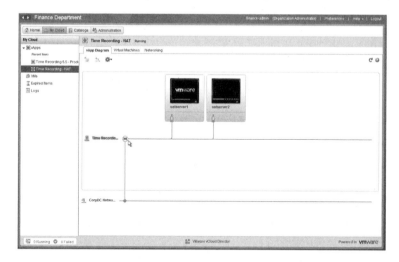

See the red firewall icon in Figure 9.47. This represents the vCNS Edge appliance that has been deployed for this vApp network.

**6.** Right-click on the icon to configure the vCNS Edge services, as shown in Figure 9.48.

**FIGURE 9.48**
Configuring vCNS
Edge services

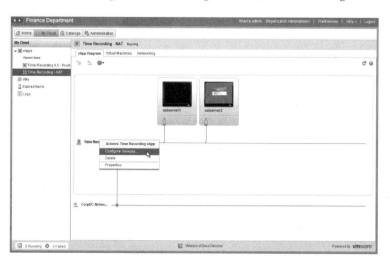

**7.** The vCNS Edge appliance provides a basic level of firewall and NAT functionality, which you can configure from the interface shown in Figure 9.49. Select the NAT tab.

**FIGURE 9.49**
NAT mappings
from the external
network to the
vApp network

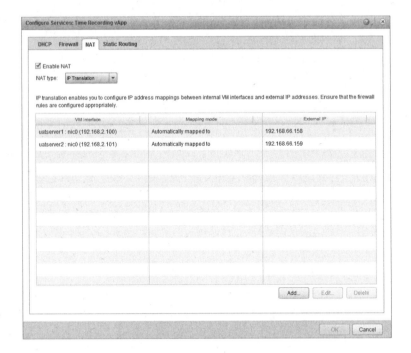

You'll see the default configuration that vCloud Director applies to the vCNS Edge appliance based on the information that was entered when the vApp was deployed. You'll see the VM interface address, which is taken from the IP range you defined for the vApp network in Figure 9.45, and the external IP address, which is taken from the org network that the vCNS Edge is attached to—in this case, the CorpDC network.

**NOTE** As long as this vApp is deployed it will retain these IP addresses. When this vApp is removed, those IP addresses will be returned to the pool and vCloud Director can reassign them to other vApps. In the Advanced Networking tab of each vApp is an option called Retain IP/MAC Resources. Click this option to ensure that the public IP address and MAC address are retained when the vApp is powered off.

**8.** You need to provide access to the web application running on each of the two VMs in the vApp, so select the Firewall tab.

You'll notice that only one rule is defined: to allow any traffic (TCP/UDP port) from any internal network (the vApp network) to any external network on any port. This means your vApp will be able to communicate with any hosts on the CorpDC network, but those CorpDC hosts will not be able to directly communicate with the two application servers in the vApp network, despite the NAT configuration shown in Figure 9.49.

The default action is Deny, which means anything that isn't explicitly allowed by a firewall rule will be denied. This includes ICMP traffic like ping, which you may use to verify connectivity.

**9.** Click Add to create a new firewall rule for HTTP traffic. The Add Firewall Rule dialog box opens.

"Internal" in the Destination field in this instance refers to the vApp network itself.

**10.** In the Destination Port field, enter **80**.

**11.** Click OK, as shown in Figure 9.50, to apply the firewall configuration.

**FIGURE 9.50**
Creating a firewall rule for HTTP access to the vApp

You should be able to connect to the web server running on both of the VMs from the corporate network using an IP address on the corporate WAN, as shown in Figure 9.51.

**FIGURE 9.51**
Accessing the vApp from the external network using NAT

The 192.168.66.158 address in this instance is a virtual IP address on the vCNS Edge appliance, which performs NAT to map traffic to the vApp network where the VM itself is configured with an IP address from a different range (Figure 9.52).

**FIGURE 9.52**
The VM list showing allocated external and internal IP addresses

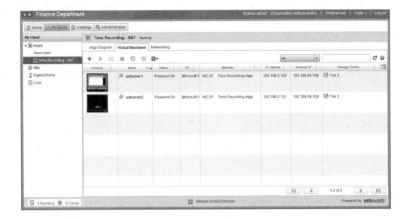

## Deploying a vApp with IP Load Balancing

Next you'll be extending the time recording vApp and using the virtual load balancer functionality of the vCNS Edge Gateway appliance to distribute traffic between these two web application servers.

The vCNS Edge appliance you deployed in the previous section offers functionality similar to a small office or home broadband router. It is capable of performing NAT and basic firewall functionality, whereas in this example the vCNS Edge Gateway is more equivalent to an enterprise-grade firewall that can be deployed in a highly available mode and that can terminate VPN connections and function as an IP load balancer.

You are assuming the role of an administrator (finance-admin) in the Finance organization with the Organization Administrator role assigned.

The user account needs to have the Organization Administrator role assigned to be able to make configuration changes to the edge gateway.

In Chapter 8 you deployed an edge gateway for the IT-Production vDC. Edge gateways are deployed per Org vDC and connect organization networks to external networks or other organization networks.

The system administrator is the only user able to create edge gateways (Figure 9.53). Organization administrators are only able to configure settings such as firewall and load-balancer rules and create organization networks that can connect to the edge gateway.

**NOTE**  Before your developers can attach machines to the edge gateway, the system administrator must have created and configured it. These steps are detailed in Chapter 8, and we assume that equivalent steps have been performed for the Finance-Development Org vDC, resulting in the following topology.

The system administrator must have created a suballocation of IP addresses for the edge gateway to use. In this example there is a suballocation of IP addresses on the CorpDC network that have been made available for the edge gateway to use. This is configured via the properties of each edge gateway, as shown in Figure 9.54. These addresses are suballocated from the pool of IP addresses already allocated to the CorpDC network.

**FIGURE 9.53**
Topology for this example showing a vCNS Edge Gateway doing IP load balancing and NAT

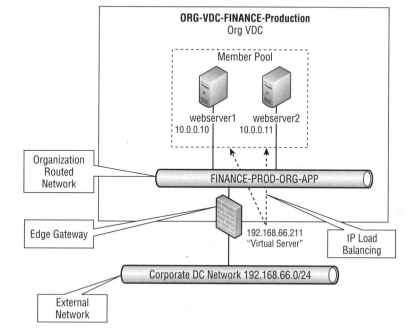

**FIGURE 9.54**
IP pool suballocation on the vCNS Edge Gateway

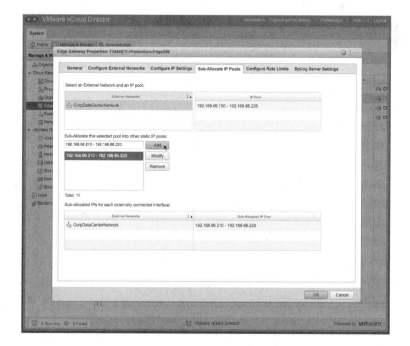

1. Navigate to the Org VDC Networks tab in the vCloud Director interface, as shown in Figure 9.55, and click Add Network.

**FIGURE 9.55**
Adding a network
to our Org vDC

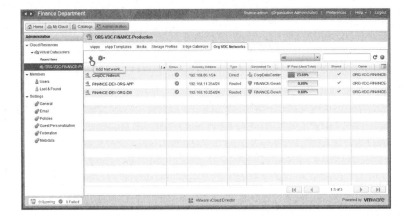

2. Add an organization network that will support production application servers and route to the CorpDC production network via the vCNS Edge Gateway; you do this by choosing to create a routed network by connecting to an existing vCNS Edge Gateway (Figure 9.56).

**FIGURE 9.56**
Routed organiza-
tion network using
an edge gateway

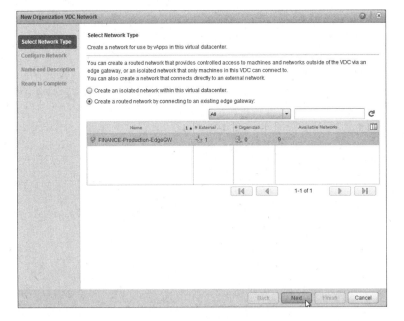

3. You are prompted for the network specifications for this organization network; you can choose whatever subnets you require here.

   In this example, dedicate a private 10.0.0.0/24 network that will contain production vApps (Figure 9.57).

**FIGURE 9.57**
Network specification for the routed organization network

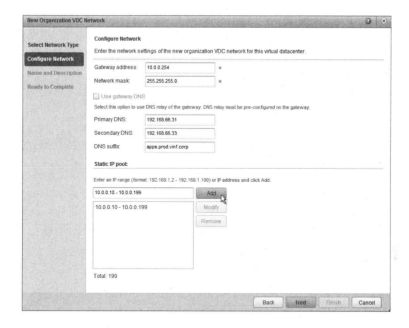

This network setup is analogous to creating a DMZ on a traditional firewall, except all the connectivity is done in software via vCloud Director.

**4.** Name the network **FINANCE-PROD-ORG-APP** (Figure 9.58).

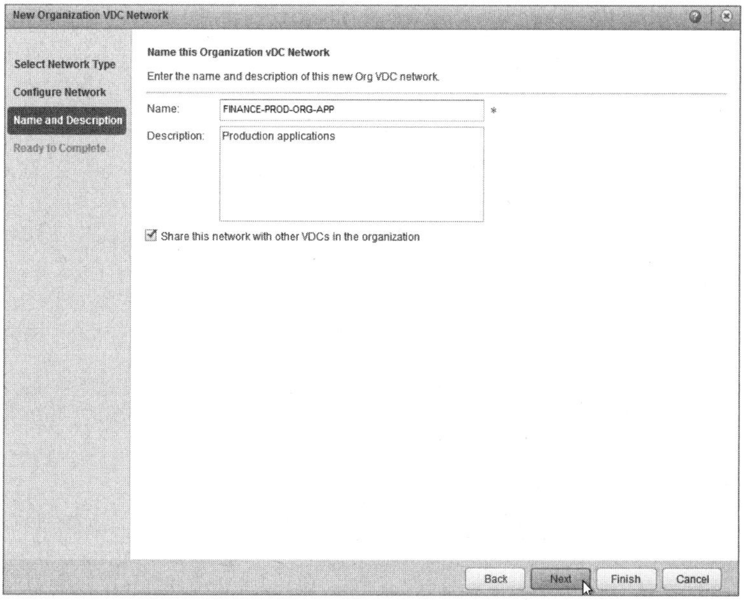

**FIGURE 9.58**
Naming the organization network

5. To reflect that this is an organization network for applications that is part of the production VDC, check the box to share the network with other vDCs in the network. This will allow you to connect vApps from the development Org vDC to the production network for testing.

   Once the organization network is created, you'll see that its type is routed (Figure 9.59). This is because it will use the edge gateway to communicate with the CorpDC network, which is a direct network to the corporate DC network.

**FIGURE 9.59**
Newly created
routed organization
network

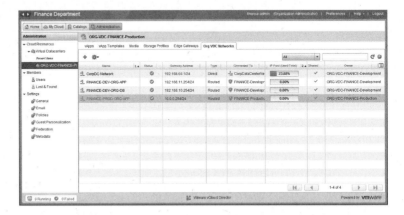

6. Right-click on the new FINANCE-PROD-ORG-APP network and choose Configure Services.

   You'll see a familiar dialog box from vCNS Edge used in the previous example, except that it has two extra tabs: VPN and Load Balancer. You'll be configuring the load balancer later in this example.

7. Now that the organization network is configured to support applications from the Home screen, click Add vApp From Catalog and choose the Finance Time Recording vApp, as shown in Figure 9.34.

8. Select the Switch To The Advanced Networking Workflow check box.

   You will choose to deploy the vApp attached to the organization routed network with a statically assigned IP address. In this example the edge gateway will provide NAT and IP load-balancing services for your vApp, which will get an IP address on a private subnet (10.0.0.0/24).

9. As with the previous example, deploy the time recording vApp from the catalog into the ORG-VDC-FINANCE-Production Org vDC, as shown in Figure 9.37.

   Note that the VM name specified has -LB appended to it to reflect that it is a load-balanced pair.

10. Select the newly created organization network and opt to use the Static - IP Pool method for IP assignment (Figure 9.60).

**FIGURE 9.60**
Attaching your
vApp to the new
network and choos-
ing the IP assign-
ment method

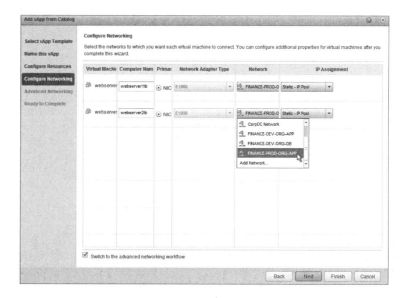

**11.** Click Finish to complete the wizard and the vApp will be deployed.

**12.** Browse to the org network you created, right-click, and choose Configure Services (Figure 9.61).

**FIGURE 9.61**
Configuring edge
gateway services

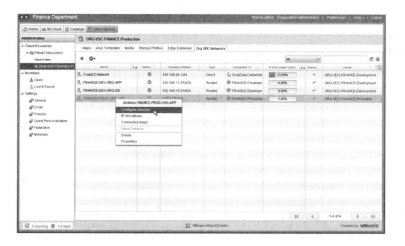

**13.** You see on the Firewall tab of the Configure Services screen that by default the vCNS Edge Gateway firewall policy does not allow ping (ICMP) traffic. To aid troubleshooting, enable it by clicking Add and creating a simple firewall rule (Figure 9.62).

**FIGURE 9.62**
Creating a rule that
allows ICMP traffic

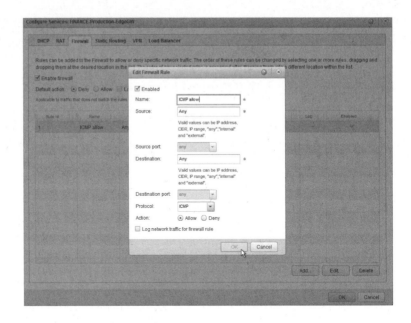

You should now be able to ping the default gateway from the VMs in your vApp, and you should be able to ping the external interface of the edge gateway (Figure 9.63). You can find the external interface of the edge gateway by right-clicking the gateway and choosing External IP Allocations.

**FIGURE 9.63**
External IP allocations for the edge
gateway

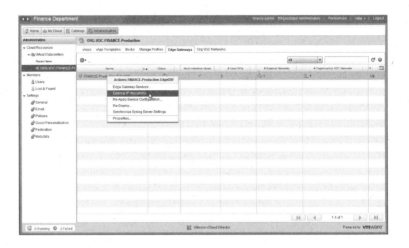

In this example, the edge gateway has been provided with an IP address on the CorpDC network, as shown in Figure 9.64.

**FIGURE 9.64**
Edge gateway IP
address

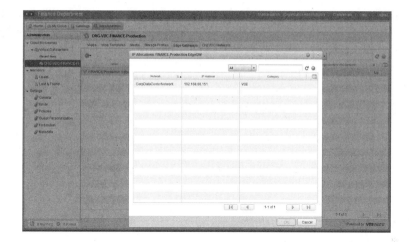

This IP address is suballocated from the CorpDC network. This suballocation is set by
the system administrator when the edge gateway is created, and non-system administrators
can only view the assigned IP address, although the system administrator can reassign it if
necessary.

Next, you need to configure the IP load balancer built into the edge gateway in order to be
able to distribute IP traffic across both web servers in the vApp:

1. Choose Configure Services on the edge gateway and navigate to the Load Balancer
   tab. Click Pool Servers at the top and click the Add button at the bottom, as shown in
   Figure 9.65.

**FIGURE 9.65**
Adding a
member pool

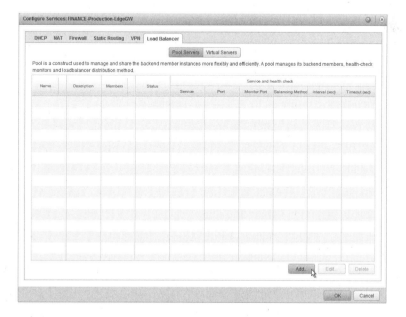

A member pool is a group of servers. This pool is then associated with one or more virtual servers. A virtual IP address is used to direct traffic to servers in the pool servers.

2. When prompted, give the member pool a descriptive name.

   You then need to configure the services your member pool will be offering and the balancing method you want to use (in this example, l).

3. Because all of your web servers have equal processing capacity, you want to load-balance HTTP connections on a round-robin basis. Using round-robin takes into account the ratio weight you assign in a later step to distribute load (Figure 9.66).

**FIGURE 9.66**
Select the load balancing method for the member pool.

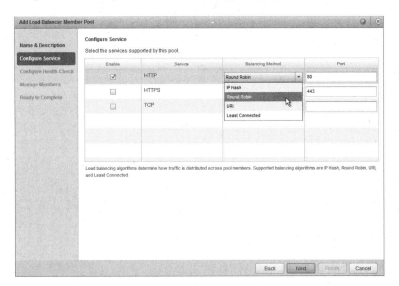

4. As shown in Figure 9.67, specify a health-check URI.

**FIGURE 9.67**
Setting health check parameters for the member pool

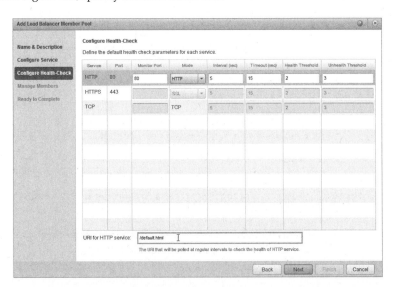

The load balancer on the edge gateway uses this URI to determine if your application server is still responding. If it does not receive a response within the timeout, it will no longer send traffic to that member of the pool because it assumes the application has failed.

You specify a URI that the load balancer will poll to determine if the application is responding or not. This may be the logon page for your application or a specific page—the exact details will depend on the application you are load-balancing.

**5.** For this example, poll for the home page of your application; if it does not respond, you know the web server has failed.

**6.** Next, you'll add servers to the member pool. Click Add and enter the IP address, port, and monitor port of each application server you wish to include in the pool (Figure 9.68).

**FIGURE 9.68**
Load-balancing port 80 HTTP traffic with equal weighting

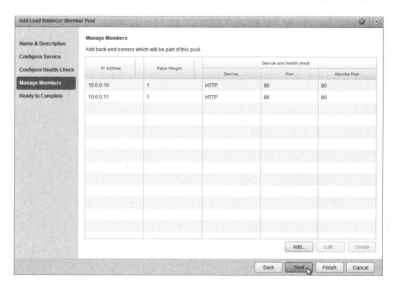

The wizard does not automatically pick up the IP addresses of the VMs in your vApp, so you will need to specify them manually.

**7.** Specify that there are two standard HTTP servers on two separate IP addresses that you intend to load-balance traffic to.

**8.** Specify a ratio weight for each server that you add to the member pool. The higher the number, the more requests will be sent to it.

You can also set Ratio Weight to 0, which will stop the load balancer from sending any traffic to the server, which could be useful for maintenance activities.

**9.** Click Finish. You now have a pool of servers with a load-balancing method and health-check mechanism specified.

The final task is to associate this member pool with a virtual server. In most other load balancers this is known as a virtual IP (VIP).

1. Click the Add button on the Virtual Servers section of the Load Balancer tab shown in Figure 9.65 and the Add Virtual Server dialog box shown in Figure 9.69 opens.

**FIGURE 9.69**
Adding a virtual server and associating it with a member pool

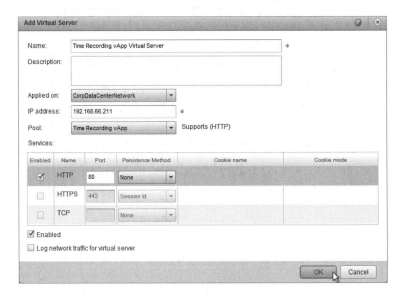

This virtual server will exist on the CorpDC network and so will be assigned a 192.168.66.0/24 network address.

2. Manually enter the IP address—the dialog box does not populate this field automatically.

   This IP address is one within the range that is suballocated to the edge gateway as shown earlier in Figure 9.54. If you enter an IP address outside of this range, a warning will appear reminding you of the available range of IP addresses that you can choose from.

3. In this example you'll be load-balancing the time recording vApp member pool, so select it from the Pool drop-down list. The application only serves HTTP requests on port 80 and does not have any persistence requirements.

---

**PERSISTENCE**

Persistence determines how connections should be directed after the initial connection. This option is useful for applications that maintain some sort of state between the client and web server. Two modes are available:

**None**   This mode will direct all requests to an available server in the member pool.

**Cookie**   This mode will use a cookie to direct sessions to the same server until it becomes unavailable.

---

The final step is to enable a firewall rule that allows HTTP traffic from the external networks to the virtual server.

**4.** The virtual server has an IP address of 192.168.66.211, so create the rule shown in Figure 9.70.

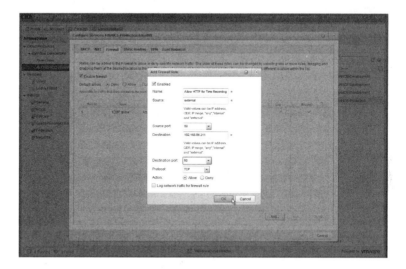

You can also find the external IP addresses configured on an edge gateway by right-clicking on it and selecting External IPA.

If you try connecting to the external IP address from a workstation on the CorpDC network, you'll find you can now connect to the load-balanced vApp. Alternate connection attempts should go to different VMs.

You have now created a simple load-balanced web application without having to deploy any hardware outside of vCloud Director or work with a network team or specialist vendor to so do. All of this functionality is enabled within the vCloud Director interface.

# Summary

Within vCloud Director, organizations can publish catalogs to other organizations in the vCloud platform. A catalog can contain vApps and media files.

In a typical deployment model for a private cloud, one organization, such as IT or corporate security, provides a set of standard, approved builds for consumers to work with. Consumers can take these building blocks and deploy them into their own catalogs and Org vDCs, where they can customize and extend them before copying them back to the organization's catalog to share with other developers.

Consumers who hold the vApp author role in vCloud Director can deploy vApps and choose which PvDC and storage tier they want to run it on. This self-service means that a consumer can specify which service level they want their vApp to run within without having to work with the infrastructure team to determine which storage LUNs, clusters, and networks their vApp needs to be deployed into. All of this is abstracted into an easy-to-understand set of objects.

vApps can be deployed directly to externally connected physical networks, such as a VLAN in a corporate datacenter. Or they can be attached to a virtual network that leverages a vCNS Edge appliance acting as a basic NAT router and firewall to isolate the vApp from the production network.

Access to vApps behind vCNS appliances is controlled by a firewall rule base, which can be edited from the vCloud Director interface. In traditional infrastructure, deploying such a topology would require input from a firewall or security team and would involve a number of configuration steps and tools. vCloud Director simplifies the process for the consumer.

vCNS Edge appliances are deployed on a per-vApp basis and support only a subset of the edge gateway functionality. For more complex network requirements, the vCNS Edge Gateway ships as part of vCloud Director. It offers the same functionality as the vCNS Edge appliance but adds the capability to support multiple network segments and VPN connections. It also provides a comprehensive IP load balancer.

The vCNS Edge Gateway can be used to provide similar functionality to a dedicated IP load balancer appliance that you'll find in many corporate datacenters. Again, the vCNS Edge Gateway abstracts the configuration and allows it to be administered from a single interface in vCloud Director.

Once the system administrator has deployed a vCNS Edge Gateway for an Org vDC, organization administrators have access to configure the vCNS Edge Gateway appliances as required. vCNS appliances can be deployed with vApps by normal consumers.

# Chapter 10

# Integrating Automation

Having successfully deployed a complete vCloud Director infrastructure, you are becoming accustomed to the day-to-day tasks associated with the maintenance of your vCloud. These tasks might range from system maintenance activities to provisioning of consumer resources. Undoubtedly you will now be looking for opportunities to enhance efficiency, ensure consistency, and increase integration through the use of automation.

This chapter highlights some of the APIs available in a vCloud and how they might be leveraged. We'll introduce commonly used automation solutions and how they could potentially be integrated into your vCloud.

In this chapter, you will learn to:

- Work with vCloud APIs

- Understand vSphere PowerCLI

- Use vCenter Orchestrator

- Work with RabbitMQ

## Working with vCloud APIs

You've learned that one of the distinguishing features of cloud computing is the opening of the infrastructure to manipulation through the use of a published API, such as the vCloud Director Representational State Transfer (REST) API. As you'll recall, a vCloud solution is constructed of several VMware products, and vCloud Director, through the use of multiple APIs, is the "glue" bonding everything together. Although the majority of vCloud automation solutions target the vCloud Director REST API, it is useful to have an appreciation of the other product APIs (see Figure 10.1).

vCloud Director includes a REST API, accessed over an HTTPS connection, for use by developers and consumers to build solutions ranging from simple scripts to more extensive integrated management systems. The vCloud API represents vCloud Director objects such as Organizations, Users/Groups, and Catalog items as Extensible Markup Language (XML) documents.

For a given vCloud Director object, the corresponding XML document will contain a number of attributes that represent key object properties: id, type, and href.

id   Represents a unique object identifier in the format of a uniform resource name (URN) that is valid for the life cycle of the object and does not get reused.

type   Defines the type of object in the format of a MIME type.

href   Represents a view of the object and is in the format of a uniform resource locator (URL) that includes the id attribute and hence is inherently valid for the life cycle of the object and does not get reused.

**FIGURE 10.1**
Individual product APIs and interdependencies

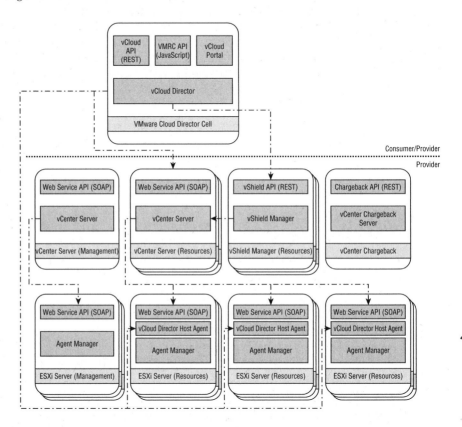

vCloud API Software Development Kits (SDKs) are available for Java, PHP, and .NET Framework. You can download them for free from the VMware website:

```
http://www.vmware.com/go/vcloudapi
```

In addition to the vCloud Director REST API, a Virtual Machine Remote Console (VMRC) JavaScript API is available. Use of this API is more common among public vCloud providers. VMRC access in vCloud Director is provided in the form of a browser plug-in, and its purpose is to integrate this functionality through a web-based interface. You can also use it to provide event notifications in case the target virtual machine state changes. The VMRC API programming guide is freely available from the VMware website:

```
http://pubs.vmware.com/vsphere-51/topic/com.vmware.ICbase/PDF/vs5_1_vmrc_prog_
guide.pdf
```

Similarly to vCloud Director, both vShield Manager and vCenter Chargeback include a REST API that is accessed over an HTTPS connection and again represents objects as XML documents. Each object is accessed via a unique resource URL—effectively the same concept as in vCloud Director. Java SDKs are available for both vShield Manager and vCenter Chargeback and are freely available for download from the VMware Developer Community website:

```
http://communities.vmware.com/community/vmtn/developer
```

vSphere provides a Simple Object Access Protocol (SOAP)-based API with Web Services Description Language (WSDL) that is accessed over HTTPS by default but can also be accessed over HTTP. The architecture of the vSphere API is based on the concept of *managed objects*, *managed object references*, and *data objects*. vSphere API SDKs for Perl, Java, and .NET exist. Again, these are freely available for download from the VMware Developer Community website.

**Managed Objects**    Managed objects represent services or components such as a virtual machine.

**Managed Object References**    Managed object references, often referred to as MoRefs, are a unique identifier for a given managed object, which persist for the life cycle of the object no matter where it's moved within the vCenter inventory. However, if a given object is removed from the inventory and then added again, a new MoRef is assigned, effectively creating a new object.

**Data Objects**    Data objects are used to define the specifications or capabilities of a given object such as a virtual machine. They exist within managed objects and can be accessed only through managed objects.

In addition to developing an appreciation of the wide range of product APIs, you should recognize the accessibility of these APIs from the perspective of a consumer or provider. We have already established that it is a requirement of cloud computing that a consumer be able to provision resources "without human interaction." The following statement relates to the requirement of APIs that allow programmatic interaction with the vCloud platform:

> *A consumer can unilaterally provision computing capabilities, such as server time and network storage, as needed automatically without requiring human interaction with each service's provider.*

> —NIST definition of cloud computing

Typically a consumer would only be granted access to the vCloud Director API, since allowing consumers access to any of the additional APIs would represent a significant risk to both the security and stability of the entire vCloud and all tenants it serves. The provider, system privileges and configuration permitting, typically has the capability to access all APIs independently, offering significant automation capabilities. But doing so has to be given careful consideration in conjunction with the security principles of "least privilege" and "separation of duties."

> *With great power there must also come—great responsibility!*

> —Uncle Ben, Amazing Fantasy

# Introducing VMware vSphere PowerCLI

VMware vSphere PowerCLI is a powerful command-line tool that lets you automate aspects of vSphere management, including network, storage, virtual machine, guest operating system, and more. More recently, following the release of vCloud Director, newer versions (5.0.1 on) of PowerCLI have introduced support for vCloud Director.

PowerCLI is distributed as a Windows PowerShell snap-in. The latest version includes over 360 PowerShell cmdlets that provide interfaces to vSphere and vCloud APIs. PowerCLI is freely available for download from the VMware website:

```
http://www.vmware.com/go/PowerCLI
```

In addition to the cmdlets distributed with the PowerCLI snap-in, VMware provides product-specific snap-ins such as the vCenter Update Manager PowerCLI and View PowerCLI cmdlets (included with the VMware View installation). Furthermore, this capability is not limited to VMware cmdlets but can be extended to include cmdlets produced by other vendors. For example, Dell provides a series of cmdlets for interaction with its Compellent storage arrays.

## Microsoft PowerShell Overview

PowerShell is a command-line shell and scripting language based on the .NET Framework. It is designed for system administrators and power users to allow command line–based management of computers within an enterprise.

Given PowerCLI is a PowerShell snap-in, it uses the same basic concepts and syntax. To work with PowerShell, you run cmdlets in much the same way you would run native Windows commands. In addition to running cmdlets, PowerShell supports the use of native Windows commands. Multiple cmdlets can be combined to form scripts or functions.

A cmdlet is a compiled piece of .NET code that performs a specific operation. All cmdlets follow a defined verb-noun naming structure, where the verb specifies an action and the noun specifies the object on which the action will be performed. This simplifies identifying which cmdlet to use, provided you know what object you wish to manipulate.

Each cmdlet will accept a series of parameters and arguments that define how the cmdlet should interact with a given object. Typically a cmdlet will contain both mandatory and optional parameters. In most cases, if a mandatory parameter is not specified you will be prompted to provide the missing parameter. Furthermore, PowerShell includes pipeline functionality that enables a cmdlet to receive an object from a previously executed cmdlet.

## Getting Started with PowerCLI

The newest version of PowerCLI (version 5.1.0 Release 1) is unique in comparison to the previous versions because it introduces two completely independent installation packages: VMware vSphere PowerCLI 5.1.0 Release 1 and VMware vSphere PowerCLI 5.1.0 Release 1 for Tenants. The former represents the latest evolution of the PowerCLI snap-in, whereas the latter is a new package aimed specifically at the needs of tenants and provides a simplified subset of cmdlets for use within a vCloud organization.

**NOTE**   The amount of effort required to start using PowerCLI is relatively low, but becoming competent will take some time and, of course, practice. The installation of PowerCLI is as simple as downloading and running an installer on a supported client machine. It is a common misconception that there are server components that require installation, but this is not the case. PowerCLI simply provides a command-line tool to interact with the existing published APIs.

To introduce the basic concepts of PowerCLI, and in particular the vCloud Director cmdlets, we'll start by examining the objects created in Chapter 8, "Delivering Services." Assuming you have managed to successfully download and run the installation package, and that you selected to also install the optional vCloud cmdlets, you should be ready to launch PowerCLI. Before trying to interact directly with vCloud Director, you should explore some of the mechanisms, in addition to the supplied documentation, for determining which cmdlets to use and how they should be used. A good example is the `Get-VICommand` cmdlet, which will retrieve a list of all of the cmdlets available with PowerCLI. But do not confuse `Get-VICommand` with the PowerShell `Get-Command` cmdlet, which will return a list of all cmdlets, including the native PowerShell cmdlets—over 700 of them!

```
PowerCLI C:\> Get-VICommand

CommandType     Name                      Definition
-----------     ----                      ----------
Cmdlet          Add-DeployRule            Add-DeployRule [-DeployRule]...
Cmdlet          Add-EsxSoftwareDepot      Add-EsxSoftwareDepot [-Depot...
Cmdlet          Add-EsxSoftwarePackage    Add-EsxSoftwarePackage [-Ima...
...
Cmdlet          Update-Tools              Update-Tools [[-Guest] <VMGu...
Cmdlet          Wait-Task                 Wait-Task [-Task] <Task[]> [...
Cmdlet          Wait-Tools                Wait-Tools [[-TimeoutSeconds...


PowerCLI C:\>
```

PowerShell also supports the use of wildcard searches within cmdlets. Using *CI* as a parameter to the previous `Get-VICommand` cmdlet, you can list a subset, but not all, of the cmdlets that are for use with vCloud Director:

```
PowerCLI C:\> Get-VICommand *CI*

CommandType     Name                      Definition
-----------     ----                      ----------
Cmdlet          Connect-CIServer          Connect-CIServer [-Server] <...
Cmdlet          Disconnect-CIServer       Disconnect-CIServer [[-Serve...
Cmdlet          Get-CIRole                Get-CIRole [[-Name] <String[...
Cmdlet          Get-CIUser                Get-CIUser [[-Name] <String[...
Cmdlet          Get-CIVApp                Get-CIVApp [[-Name] <String[...
Cmdlet          Get-CIVAppTemplate        Get-CIVAppTemplate [[-Name] ...
Cmdlet          Get-CIView                Get-CIView [-CIObject] <CIOb...
Cmdlet          Get-CIVM                  Get-CIVM [[-Name] <String[]>...
Cmdlet          Import-CIVApp             Import-CIVApp [-VM] <Virtual...
Cmdlet          Import-CIVAppTemplate     Import-CIVAppTemplate [-VM] ...
...


PowerCLI C:\>
```

Although the use of a wildcard search using *CI* can identify cmdlets for use with vCloud Director and is useful generally, it is important to recognize that not all the vCloud Director cmdlets currently include the characters CI within the name. Furthermore, over time cmdlet names may change, so it is helpful to understand how to identify cmdlets on the basis of the snap-in with which they are provided. You can do so by using the `Get-Command` cmdlet and including the `Module` parameter to specifically retrieve cmdlets for use with vCloud Director:

```
PowerCLI C:\> Get-Command -Module Vmware.VimAutomation.Cloud


CommandType       Name                      Definition
-----------       ----                      ----------
Cmdlet            Add-CIDatastore           Add-CIDatastore [[-ProviderV...
Cmdlet            Connect-CIServer          Connect-CIServer [-Server] <...
Cmdlet            Disconnect-CIServer       Disconnect-CIServer [[-Serve...
Cmdlet            Get-Catalog               Get-Catalog [[-Name] <String...
Cmdlet            Get-CIAccessControlRule   Get-CIAccessControlRule [[-E...
Cmdlet            Get-CIDatastore           Get-CIDatastore [[-Name] <St...
Cmdlet            Get-CINetworkAdapter      Get-CINetworkAdapter [-Prima...
Cmdlet            Get-CIRole                Get-CIRole [[-Name] <String[...
Cmdlet            Get-CIUser                Get-CIUser [[-Name] <String[...
Cmdlet            Get-CIVApp                Get-CIVApp [[-Name] <String[...
Cmdlet            Get-CIVAppNetwork         Get-CIVAppNetwork [[-Name] <...
Cmdlet            Get-CIVAppStartRule       Get-CIVAppStartRule [-VApp] ...
Cmdlet            Get-CIVAppTemplate        Get-CIVAppTemplate [[-Name] ...
Cmdlet            Get-CIView                Get-CIView [-CIObject] <CIOb...
Cmdlet            Get-CIVM                  Get-CIVM [[-Name] <String[]>...
Cmdlet            Get-ExternalNetwork       Get-ExternalNetwork [[-Name]...
Cmdlet            Get-Media                 Get-Media [[-Name] <String[]...
Cmdlet            Get-NetworkPool           Get-NetworkPool [[-Name] <St...
Cmdlet            Get-Org                   Get-Org [[-Name] <String[]>]...
Cmdlet            Get-OrgNetwork            Get-OrgNetwork [[-Name] <Str...
Cmdlet            Get-OrgVdc                Get-OrgVdc [[-Name] <String[...
Cmdlet            Get-ProviderVdc           Get-ProviderVdc [[-Name] <St...
Cmdlet            Import-CIVApp             Import-CIVApp [-VM] <Virtual...
Cmdlet            Import-CIVAppTemplate     Import-CIVAppTemplate [-VM] ...
...


PowerCLI C:\>
```

If you ran this cmdlet with PowerCLI 5.0.1, you'd noticed that the list of cmdlets was relatively short and that the majority of cmdlets were Get cmdlets that are used for retrieving existing objects but not for modifying or creating new objects. The reason for this is simple. When new products are released, there is a relatively short timeframe to develop and release an updated version of PowerCLI. Consequently, only a few cmdlets can be developed. In the process of developing cmdlets, the typical approach is to first create the Get cmdlets and then follow with the Set and New cmdlets in subsequent releases.

Get cmdlets represent a good starting point for anybody new to PowerCLI, since they are intended to simply retrieve information rather than create, amend, or delete vCloud Director objects.

Despite the substantial increase in cmdlets, you may encounter a case where a cmdlet to create or modify a specific object is not available. In such cases, don't dismiss the use of PowerCLI. The `ExtensionData` property, which is present on all objects returned through the use of Get cmdlets, will return cloud view objects and provide access to the vCloud API methods, thus allowing you to manipulate the associated objects. You can do the same thing by using the `Get-CIView` cmdlet.

Use of the ExtensionData property and Get-CIView cmdlet is targeted at advanced users who need access to specific cloud view objects and associated methods. In many cases, an existing cmdlet can achieve the desired result.

Once an available cmdlet has been identified, the associated parameters and how they should be applied are easily retrieved using the Get-Help cmdlet. Notice the option to specify -examples, -detailed, and -full, which allows you to tailor the type of information displayed:

```
PowerCLI C:\> Get-Help Get-VM

NAME
    Get-VM
SYNOPSIS
    Retrieves the virtual machines on a vSphere server.

SYNTAX
    Get-VM [-Datastore <Datastore[]>] [-Location <VIContainer[]>] [[-Name] <Str
    ing[]>] [-Id <String[]>] [-NoRecursion] [-Server <VIServer[]>] [<CommonPara
    meters>]
    Get-VM [-DistributedSwitch <DistributedSwitch[]>] [[-Name] <String[]>] [-Id
     <String[]>] [-NoRecursion] [-Server <VIServer[]>] [<CommonParameters>]

DESCRIPTION
    Retrieves the virtual machines on a vSphere server. Returns a set of virtua
    l machines that correspond to the filter criteria provided by the cmdlet pa
    rameters. For virtual machines with multiple NICs and multiple IP addresses
    , the IPAddress property of the VMGuest object contains all IP addresses of
     the virtual machine. The IP at position 0 is the primary IP address.

RELATED LINKS
    Online version: http://www.vmware.com/support/developer/PowerCLI/PowerCLI50
    1/html/Get-VM.html
    Remove-VM
    New-VM
    Set-VM
    Move-VM
    Start-VM
    Stop-VM
    Suspend-VM
    Restart-VM
REMARKS
    To see the examples, type: "get-help Get-VM -examples".
    For more information, type: "get-help Get-VM -detailed".
    For technical information, type: "get-help Get-VM -full".

PowerCLI C:\>
```

## PowerCLI and vCloud Director Cmdlets

Having made it this far, you should now know how to find available cmdlets and retrieve help regarding their usage. Equipped with this knowledge, you are ready to start working with your vCloud. The first stage in working with a vCloud Director Server is to establish a connection using the `Connect-CIServer` cmdlet:

```
PowerCLI C:\> Connect-CIServer -Server vcloud

Name                          User                        Org
----                          ----                        ---
vcloud                        administrator               System

PowerCLI C:\>
```

Having successfully connected to the vCloud Director Cell, it will be possible to start interrogating vCloud objects. Taking the previously created Provider Virtual Data Center (PvDC) called Bronze vDC as an example, you will first need to identify the appropriate cmdlet. As you recall, cmdlets follow a defined verb-noun naming structure, so in this instance the noun will be `ProviderVdc`, and given the intention is to get details of the PvDC, the verb will be `Get`. With the appropriate cmdlet identified, it will be necessary to supply search criteria, such as the name, to identify the specific PvDC. Using the `Get-Help` cmdlet, you will discover that there is a `-Name` parameter you can use. Alternatively executing the cmdlet with no parameters will return all PvDCs.

```
PowerCLI C:\> Get-ProviderVdc -Name "Bronze PvDC"

WARNING: column "StorageUsedGB" does not fit into the display and was removed.
Name                          Status       Enabled CpuUsedGhz   MemoryUs
                                                                 edGB

----                          ------       ------- ----------   --------
Bronze PvDC                   Ready        True    0.00 (0.0%)  0.00 ...

PowerCLI C:\>
```

You should now have a grasp of some of the fundamentals, so let's introduce some pipeline functionality to achieve something a little more meaningful. Suppose the IT-PAYG Organization vDC is running low on memory resources and you need to identify the potential culprits. To do so, you first identify the Organization (Org) vDC object and then any vApp objects and, in turn, virtual machine objects it contains. Applying the same logic for identifying the correct cmdlets, the intention is to interact with Org vDCs and vApps, so the appropriate cmdlets will be `Get-OrgVdc`, `Get-CIVapp`, and `Get-CIVM`:

```
PowerCLI C:\> Get-OrgVdc -Name "IT-PAYG" | Get-CIVApp | Get-CIVM

WARNING: 2 columns do not fit into the display and were removed.
Name                          Status              GuestOSFullName
----                          ------              ---------------
LargeVM1                      PoweredOff          Microsoft Windows...
Small VM1                     PoweredOff          Microsoft Windows...
HugeVM1                       PoweredOff          Microsoft Windows...
Small VM1                     PoweredOff          Microsoft Windows...
Small VM2                     PoweredOff          Microsoft Windows...

PowerCLI C:\>
```

In some cases the vCloud Director cmdlet names do not directly follow the expected verb-noun structure and have a CI prefix incorporated with the noun component. This is typically the case where an equivalent cmdlet already exists for vSphere.

You have now successfully identified all of the virtual machines within the IT-PAYG Org vDC, but it is not yet possible to identify how much memory they have been assigned. Wouldn't it be helpful if you could highlight the amount of memory on each virtual machine and sort the results in descending order? This is where you can leverage some of the native PowerShell cmdlets, such as `Select` and `Sort-Object`.

```
PowerCLI C:\> Get-OrgVdc -Name "IT-PAYG" | Get-CIVApp | Get-CIVM | Select vApp,
Name, MemoryMB, Status | Sort-Object -Property MemoryMB -Descending

VApp                Name                        MemoryMB            Status
----                ----                        --------            ------
MyHugevApp          HugeVM1                         4096          PoweredOff
MyHugevApp          LargeVM1                        1024          PoweredOff
MySmallvApp         Small VM2                        512          PoweredOff
MySmallvApp         Small VM1                        512          PoweredOff
MyHugevApp          Small VM1                        512          PoweredOff

PowerCLI C:\>
```

Now that you have established the fundamental aspects of using PowerCLI in the context of a few basic examples, you may have noticed that we have been using the properties of objects to select and sort results. But how do you determine what properties are available? This is where the `Get-Member` cmdlet comes in handy as it provides details regarding members of a given object:

```
PowerCLI C:\> Get-ProviderVdc -Name "Bronze PvDC" | Get-Member

   TypeName: VMware.VimAutomation.Cloud.Impl.V1.ProviderVdcImpl
Name                              MemberType Definition
----                              ---------- ----------
Equals                            Method     bool Equals(System.Object obj)
GetHashCode                       Method     int GetHashCode()
GetType                           Method     type GetType()
ToString                          Method     string ToString()
CpuAllocatedGHz                   Property   System.Nullable`1[[System.Double,...
CpuOverheadGHz                    Property   System.Nullable`1[[System.Double,...
CpuTotalGHz                       Property   System.Nullable`1[[System.Double,...
CpuUsedGHz                        Property   System.Nullable`1[[System.Double,...
Description                       Property   System.String Description {get;}
Enabled                           Property   System.Nullable`1[[System.Boolean...
ExtensionData                     Property   System.Object ExtensionData {get;}
HighestSupportedHardwareVersion   Property   VMware.VimAutomation.ViCore.Types...
Href                              Property   System.String Href {get;}
Id                                Property   System.String Id {get;}
MemoryAllocatedGB                 Property   System.Nullable`1[[System.Double,...
MemoryOverheadGB                  Property   System.Nullable`1[[System.Double,...
MemoryTotalGB                     Property   System.Nullable`1[[System.Double,...
```

```
MemoryUsedGB                     Property   System.Nullable`1[[System.Double,...
Name                             Property   System.String Name {get;}
Status                           Property   System.Nullable`1[[VMware.VimAuto...
StorageAllocatedGB               Property   System.Nullable`1[[System.Double,...
StorageOverheadGB                Property   System.Nullable`1[[System.Double,...
StorageTotalGB                   Property   System.Nullable`1[[System.Double,...
StorageUsedGB                    Property   System.Nullable`1[[System.Double,...


PowerCLI C:\>
```

You should also notice that in addition to properties of the objects the `Get-Member` cmdlet will display available methods. For example, if you were to review an Org vDC object and in particular the `ExtensionData` property, which we touched on earlier, you might notice additional methods such as `InstantiateVAppTemplate`. So for example, in the case of PowerCLI 5.0.1 where the `New-CIVApp` cmdlet did not exist, it was still possible to interact fully, but you needed to be more familiar with the vCloud API.

```
PowerCLI C:\> (Get-OrgVdc -Name "IT-PAYG").ExtensionData | Get-Member


   TypeName: VMware.VimAutomation.Cloud.Views.AdminVdc
Name                      MemberType Definition
----                      ---------- ----------
CaptureVApp               Method     VMware.VimAutomation.Cloud.Views.VAppTem...
CloneMedia                Method     VMware.VimAutomation.Cloud.Views.Media C...
CloneVApp                 Method     VMware.VimAutomation.Cloud.Views.VApp Cl...
CloneVAppTemplate         Method     VMware.VimAutomation.Cloud.Views.VAppTem...
ComposeVApp               Method     VMware.VimAutomation.Cloud.Views.VApp Co...
CreateMedia               Method     VMware.VimAutomation.Cloud.Views.Media C...
CreateMetadata            Method     System.Void CreateMetadata(VMware.VimAut...
CreateMetadata_Task       Method     VMware.VimAutomation.Cloud.Views.Task Cr...
Delete                    Method     System.Void Delete()
Delete_Task               Method     VMware.VimAutomation.Cloud.Views.Task De...
Disable                   Method     System.Void Disable()
Enable                    Method     System.Void Enable()
Equals                    Method     bool Equals(System.Object obj)
GetHashCode               Method     int GetHashCode()
GetMetadata               Method     VMware.VimAutomation.Cloud.Views.Metadat...
GetType                   Method     type GetType()
InstantiateVAppTemplate   Method     VMware.VimAutomation.Cloud.Views.VApp In...
ToString                  Method     string ToString()
UpdateServerData          Method     System.Void UpdateServerData()
UpdateServerData_Task     Method     VMware.VimAutomation.Cloud.Views.Task Up...
UpdateViewData            Method     System.Void UpdateViewData()
UploadVAppTemplate        Method     VMware.VimAutomation.Cloud.Views.VAppTem...
...
VCloudExtension           Property   VMware.VimAutomation.Cloud.Views.VCloudE...
VCpuInMhz                 Property   System.Nullable`1[[System.Int64, mscorli...
VmQuota                   Property   System.Nullable`1[[System.Int32, mscorli...


PowerCLI C:\>
```

### POWERCLI AND COMBINING vCLOUD DIRECTOR AND vSPHERE CMDLETS

Since the primary subject of this chapter is introducing automation for vCloud Director, the topic of using the vSphere cmdlets has not been covered. However, using vSphere cmdlets is, as you might expect, identical to using the vCloud Director cmdlets. An important concept worth considering is the new capability that arises through simultaneous access to both the vCloud Director and vSphere APIs. When vCloud Director is not able to support an underlying vSphere capability, PowerCLI is a potential solution. To illustrate, consider the use of Distributed Resource Scheduler (DRS) rules and the fact that they cannot currently be defined using vCloud Director.

Applying DRS rules to the VMs of a vCloud Director vApp might include some of the following key stages, with some standard PowerShell code and a simple loop to pull the process together:

Identify the vCloud Director vApp object (Get-CIVApp).

```
PowerCLI C:\> $CIVApp = Get-CIVApp –Name MySmallvApp
```

Identify the vCloud Director VM objects (Get-CIVM).

```
PowerCLI C:\> $CIVMs = $CIVApp | Get-CIVM
```

Identify the matching vSphere VM objects (Get-VM).

```
PowerCLI C:\> $VIVMs = @()
PowerCLI C:\> foreach ($CIVM in $CIVMs){
>>$VIVM = Get-VM | where {$_.Name -match ($CIVM.Id).split(":")[3]}
>>$VIVMs += $VIVM
>>}
>>$VIVMs
>>
Name                   PowerState Num CPUs Memory (MB)
----                   ---------- -------- -----------
Small VM1 (622cfb... PoweredOff 1          512
Small VM2 (ca7525... PoweredOff 1          512
```

Apply a DRS rule to the vSphere Cluster (New-DrsRule).

```
PowerCLI C:\> New-DrsRule -Cluster (Get-Cluster -Name Primary) -Name vAppKeepApartRule01
-KeepTogether $false -VM $VIVMs

Name             Enabled KeepTogether VMIDs
----             ------- ------------ -----
vAppKeepApar... False   False        {VirtualMachine-vm-6295, VirtualMachine...

PowerCLI C:\>
```

**WARNING**  Although PowerCLI reveals new capabilities for working around desired features that are missing in vCloud Director, approach with caution. Although in some cases the feature simply couldn't be incorporated within product release schedules, in other cases there may be a valid technical reason why the functionality is not present. For example, the use of Raw Disk Mappings is deliberately absent, as it would break the concept of portability between vCloud solutions or Hybrid vCloud. Consider implementing such changes outside of vCloud Director carefully so as not to inadvertently create an unsupported configuration. Detailed reporting is a great example of where the ability to interact with multiple APIs, to overcome vCloud Director limitations, offers significant benefits without the risk of implementing unsupported changes.

## PowerCLI Tools

Throughout this chapter, the examples discussed have all been based on the use of the PowerCLI command window. While PowerCLI is technically capable of creating and running more complex functions and scripts, its command-line nature does not lend itself well to this use case.

To write larger and more complex scripts, you can use any form of text editor such as Notepad, provided you then save the files with a `.ps1` extension. You can then execute these scripts from the PowerCLI command line by simply supplying the full path to the script:

```
PowerCLI C:\> C:\MyScripts\MyScript.ps1
```

The most productive method for producing PowerCLI scripts is to use an interactive editing tool such as Quest Software's PowerGUI. PowerGUI is an extremely handy tool for experts and beginners alike. It is particularly useful for beginners since it includes command keyword completion, an output window, and a hierarchy of all objects stored in variables and the ability to browse their respective properties (see Figure 10.2).

**FIGURE 10.2**
Quest PowerGUI
Script Editor

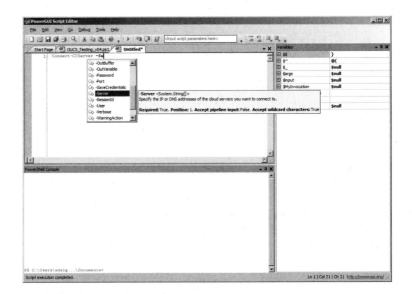

PowerGUI is available for free from here:

```
http://www.powergui.org/downloads.jspa
```

# Using VMware vCenter Orchestrator

VMware vCenter Orchestrator represents the current evolution of the Virtual Service Orchestrator (VS-O) product inherited by VMware following the September 2007 acquisition of Dunes Technologies. vCenter Orchestrator is an extreamly powerful tool that provides orchestration capabilities in the form of automated workflows. One of the many strengths of vCenter Orchestrator is the use of plug-ins that enable integration of a wide variety of solutions, in addition to the expected support for VMware products. Along with integration capabilities, plug-ins provide precreated standard workflows and in some cases workflows that can be used to assist with the initial plug-in configuration. The standard workflows include support from VMware.

Historically vCenter Orchestrator has been a relatively expensive licensed product, but in more recent years it has been bundled free with vCenter Server.

Many VMware customers do not realize the power that is just a few configuration steps away and free to use. In addition to the Windows-based installation included with vCenter Server, vCenter Orchestrator is now available as a Novell SuSE Linux Enterprise Server–based virtual appliance and is also freely available from the VMware website:

```
https://my.vmware.com/web/vmware/info/slug/datacenter_cloud_infrastructure/vmware_
vcloud_suite/5_1
```

The introduction of the vCenter Orchestrator appliance has significantly reduced the effort associated with initial deployment and configuration of vCenter Orchestrator, yet it still retains all of the features, functionality, and performance levels of the original Windows-based installation.

Despite the considerable capabilities of vCenter Orchestrator, adoption in the past has been relatively low due mainly to the lack of awareness and perceived complexity required to design and implement automated workflows. However, the drive for greater automation and integration, fueled by the industry trend for cloud computing, is leading to change. With the continuing improvements in plug-in availability, release of a virtual appliance, and further simplification introduced in the latest release acting as a catalyst, vCenter Orchestrator is undergoing a revival.

## Getting Started with vCenter Orchestrator

vCenter Orchestrator is an incredibly feature-rich and powerful product and, as a result, it will not be possible to cover all aspects of the product in this chapter. Reviewing just a subset of the functionality will almost certainly whet your appetite and encourage you to consider whether vCenter Orchestrator is the automation tool for your vCloud.

The first step in the process for using vCenter Orchestrator is to download and deploy the virtual appliance. The process for this is consistent with that of other virtual appliances and involves the simple task of downloading the Open Virtualization Format (OVF) file and associated virtual disk files, and then deploying them through vCenter Server. Following a number of relatively straightforward configuration tasks, you will be in a position to decide which plug-ins you intend to use.

### PLUG-IN OVERVIEW AND SELECTION CONSIDERATIONS

The significant capabilities of vCenter Orchestrator are a result of the flexible JavaScript API and plug-in architecture that allows for quick integration with other products and solutions. The complete selection of official plug-ins is available free for download form the VMware website:

```
http://www.vmware.com/products/datacenter-virtualization/vcenter-orchestrator/
plugins.html
```

If you were to review the available plug-ins, you would notice that plug-ins are available not only for vCloud Director but also for many other major product components that form a vCloud:

◆ vCenter Orchestrator Plug-in for vCloud Director 1.5

◆ vCenter Orchestrator Plug-in for vCloud Director 5.1

♦   vCenter Orchestrator Plug-in for vCenter Chargeback Manager 2.0

♦   vCenter Orchestrator Plug-in for vCenter Server 5.0

♦   vCenter Orchestrator Plug-in for vCenter Server 5.1

♦   vCenter Orchestrator Plug-in for Microsoft Windows PowerShell 1.0.1

These plug-ins provide vCenter Orchestrator with the capability to interact directly with the individual products. This interaction is achieved using the associated Java SDK for communication between the plug-in(s) and the REST or SOAP API of the respective products. Another significant aspect of all vCenter Orchestrator plug-ins is the inclusion of standard workflows that are supported by VMware. To put this in context, the current vCloud Director plug-in contains in excess of 160 workflows that can automate administrator actions such as the creation of new Organizations and Org vDCs to consumer-centric actions such as deploying and updating vApps.

The PowerShell plug-in is a little different from the product-specific plug-ins that enable direct product API interaction within automated workflows, since it instead enables interaction with PowerShell cmdlets or scripts from within workflows. PowerShell, complemented with product-specific snap-ins such as PowerCLI, in turn provides interaction with the product APIs. Unlike the other plug-ins, the PowerShell plug-in has an additional requirement in the form of a PowerShell host on which to execute cmdlets. The plug-in communicates with the PowerShell host using OpenSSH or Windows Remote Management (WinRM). In the case of the Windows-based installation of vCenter Orchestrator, the possibility would exist to collocate the PowerShell host with vCenter Orchestrator, but clearly this would not be possible with the Linux-based appliance. This may be an additional consideration to factor in when evaluating the benefits of the appliance against the traditional Windows-based installation.

The PowerShell plug-in supports a migration from a PowerCLI-based automation environment with reduced rework; why rewrite the scripts if you can simply run them from vCenter Orchestrator? In addition, if a specific plug-in or capability is absent from vCenter Orchestrator, such as a VMware View plug-in, then the PowerShell plug-in potentially offers the opportunity to "plug the gap."

It is generally preferable, not to mention a VMware recommended practice, to manage all aspects of a vCloud solution through vCloud Director. In light of this, it could be argued that there is no requirement to use the additional plug-ins on the basis that vCloud Director already provides that functionality. While there is some logic in this argument, the availability of the additional product plug-ins lets you perform specific configurations that cannot be achieved using vCloud Director in isolation. Though such custom implementations should be used sparingly to avoid overcomplicating an environment or inadvertently creating an unsupported configuration, there are valid use cases. vCenter Orchestrator can be used to perform the required actions by leveraging both the vCloud API and the vSphere API—remember defining a DRS rule for a vApp earlier using PowerCLI?

In addition to the VMware product-specific plug-ins, a number of additional plug-ins should also be considered in the context of extending the automation of your vCloud solution to include integration with other external applications and core infrastructure services:

♦   vCenter Orchestrator Plug-in for Active Directory

♦   vCenter Orchestrator AMQP Plug-in

♦   vCenter Orchestrator SNMP Plug-in

The Active Directory Plug-in allows vCenter Orchestrator to reference the objects of an Active Directory in the inventory and run workflows against them by leveraging Java Naming and Directory Interface (JNDI). The plug-in includes standard workflows covering common actions such as creating organization units (OUs), users and groups, and computer accounts.

The AMQP plug-in enables vCenter Orchestrator to interact with AMQP servers, sometimes referred to as brokers, such as RabbitMQ (which we will introduce later in this chapter). Using this plug-in you can subscribe to existing message queues and configure new exchanges, queues, and bindings. If these terms are unfamiliar to you, don't worry—we will cover them again later in this chapter.

The Simple Network Management Protocol (SNMP) plug-in provides vCenter Orchestrator with the capability to interact with SNMP-enabled devices such as routers, switches, and printers and define them as inventory objects. It presents the option to listen for events, referred to as "SNMP traps."

The AMQP and SNMP plug-ins are subtly different from the product-based plug-ins in the sense that they don't provide direct product automation capabilities. However, they add significant capability in the form of automated responses to defined messages or events—the basis of a self-healing datacenter?

**NOTE** Many other plug-ins are available, not specifically explored in this chapter, that present further integration opportunities with hardware and software solutions from other vendors. For example, in addition to the vCloud Director and vSphere plug-ins that leverage REST and SOAP APIs respectively, there are generic REST and SOAP plug-ins that open up almost endless integration opportunities with other applications.

It is also important to recognize the vast array of community-developed packages that can offer significant capabilities to help accelerate your path to a more automated vCloud. The perfect example is the vCloud Director blocking tasks and notification packages available from the VMware Community website:

```
http://communities.vmware.com/docs/DOC-18002
```

```
http://communities.vmware.com/docs/DOC-20446
```

The blocking tasks and notification package provides vCenter Orchestrator with the ability to react to messages from an AMQP server such as RabbitMQ and trigger automated workflows so that a defined workflow can be run on the detection of a vCloud Director blocking task or notification.

Community packages offer considerable functionality, but keep in mind they are provided "as is" and do not include any form of warranty. This is not to say they should not be used, but if the intention is to integrate them with a production solution, be sure to make an informed decision.

### ADMINISTRATION OF vCENTER ORCHESTRATOR

The configuration and administration of the vCenter Orchestrator appliance is achieved through the use of a web-based configuration interface and Java-based client application.

The web-based configuration interface provides a centralized administration point for a vCenter Orchestrator deployment. All common configuration activities are carried out from this interface. For example, this interface is used to install and configure plug-ins.

The vCenter Orchestrator Java-based client provides a simple and intuitive interface for administrators to perform day-to-day tasks such as importing packages and creating and running workflows. Though some administrative tasks can be carried out using the client, some configuration steps remain unavailable and need to be accessed from the web-based configuration interface.

### LOCATING, INSTALLING, AND CONFIGURING PLUG-INS

Following the successful deployment and initial configuration of vCenter Orchestrator, the process for deploying new plug-ins is relatively simple. Each plug-in includes associated installation and configuration guidance, but the typical process for adding new plug-ins is to download the desired plug-in, in the form of a VMOAPP file, and upload it using the plug-ins section of the web-based configuration interface (see Figure 10.3).

**FIGURE 10.3**
Uploading the vCloud Director plug-in to vCenter Orchestrator

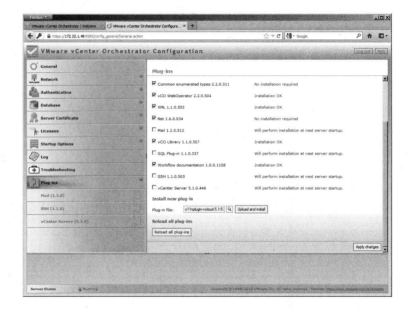

Upon completion of the upload, the vCenter Orchestrator service should be restarted from the Startup Options section—all of which is achievable in a matter of minutes. To illustrate, we will walk you through the example for deploying the vCloud Director plug-in.

The installation of the vCloud Director plug-in follows the typical process covered previously and consists of the following high-level stages:

1. Download the vCloud Director plug-in VMOAPP.

2. Open the vCenter Orchestrator web-based configuration interface.

3. Navigate to the Plug-ins section and upload the VMOAPP file.

4. Navigate to the Startup Options section and restart the vCenter Orchestrator Service.

Following installation of a new plug-in, there are generally a number of initial configuration steps required before the plug-in can be used for automated workflows. In the case of the vCloud Director plug-in, this is the process to establish a new vCloud Director connection, which includes the following steps:

1. Navigate to the vCloud Director section.

2. Select SSL Certificates and then import the SSL certificates from the vCloud Director URL.

3. Select the New vCloud Director Connection tab and define a user authentication mechanism.

When you're using Basic Authentication, two methods of authentication are available: Share A Unique Session or Session Per User. The former of these mechanisms is the more traditional approach, where vCenter Orchestrator uses a single set of credentials for connecting to vCloud Director. The latter option allows you to establish a unique session for each user connected. The release of vCenter Orchestrator 5.1 also introduced a new Single Sign-On (SSO) capability, which allows users to log on once yet be authenticated for vCenter Orchestrator, vCloud Director, and also vCenter Server. For example, this could support a user already authenticated with vSphere to run a workflow automating vCloud Director tasks while authenticated in vCenter Orchestrator and vCloud Director as the same user.

Once you complete the configuration of a vCloud Director connection, vCenter Orchestrator will be able to establish a connection to your vCloud Director Cell, browse vCloud objects, and execute automated workflows (see Figure 10.4).

**FIGURE 10.4**
Exploring the vCloud Director inventory

## AUTOMATING vCLOUD DIRECTOR WITH vCENTER ORCHESTRATOR

Now that you've installed the vCloud Director plug-in, your vCenter Orchestrator server has the capability to interact with vCloud Director. This interaction can be in the form of one of the supplied standard workflows or through the use of custom-developed workflows. The effort associated with the development of custom workflows can be significant and this topic could easily fill a chapter in its own right, but the inclusion of standard workflows provides significant capabilities out of the box. To demonstrate how this integration functions, let's go back to the objects created earlier in Chapter 8 and see how they can be automated using vCenter Orchestrator.

Let's start with something simple like the creation of a new organization, which is easily achieved through the vCenter Orchestrator Client and includes the following high-level steps:

1. Navigate to the Workflows section and expand the hierarchy (Library ⇨ vCloud Director ⇨ Admin ⇨ Organization) to reveal the Add An Organization workflow.

2. Run the Add An Organization workflow by right-clicking and selecting Start Workflow.

3. Complete the details requested in the Add An Organization wizard. You'll be prompted to define the configuration of the new Organization (see Figure 10.5).

**FIGURE 10.5**

Running the Add New Organization workflow

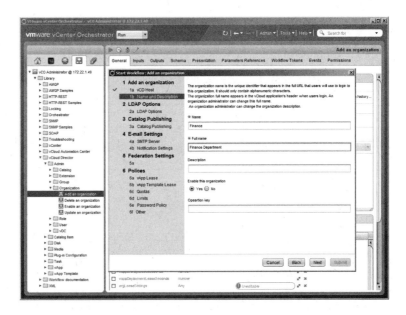

The information required, as you might expect, is the same as that required when you are using the vCloud Director portal. Upon completion of the wizard and once you've confirmed there are no validation errors, click Submit. The workflow will run and your new Organization will be created. If you navigate to the inventory section, as you did earlier to confirm the new vCloud Director Connection, you should be able to locate your new Organization. Easy, wasn't it?

Though we could review some of the other standard vCloud Director workflows—such as defining additional new users for the new Organization or creating an Org vDC—let's consider a more meaningful example like adding a new consumer or department to your vCloud. In the process of adding a new consumer, a number of tasks will be required that might include, but are not limited to, the following:

◆ Add New Organization

◆ Add A User

◆ Add A vDC

◆ Add An Organization Network

If you were to inspect the standard workflows available with the vCloud Director plug-in, you would notice that there are workflows provided for all of these tasks. So in the first instance it would be possible to simply run each of the workflows in sequence to provision a new consumer service. But wouldn't it be better if you could run just one workflow to do all of this for you? Don't forget you have the capability to create custom workflows.

The process for creating custom workflows is not for the feint hearted and will require some investment in the form of professional training or simply the time to read product documentation, community websites, and blog articles, but perhaps most importantly, it will require a development environment in which to practice. It will not be possible to cover all the individual detail of creating a custom workflow in this chapter, but we will highlight some of the key stages involved:

◆ Creating a new workflow

◆ Importing workflow elements

◆ Connecting workflow elements

◆ Defining and binding input and output parameter and attributes

The creation of a new empty workflow is simple and is achieved within the Workflows section of the vCenter Orchestrator client as follows:

**1.** Navigate to the Workflows section.

**2.** Right-click on a folder and select New Workflow.

**3.** Wait for the Workflow Editor to open automatically (see Figure 10.6).

From here the next task is to edit the workflow and import required workflow elements. You can create new folder items to organize your custom workflows.

**TIP**  Before editing the new workflow note the Version and Show Version History options, which together facilitate version control and, with the addition of the Diff Against Current option, the ability to easily highlight differences between updated workflow versions.

Having defined a new empty workflow, you must define the specific actions it should perform. You can edit workflows directly after creation or by right-clicking on the desired workflow and selecting Edit. The process of building a new workflow schema involves using the Schema tab and an intuitive drag-and-drop process of deploying elements from the left-hand side of the Workflow Editor. In the editor the elements are organized into these categories: Generic, Basic, Log, Network, All Workflows, and All Action. In this example we will focus on the Generic tab, where you can leverage predefined actions and/or workflows within your custom workflow.

The process for importing existing workflow elements is as simple as dragging the Workflow Element icon into your new workflow. You will be presented with a Chooser dialog box, which enables you to search for your required workflow (see Figure 10.7). This process can then be repeated for all other required workflow elements.

**FIGURE 10.6**
Newly created workflow and Workflow Editor

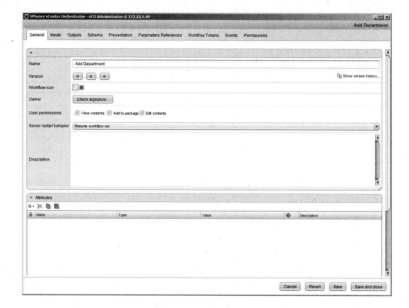

**FIGURE 10.7**
Importing existing workflows into a custom workflow

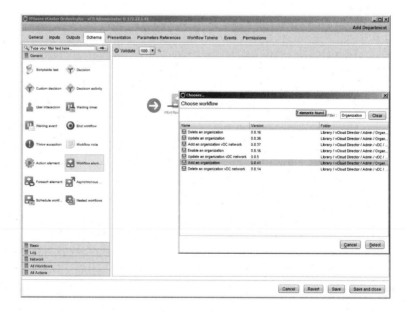

Once all desired workflow elements are imported into the custom workflow, you must define the workflow between the deployed elements. Before vCenter Orchestrator 5.1, you did so manually using the Connector Tool, which provided Microsoft Visio–like functionality for joining the workflow elements together and defining the order in which the elements should be executed (see Figure 10.8). This process is now performed automatically, but the manual capability still exists should you need it.

**FIGURE 10.8**
Defining the flow of actions within a custom workflow

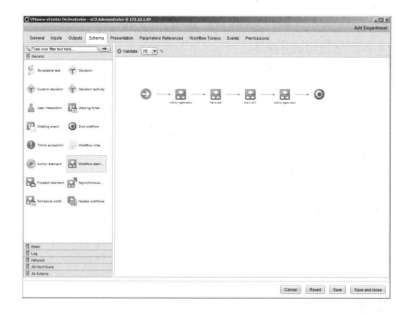

Now that all of the desired elements for your custom workflow have been imported and the execution order has been defined, things start to a get a little more involved. All workflow elements receive input parameters and generate output parameters, in much the same way as any scripted function. You will recall that upon running the Add New Organization workflow earlier, you were presented with a form enabling you to enter the characteristics of your new organization. This is the process for defining the values to be used for the input parameters required by the workflow. Since this custom workflow effectively contains four child workflows, you will need to define input parameters for all individual workflows, and this is where some of the time investment becomes more apparent.

The Promote Workflow Input/Output Parameters functionality identifies all required input parameters for a given workflow element and allows you to specify that they be automatically mapped as new input parameters on the workflow. Alternatively the input parameter can be set to Skip, resulting in a null value being assigned. Or you can set it to Value and supply an associated predetermined value (see Figure 10.9). Defining a value results in the creation of an attribute.

---

### UNDERSTANDING WORKFLOW CREATION

To illustrate why the creation of workflows can be an involved process, you should understand how the definition of input parameters was achieved prior to vCenter Orchestrator 5.1.

**1.** One option was using the Inputs section of the Workflow Editor; however, in the case of a workflow that leveraged existing workflow elements, it was generally easier to select each workflow element in turn and then review the individual in section(s), where all required input parameter names, their source parameter, and their types were defined.

**2.** From here it was possible to click the Source Parameter link. You would have been given the option to select a previously created input parameter/attribute or create one. In the case of a new custom workflow, you would have needed to create new parameters/attributes.

**3.** The process to create the parameter/attribute was initiated by simply selecting the Create Parameter/Attribute In Workflow link, which opened a dialog box where you could define a new workflow input parameter or attribute matching the name of the original workflow element input parameter. Now you can see where the perceived complication arises.

Though this functionality is still present and important to appreciate, much of this process can now be automated using the new Promote Workflow Input/Output Parameters functionality introduced in vCenter Orchestrator 5.1.

---

**FIGURE 10.9**
Defining work-
flow element
input parameters/
attributes

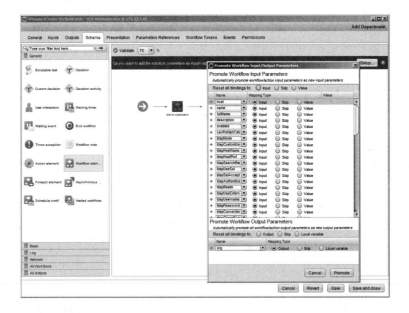

Selecting the option to define an input parameter will mean you must provide the value upon workflow execution. In contrast, if you choose to define a value, this value is predefined and will not be required at workflow execution. For example, if you only have one PvDC available, then why prompt for the same value every time? Simply define it as an attribute. This process effectively needs to be completed for all workflow elements and their respective input parameters, but there are some exceptions: common parameters.

In cases where multiple workflow elements are combined into a single custom workflow, there may on occasion be common input parameters required. In this example you are leveraging workflow elements that will create a new organization, a new user, a new Org vDC, and a new organization network. All of these elements will require the common input parameter of an organization. What you need is the capability to pass the newly created Organization object to the remaining workflow elements. vCenter Orchestrator has this covered in the form of output parameters and attributes that can be leveraged by subsequent workflow elements. As we mentioned earlier, all workflow elements accept input parameters/attributes and generate output parameters/attributes. The Visual Binding view for a workflow element presents a useful graphical representation of these bindings and also provides a drag-and-drop alternative for defining input/output parameters and attributes (see Figure 10.10).

**FIGURE 10.10**

Reviewing workflow element input parameter/attribute bindings

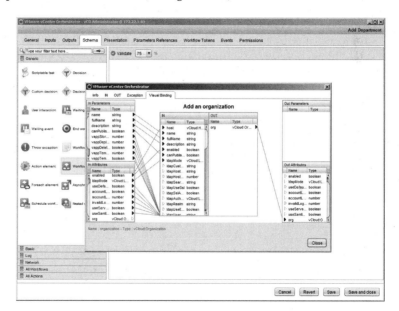

Now that you have completed the development of this custom workflow by importing the workflow elements and defining their execution order, and you have defined all the required input parameters and attributes, you are almost ready to run the new workflow. But before doing so there is one last activity: validation. Assuming all input parameters/attributes and associated bindings have been completed correctly, the validation will succeed, meaning you are ready to run the workflow (see Figure 10.11). If the validation process detects any errors, it will highlight the offending parameter/attribute, allowing you to quickly identify and fix the issue.

You should now have a completed and validated custom workflow ready to be executed for the first time. After selecting Save And Close to ensure all your efforts invested so far are preserved, you can now locate your custom workflow, right-click, and select Start Workflow. You will be presented with the Start Workflow: Add Department dialog box shown in Figure 10.12, where you supply the required information—all the values defined as parameters.

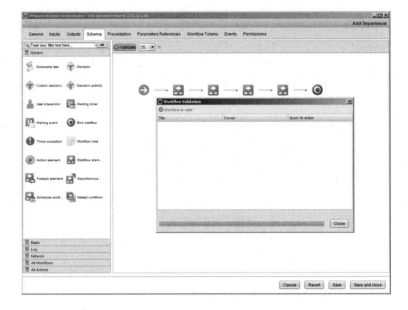

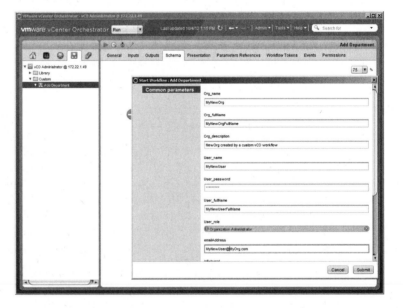

When you complete the dialog box, click Submit and wait for your new consumer department to be created in vCloud Director. You may have noticed that the dialog box presented for this workflow is cosmetically different and perhaps inferior to that for the standard workflow, the Add An Organization dialog box. The reason for these differences is the use of the Presentation functionality on the standard workflow, available in the Workflow Editor, which enables further definition and control regarding input parameters through the use of features such as dialog boxes and more detailed descriptions. Like most aspects of vCenter Orchestrator, this topic would warrant a chapter in its own right.

Now that you have stepped through the process of running a pre-created standard workflow and defining a custom workflow, you are probably beginning to realize the potential of vCenter Orchestrator and are already thinking of where it can assist you with the day-to-day running of your vCloud. Before we finish this section on vCenter Orchestrator, let's briefly explore other features that set it apart from many other automation solutions.

### vCenter Orchestrator Policies

vCenter Orchestrator includes a policy engine that enables automated workflows to be run on the basis of a given event on the vCenter Orchestrator Server or via one or more of the installed plug-ins. While a policy is running, vCenter Orchestrator reviews the policy rules and when a predefined event occurs, vCenter Orchestrator responds. For example, through the use of the SNMP and AMQP plug-ins, vCenter Orchestrator could use a policy to identify a specific message on an AMQP queue and run an automated workflow in response.

# Working with RabbitMQ

RabbitMQ is an open source message brokering solution, inherited by VMware following the acquisition of SpringSource in September 2009. RabbitMQ is built on the Advanced Message Queuing Protocol (AMQP) and provides a common platform for the distribution of messages between the individual components of your vCloud and/or external applications. RabbitMQ is freely available in a variety of formats, including a Windows executable, Linux packages, and source code.

AMQP is an open standard for messaging that enables applications and/or organizations running on differing platforms to send messages between one another. All specifications and protocol definitions are at the AMQP website:

```
http://www.amqp.org/resources/download
```

Why is RabbitMQ significant in the context of vCloud Director? vCloud Director version 1.5 introduced a new feature called Blocking Tasks And Notifications that enables vCloud Director to send AMQP messages, facilitating additional automation and integration capabilities. More specifically, Blocking Tasks represents messages sent to an AMQP broker containing details of an action in vCloud Director being blocked until a given action takes place. Notifications are simply messages containing details of a given event having taken place. AMQP messages sent by vCloud Director include a routing key, which follows this format:

```
operationSuccess.entity.org.user.subType1...subTypeN.[taskName]
```

operationSuccess is a Boolean value indicating whether the operation succeeded or failed, and entity, org, user, and subTypeN represent details of the associated vCloud Director object, its parent organization, and the action being performed. Finally taskName is applied if entity is a task or blocking task. Complete definitions for the AMQP message format and associated values are available from the vCloud Director API documentation at the VMware website:

```
www.vmware.com/pdf/vcd_15_api_guide.pdf
```

```
http://pubs.vmware.com/vcd-51/topic/com.vmware.ICbase/PDF/vcd_51_api_guide.pdf
```

Before Blocking Tasks And Notifications can be configured in vCloud Director, you must deploy an AMQP broker, such as RabbitMQ.

## Getting Started with RabbitMQ

The effort associated with deploying and configuring a RabbitMQ broker is relatively low, as the service will typically run fine using default settings. In the event you need a specific configuration or hardening, the level of effort will undoubtedly increase.

Assuming you have successfully installed RabbitMQ, including the Management Client, the process for configuring it for use with vCloud Director is straightforward. The first stage in the configuration process is to connect to the management interface and perform a number of key configuration steps:

◆ Creating a new exchange

◆ Creating a new queue

◆ Defining a new binding between the exchange and the message queue

The purpose of an exchange is to receive messages and then distribute them to queue(s) bound to the exchange. AMQP allows for a number of exchange types; Fan Out, Direct, Default, Topic, and Headers. Without delving into the details of various exchange types, you should know that the exchange type dictates the manner in which messages are distributed and to which queues. For example, a Fan Out exchange simply sends all received messages to all queues to which it is bound, whereas the Direct exchange relies on the message containing a routing key and it relies on the routing key being an identical match to that defined in the binding to pass the message to the appropriate queue.

Perhaps the most commonly used exchange for vCloud Director is the Topic exchange, which is similar to a Direct exchange, but instead of relying on an identical match, it uses routing keys separated by a period (.) delimiter. The binding key for a Topic exchange can include wildcards, such as # and *, that will match one or more words or a single word, respectively. For example, it would be possible to route vCloud Director messages on the basis of the `OperationSuccess` component of the routing key using `false.#` to identify all failed operations. Alternatively, it would be possible to identify messages associated with a specific organization using `#.<Org>`.

The purpose of the queue is to store messages routed from an exchange, where they remain until a client retrieves them. Upon retrieval of messages, a client can view those messages and then either leave them in the queue to be viewed by other clients or remove them. A given exchange can be bound to multiple queues, where it can place selected messages on the basis of the defined routing key. Returning to our earlier example, it would be possible to have defined queues for failed or successful tasks and/or individual organizations.

### PREPARING RABBITMQ FOR USE WITH VCLOUD DIRECTOR

The process for creating a RabbitMQ exchange is simple using the web-based management interface:

1. Open the RabbitMQ web-based management interface.

2. Navigate to the Exchanges tab.

3. Expand the Add A New Exchange section.

**4.** Complete the configuration details.

In this example the new exchange is named vCD and the type has been set to Topic, with the remaining settings left at their default values (see Figure 10.13).

**5.** Click Add Exchange.

**FIGURE 10.13**
Creating a RabbitMQ exchange for vCloud Director

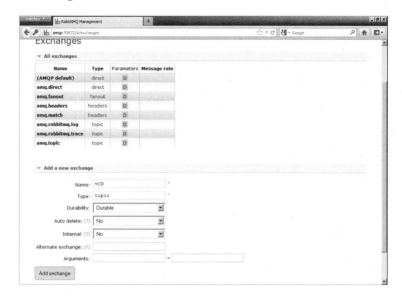

Having created a new exchange, the next step is to define a new queue, to which messages received by the exchange can be distributed. To create the new queue, select Queues, expand the Add A New Queue option, and select Add Queue. In Figure 10.14 the new queue has been named **vCO** with the remaining settings left at their default values.

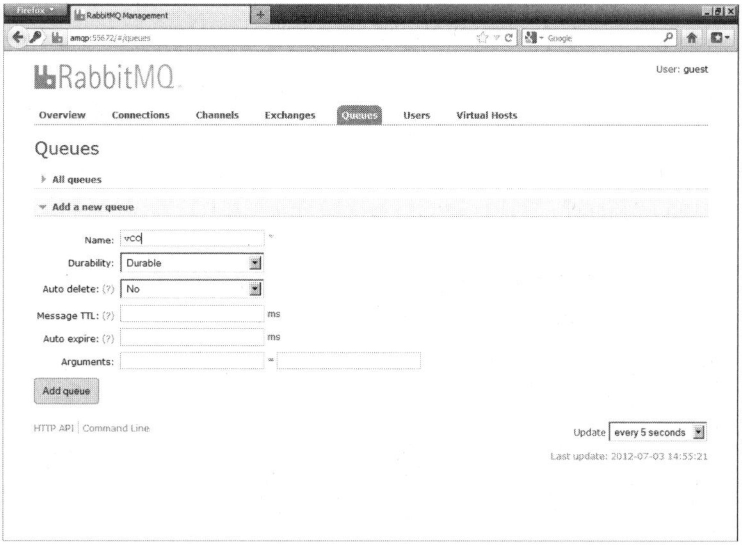

**FIGURE 10.14**
Creating a RabbitMQ queue for vCloud Director

Once you create a new exchange and queue, you have to define a new binding to specify the routing of messages from the exchange to the queue. In this example, there is only a single queue, so there's no need to define a specific routing key. Simply using # will capture all messages and send them to the vCO queue. To implement the binding, click on the new queue, locate the Add Binding section, define the previously created vCD exchange and # as the routing key, and then click Bind (see Figure 10.15).

**FIGURE 10.15**
Creating a
RabbitMQ binding

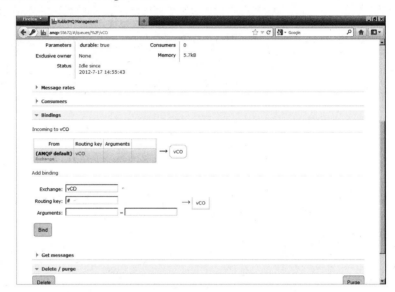

## CONFIGURING vCLOUD DIRECTOR NOTIFICATIONS

Upon completion of the initial configuration of RabbitMQ, it is now possible to set up vCloud Director so that it can send blocking tasks and notifications to the RabbitMQ server. This again is a simple task and is carried out using the System Administrator section of the vCloud Director Portal, as follows:

1. Navigate to the vCloud Director Administration section and the System Settings.

2. Locate the Extensibility options and the Settings tab.

3. Enter the details for the AMQP Host, the name of the Exchange, and finally the username and password (see Figure 10.16).

4. Click the Test AMQP Connection button to verify the configuration.

Assuming no issues were reported with the updated settings, you can now select Enable Notifications, thereby allowing your vCloud Director Cell to start sending notifications to the RabbitMQ server. Upon returning to the RabbitMQ management interface, you may notice a number of messages being queued.

The additional configuration required to enable the use of blocking tasks is simply a case of reviewing the tasks defined on the Blocking Tasks tab and selecting those for which you would want the action to be blocked pending an additional action taking place. Avoid selecting these options until the additional actions are defined and implemented; otherwise you may find a number of vCloud Director actions being blocked and eventually aborted.

Now that vCloud Director is sending Notifications and has the potential to use blocking tasks, you need a client application to consume and take action based on the messages. Wait… Didn't vCenter Orchestrator have an AMQP plug-in?

**FIGURE 10.16**
Configuring an AMQP broker in vCloud Director

### INTEGRATING VCENTER ORCHESTRATOR WITH RABBITMQ

The first step in integrating vCenter Orchestrator with RabbitMQ is to download, install, and configure the AMQP plug-in, as you did earlier for vCloud Director. The initial configuration for the AMQP plug-in is very simple and again is similar in principle to that for vCloud Director.

In essence you need to establish a connection to the RabbitMQ server and define a subscription to a queue. This is achieved as follows:

1. Navigate to the Workflows section and expand the hierarchy (Library ➪ Configuration) to reveal the sample configuration workflows.

2. Run the Add A Broker workflow by right-clicking and selecting Start Workflow.

3. Complete the details requested (name and broker connection properties) in the form that is launched.

4. Run the Subscribe To Queues workflow by right-clicking and selecting Start Workflow.

5. Complete the details requested (broker and queue details) in the dialog box that is launched.

6. Navigate to the Inventory section and verify the presence of the RabbitMQ server and queue (see Figure 10.17).

**FIGURE 10.17**

Inventory show-
ing configured
AMQP Broker and
Subscription

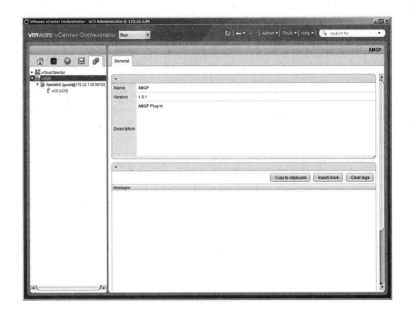

Now that you have an AMQP subscription available, you need to define a policy to detect the presence of new messages and then run the desired workflow. The process for applying a new policy is very simple and is achieved by navigating to the Policy Templates section in the client, expanding the hierarchy and locating the Subscription policy that was included with the AMQP plug-in. Applying the policy is as simple as performing a right-click and selecting Apply Policy, and then supplying the required input parameters (Name, Description, and Subscription, created earlier) when prompted. Now that the policy has been defined, it will need to be edited.

Having defined a new policy to subscribe to messages from the AMQP queue, you need to configure a trigger event. This is achieved by locating the newly created subscription policy, right-clicking, selecting Edit, locating the Scripting tab, and expanding the hierarchy. Within the hierarchy, you should be able to identify an OnMessage trigger event, which needs to be configured (see Figure 10.18).

Having identified the OnMessage trigger event and selected it, you now have the option to define a specific workflow, to be run on a new message being retrieved, by clicking the magnifying glass icon and then searching for the desired workflow. Once you complete the configuration of the policy and trigger event, all that remains is to start the policy. This is achieved by identifying the new policy in the Policies section once more, right-clicking, and selecting Start Policy. Upon starting this policy, it will run each time a new message is present in the AMQP queue. Once a new policy has been defined and started, it is possible to view progress of when the selected workflow was run by viewing the Logs tab of the policy (see Figure 10.19).

Now that you know how to subscribe to an AMQP queue, retrieve messages, and define a policy to execute workflows upon detecting a new message, you will need to invest some time in understanding, organizing, and defining specific queues to capture messages of interest by defining specific routing keys, as covered earlier in this chapter. vCenter Orchestrator can then be configured with subscriptions to each queue and will respond by running predefined workflows.

In addition to developing a series of meaningful queues, you will need to invest time developing workflows to automate the desired tasks following the detection of a new message. In the event that messages are blocking tasks, an important element that all of these workflows will need to contain is an action to fail or resume the blocked task.

**FIGURE 10.18**
Configuring the `OnMessage` trigger event to run a workflow

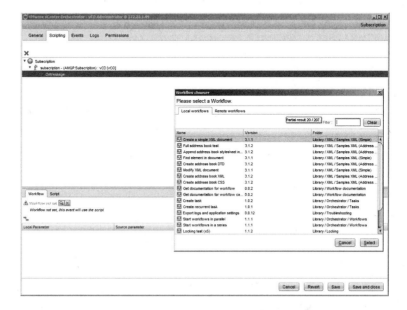

**FIGURE 10.19**
Identifying policy-based workflow executions

# Summary

In this chapter we've looked at the vCloud API; it is a REST API, accessed over an HTTPS connection, which represents objects as XML documents, within which properties are defined as elements and attributes. Unlike the other APIs available in a vCloud, it is accessible to both consumers and providers. In addition to the vCloud API is the VMRC API for facilitating integration of VM consoles within a custom portal.

vCloud components other than vCloud Director also have APIs available. Products such as vShield Manager and vCenter Chargeback have a REST API, similar to that of vCloud Director, whereas vSphere uses a SOAP-based API. These APIs are what enable vCloud Director to "glue" multiple technologies together in order to form a cohesive vCloud solution. These APIs are typically reserved for use by the provider, and in the process of releasing such capability, give careful consideration to the security principles of "least privilege" and "separation of duties." Doing so is particularly significant in environments subject to specific legislation or standards such as Statement on Auditing Standards (SAS) No. 70 and Payment Card Industry (PCI), to name but a few.

PowerCLI is a powerful utility that leverages the significant native capabilities of PowerShell and complements them with the addition of vCloud Director and vSphere-specific cmdlets that provide a quick, simplified, and yet powerful interface to the vCloud Director and vSphere APIs. Despite the simplified approach, the full capabilities of the API can be realized for the more adventurous and more capable scripter.

The capabilities of PowerCLI don't end with the VMware-developed cmdlets and can be further enhanced through the addition of cmdlets to interact with solutions from other vendors. The command line–based examples covered in this chapter are merely a starting point; in the hands of an experienced scripter, PowerCLI can be leveraged to drive highly complex solutions. A recent example is one of first vCloud Director disaster recovery solutions.

vCenter Orchestrator offers substantial automation and integration capabilities, yet it is all too often overlooked due to misconceptions around product pricing and usability. Support exists for many product components of a vCloud solution in the form of freely available plug-ins, and support can be extended with plug-ins that offer integration with core enterprise services such as Active Directory. Integration with management and messaging solutions such as SNMP and AMQP introduces the option to further enhance vCloud automation through the use of policy-driven workflows. In the few cases where a plug-in is not available, the PowerShell plug-in can be leveraged to potentially "plug the gap." In this chapter we have barely scratched the surface of the full capabilities of vCenter Orchestrator.

You should now have an appreciation of just some of the automation tools and capabilities available for use with your vCloud and should be in a position to start thinking about the capabilities you require and which type of tool may fulfill that need. Given the significant choices available, narrow down your selection to a short list and pick whichever is easiest. In the end, automation is about making life easier.

# Part IV

# Operating the Cloud

◆ **Chapter 11: Managing Your Cloud**
◆ **Chapter 12: Business Continuity**

# Chapter 11

# Managing Your Cloud

Now that you have built a vCloud Director environment to deliver services to your consumers and allowed those consumers to use the self-service portal to build vApps, we'll take a look at how best to manage your platform as an operations team.

We will cover monitoring and day-to-day operations as well as show you how and when to expand the infrastructure supporting your vCloud implementation.

In this chapter, you will learn to:

◆ Support a private cloud

◆ Manage a private cloud

◆ Perform common operational tasks and troubleshoot

## How Managing vCloud Differs from Managing vSphere

As we've discussed in earlier chapters, vCloud Director is an abstraction layer on top of vSphere that facilitates self-service and on-demand provisioning of computing, storage, and network resources for consumers to build services on. You still need to do the following:

◆ Manage the underlying vSphere implementation in a similar manner to a normal vSphere platform

◆ Keep a close eye on performance of computing and storage components to allow the load balancing functions like Distributed Resource Scheduling (DRS) and vMotion to operate correctly

◆ Patch, upgrade, and maintain hosts

You still use the vSphere client (or the web client) to manage and provision individual hosts and present storage and networks. But once hosts are allocated to vCloud Director, it handles their subdivision and allocation among various tenants, rather than the vSphere administrator doing so.

Your primary administrative interface for your private cloud is the vCloud Director user interface (UI), whereas the vSphere layer will be your interface for troubleshooting lower-level configuration or physical problems. The vCloud Director UI allows you to view any errors logged, identify the problematic subcomponent, and connect directly to it to troubleshoot further.

For example, if a vApp fails to deploy you can use the vCloud Director UI to verify that sufficient capacity exists and that the user has the proper permissions. You can also use the log files to identify which vCenter is dealing with the deployment request. You are then able to connect to that vCenter with the vSphere client to further troubleshoot the issue at the vSphere layer.

If you have a specific application-type problem with one of the vCloud Director management components, such as vCNS Manager or a cell server, you can troubleshoot such issues at the console of the relevant virtual machine or appliance directly.

You need to manage your vCloud platform in three parts:

◆ Management pod

◆ Resource pods

◆ Organization virtual datacenters (Org vDCs)

Let's explore each of these components next.

## Management Pod

The vCloud Director management pod is very much like a traditional application that you host for your organization. It consists of an allocation of resources from a vSphere cluster that provides an underlying high-availability infrastructure for an n-tier type application. vCloud Director has a browser-based application front-end, a database back-end, and various network and API interfaces to ancillary systems (like Chargeback or vCNS Manager), and you need to ensure its availability to ensure the vCloud Director platform is available to and usable by your consumers.

You can engineer resilience into most of the core components of the vCloud Director service to ensure availability. There is no real reason to deploy it on physical infrastructure rather than as virtual machines (VMs). Most of the management components of vCloud Director require more than one vCPU, so vSphere Fault Tolerance (FT) is of limited use to protect these components.

Generally your management pod will be quite static, with infrequent changes. It should come under the scope of tight change management to ensure a good level of security and availability.

## Resource Pod

You will have one or more resource pods. Each pod contains clusters with varying levels of resilience, capacity, or capability that map to your Provider Virtual Datacenter (PvDC) objects in vCloud Director. These PvDC objects and the underlying ESX host clusters will run the vApps that your consumers will build and use.

The resource pods will be managed and configured in the traditional manner via vCenter. However, the management team is also responsible for ensuring that there is sufficient capacity to meet demand, and the team deals with any underlying platform issues, such as hardware failures, security patching, and host upgrades. Because a key principle of cloud computing is self-service, your consumers will be managing, uploading, and deploying vApps using the template and catalog capabilities provided by vCloud Director.

As part of an operations team running a vCloud Director platform, you would not typically be involved in building, configuring, and deploying VMs for your end users beyond possibly setting up the initial catalogs and objects in vCloud Director. Likewise, for networking on a day-to-day basis port groups are allocated and created for your consumers on demand by vCloud Director from the network pool you created at setup time.

In a regulated environment where you need to comply with commercial or government regulations, your system administrators may not be allowed access inside VMs deployed by your consumers. vCloud Director allows the owners of these VMs to deploy, configure, and administer them independently of the team responsible for managing the underlying infrastructure.

Your resource pods will generally have a higher level of change than the management pods. You will be continually managing capacity and performance of the platform, and as such, you may need to frequently add/remove and reallocate hosts among your various PvDCs. Native vSphere platform features like maintenance mode, vMotion, and DRS mean you can do this online in a nondisruptive manner.

## Org vDCs

You will have a number of tenant organizations, each with its own allocation or share of pooled resources. Much of the control and management of the vApps your consumers deploy within their Org vDC is delegated to the consumer. Therefore, they are responsible for ensuring their software solutions are available and meet the demands of their user community.

These containers will have a high level of change, so much of the change management should be focused on the end user rather than technical/platform impacts. vCloud Director provides a determinate level of performance through its Org vDC constructs. These can be increased on request if further resources are required from the platform to meet application demands. Consumers and end users do not need to get bogged down in the technical aspects of such changes—such issues are dealt with lower down the stack by the platform team—but requests for more or fewer resources can be expressed in easily understandable units like GHz, GB, and IOPS.

Rather than consumers saying "My application is slow," it's easier to get a view of how many resources are allocated to a vApp and how much is reserved compared to consumed. This allows you to quickly determine whether adding more resources will in fact improve performance or whether the problem lies elsewhere.

# Understanding Change Management

Change management is important in any production system, but you need to take a pragmatic approach to its implementation in a cloud environment, which is geared up for agility and flexibility.

Figure 11.1 illustrates management layers with a strictly defined approval and control process. Note there are decreasing levels of change control to allow more agile adjustment of capacity at the resource level, and no change control is enforced by the cloud provider at the consumer level.

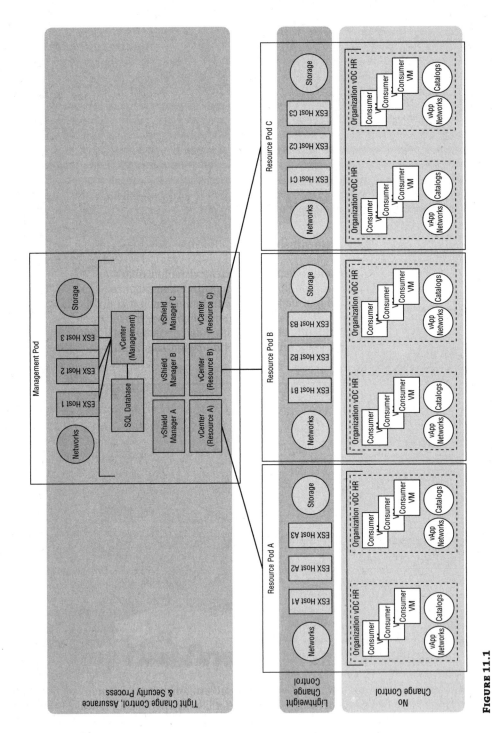

**FIGURE 11.1**

The various levels of change control from management to consumer

Particularly with regard to the resource pod layer, you should adopt the concept of preapproved changes and capped quantities. You can have a number of standard changes (such as adding datastores or hosts) that can be fast-tracked through the change process because they can be done online with no disruption to service. However, the schedule and process is communicated to infrastructure stakeholders for information only.

Likewise, you should maintain a quota of preapproved changes. For example, the operations team could have the authority to add hosts to a resource pod up to a predefined design limit before they need to seek further design or financial approval.

## Capacity Planning

Whenever a new host is added, the addition of the host feeds into the capacity-planning teams, who review the current and projected footprint against the overall architectural and financial plan to ensure that technical or financial constraints are not breached. By maintaining this buffer capacity, or "headroom" of capacity/approval, you can still deliver most of the agility wanted by consumers while maintaining control and assurance of the underlying platform.

The amount of headroom you maintain in the platform depends on your business plans and desire to overcommit resources. Your capacity plans will evolve over time in line with business, technical, and operational change. As such, the capacity-planning role needs to pay close attention to planned projects as well as closely monitor actual usage to ensure capacity keeps ahead of potential demand (see Figure 11.2).

**FIGURE 11.2**
Headroom capacity delivered by expansion vs. consumer workload over time

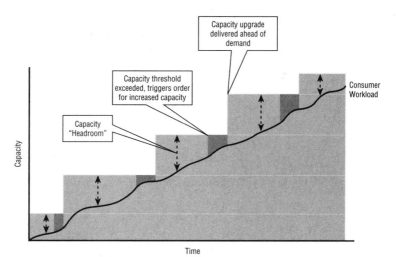

# Team Structure

Deploying a private cloud in your enterprise means a slight shift in the mindset of your organization and how it performs conventional operations, from supporting and managing end users to enabling and empowering consumers. IT capability is provided in a less prescriptive manner, which means IT departments can relax their control over the systems and solutions the consumer chooses to deploy. Such transformation can be hard, and you need to ensure your organization and teams give the concept their buy-in. Some tactics for winning this buy-in are outlined in Chapter 2, "Developing Your Strategy."

A common strategy for operating your private cloud is to split the team into two functions:

**vCloud Operations**   Members of this team are responsible for supporting vSphere and vCloud and for ensuring capacity and availability.

**Transition Support**   This team works in the business, helping consumers bring their solutions on board and understand how best to use vCloud and your private cloud facility at a technical level. This may involve liaising with developers and assisting with integration with the vCloud API. It also may involve advising your consumers on how they should best build their solutions and applications to ensure availability and performance.

**NOTE**   In smaller organizations, the transition team role may be virtual and fulfilled by a member of the core team responsible for working with and advising consumers.

You should also be prepared to have the transition team work with third parties, business partners, suppliers, and customers where appropriate and work to align them closely with projects that build new solutions on your private cloud to ensure success.

Operations are a critical part of the overall team, charged with building, maintaining, and operating the platform. The operations manager role is a key part of this management team and is responsible for delivering infrastructure that can meet the service levels offered to consumers.

As we've discussed, if your organization is reasonably experienced at operating vSphere, then you'll find that operating a vCloud platform isn't totally different from what your existing vSphere operations team does on a day-to-day basis:

◆   Hosts will still need to be patched.

◆   Failures will need to be resolved.

◆   Upgrades and enhancements will be continual.

However, there is less reliance on building VMs and directly serving requests from end users; much of this is dealt with through self-service.

In a vCloud environment, your team will be serving two types of consumer:

◆   End users creating and deploying vApps

◆   Autonomous systems consuming the APIs you provide

For example, consumers are free to build applications that interact with the vCloud infrastructure via its API to request more instances of a vApp or even to change network and firewall rules (depending on the levels of permissions granted). This level of integration doesn't often happen in traditional vSphere deployments and will thus bypass any manual process for change control, capacity planning, and so forth. In such instances, you are relying on the quotas put in place by the capacity-planning function and configured on an Org vDC to meet the demands of your consumers until they request further resources.

vCloud Director does an excellent job of creating abstractions of the complex permissions required to deliver such functionality in a secure manner within the underlying vSphere platform. These abstractions are known as *roles* and can easily be used by your vCloud operations team as building blocks to control consumer access. That way, your team does not have to spend significant time building and testing low-level access control lists.

Depending on the size of your deployment, you will have a number of subject matter expert (SME) roles within your team. SME roles may be held by a couple of individuals, or you may have dedicated SMEs in larger deployments. The SMEs provide expertise on the following areas:

◆ Storage—FC, NAS, SCSI, IOps/performance troubleshooting

◆ Servers/virtualization—vSphere

◆ Network—VLAN, switching, vDS, routing, firewalls, and load balancers (physical and virtual)

◆ Automation—API support, integration of end-to-end automations

## Monitoring Performance and Availability

The private cloud is very much about offering a product to your internal consumers. Part of that product specification is a service level agreement (SLA). To ensure that you are conforming to that SLA, it's important to be able to monitor performance and availability.

vCloud and the underlying vSphere platform has many "moving parts": servers, networks, storage, applications, and so forth. These components may make it difficult to provide an end-to-end picture of a solution.

There is no one-size-fits-all solution. Your solution depends on your individual vendors, but it's likely that you'll need to build your own solution. The architecture shown in Figure 11.3 shows the split between consumer and provider monitoring solutions.

This model reinforces the concept that the consumer cannot see or access the underlying infrastructure components for monitoring and that the provider generally has no visibility into the consumer workload.

VMware provides the vCenter Operations Management Suite (vCOPS), which can provide detailed analysis of the virtual workload. This tool has an extensible adapter architecture that allows integration with vCloud Director as well as hardware vendors like EMC or NetApp for storage monitoring and alerting. However, it's important to note that vCloud integration for these tools is an ongoing process and they currently do not integrate with the native vCloud portal. They have their own interfaces and consoles, which would form part of your management platform.

If you want to build access to these tools for your consumers, you'll likely need to build some custom dashboards within those products and publish them to your consumers. vCOPS isn't yet a multitenant solution, so this could be an issue in a private cloud scenario if you have security requirements to separate visibility of those dashboards between consumers.

vCDAudit is a community-built plug-in for the popular vCheck PowerShell toolkit. This plug-in generates easily customized reports on vCloud workloads and configurations. If your requirements are simple or you need a high level of customization, we recommend you use vCDAudit.

You can download vCDAudit from Alan Renouf's blog at www.virtu-al.net/2012/03/13/vcdaudit-for-vcloud-director/.

**FIGURE 11.3**
Demarcation
between consumer
and provider
monitoring

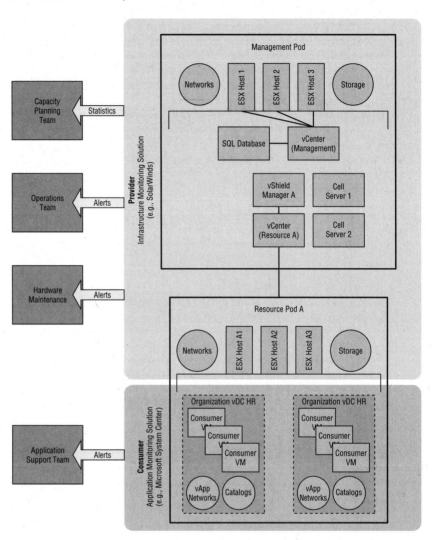

## Using Malware Protection

Malware protection is important in any production environment and is often a compliance requirement if you operate in a regulated industry. As with traditional vSphere environments, antimalware vendors are starting to integrate their products with hypervisors, having recognized that traditional pure in-guest solutions are inefficient and difficult to manage when using virtualization with no control inside the guest OS.

Currently none of the hypervisor-integrated solutions are supported by vCloud. This is generally because they rely on special network-level filter drivers or appliances on ESX hosts that are not understood by vCloud Director's networking automation.

vCNS Edge and Gateway currently provide network-level firewall functionality and packet filtering. However, you'll need to stick with in-guest solutions like antimalware tools and built-in Windows or Linux firewalls as part of your strategy for virtual workload protection until those products are released with the ability to be controlled from vCloud Director.

# Balancing Capacity and Demand

As discussed earlier, your resource pods will likely experience a higher level of change than your management pods. You may need to add more hosts to increase capacity or move hosts between clusters to balance capacity and demand.

Having a consistent configuration for your ESX hosts is critical for vSphere clusters. When you are aggregating multiple hosts and clusters into a computing pool managed by vCloud Director, a consistent configuration is even more important because all of the network and storage settings will need to be identical on all hosts to ensure consistent performance and reliability. As such, you should apply an automated method to get a consistent configuration on your hosts. For example, you might use vSphere host profiles or a PowerShell script to ensure that all port groups and datastores are named and configured consistently.

Using the new Storage DRS functionality of vSphere 5 makes scaling and maintaining storage simple. You just add or remove storage to the clusters and storage DRS (SDRS) automatically takes care of distributing load. Likewise, if you need to reallocate storage between clusters at the vSphere layer, you can use SDRS maintenance mode to automatically move VMs to alternative datastores so you can work on the datastores in maintenance mode without impacting the VMs that were originally stored there. This all happens transparently to vCloud Director and can be carried out by a vSphere administrator as part of business-as-usual activities.

## Adding More ESX Hosts to a PvDC

As part of your capacity-planning process, you may decide that you need to add more ESX hosts to your clusters to increase capacity available to PvDCs.

1. Add another host to an existing vSphere cluster using the vSphere client by right-clicking on the cluster and choosing Add Host; supply the connection details and confirm that the host was added successfully to the cluster.

2. Ensure that the host is configured consistently with the other nodes, either by applying a host profile or by using a script.

   Once the new host is added to the cluster and ready for use, you need to "prepare" it for use with vCloud Director.

3. Deploy an agent to the new host. You can do so from the vCloud Director UI. If you are using a scripted or stateless automatic method to deploy your hosts, you need to deploy the vCloud Director vSphere Installation Bundle (VIB) to each host.

   As you can see in Figure 11.4, vCloud Director knows when a host has been added to a PvDC but isn't yet ready for use.

**FIGURE 11.4**
A new unprepared
host has been
detected by vCloud
Director.

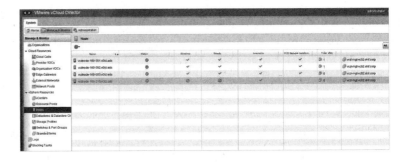

vCloud Director has detected a host in the cluster that hasn't been prepared for use. Note that it is not enabled or ready and does not support vCloud Network Isolation (VCNI).

The agent that is deployed by vCloud Director to each host installs extra networking components to support VCNI and VXLAN network encapsulation between hosts (for more information on these technologies, see Chapter 5, "Platform Design for vCloud Director").

   4. To prepare a host for use with vCloud Director, right-click on the host and choose Prepare Host, as shown in Figure 11.5.

**FIGURE 11.5**
Preparing a host
for use with vCloud
Director. This step
initiates the instal-
lation of the vCloud
Director agent to an
ESX host.

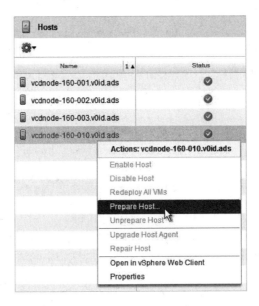

   5. You are prompted for credentials for the ESX host to install the agent (Figure 11.6). This automatically puts the host into maintenance mode, installs the driver, and then exits maintenance mode.

   6. Click OK. The cell servers initiate a connection to the individual ESX host to install the driver (Figure 11.7).

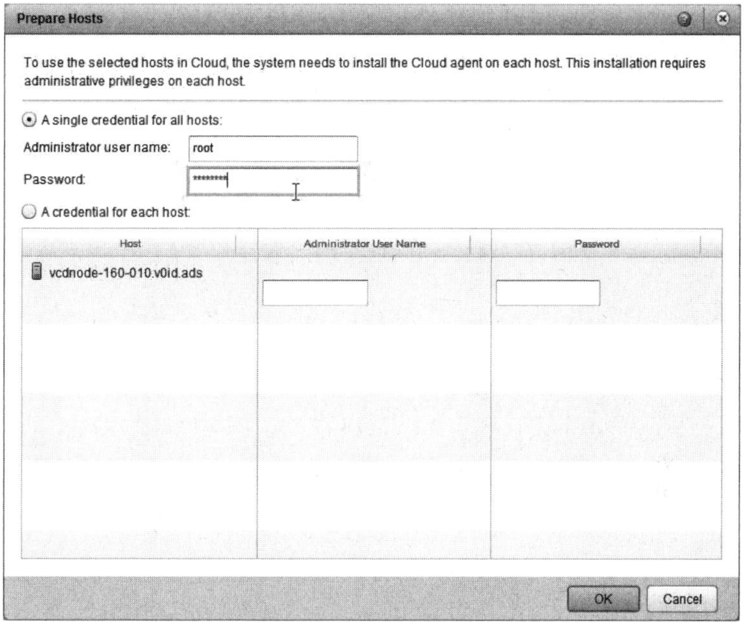

**FIGURE 11.6**
Entering root credentials to connect to an ESX host

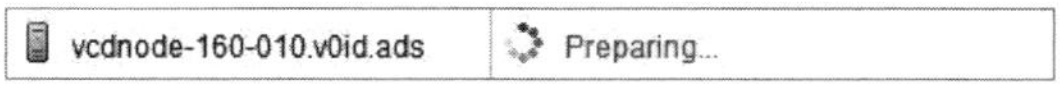

**Prepare Hosts**

To use the selected hosts in Cloud, the system needs to install the Cloud agent on each host. This installation requires administrative privileges on each host.

⦿ A single credential for all hosts:

Administrator user name: root

Password: ********

◯ A credential for each host:

| Host | Administrator User Name | Password |
| --- | --- | --- |
| vcdnode-160-010.v0id.ads | | |

OK   Cancel

**FIGURE 11.7**
A host is being prepared for use with vCloud Director.

vcdnode-160-010.v0id.ads   Preparing...

The message may mention enabling host spanning (Figure 11.8). This is the network driver that provides VCNI and VXLAN functionality on each ESX host.

**FIGURE 11.8**
Enabling host spanning task during agent installation

vcdnode-160-010.v0id.ads   Enabling Host Spanning...

Once the process is complete, the host is ready for use (Figure 11.9). DRS will distribute VM workloads to the host automatically if configured to do so.

**FIGURE 11.9**
Host preparation completed

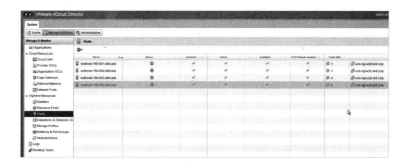

## Removing ESX Hosts from a PvDC

You may find it necessary to move one or more physical vSphere hosts to a different cluster or to remove the hosts entirely. vCloud Director is connected to your vCenter servers, so if you put a host into maintenance mode, vCloud Director detects this fact automatically and marks the host as unavailable until you exit maintenance mode (Figure 11.10).

**FIGURE 11.10**

vCloud Director detects a host has been placed into maintenance mode.

However, vCloud Director does not automatically remove a host from the inventory if you move the host to a different vSphere cluster or remove it entirely.

So, to remove a host you need to do the following:

1. Disable the host in vCloud Director, as shown in Figure 11.11, by right-clicking on the host.

**FIGURE 11.11**

Disabling a host

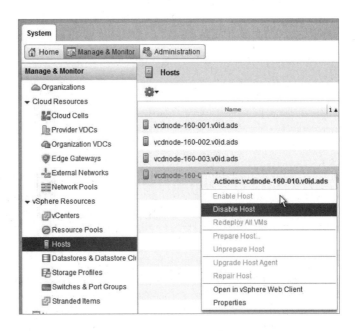

2. Click Unprepare Host by right-clicking on the host, this action will remove the vCloud Director agent from the host (Figure 11.12).

**FIGURE 11.12**
Choose Unprepare Host from this menu.

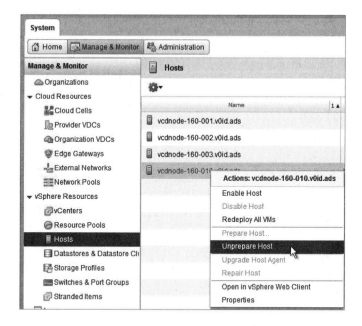

**3.** You can now safely remove the host from vCenter and it will no longer show as part of vCloud Director.

---

**MOVING HOSTS BETWEEN PHYSICAL CLUSTERS**

If you are going to move hosts between physical clusters, and thus PvDCs, you can do so within vCenter by putting the host into maintenance mode and moving it. You don't need to prepare/unprepare the host; vCloud Director will automatically pick up the change. This capability is useful if you have identical hosts and need to balance the capacity between different PvDCs.

---

## Adding Datastores

Use the Storage Profiles feature of vSphere to create storage profiles. This feature provides a further level of abstraction to vCloud Director and allows your cloud to consume storage of a particular profile without having to select individual logical unit numbers (LUNs). For example, you can group LUNs with particular capabilities (such as performance, array-based encryption, or different levels of redundancy) into storage profiles.

Figure 11.13 illustrates the mapping of physical disks to storage profiles by capability tags and ultimately into storage that is abstracted to consumers in Org vDCs.

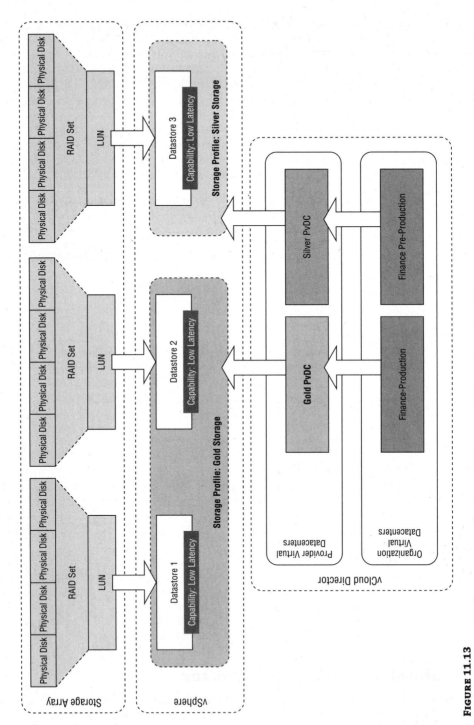

**FIGURE 11.13**

Mapping of physical disks to storage profiles by capability tags and abstracting to Org vDCs

The process for adding more storage to your vCloud environment includes two steps. First, the storage needs to be presented at the vSphere layer, as you would for a traditional vSphere environment. LUNs are zoned and masked to a cluster. The vSphere administrator scans for new LUNs and formats them. These LUNs are then added to a storage profile using either user-assigned capabilities or automatically detected capabilities. If you have a storage array that supports vStorage APIs for Storage Awareness (VASA), you can use the automatically detected capabilities to define a storage profile.

Second, if you are using storage profiles as shown in Figure 11.14, LUNs with common capabilities or properties are automatically able to be used by vCloud Director as you associate a PvDC and its associated Org vDCs with storage profiles. vCloud Director is then able to consume whatever is provided within each storage profile.

**FIGURE 11.14**
vSphere storage profiles

Using storage profiles means that as soon as datastores are added at the vSphere layer they are automatically available to vCloud Director for consumption unless they are in maintenance mode.

### Adding Additional vCenter Servers

As your environment grows, you may start to approach the configuration maximums of a single vCenter in a vCloud deployment in terms of the number of VMs or hosts that you can support. Scaling further will require another vCenter server. Or you may have a workload that has a different security profile, which means you'll need to deploy a dedicated vCenter and set of resource pods (clusters).

Deploying a dedicated vCenter and set of resource pods is a straightforward process and is just a case of adding another vCenter and vCNS Manager to your vCloud console. You'll remember from Chapter 3, "Introducing vCloud Director," that vCloud Director aggregates multiple vSphere resources into a common management and orchestration function. This is how vCloud is able to scale to a significant number of VMs. The process of adding further vCenter servers is the same as the steps shown in Chapter 8, "Delivering Services," for attaching the first vCenter.

## Troubleshooting vCloud Director

From time to time you may encounter issues with your vCloud Director environment. Most of the "brains" of vCloud Director reside in the code running on the cell servers and are quite straightforward to troubleshoot.

vCloud Director provides a number of logs that are accessible to administrators via the vCloud Director interface. As you can see in Figure 11.15, these logs include tasks and events that are generated by vCloud Director across the implementation. Double-clicking on a task will display more details about the error, as shown in Figure 11.16.

**FIGURE 11.15**
vCloud Director
logs: tasks and
events

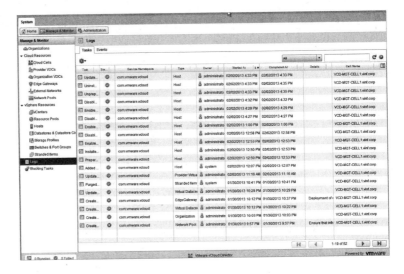

**FIGURE 11.16**
Task details

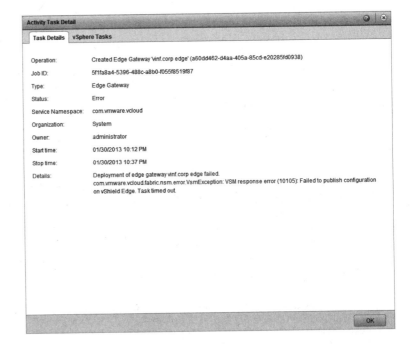

Often it's useful to be able to track vCloud Director–created objects in vSphere. In the properties dialog box of a VM, you'll be able to find its vSphere name toward the bottom of the screen, as shown in Figure 11.17. You can then locate this object in the vSphere client and troubleshoot any issues with that VM at the vSphere layer, as shown in Figure 11.18.

**FIGURE 11.17**
Locating the vSphere object name in the VM's properties dialog box

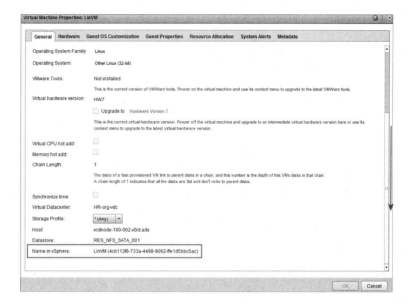

**FIGURE 11.18**
vCloud Director managed object viewed from vSphere

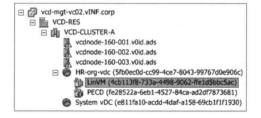

If you experience problems connecting to the vCloud Director interface, this is often a sign of an issue with one or more of your cell servers. Each cell server maintains a number of local log files. You can view these files by creating a Secure Shell (SSH) connection to the cell server and viewing the log files. The log files are held in /opt/vmware/vcloud-director/logs (see Figure 11.19).

The most useful log files for day-to-day running are the cell.log and vcloud-container-debug.log files. If you are experiencing issues, you should review these files first for recent events and errors.

There are not many controls you can use to adjust the function of a cell server while it is online, and it may be necessary to restart the vCloud Director software running on a cell server if you have problems.

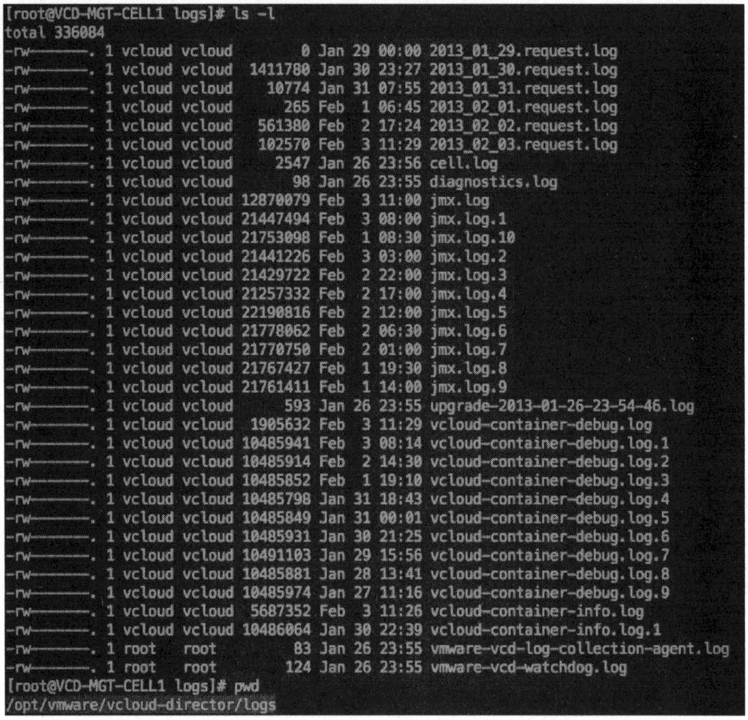

**FIGURE 11.19**
vCloud Director cell
server log directory

```
[root@VCD-MGT-CELL1 logs]# ls -l
total 336084
-rw-------. 1 vcloud vcloud        0 Jan 29 00:00 2013_01_29.request.log
-rw-------. 1 vcloud vcloud  1411780 Jan 30 23:27 2013_01_30.request.log
-rw-------. 1 vcloud vcloud    10774 Jan 31 07:55 2013_01_31.request.log
-rw-------. 1 vcloud vcloud      265 Feb  1 06:45 2013_02_01.request.log
-rw-------. 1 vcloud vcloud   561380 Feb  2 17:24 2013_02_02.request.log
-rw-------. 1 vcloud vcloud   102570 Feb  3 11:29 2013_02_03.request.log
-rw-------. 1 vcloud vcloud     2547 Jan 26 23:56 cell.log
-rw-------. 1 vcloud vcloud       98 Jan 26 23:55 diagnostics.log
-rw-------. 1 vcloud vcloud 12870079 Feb  3 11:00 jmx.log
-rw-------. 1 vcloud vcloud 21447494 Feb  3 08:00 jmx.log.1
-rw-------. 1 vcloud vcloud 21753098 Feb  1 08:30 jmx.log.10
-rw-------. 1 vcloud vcloud 21441226 Feb  3 03:00 jmx.log.2
-rw-------. 1 vcloud vcloud 21429722 Feb  2 22:00 jmx.log.3
-rw-------. 1 vcloud vcloud 21257332 Feb  2 17:00 jmx.log.4
-rw-------. 1 vcloud vcloud 22190816 Feb  2 12:00 jmx.log.5
-rw-------. 1 vcloud vcloud 21778062 Feb  2 06:30 jmx.log.6
-rw-------. 1 vcloud vcloud 21770750 Feb  2 01:00 jmx.log.7
-rw-------. 1 vcloud vcloud 21767427 Feb  1 19:30 jmx.log.8
-rw-------. 1 vcloud vcloud 21761411 Feb  1 14:00 jmx.log.9
-rw-------. 1 vcloud vcloud      593 Jan 26 23:55 upgrade-2013-01-26-23-54-46.log
-rw-------. 1 vcloud vcloud  1905632 Feb  3 11:29 vcloud-container-debug.log
-rw-------. 1 vcloud vcloud 10485941 Feb  3 08:14 vcloud-container-debug.log.1
-rw-------. 1 vcloud vcloud 10485914 Feb  2 14:30 vcloud-container-debug.log.2
-rw-------. 1 vcloud vcloud 10485852 Feb  1 19:10 vcloud-container-debug.log.3
-rw-------. 1 vcloud vcloud 10485798 Jan 31 18:43 vcloud-container-debug.log.4
-rw-------. 1 vcloud vcloud 10485849 Jan 31 00:01 vcloud-container-debug.log.5
-rw-------. 1 vcloud vcloud 10485931 Jan 30 21:25 vcloud-container-debug.log.6
-rw-------. 1 vcloud vcloud 10491103 Jan 29 15:56 vcloud-container-debug.log.7
-rw-------. 1 vcloud vcloud 10485881 Jan 28 13:41 vcloud-container-debug.log.8
-rw-------. 1 vcloud vcloud 10485974 Jan 27 11:16 vcloud-container-debug.log.9
-rw-------. 1 vcloud vcloud  5687352 Feb  3 11:26 vcloud-container-info.log
-rw-------. 1 vcloud vcloud 10486064 Jan 30 22:39 vcloud-container-info.log.1
-rw-------. 1 root   root        83 Jan 26 23:55 vmware-vcd-log-collection-agent.log
-rw-------. 1 root   root       124 Jan 26 23:55 vmware-vcd-watchdog.log
[root@VCD-MGT-CELL1 logs]# pwd
/opt/vmware/vcloud-director/logs
```

**WARNING**    Restarting the cell service will prevent consumers from accessing the vCloud UI
until it restarts but will not affect their vApps, which will continue to run as normal. If interruption to the vCloud UI is an issue, you can implement multiple cell servers and an IP load balancer
to provide high availability.

You can perform a full restart of the vCloud Director cell software on a single server by issuing the following command as root (see Figure 11.20). Note that this command will terminate
any currently running jobs.

```
service vmware-vcd restart
```

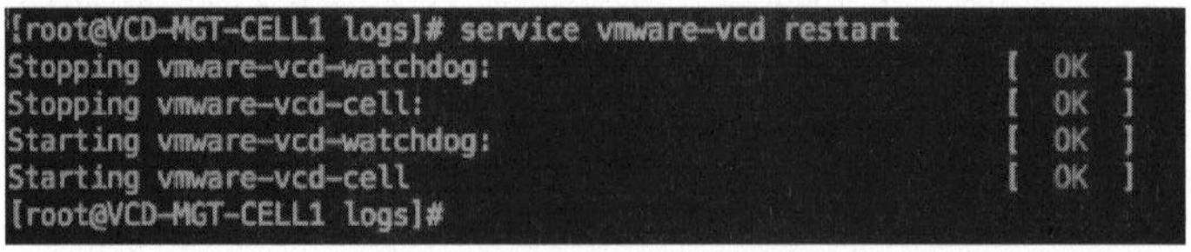

**FIGURE 11.20**
Restarting vCloud
Director software
on a cell server

```
[root@VCD-MGT-CELL1 logs]# service vmware-vcd restart
Stopping vmware-vcd-watchdog:                              [  OK  ]
Stopping vmware-vcd-cell:                                  [  OK  ]
Starting vmware-vcd-watchdog:                              [  OK  ]
Starting vmware-vcd-cell                                   [  OK  ]
[root@VCD-MGT-CELL1 logs]#
```

Although the console reports back reasonably quickly that the service has restarted, the actual
vCloud Director software is still carrying out its initialization processes in the background. You
can check on the progress of this task by viewing the cell.log file (see Figure 11.21). If you use
the tail -f command, you will see real-time updates to this log file on the console without having to reopen the file.

**FIGURE 11.21**
The cell.log
file on a vCloud
Director cell server
during service
initialization

```
[root@VCD-MGT-CELL1 logs]# tail -f /opt/vmware/vcloud-director/logs/cell.log
Application Initialization: 47% complete. Subsystem 'com.vmware.vcloud.fabric.foundation' started
Application Initialization: 52% complete. Subsystem 'com.vmware.vcloud.fabric.storage' started
Application Initialization: 58% complete. Subsystem 'com.vmware.vcloud.fabric.compute' started
Application Initialization: 64% complete. Subsystem 'com.vmware.vcloud.fabric.net' started
Successfully verified transfer spooling area: /opt/vmware/vcloud-director/data/transfer
Application Initialization: 70% complete. Subsystem 'com.vmware.vcloud.backend-core' started
Application Initialization: 76% complete. Subsystem 'com.vmware.vcloud.ui.configuration' started
Application Initialization: 82% complete. Subsystem 'com.vmware.vcloud.imagetransfer-server' started
Application Initialization: 88% complete. Subsystem 'com.vmware.vcloud.rest-api-handlers' started
Application Initialization: 94% complete. Subsystem 'com.vmware.vcloud.jax-rs-servlet' started
Application Initialization: 100% complete. Subsystem 'com.vmware.vcloud.ui-vcloud-webapp' started
Application Initialization: Complete. Server is ready in 1:22 (minutes:seconds)
Successfully initialized ConfigurationService session factory
Successfully posted pending audit events: com/vmware/vcloud/event/cell/start
Successfully started scheduler
Successfully started remote JMX connector on port 8999
```

If you have problems with the vCloud cell server initializing correctly, you should further investigate the log files and verify that you have connectivity to the server where the vCloud database is held and that DNS resolution is functioning correctly.

You can also gracefully shut down a cell server. Doing so allows running processes to complete but disables new connections to the cell server. This approach is useful for performing online maintenance.

You can stop any new jobs from being scheduled on an individual cell server with the following command:

```
cell-management-tool -u UserName -p YourPassword cell -q true
```

You can query the number of active jobs using this command (see Figure 11.22):

```
cell-management-tool -u UserName -p YourPassword cell -t
```

**FIGURE 11.22**
Querying the cell
service

```
[root@VCD-MGT-CELLB1 bin]# ./cell-management-tool -u cloudadmin -p _g4rbl3D cell -t
Job count = 0
Is Active = true
```

When the job count equals 0, you can stop the cell server with the following command (see Figure 11.23):

```
cell-management-tool -u UserName -p YourPassword cell -s
```

**FIGURE 11.23**
Cell service with no
active jobs

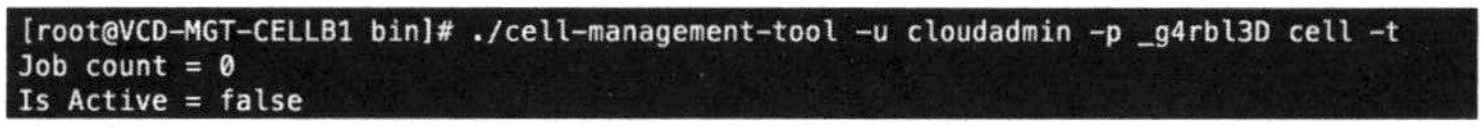

```
[root@VCD-MGT-CELLB1 bin]# ./cell-management-tool -u cloudadmin -p _g4rbl3D cell -t
Job count = 0
Is Active = false
```

Note you have to run this command twice:

◆ The first time, it shuts down the watchdog service.

◆ The second time, it shuts down the actual cell service.

You can double-check the status of the cell service using the following command. The results in Figure 11.24 show the vCloud services are stopped after being gracefully shut down.

```
service vmware-vcd status
```

**FIGURE 11.24**

vCloud services
stopped after grace-
ful shutdown

```
[root@VCD-MGT-CELLB1 bin]# service vmware-vcd status
vmware-vcd-watchdog is not running
vmware-vcd-cell is not running
```

Once you have completed your maintenance, you can restart the cell service by using this command:

```
Service vmware-vcd start
```

## Summary

Managing your vCloud environment isn't drastically different from managing traditional IT infrastructure, except much of the focus of the operations teams is shifted to capacity planning and management, rather than day-to-day provisioning activity for customer VMs and applications.

Change control allows you to enforce a level of diligence and planning for change. As such, we suggest that you apply change control in varying levels. Apply the tightest level of governance and control to the management elements of the platform.

To retain agility around the infrastructure elements that service customer workloads directly (the resource pods), we recommend that you develop a set of preapproved changes and processes that are available to the operations teams to invoke as required without having to go through a full change control or approval process.

From a provider point of view, no change control is provided or enforced on consumer workloads. Consumers have a self-service interface to the platform and can create and destroy their own systems as they see fit.

Monitoring is split into two elements: platform (vCloud, vSphere, network, storage) and consumer workload (vApps). The provider is typically interested in monitoring platform performance, ensuring the infrastructure is available and performing to the required SLA.

In an IaaS offering like vCloud, the consumer workload is typically managed and monitored by the consumer. The infrastructure is not visible to the customer, who must rely on the provider to deliver the required (or even contracted) SLA. To manage and monitor vApp performance and availability, the consumer would have to implement their own solution in their Org vDC or integrate the vApps with an existing external enterprise monitoring solution.

Likewise, there are no vCloud-integrated antimalware solutions available as of this writing, but this does not prevent consumers from implementing antimalware solutions in their vApps.

From time to time there may be issues with the vCloud cell servers or database connections they rely on. Restarting the cell service is a straightforward process. If there are multiple cell servers, any outage to consumers can be avoided by implementing an IP load balancer to distribute connections to the cell servers.

Issues with the underlying vSphere platform can be investigated and resolved using the vSphere client. Both vCloud and vSphere maintain a comprehensive set of logs, particularly if you use a syslog server to correlate alerts and event messages.

# Chapter 12

# Business Continuity

Business continuity is a key consideration for any infrastructure, and this also holds true for a vCloud solution. Business continuity is an umbrella term for all the activities you need to perform to ensure availability of your vCloud solution for consumers. The design, deployment, and operation of a vCloud solution must incorporate specific considerations in order to support the wider business continuity plan for your organization.

In this chapter we will focus on a small subset of the entities encompassed within a business continuity plan, with particular focus on topics where the move from the more traditional vSphere environment to a vCloud environment has introduced new challenges.

In this chapter, you will learn to:

- ◆ Evaluate backup strategies for your cloud

- ◆ Back up consumer workloads

- ◆ Understand disaster recovery strategies

## Backing Up Consumer Workloads

Before the introduction of virtualization solutions such as vSphere, the typical approach to backing up and restoring data was to use *LAN-based* (sometimes referred to as *agent-based*, although that term does not always infer LAN-based) backup solutions. These two terms arose from the fact that backup data was sent over the network to a backup server and that the scheduling, selection, and transfer of such data was initiated using locally installed software in the form of a solution-specific backup agent. Although agent-based backups in virtual machines function in the same way as those for physical servers, the introduction of virtualization created new challenges.

During a backup, an agent-based solution ties up resources in the form of processor time, storage, and network I/O. When used with physical servers, resource consumption is limited to that of a single agent. The consolidation of multiple virtual machines, each running independent agents, onto a single physical host system compounds the resource usage.

To address the challenges associated with agent-based backups in virtual machines running on ESX Server or ESXi Server hosts, VMware introduced VMware Consolidated Backup (VCB) with ESX Server 3 in 2006, which offloaded much of the resource demands to a VCB backup proxy server. Virtual machine filesystem (VMFS) datastores would be mounted directly from the backup proxy, enabling it to copy virtual machine files (image-level backup) or, for supported Microsoft Windows operating systems, mount the virtual disk file and take copies of individual files (file-level backup) from the guest operating system. Throughout its life cycle, many major storage vendors developed integration points for VCB.

The May 2009 release of vSphere 4.0 included the vStorage APIs for Data Protection (VADP), which offered functionality equivalent to that of VCB and also introduced new capabilities such as incremental backup and the ability to restore through the use of *changed block tracking*. In addition, the VMware Data Recovery (VDR) appliance was released. The two solutions combined would ultimately replace VCB, which went out of general support in July 2010.

The vDR appliance leverages support for VADP and integration with vCenter Server to provide centralized administration and scheduling of virtual machine backups. In addition, vDR supports Volume Shadow Copy Service (VSS) in Windows operating systems and provides data de-duplication. All backup data is stored to a virtual disk, using any ESX/ESXi Server-supported format, attached to the appliance. Unfortunately, vDR is not integrated or supported with vCloud Director.

**NOTE** Following the release of vSphere 5.1, the vDR appliance has been replaced with vSphere Data Protection (VDP), which was developed in conjunction with EMC and is based on EMC Avamar. Like vDR, VDP is deployed as a virtual machine appliance. Although VDP does not currently support vCloud Director, technology previews of PowerShell cmdlets for automating VDP show potential for accelerating such integration in the near future.

## The New Challenge

Despite the shift away from the more established agent-based backups in favor of solutions more suited to virtualized servers, history is repeating itself. The introduction of new technology, in this case vCloud Director, although it adds significant value, has also introduced new challenges for backup and recovery. To understand the challenge, you first need to have a better appreciation of vApps, how they differ from virtual machines, and the impact they have on backup solutions.

Virtual machines are a software representation of a physical server and as such include virtual hardware in the form of virtual processors, virtual memory (not to be confused with swapping or paging), virtual network adapters, and virtual disks. The virtual hardware configuration of a virtual machine is stored within the VMX file, and the guest operating system and application data is stored within the virtual disks. To take a complete image-level backup of a virtual machine, you simply need a copy of all of the virtual machines files, which are typically located in a single directory on a single VMFS or NFS datastore. In contrast, to perform file-level backups you need to implement a traditional agent-based backup solution or a more virtualization-aware VADP-based solution from one of the major storage or software vendors such as Symantec, Computer Associates, CommVault, EMC, IBM, HP, or Quest, to name just a few.

vCloud Director vApps represent a virtual system that contain one or more virtual machines—up to 128 as of vCloud Director version 5.1—and are the standard unit of deployment within a vCloud. In addition to virtual machines, a vApp will contain configuration details regarding defined power on/off sequences and network connectivity. In cases where vApp networks are routed or fenced, the associated network information is potentially more complex as a result of the requirement for vShield Edge appliances and associated configuration.

---

**vApp Differences**

Although a vCloud Director vApp can be exported as an Open Virtualization Format (OVF) package, it is subtly different from a vSphere vApp. The primary difference is that vCloud Director, unlike vSphere, does not currently support all sections defined in the OVF standard.

◆   `AnnotationSection`

◆   `DeploymentOptionSection`

◆   `InstallSection`

◆   `ProductSection`

◆   `ResourceAllocationSection`

You'll find full details of the OVF format specification at the Distributed Management Task Force (DMTF) website:

   `www.dmtf.org/sites/default/files/standards/documents/DSP0243_1.0.0.pdf`

---

So what does all this mean? In short it means that backups are now more difficult due to the need to address the data of multiple virtual machines. Perhaps more important, backups must account for the additional configuration data associated with the vApp construct, which today is stored in the vCloud Director database. vCloud Director 5.1 introduced the Preserve Identity Information option for vApp exports; the option is designed to enhance the OVF descriptor to include network configuration details (vCloud API `NetworkConfigSection`). However, this option is accessible only when the vApp is powered off and available as a catalog item. The reality is that a given backup solution would still need to access this information from the vCloud API.

Finally an additional challenge, which was touched on in Chapter 10, "Integrating Automation," is the concept of provider- and consumer-driven control. In a traditional vSphere environment, backup and recovery are managed by the provider; however, the nature of a vCloud solution often raises the question of who is responsible for backup and recovery. Consumer requests for self-driven vApp backup solutions are on the increase, but this situation is typically associated with consumers of a public vCloud solution. In the case of a private vCloud solution, the typical consumer expectation is more likely to assume that the provider manages backup and recovery, as was the case for their previous vSphere or physical workloads.

## Assessing Current Backup Options

You should now appreciate why additional challenges are associated with the backup and recovery of vApps in comparison to traditional virtual machines. To fully understand these challenges, let's consider some sample use cases. We'll review how currently available backup solutions can be applied, and we'll highlight the potential challenges.

Unfortunately, from the initial release of vCloud Director integrated backup solutions have been slow to materialize. The situation today is that although many vCloud Director-aware backup solutions are emerging, they are relatively immature and, as a result, contain some limitations. These solutions are continually improving; be sure to review them at the time of your implementation so that you base your decision on the latest software versions. Because of this slow emergence of vCloud Director backup solutions, many organizations have already had to implement their own solutions or have chosen to leverage their current backup solutions.

---

**Is Backing Up Really Necessary?**

Before delving into the details of various backup solutions and how they might be applied, don't overlook the simplest but perhaps less obvious solution available: doing nothing. Upon initial consideration this may seem unthinkable, but you should not forget that in moving to a vCloud service offering, you have changed the manner in which services are delivered to your internal consumers, and for some use cases, backup and recovery may not be required—it would heavily depend on the nature of your consumers.

For example, in a test and quality assurance (QA) use case, the core intellectual property, the source code, will likely be stored in a code repository, which will almost certainly be backed up. Your vApps are then simply a tool on which code is tested, in which case they can be redeployed if inadvertently deleted (provided your catalog images are protected). Similarly, consider a "cloud bursting" use case, where an existing business application experiences cyclical load and needs to deploy a series of additional "worker nodes" implemented as vApps to expedite number crunching. In such cases the core data is likely held in an application database, and the worker contains only an allocated work package. The default functionality of a vCloud solution is that the consumer can export and import their workloads. For example, if the consumer were to export a given vApp on a daily basis, this could constitute a daily image-based backup—granted, a fairly crude one.

---

## Agent-Based Backups

Although agent-based backups, which we introduced at the beginning of this chapter, have become less common in virtualized environments, they can still represent a valid solution. Furthermore, they can also be applied in a vCloud Director environment. When you're using agent-based backups with vCloud Director, the same vSphere resource usage issues apply and potentially become a little more challenging due to the delegated control of vApps to consumers and their less predictable usage patterns. Perhaps more significant is the potential complication introduced as a result of the virtual networking and, in particular, the use of vShield Edge appliances.

Application agents, including backup agents, typically operate using one of two modes: push or pull. In *push* mode, jobs are initiated from a management server, which then establishes a connection to the locally installed agent and instructs it to execute a given task. Upon completion of the task, the agent establishes a connection to the management server to report the status of the assigned task. In contrast, *pull* mode starts with the locally installed agent connecting, and in many cases regularly polling, the management server to check for assigned tasks. Having retrieved and executed a given task, the agent will report the status of the assigned task. In the case of both pull and push modes, backup agents also have a requirement to transfer large quantities of data from the agent to storage media that can be local, accessible via the management server or, depending on the backup solution and associated terminology, an alternative server such as a media server. To better understand how agent-based backups can be employed in a vCloud environment, let's consider these use case examples:

- Direct-attached vApp and direct-attached organization external network
- Direct-attached vApp and routed organization external network

◆ Routed vApp and direct-attached organization external network

◆ Routed vApp and routed organization external network

The use case of both a direct-connected organization external network and a vApp network represents the simplest situation in which to deploy agent-based backups and represents little or no change from being deployed in a physical or vSphere virtualized environment. Since all components are connected to the same network segment (see Figure 12.1), communication between the backup agents installed in virtual machines and the management server is unencumbered. Furthermore, any registration process required between the agent and the management server will record the valid network specifics, such as the IP address or MAC address, of the virtual machine. The deployment of direct-connected networks is common in private vCloud deployments.

**FIGURE 12.1**
Direct-attached
vApp and organiza-
tion network

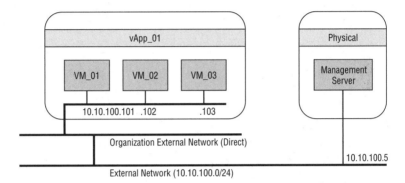

**NOTE**   Depending on the specifics of your backup solution and, in particular, the supporting network configuration, multiple virtual network adapters may be required in virtual machines. This is a common configuration when LAN-based backups are used.

The deployment of routed organization external networks, when deploying agent-based backups in vCloud Director, introduces additional challenges. The vShield Edge appliance managing connections between the organization external network and the external network (see Figure 12.2) results in connectivity between the backup agents and the management server being interrupted through the use of network address translation (NAT) in the form of IP translation or port forwarding—sometimes called port address translation (PAT).

**FIGURE 12.2**
Direct-attached
vApp and routed
organization
network

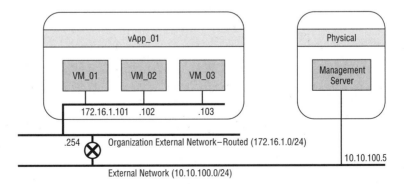

### ROUTED ORGANIZATION NETWORKS

vCloud Director routed networks offer IP translation and port forwarding capabilities. IP translation results in a one-to-one translation of the IP addresses when packets traverse the vShield Edge. So, applied in the context of a vCloud Director vApp, the constituent virtual machines would each be assigned an IP address from the external network on the external interface of the vShield Edge that is then translated to the actual IP address of the virtual machine that is connected to the organization network.

Port forwarding results in the translation of the IP address and/or port number when packets traverse the vShield Edge. So the constituent virtual machines of the vApp may be assigned a single IP address from the external network and specific individual ports, an IP address each and a specific individual port, or a combination in between.

The deployment of routed organization networks is less common in private vCloud deployments, but it's not unheard of. It is typically seen in cases where isolation is required between internal departments or subsidiary business units. This deployment is common in public vCloud deployments because the external network in such cases is typically a shared, and hence untrusted, public network.

Depending on the nature of the selected agent-based backup solution, whether it operates in push or pull mode, and the type of IP translation and port forwarding in place, there can be a number of challenges. The push model is generally more susceptible to issues that might include the following:

- The management server fails to register multiple agents with the same NAT IP address.

- Upon registering, the agent supplies its actual IP instead of the assigned NAT IP, leading to connectivity issues.

The severity of these issues will vary between different solutions. To address them you will need to refer to vendor and product-specific documentation in relation to deploying backup agents behind a firewall or in a demilitarized zone (DMZ).

It is very important to recognize that the use of a vShield Edge appliance between vApp and organization networks can be implemented in one of two ways: routed or fenced. The use of routed vApp networks essentially introduces the same challenges as those of the direct-attached vApp network and routed organization external network. Upon first inspection, you could be forgiven for thinking the major difference is the location of the router (see Figure 12.3); however, an additional consideration is the router ownership. In this instance, it is the consumer and not the provider, which should factor heavily in any decision regarding agent-based backup solutions in order to ensure adequate control and achieve SLAs.

It is a common misconception that the use of a fenced network during the deployment of a vApp is the same as a routed network. They are actually subtly different. When Fenced is selected, the vShield Edge is configured not only for NAT but also Proxy-ARP (Address Resolution Protocol). Proxy-ARP is used to allow a device to answer ARP requests for another network device by assuming the identity of that device and thereby taking responsibility for forwarding network packets. The key point to note is that the virtual machines share the same IP subnet as that of the external network (see Figure 12.4)—the exception being when Fenced is not configured during vApp deployment. A good explanation of Proxy-ARP is available at the Cisco website:

www.cisco.com/en/US/tech/tk648/tk361/technologies_tech_note09186a0080094adb.shtml

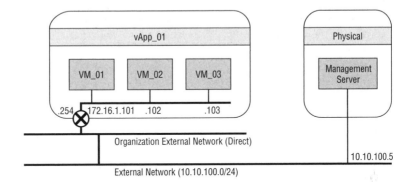

**FIGURE 12.3**
Routed vApp and direct-attached organization network

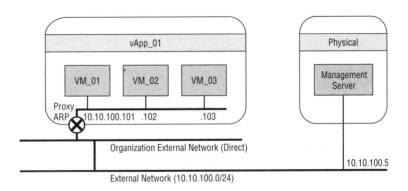

**FIGURE 12.4**
Fenced vApp and direct-attached organization network

The use of fenced networks is relatively common in addition to the use of direct-attached organization external networks in a private vCloud deployment. In particular, it is typically implemented for the use case of test and development environments, because it permits deployment of duplicated vApps without the need to customize the constituent virtual machines. Given that fenced networks are used to permit the use of duplicate virtual machines, it is unlikely you would wish to back them up; instead, the source vApp template should probably be backed up. In the unlikely event fenced virtual machines did need backing up, the challenges are similar to those of the routed vApp network and direct-attached vApp network combined with a routed organization external network.

The use of vApp level routed networks in conjunction with routed organization external networks presents the same challenges as those for the use of routed organization external networks or routed or fenced vApp networks, but an order of magnitude more complicated due to the "double NAT" that results from combining the two (see Figure 12.5) approaches. Furthermore, this could be compounded by the blurred lines of demarcation between provider- and consumer-configured devices. Although theoretically possible, using agent-based backups in this scenario would become somewhat unwieldy and is probably better avoided other than for low-volume exception cases.

**FIGURE 12.5**
Routed vApp and
organization
network

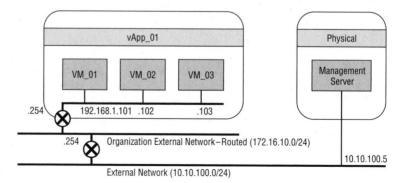

In addition to the use of direct or routed organization external networks and vApp networks, vCloud Director can support the use of isolated networks. Given these network types offer no connectivity to an external network, the use of agent-based backups will not be applicable, so take this factor into account if you are considering the use of agent-based backups.

Throughout this section we have reviewed potential network complications associated with the use of vShield Edge appliances and agent-based backups, but we have not yet considered the potential restrictions on throughput. vShield Edge appliances are small appliances with relatively low computing resources when compared with typical virtual machines and hence could present a bottleneck when running agent-based backups. Previously the unofficial guidance was that vShield Edge devices are typically limited to a maximum 4 GB per-second throughput, but this was based on the implementation of vShield Edge used with vCloud Director 1.0/1.5. This improved with the release of vCloud Director 5.1 and in particular the introduction of *compact* and *full* vShield Edge configurations, both offering identical security features but the full configuration providing increased performance and capacity. Although the revised vShield Edge implementation will undoubtedly reduce bottlenecks, actual throughput figures have not yet been publicly released by VMware.

## AGENT-BASED BACKUPS AND BACKUP NETWORKS

Now that we have established some of the potential challenges associated with the deployment of agent-based backups in a vCloud and in particular the deployment of vShield Edge appliances and the introduction of NAT configurations or potential throughput restrictions, what options exist to mitigate this? The simplest solution is to deploy a dedicated backup network (see Figure 12.6) in the form of an additional external network in vCloud Director—just as we used to do in the physical world.

Although the addition of an extra external network, dedicated for use with backups, appears to be a simple solution to the challenges of running agent-based backups through vShield Edge appliances, this can present new security issues. Implementing a new backup network using direct connectivity essentially places all of the virtual machines in the same Layer 2 network and broadcast domain. Depending on the nature of your consumers and any specific security requirements, this may not be acceptable. After all, if it was deemed necessary to deploy vShield

Edge devices, it is unlikely that the use of a shared Layer 2 backup network will be acceptable. This certainly would not be acceptable in a public vCloud where multiple tenants leverage the same infrastructure and may also be unacceptable for a private vCloud if different departments or subsidiary business units require segregation. So how can this be resolved? You need to introduce some additional network security controls; two possible examples are private VLANs or VMware vShield App.

**FIGURE 12.6**
vApp backup
network

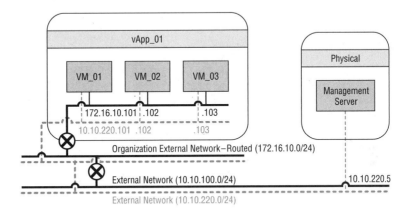

## Securing Backup Networks with Private VLANs

Private VLANs (PVLANs) allow you to subdivide a single VLAN into a series of isolated broadcast domains, in effect creating a VLAN within a VLAN. Similar to traditional VLANs that represent a single broadcast domain, PVLANs further divide a VLAN into smaller broadcast domains, but they offer the capability to support different types of subdomains. Three different port designations exist within a PVLAN and dictate what level of connectivity is permitted between devices within the same PVLAN. The three port designations include the following:

**Promiscuous**   Promiscuous ports are permitted to communicate with any device within the PVLAN, and as such this port designation is typically reserved for default gateways or common management devices.

**Isolated**   Isolated ports are permitted to communicate only with devices connected to a promiscuous port.

**Community**   Community ports can communicate with devices that are connected to ports within the same community or devices connected to promiscuous ports. Further details are available in RFC5517: http://tools.ietf.org/html/rfc5517.

Although vCloud Director does not provide any specific mechanism for configuring PVLANs, they have been supported by vSphere since the introduction of the vNetwork Distributed Switch (vDS) back as far as Sphere 4.0. Given the use of external networks in vCloud Director simply involves specifying a vSphere port group, it is simple to create an external network that is backed by PVLANs.

Although the capability of PVLANs to further segregate traditional VLANs into smaller subdomains does offer some security at a basic level, it is important to recognize that PVLANs were not primarily designed as a security mechanism and hence are subject to a number of limitations. The most common concern is spoofing.

*Spoofing* occurs when a network device successfully imitates another by using false data. For example, a device connected to an isolated port will not be permitted to communicate with any other device, other than those connected to a promiscuous port. However, if the same device sent a packet to the MAC address of the default gateway connected to a promiscuous port, and it included the IP address of a device connected to an isolated port, then the packet would be passed. To mitigate this, you need additional access lists or firewalling.

### Securing Backup Networks with vShield App

VMware vShield App (vShield App) is a hypervisor-based firewall that leverages the VMSafe API. vShield App provides the monitoring and control of ingress and egress traffic from ESXi Server hosts and virtual machines in the form of a virtual network adapter (vNIC)-level firewall. Unlike traditional firewalls that define rules in the format of source address, source port, destination address, destination port, and action (referred to as 5-tuple), vShield App allows policies to be defined based on containers such as datacenters, clusters, resource pools, and network objects such as port groups.

The deployment of vShield App is managed through vShield Manager, which you should recall from Chapter 3, "Introduction to vCloud Director," which is a mandatory component of a vCloud infrastructure. The use of vShield App involves the installation of a vmkernel module and appliance on each protected ESXi Server host within a given cluster.

To illustrate how vShield App could potentially be used as an alternative to using PVLAN for a multitenant external network, we'll work through a high-level example based on the previous vApp configuration (see Figure 12.6) and in particular the use of a common backup network. Given the installation process for vShield Edge is relatively simple, for the purposes of this worked example we'll focus on the construction of the rule sets and assume that the installation steps have already been carried out.

The primary requirement in this case is to allow the individual virtual machines, contained within the vApp, to communicate with the backup server while still ensuring they cannot communicate with each other or any device on the same network. To implement such rules, you first need to determine the best container to which the rules should be applied; in this case the requirement is to apply rules to a vCloud Director External Network. But vShield App does not directly integrate with vCloud Director. Although this is true, a vCloud Director external network is essentially a vSphere port group, and vShield App does integrate with vSphere.

The process for defining rules using vShield App is relatively straightforward and is easily achieved by logging into the vShield Manager appliance via the web-based management interface and following these steps:

1. Use the View drop-down to select the most appropriate view; in this case, choose Networks.

2. Identify and select the appropriate port group—in this case, the external network for vCloud Director backups.

3. Locate the Layer 3 rules (labeled "L3" on the right-hand pane), and then select Add Rule.

4. Use the Add L3 Rule – IP Protocols dialog box to define your rule (see Figure 12.7).

**FIGURE 12.7**
Creating a vShield
App Layer 3 rule

Add L3 Rule - IP protocols ✕

| | |
|---|---|
| Source: | LAN_10_10_220_0-24 ❓ |
| | *Leave blank to indicate any source* |
| Source boundary: | ⦿ Inside ◯ Outside |
| Source ports: | |
| | *(e.g 8001, 9000-9010 or leave blank to indicate any port)* |
| Destination: | BackupServers ❓ |
| | *Leave blank to indicate any destination* |
| Destination boundary: | ⦿ Inside ◯ Outside |
| Type of traffic: | ⦿ Known Application ◯ Protocol |
| | EMC Networker |
| | *Leave blank to indicate any protocol* |
| Action: | ◯ Block ⦿ Allow |

OK    Cancel

The process for adding a new rule is logical and similar in nature to a traditional firewall in the sense that you must define the following:

**Source**    In this case, the source is not a specific device but any virtual machine contained within the selected port group. The benefit here is that this will capture any virtual machine connected to this port group, so there's no ongoing process to add new virtual machines.

**Destination**    The destination represents the target backup server(s). In this case, the Grouping feature has been used to defined a logical grouping of server devices (using IP addresses) to ease rule creation.

**Type Of Traffic**    Type Of Traffic is used to define a collection of protocols and ports that will be set to Block or Allow. In this case, the Applications feature has been used to logically group a series of protocol and port requirements into a single logical application to simplify rule creation. So in the case of our example you would have to create rules permitting traffic from virtual machines within your vSphere Port group to your defined backup servers (see Figure 12.7), and the reverse equivalent.

**Action**    The desired action reflects how packets matching the defined rule, comprising source, destination, and type, should be treated. The options are Block or Allow. The former will result in packets being dropped, whereas the latter will result in packets being passed.

Having defined the permitted applications or protocols, you must next define a default rule to block any traffic that doesn't match. Rules are applied in a top-to-bottom order.

Now that you've created a series of Layer 3 rules, you can use the same process to define Layer 2 rules. Similarly, these are created by defining source, destination, protocol, and desired action (see Figure 12.8), but there are some subtle differences. The destination again represents the target backup server(s), using the Grouping feature, but the server devices are now defined using MAC addresses.

Multiple Layer 3 and Layer 2 rules are combined to form a complete rule set (see Figure 12.9). Furthermore, in both cases it is possible to define whether a specific rule is enabled or disabled, which can be useful for troubleshooting. In our example we also defined two additional rules for Internet Control Message Protocol (ICMP) ready for configuration testing and troubleshooting, but have left them disabled for day-to-day use.

**FIGURE 12.8**
Creating a vShield
App Layer 2 rule

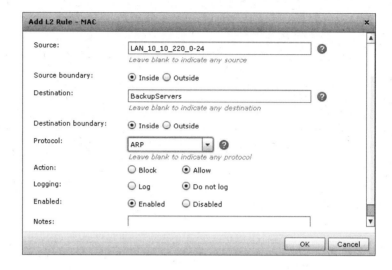

**FIGURE 12.9**
Completed set of
vShield App rules

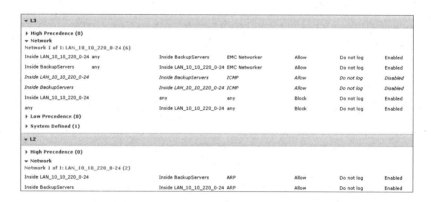

**TIP** Use the Grouping feature to define logical groups of servers using IP/MAC addresses and the Applications feature to define a logical application consisting of multiple protocols and ports.

## VADP-DERIVED BACKUPS

VADP represents the latest evolution of VMware's framework to support the development of LAN-free backups for vSphere. It enables virtual machine backups, without the need for downtime through the use of the snapshot functionality available in vSphere—in principle, the same concept employed with VCB. Backup products leveraging VADP, depending on the specific vendor/product, will typically support these features:

- Image-level backup and restore
- Incremental image-level backup and restore
- File-level backup for Windows and Linux guests
- File-level restore for Windows and Linux guests (requires installed agent)

**WARNING** Upon first inspection, VADP-based backup solutions may appear to not be susceptible to the issues associated with agent-based backups, since they are LAN free. However, in some cases you may need installed agents in order to support file-level backup and restore, which may result in some of the same challenges you'd encounter with agent-based backups.

Regardless of the vendor/product selected, all VADP-based backup solutions will follow a common set of high-level steps to perform the backup of a virtual machine:

1. Connect to the vCenter Server managing the virtual machine.
2. Issue a request to create a new virtual machine snapshot.
3. Capture the virtual machine configuration and virtual disk data.
4. Remove the virtual machine snapshot.

In contrast, the restore process for a virtual machine will again follow a common set of high-level steps:

1. Connect to the vCenter Server managing the virtual machine.
2. Issue a request to power off the virtual machine.
3. Create a new virtual machine (optional, if a full-image restore is supported).
4. Restore the virtual machine virtual disk data.

Today there are a variety of VADP backup solutions, each with their own differentiating features, from major storage/software vendors such as Symantec, Computer Associates, CommVault, EMC, IBM, HP, and Quest, to name just a few.

Despite the comprehensive capabilities available through VADP, it does not solve the issues of vCloud Director vApp backups. VADP is a virtual machine–centric solution, designed prior to the release of vCloud Director, and does not include the capability to offer backup and restore of the additional configuration data associated with the vApp construct. Vendors have to combine support for VADP with the addition of vCloud Director API integration to bridge the gap. A number of the major vendors have offerings that include vCloud Director support. These include:

- EMC Avamar
- CommVault Simpana
- Symantec NetBackup and Backup Exec

◆ Acronis Backup & Recovery

◆ HP Data Protector

Although many vendors claim vCloud Director support, it is important to fully evaluate each solution because in some cases the level of integration with vCloud Director is minimal. Most solutions offer the capability to identify and back up vCloud Director virtual machines, but the level of integration varies significantly and is sometimes limited to the selection of virtual machines—that is, the virtual machine is selected through some form of vCloud Director plug-in but the backup process is simply the same as that already employed for vSphere. The result is that additional vApp construct configuration data is not necessarily captured. This is significant because it means that the backup solution will be dependent on the existence of the original vApp in order to restore data to a backed-up virtual machine. That means that if the vApp is deleted or even partially deleted, it may not be possible to recover the vApp without significant manual intervention. Furthermore, for the most part, these solutions are provider-centric and don't offer consumer-level functionality.

Although the majority of vCloud Director–enabled backup solutions include a number of limitations, it is important to recognize that these are early releases of products and integration will undoubtedly improve with later releases. The key takeaway here is that although many backup solutions claim vCloud Director support, you should clarify the extent of this support, the product roadmap to fulfill any missing features, and how it fits with your vCloud strategy.

## OTHER BACKUPS

Having reviewed the current backup solutions available for vCloud Director, you may decide that none of the solutions fulfill your current requirements and that you need something custom or you need a solution to offer consumer-driven backups. A custom-built solution could range from something as simple as replicating vApps to alternative organization virtual datacenters or fully developed solutions leveraging a combination of VADP and the vCloud Director API or anything in between.

Although not particularly efficient in terms of storage utilization, a simple approach to vApp backups is to use a manual or automated solution, such as PowerCLI and/or vCenter Orchestrator, to create vApp backups by using the Export or Full Clone features at scheduled intervals.

Given the extensive APIs available with the VMware products that comprise a vCloud solution, it would be entirely possible to create a custom-built vCloud Director backup solution. However, this approach would undoubtedly involve significant effort. Consider the level of effort and time required to develop such a solution along with the roadmap projections of vendor solutions. Unless you have specific or unorthodox requirements, it is likely that you will decide against the custom-built option since in most cases the vendors solutions will evolve sufficiently to meet your requirements within the timescales it would take you to develop something from the ground up.

# Understanding Disaster Recovery Strategies

Today businesses are increasingly dependent on the availability of IT systems in order to maintain day-to-day operations. As a result, disaster recovery in infrastructures today is nearly always a mandatory requirement, no longer a "nice to have." Historically the only way to ensure successful recovery was to ensure both the protected site and recovery sites were equipped with identical hardware. Typically the duplicated hardware at a recovery site would remain dormant until a disaster recovery process was initiated—an extremely expensive approach in terms of hardware and datacenter space, power, and cooling. Typically a disaster recovery solution is based on the foundation of one of a small number of common strategies:

◆ System and data backups written to local media and then sent offsite

◆ System and data backups written to offsite media (for example, disk)

◆ System data replicated offsite (for example, storage array replication)

◆ Highly availability solutions spanning multiple sites

The type of disaster recovery strategy is generally driven by the business continuity plan of your organization. In particular, the two primary considerations when designing a disaster recovery solution are as follows:

**Recovery Point Objective (RPO)**  The RPO represents the maximum window of time during which data loss is tolerable.

**Recovery Time Objective (RTO)**  The RTO represents the maximum window of time in which a system should be recovered.

See Figure 12.10 for an illustration of the two.

**FIGURE 12.10**
RPO and RTO
timeline

For example, let's consider the RPO and RTO in the context of some the common disaster recovery strategies introduced earlier. We'll start with the system backups being written to local media.

The majority of backup strategies follow the principle of a weekly full backup (a complete system image) followed by an incremental backup (which saves data changes since the last backup) or differential backup (which saves data changes since the last full backup) in between. For example, a full backup may be taken on a Sunday with incremental or differential backups taking place Monday through Saturday. Given the timeframe between each backup, regardless of type, the result is an achievable RPO of 24 hours. If a disaster event were to occur just before a scheduled backup, then it is conceivable that 24 hours' worth of data would be lost.

Continuing the same example, and assuming we already have duplicate hardware ready, a recovery process would involve restoring data from the backup media to the duplicate hardware in a recovery site. In essence, this process would involve initially restoring the last full backup and then restoring the incremental (one for each day since the last full backup, up to 6 days) or differential (one since the last backup) backups to bring the system up to the state of the latest backup. The amount of time to perform the restore process will ultimately depend on the specific hardware in place and the amount of data to be restored.

For the purposes of this example, let's consider a single server with 100 GB of data to be restored and a backup solution using a Linear Tape-Open (LTO)-4 drive with a theoretical transfer rate of 120 MB per second, or approximately 420 GB per hour. In this case, the theoretical restore time for the full backup would be about 14 minutes (total data/transfer rate). Following the restore of the full backup, we need to restore the incremental or differential backups, which could take a further 17 minutes ([total data × 0.2]/transfer rate) based on the assumption of 20 percent daily change. Clearly the process of restoring incremental backups would be longer than that for differential due to the multiple restore processes required to recover the same volume of data. Therefore, for this single system a theoretical RTO of 31 minutes is achievable. Obviously this should be considered in conjunction with the "bigger picture" of your organization: the time required to invoke disaster recovery plans, to restore data for multiple systems comprising a given business application, and to perform validation. This means the actual RTO for a given business application would more likely be measured in hours.

At the other end of the spectrum of the common disaster recovery strategies, we have the method of replicating system data offsite, an approach common in virtualized environments. In comparison to our previous example, these solutions are typically capable of both low RPO and RTO. This is because data is being continually replicated offsite, meaning data is already in place at the recovery site without the need for it to be restored from tape or disk. Therefore, the time required to recover systems is significantly reduced. So why doesn't everybody use this approach? Quite simply, RPO and RTO have an inverse correlation with cost. In other words, as RPO or RTO are reduced, cost is increased, with the increase typically exponential in nature and not linear (see Figure 12.11).

**FIGURE 12.11**
RPO and RTO
impact on
solution cost

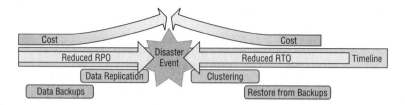

Before focusing more closely on how disaster recovery can be achieved in vSphere and vCloud Director environments, we should establish some high-level foundation with regard to the definition of a disaster. Disasters are disruptive unplanned events that typically fall into one of two categories: natural disasters and man-made disasters. Regardless of the category of disaster, for the purposes of this chapter we will consider a disaster to be any event resulting in the complete loss of an entire site. A natural disaster such as a flood is a good example. This is an important distinction to make because it typically rules out the use of VMware technologies such as vSphere High Availability (HA), which is often incorrectly considered a disaster recovery solution; vSphere HA is designed to protect against localized ESXi Server host failure.

## VMware vSphere Disaster Recovery

Before focusing on some of the specific considerations regarding vCloud Director disaster recovery, it makes sense to build some foundation knowledge in relation to vSphere and disaster recovery. After all, it is vSphere resources that vCloud Director presents to your consumers, and as a result, any vCloud Director disaster recovery solution will likely be derived from an existing vSphere solution.

Virtualization solutions such as vSphere offer simplification of disaster recovery processes by relaxing the traditional requirement for identical hardware in both the protected and recovery sites and furthermore, they reduce the need for system reconfiguration. This is achievable because virtual machines are independent from the underlying physical infrastructure and hence can be moved from one type of physical server to another without having to update device drivers and/or operating system configuration. In essence, virtual machines are simply a collection of files.

Although this simplification theoretically allows organizations to reduce costs through repurposing previous hardware equipment for disaster recovery, this approach has become less common in favor of identical ESXi Server host platforms at both protected and recovery sites. This is undoubtedly a result of the increased reliance on virtualized infrastructures and the growing demand of business to ensure that recovered system performance is comparable to that of the original protected system. Furthermore, many organizations now leverage the recovery hardware for alternative less critical services in day-to-day operations and simply shut the services down if disaster recovery is invoked.

It is often overlooked that disaster recovery of vSphere environments can be achieved using the same core principles identified earlier, in much the same way as physical environments. For example, in the case of a backup and restore methodology, the key factors to consider are as follows:

◆ The size of VMFS or NFS datastores

◆ The transfer rate of the backup solution and how this fits with the required RPO and RTO

For example, if we were to revisit our earlier example of using an LTO-4 drive to restore a single VMFS volume of 1 TB, then the achievable RTO would be in the order of 2.5 hours.

The vast majority of virtualized systems deployed today leverage the use of a shared storage solution in the form of a storage area network (SAN) in order to realize the key benefits of virtualized environments. For example, vSphere HA, vSphere Distributed Resource Scheduler (DRS), and vSphere vMotion require shared storage as a prerequisite. Given most organizations already have a SAN solution deployed, the logical approach to realizing a disaster recovery capability is to leverage some form of SAN-level storage replication. Storage replication is typically divided into two main categories based on how write operations are managed: synchronous and asynchronous.

**STORAGE REPLICATION**

Synchronous replication results in a write being committed to both the local storage and the remote storage, with writes not considered complete until acknowledged by both the local and remote systems. Although synchronous replication offers an RPO of 0, it is constrained to locations within close proximity. The distance limitation arises from the performance penalty of latency due to the requirement to receive acknowledgment of the write to remote storage.

Asynchronous replication results in writes being committed to the local storage, with the remote storage updated at a later point in time. Since writes are considered complete following acknowledgment from the local storage, the distance limitations of synchronous replication are removed but at the expense of increased RPO. The lag between the writes to the local and remote storage means there is an inherent risk of data loss and the resulting RPO will be equivalent to the time lag.

In addition to synchronous and asynchronous replication, there are other variations such as semi-synchronous, snapshot, and journal replication. These variations are typically aimed at achieving RPO benefits close to that of synchronous or the option for multiple recovery points. Ultimately these solutions are similar to asynchronous replication in the context that, without writes being acknowledged by both the local and remote systems, they do not offer an RPO of 0.

Now that you understand why most vSphere disaster recovery solutions depend on SAN-based replication and are familiar with the primary replication types available, we will explore the "under the covers" principles of a vSphere disaster recovery solution that is based on the use of an underlying storage replication solution. The high-level steps, regardless of any additional products or management solutions, typically include the following:

1. Disable replication and map replica volumes to ESXi servers at the recovery site.

2. Mount the replica volumes to ESXi servers at the recovery site.

3. Discover virtual machines on the replicated volumes.

4. Register virtual machines in vCenter Server at the recovery site.

5. Perform any required reconfiguration.

6. Power on recovered virtual machines.

7. Perform any guest reconfiguration.

The specific approach and terminology associated with disabling array replication and mapping replicated volumes as read/write to ESXi Server hosts at the recovery site will differ between array vendors. Despite differences in array vendor, model, and management utilities, the end result should be the same: Replica volumes containing a block-level copy of volumes from your protected site will be presented to ESXi Server hosts at the recovery site with read/write access.

Having presented the replica volumes to the ESXi Server hosts at the recovery site, the volumes need to be mounted as VMFS datastores so that the virtual machine files they contain can be accessed.

## MANAGING DUPLICATE VMFS DATASTORES

When an ESXi Server host is presented with a replica VMFS datastore, by default it will not be mounted. This is a symptom of a built-in vSphere protection mechanism designed to prevent the data corruption that could occur in the event that both the original and replicated VMFS datastores were to be presented to the same ESXi Sever host. Replica VMFS datastores are detected during the rescan process for new VMFS datastores, during which the Logical Volume Manager (LVM) Header is inspected for the device ID that was written when the VMFS volume was created. In the case of a replica VMFS datastore, the device ID will not match that of the underlying volume. When a mismatch is detected, the VMFS datastore is not mounted.

If a VMFS datastore is detected as a replica, two resolution options are available: Resignature or Force-Mount (within the vSphere Client these options are identified as Assign A New Signature and Keep Existing Datastore Signature, respectively). The former of the two options results in the VMFS datastore being assigned a new universally unique identifier (UUID) and a new VMFS label and being mounted as a distinctly new datastore. As a consequence, a new managed object reference (MoRef) will also be assigned. The latter option overrides the detected device ID mismatch and results in the replica VMFS datastore being unaltered and mounted with both reads and writes being permitted.

Typically the decision regarding which option to use is based on whether the original VMFS datastore is currently or ever likely to be presented to the same ESXi Server host. If the original VMFS datastore will be presented, then the replica VMFS datastore must be "resignatured."

NFS datastores do not suffer from this issue because they are mounted using a server hostname and directory path, duplicates of which would not be possible.

Once the ESXi Server hosts can read from VMFS datastores, virtual machines can be discovered by searching for virtual machine configuration files (identified with a .vmx extension). The configuration files can be used to register the virtual machines in the inventory of the vCenter Server at the recovery site. Typically this is an existing vCenter Server deployed in the recovery site, but it could be the vCenter Server from the failed site provided an additional procedure is in place to recover it before the remaining virtual machines.

Once you've registered the discovered virtual machines, you can manage them just as you did at the protected site. In effect, new virtual machines have been created that just happen to be exact replicas of those at the protected site. At this point, any required virtual hardware reconfiguration can take place. For example, you could connect the virtual machine to a different virtual port group due to different network configuration at the recovery sites.

Following any required virtual hardware reconfiguration, you can power on the virtual machines. Once you do, you can perform any final reconfiguration of in-guest parameters. For example, you can revise the IP address configuration to match the new virtual port group.

The process for vSphere disaster recovery can be performed manually, but in the vast majority of cases such processes are automated. Executing such steps manually for more than a handful of virtual machines would be very error prone (human error) and undoubtedly result in a significant RTO. You can automate such steps by using a number of methods, including scripting tools such as PowerCLI, orchestration tools such as vCenter Orchestrator, or more commonly, product-based solutions such as VMware Site Recovery Manager (SRM). SRM is a popular choice for vSphere-based disaster recovery solutions.

## vCloud Director Challenges

When reviewing the available options to provide a vCloud Director disaster recovery solution, establish which aspects of your vCloud solution you intend to protect against disaster: the management cluster or resources cluster(s). It is highly likely that you'll wish to protect both to an equal degree. Protecting one without the other, other than in a small number of exception cases, wouldn't make a great deal of sense. However, you may decide to protect the different clusters using different solutions, an approach that will make more sense as you progress through the remainder of this chapter.

It would be natural to assume that vCloud Director, being built on the foundation of vSphere, can be deployed with provision for disaster recovery using SRM, but unfortunately this is not the case. Before dismissing the use of SRM altogether, we should dispel the misconception that SRM cannot be used with vCloud Director at all: It can be used to protect a management cluster, as you'll learn later in this chapter.

However, SRM cannot be used to protect vCloud Director managed resource cluster(s) that, like virtual machine backups, have introduced new challenges for solution integration. Before reviewing available options, we will explore the specific challenges, but first we will demonstrate how vCloud Director integrates with vSphere and examine some of the key architectural characteristics of an SRM deployment.

### vCloud Director Integration with vSphere

In Chapter 3, we explained that vCloud Director integrates with vSphere to manage vSphere clusters, or resource pools, and present them as provider vDCs for consumption by your vCloud consumers. vCloud Director maintains inventory data regarding vSphere objects and is heavily reliant on the vSphere MoRef, as shown in Figure 12.12. The use of MoRefs for managing vSphere resources goes beyond clusters to include, though not limited to, datacenters, folders, resource pools, datastores, and port groups. In principle, wherever a vSphere object is managed there will almost certainly be a database record of the MoRef. Unfortunately, vCloud Director is intolerant of unexpected (initiated independently of vCloud Director) MoRef changes, and in cases where this occurs, the result is typically that vCloud Director is unable to manage the affected objects.

**FIGURE 12.12**
MoRef values in the vCloud Director database

### VMware Site Recovery Manager

SRM provides an out-of-the-box solution for vSphere disaster recovery and is built on the foundation of an underlying storage replication solution and, in conjunction with many more additional capabilities, follows many of the high-level steps discussed previously (see Figure 12.13). One of the main architectural requirements of SRM is the use of separate vSphere infrastructures, managed by separate vCenter Server instances at the protected and recovery sites. An SRM server instance is deployed at each location, where it integrates with the local vCenter Server.

**FIGURE 12.13**
SRM architecture
overview

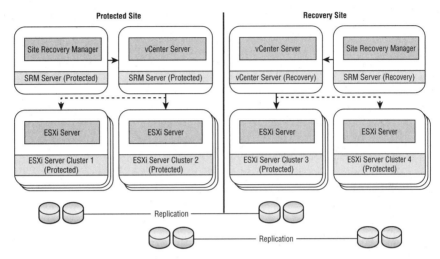

To fully understand the root cause, let's revisit the high-level steps behind a vSphere disaster recovery solution, introduced earlier, but this time in the context of an SRM initiated recovery. In particular there are a number of key stages in the recovery process to consider: mounting the replicated volumes to ESXi Servers at the recovery site and registering virtual machines on vCenter Server at the recovery site.

For the automation of disabling replication jobs and presenting volumes to ESXi Server hosts at a recovery site, SRM employs a storage replication adapter (SRA). The SRA is provided by the storage array vendor and is used to control the underlying storage array. The SRA could be considered a plug-in that allows SRM to interface with storage array APIs.

Following the successful use of the SRA to disable storage replication and present replica volumes as read/write to the designated recovery ESXi Server hosts, SRM needs to define how the ESXi Server hosts should handle the detected replica VMFS volumes before they can be mounted. In the case of NFS datastores, this stage is not required. Unfortunately, SRM does not present any configurable option and will always use the Resignature option, resulting in a change in MoRef. Though that's a genuine issue, another more fundamental point is that VMFS datastores are being mounted on ESXi Server hosts managed by a different vCenter Server. This means that even if it were possible to configure SRM to use the Force-Mount option, the datastores would still effectively be new datastores with a new MoRef; this applies for both VMFS and NFS datastores.

**NOTE**  You should recall from Chapter 10 that a MoRef is a unique identifier for a given managed object, which persists for the life cycle of the object whether or not it is moved within the vCenter inventory. However, if a given object is removed from the inventory and readded, a new MoRef is assigned, effectively creating a new object.

Similarly to the situation mentioned earlier for VMFS datastores, virtual machines recovered from the replicated VMFS volumes will be registered in the inventory of a different vCenter Server. This again means they too will effectively be new virtual machines with a new MoRef. The same challenges regarding MoRef changes will also apply to other vSphere objects, and hence the fundamental point is that SRM, in its current form and using its standard architecture, cannot be used to recover vCloud Director consumer workloads. The key issues are that the SRM architecture is reliant on multiple vCenter Server instances and the default "Resignature" approach is used to handle replica VMFS datastores.

## Current Options

Now that you have a basic understanding of how typical vSphere disaster recovery solutions work under the covers and have explored the challenges with implementing a vCloud Director disaster recovery solution, let's cover the possibilities that do exist.

### VMWARE SITE RECOVERY MANAGER

Previously we looked in detail at some of the reasons SRM cannot be used to provide a disaster recovery solution for vCloud Director consumer workloads. However, we did not look in any detail at the potential for SRM to provide disaster recovery for the management components of a vCloud infrastructure. In Chapter 3, we identified the constituent parts of vCloud Director deployment:

◆   vCloud Director cell server(s)

◆   vShield Manager appliance

◆   Database server(s)

◆   vCenter Server(s)

◆   vCenter Chargeback Server

Although the sum of these constituent parts is a complex vCloud solution, when broken down to the basic virtual machines, these parts are simply a series of Linux and Windows-based guest operating systems running production applications. Since these parts are not actually managed by vCloud Director, the issues associated with MoRef changes are not applicable. Therefore, nothing prevents these virtual machines from being protected against a disaster recovery event using SRM.

**NOTE**   A vCloud Director management cluster is effectively a series of production virtual machines that happen to manage a vCloud environment, and as a result SRM is a viable option for protecting the management components in the event of a disaster.

Given SRM does not support the complete recovery for a vCloud Director solution, why should it be considered further? Despite the lack of support for vCloud Director resource cluster recovery, SRM offers a relatively quick and simple way to retrofit the solution for management cluster recovery (assuming you already have a supported storage replication solution). Furthermore, SRM facilitates simple control through the use of recovery plans to facilitate virtual machine recovery and power-on priorities—which are important for ensuring the successful restart of vCloud Director components following a recovery.

An additional feature within SRM is the ability to add custom recovery plan steps that give the potential to introduce some additional custom-built functionality by enabling commands to be executed on a recovered virtual machine or on the SRM Server itself.

### CUSTOM-BUILT SOLUTIONS

Before the release of VMware Site Recovery Manager, vSphere disaster recovery had to be performed manually, using automation products or by writing scripts using one of the vSphere API SDKs available at the time. Despite becoming the de facto standard for vSphere disaster recovery, SRM cannot cover all scenarios, and as a result there are occasions when only a custom-built solution can meet the requirement—vCloud Director is an example of where a custom-built solution would be required.

It will not be possible to cover all the aspects of building a custom vCloud Director disaster recovery solution; doing so would fill an entire chapter. What we can do is review some of the key concepts. Before diving into the details, let's recap the primary challenges associated with the use of SRM that you will need to overcome. Working on the assumption that you will follow the high-level vSphere disaster recovery steps covered earlier, the key issues to be addressed are "resignaturing" replica VMFS datastores and recovering vSphere objects to a new vCenter Server.

Following a successful process to disable storage replication and map replica volumes to ESXi Servers at the recovery site, you need to define how ESXi Server should treat the VMFS datastores when they are detected as a replica. Specifically you must ensure that they are "force-mounted." To show how this is achieved, we will briefly discuss the vSphere API.

Adopting the terminology of the vSphere API, you need to identify any UUID conflicts (the mismatch in device ID between the LVM Header and the underlying physical volume) following the rescan for the presented replica VMFS datastore. Having identified the affected VMFS datastores, you then need to resolve the conflict. To achieve this, use the methods `QueryUnresolvedVmfsVolumes` and `ResolveMultipleUnresolvedVmfsVolumes`. These methods can be leveraged through the use of the automation tools we discussed in Chapter 10.

Having identified that scripting can be used to overcome the inability of SRM to use the Force-Mount option for replica VMFS datastores, you next address the fundamental incompatibility between the SRM architecture and vCloud Director—more specifically, the SRM requirement for two vCenter Server instances, the associated MoRef changes, and how these changes can be avoided. The answer to this problem is simple: Don't register the recovered vSphere objects in a new vCenter Server. But how can you achieve this?

The statement "Don't register the recovered vSphere objects in a new vCenter Server" may seem a gross oversimplification, but this is in fact the answer to the vCloud Director disaster recovery challenge. It can also apply to other VMware solutions, such as VMware View, that suffer similar challenges. This concept is discussed in the VMware vCloud Director Infrastructure Resiliency Case Study available for download at the VMware website:

```
http://www.vmware.com/files/pdf/techpaper/vcloud-director-infrastructure-
resiliency.pdf
```

To understand why this works, again revisit the high-level vSphere disaster recovery steps we covered earlier and in particular the activities associated with vCenter Server at the recovery site. You should take these steps into account with regard to the recommended deployment model for a vCloud and more specifically the use of separate management cluster and resources cluster(s).

The natural assumption would be to assume that the execution of the high-level recovery steps for vSphere disaster recovery always take place against a new vCenter Server instance already deployed at the recovery site—exactly as SRM does today. However, if the vCenter Server instance that manages vCloud Director–owned vSphere objects could be recovered before the recovery of the consumer workloads, the challenges with MoRef changes would no longer exist. Given that the vCenter Server(s) managing vCloud Director consumer workloads are virtual machines running in the management cluster, and hence themselves are managed by an independent vCenter Server instance, this is entirely possible—remember that the management cluster can be protected by SRM.

The remaining piece of this puzzle is how you tie this together with the "force-mounted" VMFS datastores. Again the natural assumption is that the replica VMFS datastore would be replicated to ESXi Server hosts in a cluster at the recovery site—again, as SRM does today. The key to maintaining the validity of MoRef and vCloud Director construct references is to ensure that the replica VMFS datastores are presented to ESXi Server hosts in the same cluster. But how do you do this? You have two options:

◆ Placing ESXi Server hosts in the recovery site in the same cluster (often referred to as a "stretched" cluster) but ensuring they are unused (for example, in Maintenance Mode) until disaster recovery is initiated

◆ Assigning ESXi Server hosts to the same cluster following the recovery of the vCenter Server instances but prior to the mounting of VMFS datastore replicas

If you choose the first option, you can leverage vSphere HA to power on virtual machines; we'll come back to this point shortly.

To avoid any potential confusion, let's recap the topics covered in this section, relate them to the high-level vSphere disaster recovery steps we discussed earlier, and formulate a revised set of high-level disaster recovery steps tailored to vCloud Director:

1. Recover the management cluster using SRM or a custom-built solution derived from the high-level vSphere disaster recovery steps.

2. Recover vCenter Server instances managing resource clusters; virtual machines are "inactive" since VMFS datastores are inaccessible.

3. Disable resource cluster storage replication and map replica volumes to ESXi servers at the recovery site.

4. Mount the replica volumes to ESXi servers at the recovery site, ensuring they are "force-mounted."

5. Verify the virtual machines on the replicated volumes are now "active."

6. Power on recovered virtual machines in one of two ways:

   a. Using vSphere HA

   b. Using custom scripting

You'll decide between these two power options based on the RTO for your organization and the desired state following recovery from a disaster. The use of vSphere HA to power on the recovered virtual machines offers a simple recovery process with a comparably quick RTO to further custom scripting. When ESXi Server hosts are removed from Maintenance Mode, the virtual machines are restarted as if there had simply been one or more physical server failures. The alternative is to use the vCloud Director API to start specific vApps in a priority order and to honor defined power-on sequences within vApps. This is at the cost of additional complexity and increased RTO.

## HIGH-AVAILABILITY METRO CLUSTERS

An alternative approach to achieving a disaster recovery solution is to implement a multisite high-availability solution or vSphere Metro Storage Cluster (vMSC), leveraging a storage virtualization technology. Before going into more detail on how such a solution might look, let's review three key principles to which you must adhere in order not to impact vCloud Director: The vCenter Server instances managing the resource clusters must be recovered, the replica volumes must be mounted to ESXi Server hosts in the same cluster, and replica VMFS datastores must not be "resignatured."

Several vendors now offer storage virtualization technologies. Some of the more widely known solutions are EMC VPLEX, NetApp MetroCluster, and Hewlett-Packard (HP) LeftHand Multi-Site. Without going into the technical details of the technology, the key takeaway is that the capability to leveraging storage from multiple arrays in multiple sites exists and can be supported. This concept is discussed in the VMware vSphere Metro Storage Cluster Case Study available for download at the VMware website:

```
http://www.vmware.com/files/pdf/techpaper/vSPHR-CS-MTRO-STOR-CLSTR-USLET-102-HI-
RES.pdf
```

The deployment of a vMSC solution removes some of the concerns about volumes being mounted to ESXi Server hosts in the same cluster and replica VMFS datastores being "resignatured." In effect, the VMFS datastores are never lost.

Using storage virtualization technology facilitates the deployment of ESXi Server clusters stretched between two physical locations (Figure 12.14)—but hasn't this always been possible? Although the deployment of ESXi Server clusters stretched between multiple physical locations has been achievable for some time, the fundamental difference is that the storage was presented from a single location. If the physical location housing the storage were to fail, then ESXi Server hosts at the remote site lost access to the storage—unless an underlying replication technology was used, in which case storage had to be recovered in the same manner as an SRM solution.

In the case of storage virtualization technologies, a disaster resulting in site failure will still cause I/O access to the failed site to be lost, but in this case it will be continued from the surviving site. As a result, all virtual machines running on ESXi Server hosts within the impacted location will fail, but they will be automatically restarted on ESXi Server hosts in the surviving site—in effect providing vSphere HA protection across datacenter locations. In relying on vSphere HA to initiate virtual machine, keep in mind that the ability to define restart priorities is limited to the native functionality of vSphere HA and that the ability to honor defined power-on sequences within vApps is not present. If this automated restart is a requirement, additional custom scripting is needed, in which case the original, simpler high-availability solution starts to become comparable in complexity to a custom-built disaster recovery solution.

Although a vSMC solution initially appears to be the simplest route to a achieving a disaster recovery solution, there are some additional considerations worth noting. To provide access to physical storage from multiple arrays in multiple sites, you generally need some form of synchronous replication. Earlier we mentioned that synchronous replication is constrained to locations within close proximity due to the impact of latency. Each storage vendor will provide specific recommendations on this topic; for example, the EMC VPLEX Metro solution requires a roundtrip time (RTT) of less than 5 ms. In addition, there are considerations regarding ESXi Server management networks; these are documented in the VMware vSphere Metro Storage Cluster Case Study.

**FIGURE 12.14**
Stretched cluster overview

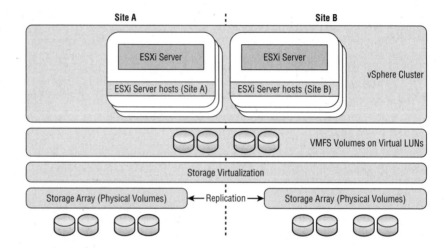

## NON-VMWARE SOLUTIONS

In this chapter we have focused heavily on the VMware-based options for achieving disaster recovery capabilities for vCloud Director. This is because deploying such a solution is challenging, and in most cases there will be a requirement for some custom-built components to "plug gaps" in product capabilities. There is, however, another solution worth mentioning: Zerto Virtual Replication.

Virtual Replication is a software-only LAN/WAN-based solution that uses a hypervisor-based replication technology to offer an array-agnostic solution for multisite and multitenant disaster recovery. This is achieved using a virtual replication appliance (VRA) deployed on the ESXi Server host(s) at the protected and recovery sites. The VRA running at the protected site intercepts writes to protected virtual machines, then compresses and prioritizes the data before asynchronously replicating it to ESXi Server host(s) at a recovery location. Journal-based writes are used at the recovery site to enable point-in-time recovery capabilities.

Virtual machines are replicated in groups known as virtual protection groups (VPG), upon which it is possible to define specific RPO parameters in order to influence the frequency of checkpoints being written to the journal.

Given Virtual Replication is a relatively new product, it is likely to evolve significantly. Check it out at the time of your implementation to make sure you base your decision on the latest software version.

# Summary

In this chapter, we've looked at how backup solutions have evolved with the introduction of virtualization solutions. Vendor solutions that originally used an agent-based architecture, driven by increased adoption of virtualization, have evolved to include LAN-free solutions such as VCB and more recently VADP.

Despite the evolution of backup solutions that offer greater support and integration of virtualized solutions, the release of vCloud Director has introduced additional challenges. vApps are more complex than virtual machines and contain additional configuration details, stored within the vCloud Director database, that also require backup. Current backup solution options include the use of more traditional agent-based solutions, VADP API solutions, or other custom-built solutions.

Agent-based backups can be implemented in vCloud Director but suffer the same resource consumption issues that led to the evolution of LAN-free backups. Also, agent-based backups can become complex when used in conjunction with routed networks. Although the complexity of routed networks can be overcome by implementing dedicated backup networks, without routing this exposes security concerns that may necessitate the deployment of network segregation and security technologies such as PVLANs or vShield App.

Backup solutions leveraging VADP are still in their infancy, and though many claim to offer vCloud Director integration, this integration is often limited to the selection of virtual machines to back up and often does not include the additional configuration data associated with the vApp construct. As a result, many of the available solutions cannot fully recover deleted or corrupted vApps; instead, they can recover the data associated with the constituent virtual machines provided the vApp still exists.

Other backup options include manual or automated exporting and cloning of vApps in order to create the equivalent of a system-level image of a vApp that can be restored. Alternatively, the extensive set of APIs available with the vCloud Director products that constitute a vCloud can be leveraged in conjunction with VADP to create a ground-up custom-built backup solution—provided you are willing to invest significant effort.

Disaster recovery solutions are no longer a "nice-to-have" but are increasingly a mandatory requirement, and they can range in complexity from a predefined backup and restore to duplicate equipment in a recovery location to intricate solutions heavily dependent on storage replication technologies. The type of disaster recovery right for you will depend on the RPO and RTO desired by your organization.

Although vSphere disaster recovery solutions can be built on the same core strategies as those used extensively for physical environments, the most common approach is to use a storage-based replication technology to replicate VMFS datastores, containing whole virtual machines, between protected and recovery sites. With replicated copies of entire virtual machines available at a recovery site, you can use manual effort, custom scripts, or a product solution such as SRM to execute a relatively common recovery process.

Despite building on a vSphere foundation, the same principles that apply to vSphere disaster recovery solutions cannot be directly applied to vCloud Director. This is due to its heavy reliance on MoRefs to manage vSphere resources and the intolerance to these being changed unexpectedly. SRM, although the de facto standard for vSphere disaster recovery, can only be used to protect vCloud Director management cluster virtual machines but not resource cluster virtual machines.

The only viable option to provide disaster recovery for vCloud Director resource clusters is to implement a custom solution that recovers vCenter Server instances, that manage consumer resources, and allows VMFS datastores to be mounted without being "resignatured." This alternative can only be achieved through the use of custom scripting or a specific high-availability solution in the form of a vSphere Metro Storage Cluster. Both can be combined with SRM in a hybrid solution.

The use of SRM and a custom-built resource cluster recovery process is covered in the VMware vSphere Metro Storage Cluster Case Study, available for download at the VMware website:

```
http://www.vmware.com/files/pdf/techpaper/vSPHR-CS-MTRO-STOR-CLSTR-USLET-102-HI-
RES.pdf
```

# Index

# Index

**Note to reader:** Bolded page numbers indicate main discussions of a topic. *Italicized* page numbers indicate illustrations.